The First Book of
Microsoft® Publisher

Ralph Roberts

SAMS
A Division of Prentice Hall Computer Publishing
11711 North College, Carmel, Indiana 46032 USA

©1992 by SAMS

All rights reserved. No part of this book shall be reproduced, stored in a retrieval system, or transmitted by any means, electronic, mechanical, photocopying, recording, or otherwise, without written permission from the publisher. No patent liability is assumed with respect to the use of the information contained herein. While every precaution has been taken in the preparation of this book, the publisher and author assume no responsibility for errors or omissions. Neither is any liability assumed for damages resulting from the use of the information contained herein. For information, address Sams, 11711 North College Avenue, Suite 141, Carmel, Indiana 46032.

International Standard Book Number: 0-672-27399-3
Library of Congress Catalog Card Number: 91-67081

95 94 93 92   8 7 6 5 4 3 2 1

Interpretation of the printing code: the rightmost double-digit number is the year of the book's printing; the rightmost single-digit number is the number of the book's printing. For example, a printing code of 92-1 shows that the first printing of the book was in 1992.

Screen reproductions in this book were created by means of the program Collage Plus from Inner Media, Inc., Hollis, NH.

Printed in the United States of America

Publisher
Richard K. Swadley

Associate Publisher
Marie Butler-Knight

Managing Editor
Marjorie Hopper

Acquisitions Editor
Mary Terese E. Cozzola Cagnina

Development Editor
Lisa Bucki

Technical Editor
C. Herbert Feltner

Manuscript Editor
Joe Kraynak

Book Designer
Scott Cook

Cover Design
Dan Armstrong

Indexer
Johnna VanHoose

Production
*Claudia Bell, Scott Boucher, Michelle Cleary, Mark Enochs,
Brook Farling, Audra Hershman, Betty Kish, Bob LaRoche,
Laurie Lee, Anne Owen, Juli Pavey, Cindy L. Phipps, Bruce Steed,
Lisa Wilson, Phil Worthington, Christine Young*

Special thanks to C. Herbert Feltner for ensuring the technical accuracy of this book.

Contents

Introduction, xiii

1 *Introduction to Microsoft Publisher, 1*

What Is Microsoft Publisher?, 1
A Desktop Publishing Program That's Inexpensive and Easy To Use, 3
What You Need To Use Publisher, 4
What Is Microsoft Windows?, 4
Basic Windows Techniques, 5
Starting Microsoft Publisher, 17
Using Publisher's Window, 19
Using Publisher's Dialog Boxes, 28
The Publisher Mouse Pointer, 32
On-line Help, 34
Exiting Publisher, 37
What You Have Learned, 38

2 *A Quick Start to Publishing with PageWizards, 39*

Desktop Publishing Right Out of the Box, 39
Using PageWizards within Other Publications, 42
Available PageWizards, 43
Starting a PageWizard, 45
Your First Project: Creating a Fax Cover Sheet, 48
Saving Your Files, 56
Quick Printing, 61

Using the Other PageWizards, 61
What You Have Learned, 71

3 Setting Up a Document from Scratch, 73

Starting a New Document, 73
Setting Up Your Printer, 74
Creating a Blank Page, 77
Changing Page Orientation, 78
Setting Up a Page, 79
Using Guides on a Page, 86
Using the On-Screen Rulers, 90
Changing the Page View, 93
Specifying Units of Measurement, 95
Using the Background, 97
What You Have Learned, 99

4 Adding Text to a Document, 101

Assembling a Page, 101
The Seven Basic Objects, 102
Using Text Frames, 104
Creating Text Frames, 104
Selecting a Text Frame, 108
Selecting Multiple Frames, 108
Entering Text in a Text Frame, 109
Too Much Text in a Text Frame?, 116
Editing Text, 119
Searching for Text, 127
Checking Your Spelling, 130
Moving, Resizing, and Reshaping Frames, 133
Making Frames Transparent, 134
Deleting Text Frames, 135
What You Have Learned, 136

5 Formatting Text, 139

Setting Your Own Type, 139
Formatting Text, 140

Controlling Type Style, 141
Using Fonts to Communicate, 145
Indents, Line Spacing, Tabs, and Other Text Formatting, 158
What You Have Learned, 170

6 *Creating Objects with the Drawing Tools, 173*

The Four Drawing Tools, 173
Drawing Objects, 175
Selecting Drawn Objects, 179
Selecting Multiple Objects, 180
Combining Drawn Objects, 189
What You Have Learned, 192

7 *Adding Pictures to a Document, 193*

Working with Graphics in Publisher, 193
Pictures and Picture Frames, 194
Importing Pictures with and without Picture Frames, 194
Importing Pictures, 198
Cropping Images, 209
Moving, Resizing, and Copying Picture Frames, 210
Deleting Picture Frames, 214
What You Have Learned, 215

8 *Creating Special Frame Effects, 217*

Designing Frames, 217
Working with Borders, 218
Adding a Simple Line Border, 218
Understanding BorderArt, 220
Where To Use BorderArt, 221
Using BorderArt, 223
Enhancing BorderArt, 226
Removing BorderArt, 228
Overlapping Frames for Special Effects, 229

Shading a Frame, 231
Adding a Shadow to Any Frame, 234
What You Have Learned, 235

9 Creating Special Text Effects, 237

Breathing Life into Your Text, 237
What Is WordArt?, 238
Using WordArt, 240
Editing Your WordArt Objects, 249
Other Text Effects, 250
Making Your Own Ads, 256
What You Have Learned, 259

10 Working with Pages, 261

Going Beyond the Page, 261
Inserting Pages, 262
Deleting Pages, 264
Working with Publisher's Background, 264
What You Have Learned, 272

11 Printing with Publisher, 275

The Importance of Printing, 275
Selecting a Printer, 276
Checking Your Printer Setup, 277
Calibrating Your Printer, 278
Printing for Color Reproduction, 283
What You Have Learned, 289

12 Working with Publication Files and Templates, 291

Working with Existing Files, 291
Opening an Existing File, 292
Understanding Templates, 294
Managing Your Directories and Files, 303
What You Have Learned, 308

13 Professional Techniques: Newsletters, Brochures, and Business Forms, 309

Making Publisher Pay for Itself, 309
Tips on Newsletters, 310
A Newsletter Framework, 311
Customizing the Newsletter, 313
Tips on Brochures and Flyers, 322
Tips on Bids, Quotes, and Proposals, 326
Tips on Other Business Forms, 328
Tips on Business Cards, 329
Putting the Promotions Together, 331
What You Have Learned, 331

A Installing Microsoft Publisher, 333

What You Need, 333
Running the Installation Program, 333

Index, 337

Introduction

Although desktop publishing (DTP) programs have been around for years, most of them are too complicated or too expensive for the average computer user. If you could afford one of the high-end programs (such as PageMaker or Ventura Publisher), you probably couldn't afford the time to learn how to use it. If you opt for a cheaper publishing program, you get a cheaper interface, an erratic mouse, scrappy clip art, and more desktop publishing problems than solutions.

Microsoft Publisher fills the void that exists between these high-end and low-end products, by giving you a powerful, easy-to-use program that's affordable, as well. Publisher helps you design and build professional-looking newsletters, flyers, calendars, greeting cards, and a wide array of standard business forms. With Publisher, you won't have to seek out professional help to publish your own material; the professional help is right there—on your computer screen. Here are some of the features that give *you* this publishing power:

- ▶ A Windows interface with easy-to-use pull-down menus, icons, dialog boxes, scroll bars, message bars, and WYSIWYG (*what you see is what you get*) display.
- ▶ *PageWizards*—Smart templates that let you build custom documents such as newsletters, calendars, and business forms simply by answering a few design questions. PageWizards lead you through the process of creating customized publications.
- ▶ *Templates*—A complete library of predesigned templates for creating mailing labels, envelopes, letterhead, flyers, business cards, brochures, catalogs, resumes, and more. You can use the templates over and over to create as many customized publications as you need.
- ▶ A built-in word processor with spell checker and search and replace features gives you complete control over editing your text. You can also import text from all major word processing applications.

- An *autoflow* function links text that won't fit on one page with text on other pages. An *autowrap* function wraps text automatically around graphic illustrations or other frames for eye-catching professional effects.
- Easy-to-use page layout tools do away with scissors, messy paste pots, layout tables, and metal rulers. Publisher gives you all you need right on your computer screen. A complete tool palette allows you to create *frames* for importing text and graphics. A unique *scratch area* feature allows you to lay pieces of text off to the side for paste-up. Movable rulers and grid lines help you position objects on the pages. And *background pages* allow you to print the same information and designs on every page of your publication.
- Graphics tools give you control over the visual impact of your publication. Publisher's drawing tools allow you to draw lines, rectangles, and ovals. The *BorderArt* gallery allows you to add decorative borders, and the *ClipArt* library offers scores of ready-to-use images that you can easily size to fit your needs. You may also import graphic files from other sources in many popular formats, including scanned images (if you have a scanner).
- The *WordArt* feature allows you to spark up your documents using a library of fancy graphic fonts. With WordArt, you can create a number of special effects, including slanted, arched, and upside-down text. You can add drop shadows for a three-dimensional effect and create button text like the text used on campaign buttons and badges.

This book introduces you to Microsoft Publisher, and helps get you up to speed using it. We promise you explanations in plain English and generous helpings of ideas to get your own creative juices flowing. Publisher gives you a lot of power in designing and building documents. You're going to have fun!

Who Should Use This Book

Microsoft Publisher is for the small-business or home user who needs to produce professional-quality publications quickly and easily. That covers just about *all* of us. This book is written to make learning Publisher easy and to help you get up and running with the program quickly. No knowledge of computers or desktop publishing is required to use this book.

If you are a small-business person, you *need* Publisher's help in producing the many things that can enhance your business. These include flyers, tent cards, brochures, letterhead, business cards, camera-ready ads, and much more. Yet, by the very nature of being in business, you simply don't have the time (time *is* money) to explore a huge reference book on the program to find the few things you need. This book is intentionally brief and concise. It is specially designed to bring you rapidly up to speed using Publisher without swamping you with a lot of extraneous detail.

The same holds true for the home user who just wants to spiff up his or her correspondence or to prepare a handsome resume. This book is not meant to replace the technical manual provided with Microsoft Publisher, but rather to help you understand it and see how Publisher's tools apply to real publications.

Conventions Used in This Book

This book provides several features designed to make learning Publisher easy and to give you fast access to useful information. These features include:

Quick Steps—Look for this icon to find the steps you need to perform to accomplish a task quickly. Quick Steps give you step-by-step instructions for accomplishing often-used procedures such as inserting text and graphics, using special features like WordArt, changing the BorderArt, and much more. A listing of these Quick Steps is on the inside front cover of this book.

The *Tip* icon calls attention to tips that will help you use Publisher's special features more efficiently.

The *For Your Information Idea* icon points out professional desktop publishing ideas that you can use in your own publications.

Caution icons warn you of what to watch out for while performing a task or using a feature. These cautions prevent you from running into problems.

Illustrations of various useful documents created using Microsoft Publisher are included. You'll see examples of letterhead, brochures, newsletters, calendars, business forms, and a few things for fun's sake.

Chapter summaries are included to help you review what you've learned and to help you check your progress.

Screen messages or prompts appear in `computer type`.

Text that you will type appears in colored `computer type`.

Option Names and Menu Names appear with the first letter in each word of the name capitalized. If you can select an option by pressing an underlined letter in the option's name, that letter appears underlined in the text.

Acknowledgments

Although only one name appears on this book as author, it is very much a team effort. Special thanks go to those wonderful and erudite editors: Mary-Terese Cozzola Cagnina and Lisa Bucki. And thanks to Herb Feltner for testing the manuscript and ensuring its technical accuracy.

Thanks also to the kind folks at Microsoft who made Publisher possible, and especially to Bill Gates and Christy Gersich.

And a heartfelt *thank you* to the legion of professionals over the years who have shared with me their knowledge of layout, typography, editing, and all the other things that are part of the magical process of creating and publishing documents.

Trademarks

All terms mentioned in this book that are known to be trademarks or service marks are listed below. In addition, terms suspected of being trademarks or service marks have been appropriately capitalized. Sams cannot attest to the accuracy of this information. Use of a term in this book should not be regarded as affecting the validity of any trademark or service mark.

CorelDRAW! is a trademark of Corel Systems.

Hercules Graphics Card is a trademark of Hercules Computer Technology.

HP is a registered trademark and HP DeskJet is a trademark of Hewlett-Packard Co.

IBM is a registered trademark of International Business Machines Corporation.

MS-DOS, Microsoft Excel, Microsoft Windows, Microsoft Word, Microsoft Word for Windows, Microsoft Paintbrush, and Microsoft Publisher are registered trademarks and Windows and Toolbar are trademarks of Microsoft Corporation.

PostScript is a registered trademark and Adobe Type Manager is a trademark of Adobe Systems, Incorporated.

Sprint is a registered trademark of Borland International.

WordStar and WordStar 2000 are registered trademarks of MicroPro International Corporation.

Ventura Publisher is a registered trademark of Ventura Software, Inc.

WordPerfect is a registered trademark of the WordPerfect Corporation.

Chapter 1

Introduction to Microsoft Publisher

In This Chapter

▶ What Microsoft Publisher does
▶ Moving around in Microsoft Windows
▶ Starting Microsoft Publisher
▶ Understanding and using the items on the main screen
▶ Using Publisher's on-line help system
▶ Exiting Publisher

What Is Microsoft Publisher?

Microsoft Publisher is a desktop publishing (DTP) program. Such programs allow you to use your personal computer to do what in the past only professional print shops could do: combine text and artwork on the same page and print out the resulting document. In the past, print shops would prepare pages for publication by pasting sections of text and pictures onto a *layout board*, as shown in Figure 1.1. With a DTP program, such as Publisher, you perform the same process electronically, eliminating the need for scissors, paper, tape, and messy pots of glue.

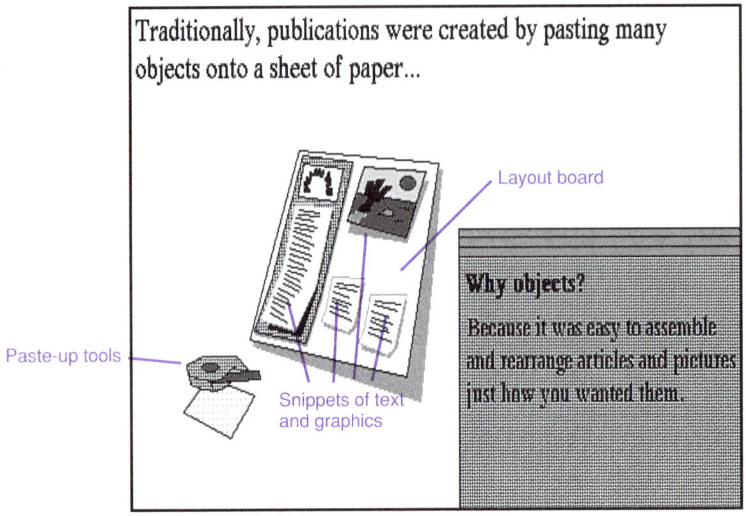

Figure 1.1 Traditional publishing required you to paste pictures and pieces of text onto a layout board.

Desktop publishing is now one of the most popular and useful types of business software on the market. Coupled with recent advances in hardware technology, DTP programs allow you to turn your computer into your very own print shop, giving you control over the design, production, and cost of your publications.

A small business can save hundreds or thousands of dollars every year by producing its own brochures, letterhead, invoices, statements, advertisements, business cards, and other customized publications. Instead of having to pay a business-forms dealer or print shop to design and print a custom form, and then having to wait for delivery, any business can design and produce its own layout, creating just the right form. When the form is perfect, the business can then run off copies on its own copy machine or take the form to the corner copy shop. If the form requires a change, the business can modify the form in-house and print the new form immediately.

Home users can save money, too, by being able to make their own greeting cards, personalized notepaper, yard sale signs, club newsletters, job resumes, and much more. And because the user has complete control over the content and design of the form, the user can add that wonderful personal touch to any correspondence.

Yes, desktop publishing can be and should be fun, but *only* if it's easy. Luckily, technology is now at a point where you don't have to be a rocket scientist to create and publish professional-looking documents. In fact, pushing a mouse (that little device that sits on the desk by your computer) to move an arrow around on the screen and clicking a button is about the highest level of computer expertise you'll need.

A Desktop Publishing Program That's Inexpensive and Easy To Use

Desktop publishing started on the Macintosh, a computer on which the intuitive ease of *point and click* techniques first became popular. Because every Macintosh uses a mouse, the Macintosh was a natural at allowing the user to cut, paste, and arrange blocks of text and pieces of artwork on-screen. To give IBM-compatible PCs this same power, Microsoft Corporation developed the Windows environment, a graphical user interface which now rivals the Macintosh interface in popularity and usability.

Microsoft Publisher works in this graphical environment, allowing the user to cut and paste text and graphics from various programs onto pages by simply selecting the appropriate commands from a series of menus. Once the text and graphics are on the page, the user can arrange and modify the text and graphic objects by dragging them across the screen with a mouse. In addition, Microsoft Publisher provides predesigned layouts that *help* you create simple page designs, such as those used for business forms, greeting cards, newsletters, stationery, and much more. With Microsoft Publisher and Windows, you won't need to know much about page layout or even about using a computer.

Of course, other desktop publishing programs exist, so why choose Microsoft Publisher? The reason is that, dollar for dollar, Microsoft Publisher delivers more desktop publishing power than its rivals. Desktop publishing programs typically fall into two groups—high end, technically complex programs, which sell for around $700, and entry-level products for around $200. The high-end products offer a number of bells and whistles, but they tend to be more difficult to learn and more powerful than most users need.

The entry-level programs, although easy to learn, often provide a sloppy user interface and few options. Microsoft Publisher offers the best of both at a price around $200, and it's Windows-compatible as well.

What You Need To Use Publisher

Not all computers can run Microsoft Publisher. In order to run the program, you need the following:

- ▶ An IBM PC-compatible computer running Microsoft Windows 3.0 or higher, and having at least one megabyte of RAM (random-access memory).
- ▶ A hard disk with at least four megabytes of free space. The desktop publishing documents and picture files you will be generating take up *a lot* of space. An 80, 120, or even larger hard disk, although not essential, is highly recommended.
- ▶ A graphics display of at least EGA quality, preferably VGA.
- ▶ A printer with graphic capabilities installed in Windows (although you can print to disk and take those disks to other computers for print out).
- ▶ A mouse or similar pointing device.

> **Tip:** While anyone can do all the moving and selecting described in this section in Publisher with a keyboard, there are several techniques, such as selecting and dragging objects on-screen, that you cannot do without a mouse. Thus, having a mouse installed in your computer is a requirement for using Microsoft Publisher.

What Is Microsoft Windows?

Microsoft Windows is a graphical user interface (GUI) which runs on top of DOS (your computer's Disk Operating System). Although DOS is still running and performing the necessary tasks, Windows hides DOS, providing you with a simple way to enter commands.

With a graphical user interface, you don't have to type commands. Instead, you use a pointing device, usually a mouse, to select the command from a menu or to select a graphic symbol (icon) from the screen. In addition, Windows sets a standard for the commands used in Windows-compatible programs; you enter the same commands to perform the same tasks no matter which program you're using. For example, if you want to save a file in any Windows-compatible program, you pull down the File menu and select Save. This standard scheme of commands makes learning new Windows programs easy.

Just as Windows runs on top of DOS, an application program such as Publisher runs on top of Windows. (An application is a program that does a major task, such as word processing, bookkeeping, or desktop publishing.) Publisher uses Windows' advanced display capabilities to display graphics and text on-screen that closely approximate how they will look in print. This display capability is called *What You See Is What You Get* (WYSIWYG, pronounced WizzyWig).

Basic Windows Techniques

To activate windows, type `win` at the DOS prompt (usually C:>) and press Enter. The Windows title screen appears briefly, and then a box (called a *window*) appears, as shown in Figure 1.2; this is the Program Manger window. The Program Manager lets you choose and run applications in Windows; it acts as an Applications Coordinator. Overlaying this window is a smaller window entitled Main. You can think of the Main window as your main menu. If you don't see the Main window, press Alt+W to pull down the Windows menu, and then select Main. (You'll learn more about selecting items from menus later in this chapter.)

Why all the windows? The power of Windows comes from its ability to have several applications running at the same time. Each application runs in its own *window*. You can even have several copies of the *same* application open at once, such as three copies of Publisher, each in its own window. You can then edit different sections of the same document or three different documents (this does require a lot of memory, at least two megabytes, in your computer to run effectively). You can arrange these windows in any number of ways, just as you may lay various documents on your desk. You can even reduce a window to the size of an *icon* to "put the document away."

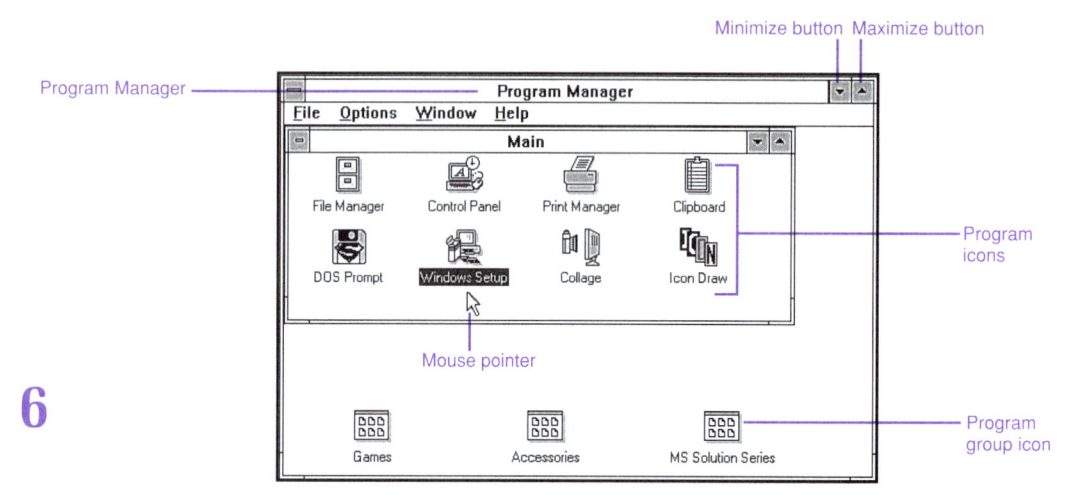

Figure 1.2   The Windows Program Manager, with the Main program group window open.

Icons are the small graphic symbols on the screen. Each icon represents a *program* or *program group*. Clicking twice quickly on a program group icon opens another window containing other program icons. To run a program, you move the mouse pointer over the program's icon and click the left mouse button twice quickly. This loads the program into your computer's memory and opens an application window, which allows you to start using the program.

The following sections explain the basics of using Windows and Microsoft Publisher. You are encouraged to follow along on your computer as this text leads you through the basics. If you haven't installed Publisher yet, refer to Appendix A, "Installing Microsoft Publisher."

Pointing and Selecting in Windows and Publisher

Whatever you do in Windows, you do by *pointing* and *selecting*. To start a program, you point to its icon and select it. To enter a command, you point to it on its menu and select it. To enter text, or draw a picture, you point where you want it to appear and select that point. Because these two actions are so essential for using Windows and any Windows-compatible program, you need to learn how to point to and select items on-screen.

There are two basic ways to move around in Windows—with a mouse or a keyboard. Using a mouse is easier, because Windows is designed for mouse use; the mouse pointer passes over other objects on its way to the object you want to select. With the keyboard, you have to move through one or more objects to get to the object you want. However, if you don't have a mouse or your mouse breaks, you can still use Windows programs, including Publisher, through your keyboard. If you have both a keyboard and mouse, you may use them together to develop a system that's faster than using the mouse alone.

The rest of this chapter describes how to move around in Windows and Publisher and select items with both the keyboard and mouse. Each method is explained in detail. Later in the book, you will see general terms such as "Select." You can then select an icon, command, or option using either the keyboard, the mouse, or both, depending on the method that's easiest and fastest for you.

Using the Mouse

A *mouse* is a small plastic device that fits in your hand and rolls around on your desk. As you roll the mouse, a small symbol (usually an arrow) moves in the corresponding direction on-screen. This symbol is called the *pointer*. Placing the pointer on top of an item on the screen, such as a command name or an object to be manipulated, is called *pointing*.

To *select* an item on-screen, you must first point to the item (move the mouse pointer over it) and then press the specified button on the mouse. Most mice have two or three buttons. The left button is used most often for selecting items. The right button is used less often to enter special commands. The middle button (on a three-button mouse) is rarely used.

Chapter 1

When you select an object, it will change color or give some other indication that it has been selected. In the case of icons, the icon's name appears in reverse video (white on black instead of black on white). If you select a window, that window is highlighted and moved to the front of any other windows on-screen. The selected window is then said to be *active*.

You select menus in the same way. To open a menu from the pull-down menu bar at the top of the window, you move the mouse pointer over the menu's name and press the mouse button. The selected menu is then pulled down from the menu bar and overlaps a small portion of the screen. To execute an option on the menu, you move the mouse pointer over the desired option and press the mouse button twice in quick succession.

You can press mouse buttons and move the mouse in various ways to change the way it acts. Throughout this book, you should be aware of the following mouse terminology:

- ▶ *Point* means to move the mouse pointer onto the specified item. Part of the mouse pointer must be touching the item; you cannot simply point *at* an item.
- ▶ *Click on an item* means to move the pointer onto the specified item and press the mouse button once. Unless specified otherwise, use the left mouse button.
- ▶ *Double-click on an item* means to move the pointer onto the specified item and press and release the mouse button twice in quick succession. Unless specified otherwise, use the left mouse button.
- ▶ *Drag* means to move the mouse pointer onto the specified item, hold down the mouse button, and move the mouse while holding down the button. This is used for moving or stretching objects or selecting a group of objects. Use the left mouse button unless specified otherwise.

> **Tip:** To program your mouse for left-handed use, double-click on the Main program group icon in the Program Manager window. Double-click on the Control Panel icon. In the Control Panel window, double-click on the Mouse icon. In the box that appears, point and click on the small box entitled `Swap Left/Right Buttons` to put an X in the box. This change applies to only those programs you run under Windows. Click on the OK button to close the box. When you exit Windows, be sure to click on the Save Changes check box to save your mouse setup.

Common Mouse Woes

Although using the mouse is by far the easiest way to navigate Windows, first-time users often have trouble getting accustomed to its moods. If this is your first encounter with Windows, keep the following tips in mind.

Hold still when selecting. Many users have trouble selecting items because they move the mouse when pressing the mouse button. This moves the mouse pointer off the item they want to select. Be sure to hold the mouse still when pressing a button.

Click to select, double-click to activate. There is an important difference between *selecting* and *activating*. The basic difference is that you click to select and double-click to activate. Program icons offer an excellent example. When you point and click on an icon, the name below it switches to reverse video, showing it has been selected. However, simply selecting a program's icon does not activate the program; you must double-click on the program to activate it, even if it is already selected.

Keep an eye on the other cursor. When you're working with text, two cursors appear on-screen: the mouse pointer and a text cursor (often shaped like a vertical bar and referred to as the *insertion point*). When you start typing, text is entered at the text cursor, not at the mouse pointer. To move the text cursor, you must use the mouse to click on the part of the screen where you want the text cursor to move.

Quick with the double-click. Two clicks is not the same as a double-click. When you double-click on an item, you must press and release the mouse button twice in quick succession without moving the mouse. If you press the mouse button twice slowly, Windows interprets this as two single clicks rather than as a double-click.

Tip: If you are having trouble getting double-clicking to work, you can adjust the speed at which Windows recognizes a double-click. Double-click on the Main program group icon in the Program Manager window. Double-click on the Control Panel icon. In the Control Panel window, double-click on the Mouse icon. A box appears that lets you adjust both the mouse tracking speed (how fast it moves the pointer), and the double-click rate. After making your changes, click on the OK button.

Using the Keyboard

Although Windows favors a mouse or similar pointing device, you can use Windows with only a keyboard or with both a keyboard and mouse. Windows offers several keyboard shortcuts that allow you to bypass the time-consuming menu system required by a mouse.

Just as you can move among windows and icons with a mouse, you can move around in Windows using the keyboard. To cycle through program group windows and *document icons* (program group windows that have been reduced to icons), press Ctrl+F6. The title bar of the selected window appears highlighted to show it is active. If you move to a program group window that has been minimized to an icon, you can restore the window to its original size by pressing Enter.

Pressing the Alt and the Esc key at the same time lets you cycle through application windows and icons. Pressing Alt+Esc moves to the next active application window or icon. If the application window is reduced to an icon at the bottom of the screen, you can restore the application window to its original form by pressing Enter.

Once a program group window is active, you can move from one application icon to another within that window by pressing the arrow keys: ← → ↑ ↓ on the *cursor keypad*. Many keyboards have a separate cursor keypad that contains these four keys. Other keyboards place these keys on the *numeric keypad* on the far right of the keyboard. For the arrow keys on the numeric keypad to work, you must press the Num Lock key. This turns the Num Lock indicator light that's on the keyboard off and allows you to use the number keys (2, 4, 6, and 8 on the numeric keypad) to move the cursor. The Num Lock key is said to *toggle* Num Lock on and off; that is, pressing the key once turns Num Lock off, pressing it again turns Num Lock on.

With the cursor keys, you have no pointer as you do with the mouse. The name of the selected icon is in reverse video, indicating the current position of the "cursor." If you press the → key, the selected icon changes back to normal, and the icon to the right of it appears in reverse video. Instead of double-clicking on an icon to activate a program, you press Enter after highlighting the icon.

In addition to activating windows and programs, you can use the keyboard to open pull-down menus and select commands. To open a menu, you must first activate the pull-down menu bar at the top of the screen by pressing the Alt (alternate) key or the F10 function key. This highlights the first menu name in the bar, usually

File. You can then use the ← and → keys to move along the menu bar. The name of the currently selected menu will go to reverse video to show that it is selected. Pressing the Enter key causes that menu to drop down over a small area of the screen.

To highlight a command on the menu, use the ↑ and ↓ keys. To execute the highlighted command, press Enter. The Esc (Escape) key cancels a pulled-down menu. To pull down a specific menu with a single keystroke, hold down the Alt key and press the key that corresponds to the underlined letter in the menu's name. For example, to pull down the File menu, you hold down the Alt key and press F. To select a command from the menu, press the underlined letter in the command's name.

Understanding the Desktop

In addition to a graphical interface, Windows provides you with a work area called a *desktop*, as shown in Figure 1.3. This desktop allows you to open several files at once and use a number of tools, just as you would on a real desk top. For example, on a real desk, you might have a notepad, a calculator, a clock, an appointment calendar, and a Rolodex. With Windows, you can use a similar configuration that operates electronically. You may have a word processing program in one window, a calculator in another window, a clock in another window, and so on. You can then change each Window's size and rearrange the windows, just as you would rearrange items on your desk. You can even lay windows and icons on top of other windows you're not using at the moment. The following sections describe the most important features of a window.

Parts of a Window

When you load an application, Windows creates an *application window* on the desktop. Figure 1.4 shows the Windows desktop with an application window open for Publisher. This window contains the same elements included in any application window.

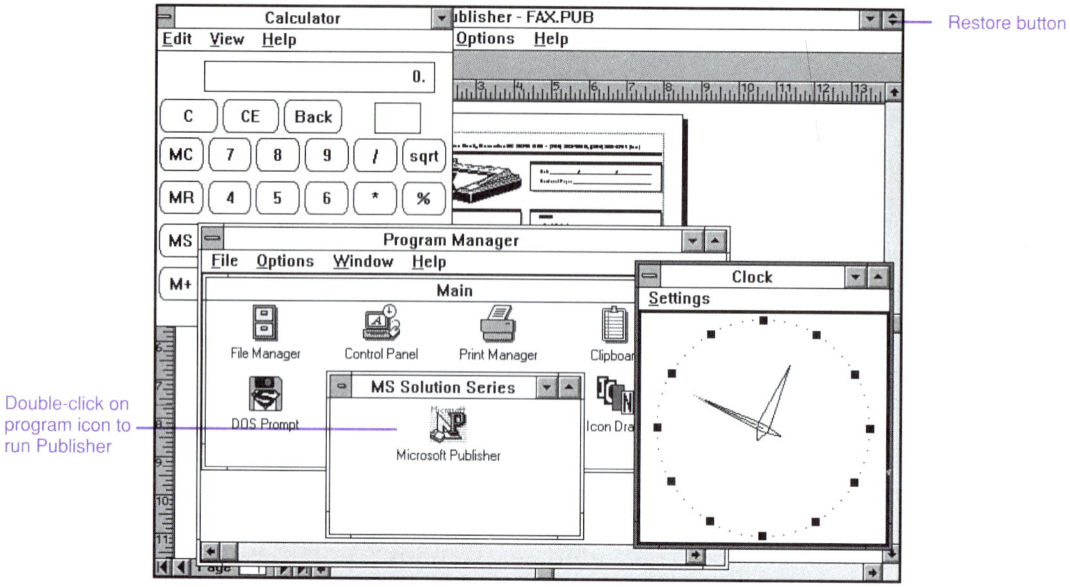

Chapter 1

Figure 1.3 Windows turns your computer screen into an electronic desktop, complete with a variety of tools.

This window contains the following elements:

▶ *Title bar.* At the top of the window is a title bar. This bar contains the name of the program and the name of the data file that's currently open in the program. In Figure 1.4, the file has not yet been named, so (Untitled) appears in place of the file's name.

▶ *Sizing Buttons.* At the far right of the title bar are the *Minimize* and *Maximize* buttons. The first button (the one with the down-pointing triangle) shrinks the application down to the size of an icon, as shown in Figure 1.5. The second button expands the window to take up most of the screen. The button then changes to a double-headed *Restore* button, which allows you to return the window to its original size.

▶ *Control-menu box.* At the upper left corner of all application windows is the Control-menu box. You can activate this box by clicking on it or pressing Alt+spacebar. This pulls down a menu which allows you to control the size and location of the window (see Figure 1.6). If you have a mouse, you can bypass this menu and use the mouse to move and resize windows more quickly.

▶ *Menu bar.* Just below the title bar is the pull-down menu bar. This bar contains a list of the pull-down menus available in the application.

▶ *Mouse Pointer.* Somewhere on the screen, a mouse pointer should appear (a mouse is required to use Publisher). If you don't see it right away, move the mouse to bring the pointer into view. The pointer's symbol varies depending on the function you're performing.

▶ *Work Area.* The space in the middle of an application window is the *work area*. This is where you actually do your work, such as typing text, drawing sketches, and rearranging the content of a file.

▶ *Scroll bars.* Below the work area and to the right of it are scroll bars, which allow you to view any part of a file that does not fit on the screen. The scroll arrows on each end of the scroll bar allow you to scroll incrementally. The scroll box allows you to scroll more quickly; for example, you can drag the scroll box halfway down the scroll bar to go to the middle of the file. You can also click inside the scroll bar, on either side of the scroll box, to move one screen at a time.

▶ *Size box.* At the lower right corner of the window is a box that allows you to change the size of the window easily using your mouse.

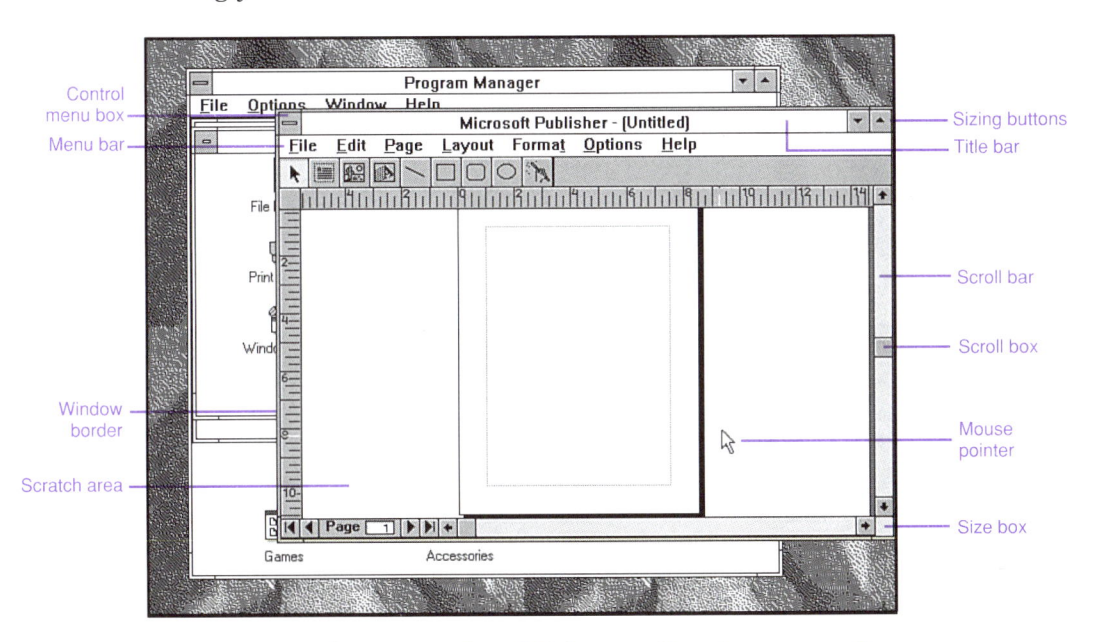

Figure 1.4   The Microsoft Publisher application screen shows the basic elements of any application window.

Chapter 1

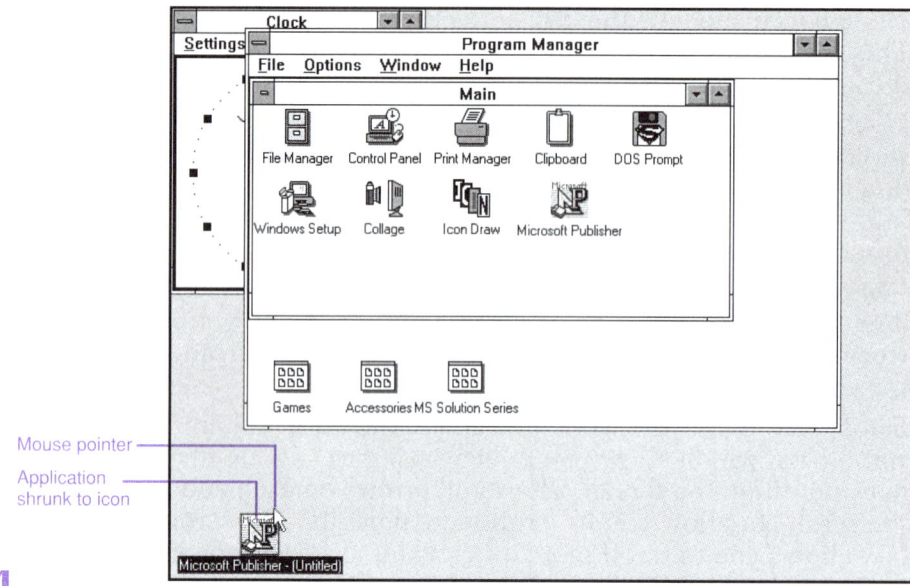

Figure 1.5 The Minimize button shrinks the application window down to the size of an icon.

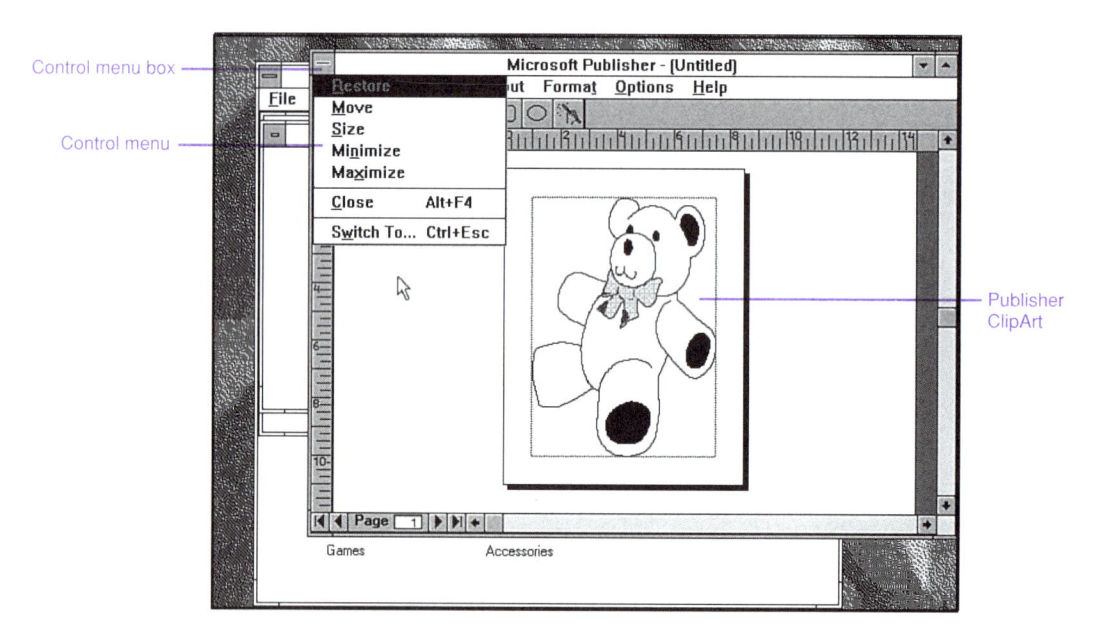

Figure 1.6 The Control menu allows you to control the size and location of the application window.

Activating an Application Window

The *active window* is the frontmost, highlighted window on the screen. Any command you enter will affect the active window. You can activate a different window using either the mouse or keyboard. With a mouse, part of the window you want to activate must be visible. Click on any part of the window you see, and the window will move to the front of the stack. If the application has been reduced to an icon, double-click on the icon to restore the window and make it active.

To activate a window using the keyboard, press Alt+Esc to cycle through the application windows and icons. When an application *window* is highlighted, you can work with that application; it is activated. When an application *icon* is highlighted, you must restore the application to window size before you can work in it. To restore an application, highlight its icon and then press Enter. You can also cycle through the application windows and icons by pressing Alt+Tab (the Tab key). If you highlight an application icon in this way, you can restore the application simply by releasing the Alt key.

You can also move to another active application by choosing the S*w*itch To command from a window's Control menu. To open the Control menu, click on the Control-menu box in the upper left corner of any window or press Ctrl+Esc. A dialog box entitled `Task List` pops up. To switch to another window, double-click on an application with your mouse or highlight the application with the arrow keys and press Enter.

Moving and Resizing Windows with the Mouse

At the top of every application window is a title bar. You can use this bar to move the window with your mouse. Move the mouse pointer anywhere inside the title bar, hold down the mouse button, and drag the mouse. As you drag, the window moves. Release the button when you're done.

Every application window is surrounded by a thin *border*, which you can use to stretch the window to the desired dimensions. To change the dimensions of a window, move the mouse pointer to the left, right, or bottom border. When the mouse pointer is over the border, it changes to a two-headed arrow, as shown in Figure 1.7. You can now *grab* the border. Hold down the mouse button and drag the mouse to move the border in or out. To make a box wider or narrower, drag the left or right border. To make it longer, drag the bottom border. If you grab a corner of the border, you can change both the length and width of the window.

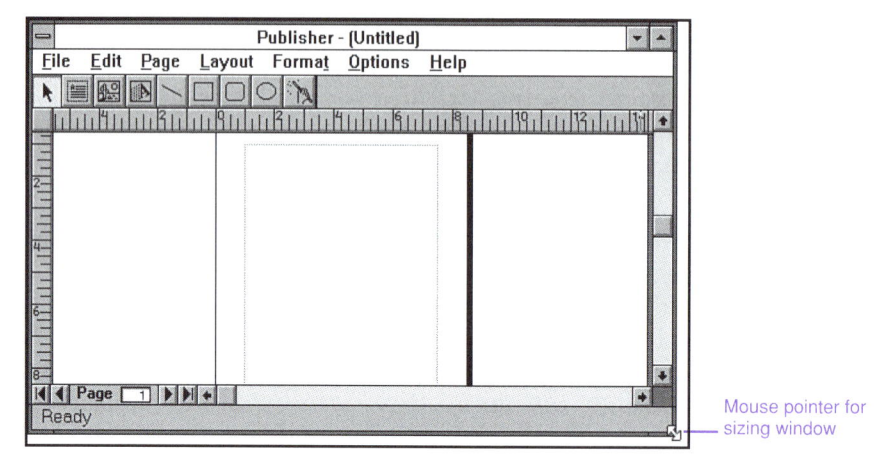

Figure 1.7 You can resize a window by dragging its border.

Moving and Resizing Windows with the Control Menu

Although it's easiest to move and resize windows with a mouse, you can perform the same operation with the keyboard. First, make sure the window you want to modify is active. You can then pull down that window's Control menu by clicking on the Control-menu box or pressing Alt+spacebar. The Control menu drops down, as shown in Figure 1.6. This menu contains several commands that let you control the size and location of the window:

▶ Restore restores the window to its original size. If you select an application that's been reduced to an icon, you can restore its window by selecting this option.

▶ The Minimize and Maximize options operate just like the Minimize and Maximize buttons described earlier. Maximize expands the window so it fills most of the screen. Minimize reduces the window to an icon.

▶ Move allows you to use the arrow keys to move the window up, down, left, or right.

▶ Size allows you to move the right border in or out, changing the window's width, or move the bottom border up or down to change its height.

The following Quick Steps lead you through the process of resizing a window.

Q Resizing a Window

1. Move the mouse pointer to an edge of the window to be resized. You can move to a corner to change the width and height of the window at the same time.

    The mouse pointer changes to a double-headed arrow.

2. Hold down the left mouse button and drag the mouse pointer to change the size and dimensions of the window.

    The selected side of the window is moved in the direction you drag the mouse.

3. Repeat steps 1 and 2 for the other sides of the window until you are satisfied with the new size.

    You may have to move the window in order to create more room for changing its size. The window is now resized.

    □

Starting Microsoft Publisher

Now that you know the basics of working with the Windows graphical interface, you'll find it easy to learn the basics of working in Publisher. But first, you have to get Windows and Publisher up and running.

If Windows is not running, start Windows from the DOS prompt by typing `win` and pressing Enter. The Windows opening screen appears momentarily, and then the Program Manager is displayed. If you have just installed Publisher, the MS Solution Series window is active, and the Microsoft Publisher icon is high-

Chapter 1

lighted. If the MS Solutions Series window is not displayed, double-click on its program group icon, if the icon is visible. If you cannot see the icon, pull down the Windows menu and select MS Solution Series.

To start Publisher, double-click on the Microsoft Publisher icon or highlight the icon using the arrow keys and press Enter. The Publisher title screen appears briefly, then the Publisher application window appears. It initially occupies the entire desktop, but you can resize it.

In the center of the application window is the Start Up dialog box, as shown in Figure 1.8. At the top of the box are the following four option buttons: PageWizards, Templates, Blank Page, and Open. You will use these buttons to tell Publisher the initial page layout you want to use to start working:

PageWizards is a collection of smart templates that lead you through the process of creating and customizing popular publications, such as newsletters and brochures. Because PageWizards is selected by default, a list of PageWizard options appears in the list box. The next chapter will discuss PageWizards in more detail.

Templates provides a list of predesigned layouts from which you can choose, including layouts for envelopes, letterhead, and much more. You can use the selected template as is or customize it.

Blank Page displays (you guessed it) a blank page. This allows you to start a layout from scratch. Pressing the Cancel button at the bottom of the dialog box also displays a blank page. Figure 1.9 shows how the screen looks when you select this option.

Open allows you to work with a layout or publication that you have already created and saved to disk. You may then print the publication or modify it.

To select one of these options, perform the following Quick Steps:

Selecting a Start-Up Option

1. Select the option button you want to use by clicking on it or holding down the Alt key and pressing the underlined letter in the option's name.

    The selected button appears pushed-in.

2. If the selected option displays items in the list box, select one of the items listed.

    For example, if you choose Templates, select a type of template from the list.

3. Press Enter or click on the OK button.

    The dialog box disappears, and Publisher displays the selected file or layout. □

Using Publisher's Window

The Publisher Window is basically the same as the other application windows discussed so far. You can resize, move, maximize, minimize, and close this window just as you can any other application window.

Along the top of the Publisher window, between the Control-menu box and the minimize and maximize buttons is the title bar. When the program first loads, the title here is `Publisher-(Untitled)`, because no file has been opened in Publisher.

Publisher's application window contains a few extra items that you may not have seen on other application windows:

- ▶ *Menu bar.* Contains seven menus which you can pull down to access Publisher's commands and to get help.
- ▶ *Toolbar.* Contains several tools that let you add text and pictures to your pages, draw graphic objects, and access some of Publisher's more advanced features.
- ▶ *Rulers.* At the top and left side of the window are rulers which allow you to place objects in precise locations on pages.

Chapter 1

- *Work area.* Consists of a page surrounded by a *scratch area.* You paste text, pictures, and other objects on the page to create your publications. The scratch area gives you more room to work, allowing you to place objects off to one side before pasting them down.
- *Scroll bars.* Allow you to move the page to focus on various areas of the page.
- *Paging control.* Lets you flip through the pages of your publication.

The following sections explain the various parts of Publisher's application window in greater detail.

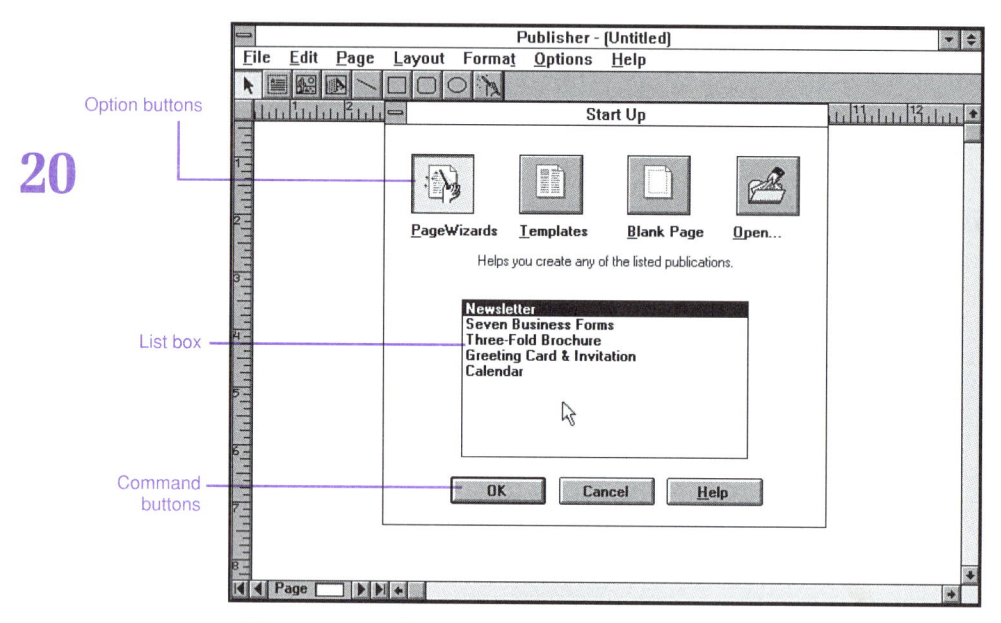

Figure 1.8 The opening Publisher screen displays the Start Up dialog box, prompting you to select a starting page layout or file.

The Menu Bar

Directly below the Title bar is Microsoft Publisher's pull-down menu bar. This bar contains a list of the pull-down menus you can access in Publisher: File, Edit, Page, Layout, Format, Options, and

Help. To pull down a menu, click on menu's name or press Alt plus the underlined letter in the menu name. Another way to open a menu is to press Alt or F10 to activate the menu bar, use the ← and → keys to highlight a menu name, and press Enter.

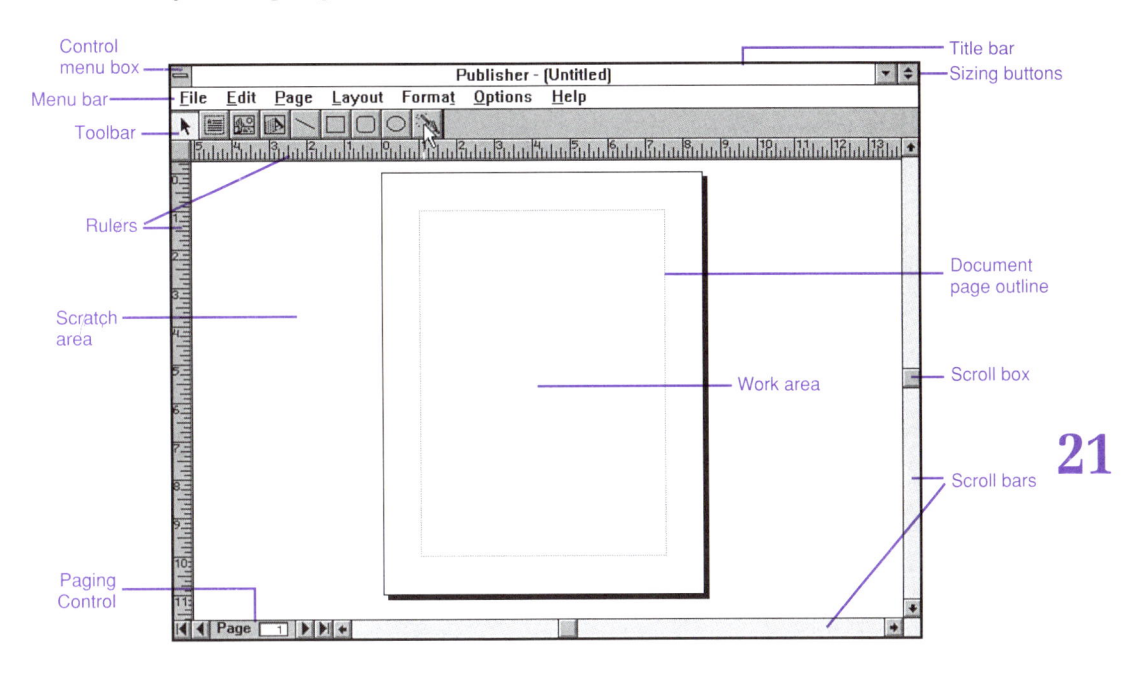

Figure 1.9 Parts of the Publisher application window.

To close a menu without making a selection, press Alt or F10 or click on any blank space outside the menu. Pressing Esc will close the menu and leave the menu bar active so you can make another selection.

Each menu contains a list of related options. For example, the File menu (shown in Figure 1.10) contains a list of options for working with files. This list includes saving files, opening existing document files, printing files, and exiting the program. At the bottom of the File menu is a list of files you worked on most recently; this list provides quick access to these files. Just as the File menu contains file-related options, the Edit menu has editing-related commands, the Page menu gives you control over page formatting, and so on. More detailed information about the pull-down menus is given in Chapter 3.

Chapter 1

Figure 1.10 Publisher's File menu provides a list of options for working with files.

Choosing Menu Options

Once you've pulled down a menu, you'll see a series of commands from which to choose. Before you choose an option, you should know a little about the various conventions Windows uses to display menu options and what those conventions mean. Table 1.2 provides a list of conventions. Refer to Figures 1.10 and 1.11 to see how these conventions appear on-screen.

Table 1.2 Microsoft Publisher's menu conventions.

Convention	Meaning
Underlined letter	To select a command with the keyboard, you can press the key that corresponds to the underlined letter in the option's name.
Dimmed command name	The command is not currently available. Before you can use the command, you may have to perform some other action, such as selecting a text or graphic object.

Convention	Meaning
Ellipsis (...) after name	Selecting this option will display a *dialog box* asking for addition information. Dialog boxes are discussed in the next section.
Checkmark next to name	The command is active. It is used for options that toggle between on and off states.
Shortcut key combination after name	A key combination after the name, such as Ctrl+S, shows that you can bypass the pull-down menu by pressing a *shortcut* key combination. This works only if no menu is open.

To choose a command from a pull-down menu, take the following Quick Steps. Keep in mind that you can close a menu at any time by clicking outside the menu or pressing Esc.

Selecting an Option from a Pull-Down Menu

1. Pull down the menu that contains the command or option you want to choose.

   The selected menu is pulled down, and its options are visible.

2. Click on the option you want to choose or press the highlighted letter in the option's name.

   The option or command is executed.

3. If a dialog box or message appears, follow the on-screen messages to complete the action.

   ☐

You can also select an option from the pull-down menu by using the arrow keys to highlight the option and then pressing the Enter key.

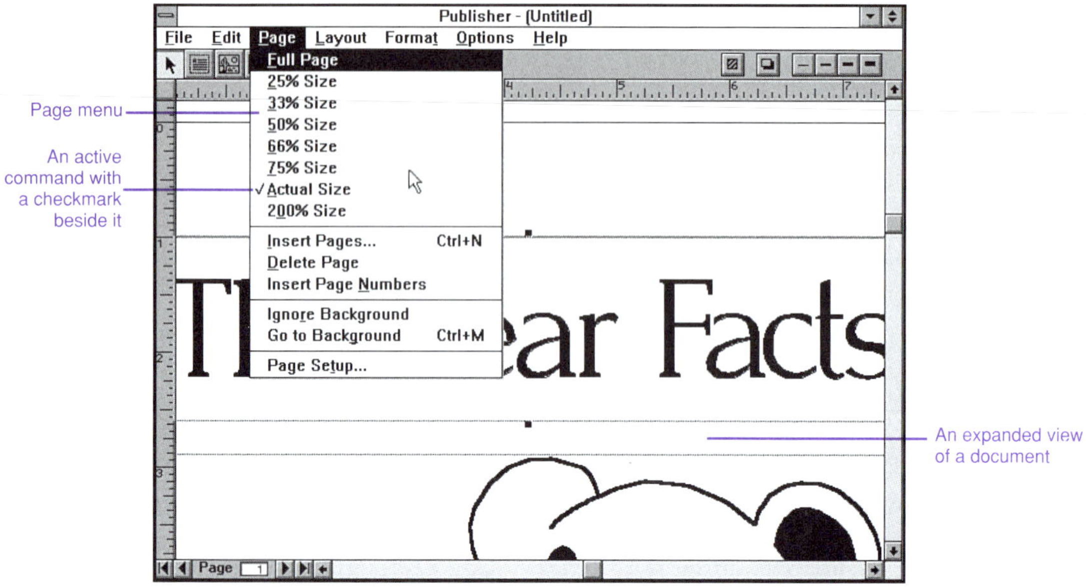

Chapter 1

Figure 1.11 Each pull-down menu contains a list of related commands.

Using the Toolbar

Just below the pull-down menu bar is the *Toolbar*, which you can see in Figure 1.9. This bar contains several tools to help you draw boxes, change line thickness, control shading, change the style of text, and perform other common page-layout activities.

Eight tools (on the left) are always there. Others tools appear on the right end of the bar depending on the selected object. For example, if you select a text frame, a set of tools appears as in Figure 1.12, allowing you to format the text. If you select a graphic object, a different set of tools appears, allowing you to modify the graphic image.

Creating a document from scratch is simply a matter of choosing a tool and creating an object (you'll learn about the basic objects that make up a Publisher document beginning in Chapter 3). Once you've created the objects you want included on a page, you can rearrange them just as printers used to arrange bits of text and artwork on layout boards for newspapers and magazines. But you will do it all electronically, and with a lot less hassle. No more sticky fingers from hot wax or globs of paste falling on your shoes.

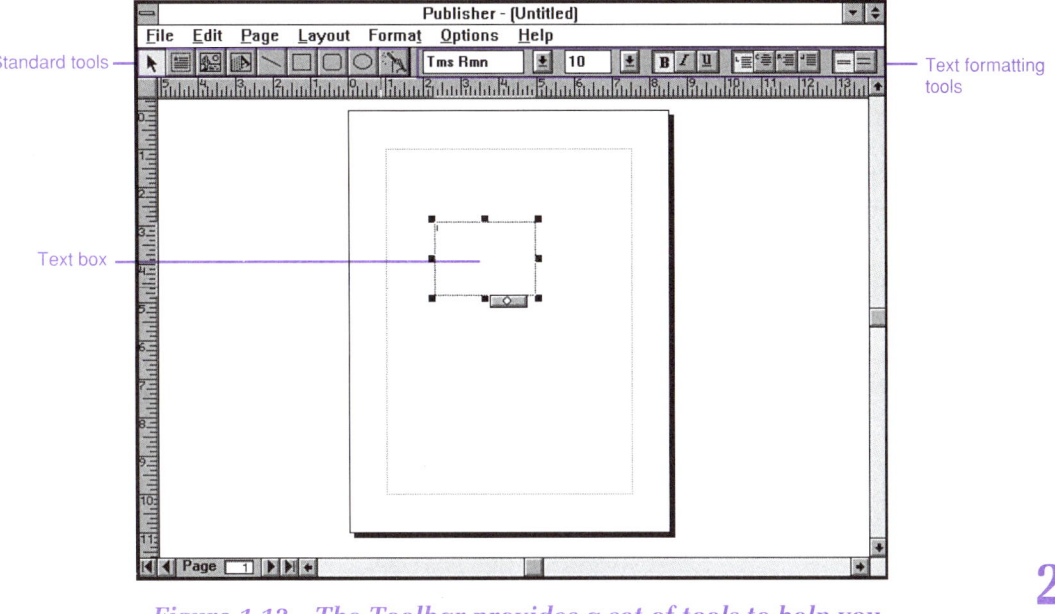

Figure 1.12   The Toolbar provides a set of tools to help you perform common page-layout activities.

Using Rulers

When you first use Publisher, you'll notice two rulers: a vertical ruler along the left side of the screen, and a horizontal ruler along the top (see Figure 1.9). These are calibrated initially in inches, but you can change the unit of measurement as you'll see in Chapter 3. When you move or size an object, lines appear in the rulers to show the precise location of the cursor and of the object's edges. These markings allow you to move the object to an exact location and to size and object to precise specifications.

You may not need rulers on the screen all the time. To remove the rulers from the screen, press Ctrl+K or pull down the Options menu and select Hide Rulers. This gives you more room on-screen for manipulating your document. To display the rulers, press Ctrl+K or pull down the Options menu and select Show Rulers.

Understanding the Work Area

Publisher's work area consists of two basic parts: a page and a scratch area that surrounds the page (refer to Figure 1.9). On the page, you will import, create, and paste various objects in order to prepare a page for publication. This page acts as your layout board—it holds all the objects that will be printed.

The scratch area, outside the page, acts as your desk. You can lay the various objects you are working with off to the side in this scratch area, just as you can lay bits of paper and photos on a desk. You can then turn to the page on which you want to paste an object and then drag the object from the scratch area onto the page for paste-up.

Using Publisher's Scroll Bars

The real drawback in computerized document processing has always been the limited viewing area of the screen. Although a physical page can be 66 lines or more, you can view only 22 lines or so on-screen. Likewise, if you have a wide document, you can view only a portion of it at a time. And if you want to view pages side-by-side, forget it!

With desktop publishing, the limitations are even more apparent and more frustrating. Although you want to see what the type and graphics will look like full-size, you need a bird's-eye view of the pages as well.

Publisher overcomes the view limitations in two ways. First, Publisher allows you to view a page in various sizes. The page size options are listed on the Page menu. For example, you can select Full Page to view the overall layout of the page, although in this view you won't be able to read the text. When you choose a larger view such as Actual Size, you can read the text and see how it will appear in print, but you see only a portion of the page.

When the page is too large to fit entirely on the screen, you need some way to move to other sections of the page. The *scroll bars* allow for this movement. You can use the scroll bars in the following ways to move to a different portion of the page:

Scroll arrows. Scroll arrows are on both ends of the vertical and horizontal scroll bars. Click once on an arrow to scroll incrementally in the direction of the arrow. Hold down the mouse button to scroll continuously in that direction.

Scroll box. The scroll box is a small box inside the scroll bar. Drag the scroll box along the scroll bar to the area of the page you want to view. For example, to move to the middle of the page, drag the scroll box to the middle of the scroll bar.

Scroll bar. Click once inside the scroll bar on either side of the scroll box to move the view one screenful at a time. For example, if you click once below the scroll box, you'll see the next screen.

Paging

The documents you create in Publisher may consist of many pages, but you see only one page at a time. To flip to another page, use the *page control* in the lower left corner of the Publisher window. When you first open a document, you'll see a 1 in the Page box, which indicates you are on the first page.

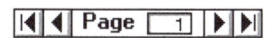

On each side of the Page box are two arrow buttons facing away from the number. The buttons to the left allow you to move to previous pages; the buttons to the right allow you to move to following pages. The two buttons that have only arrowheads (no vertical bar) flip pages one at a time. The two buttons that have arrowheads and vertical bars flip to the first or last page of the document.

You may also change pages by clicking on the page number that's displayed in the box. This selects the text box, turning the page number to reverse video. Just type the page number you want to go to and press Enter.

Chapter 1

Reading the Status Bar

On the very bottom line of the Publisher applications window is the *Status Line*, where helpful hints appear. For example, if you select an object on the screen, this line might read

```
Hold down the mouse button and drag to move the
selection.
```

When you're first starting out in Publisher, you'll find that this line often provides just the information you need. As you get more experienced, you won't even notice the messages, but they still take up screen space. To remove the status line, pull down the Options menu and select Hide Status Line. To turn the status line on again, pull down the Options menu and select Show Status Line.

Using Publisher's Dialog Boxes

A *dialog box* in a Windows application allows you to carry on a conversation with the application. The box provides you with information and prompts you to respond in some way. Should Windows need additional information to execute a command, a dialog box will pop up, and you can then type whatever is needed. An ellipsis (three dots . . .) after the command's name alerts you that activating that command brings up a dialog box. In the case of commands like Save, the dialog box appears only if Publisher needs additional information.

For example, say you've created a document in Publisher and want to save it to disk. You pull down the File menu and choose Save. Because this document has never been saved before, Publisher wants to know what name to save it under, so a dialog box appears, as in Figure 1.13. You type the filename and click on the OK button in the box or press Enter to save the now-named file. The next time you save the document, no dialog box appears because Publisher knows its name and address on the disk.

Most dialog boxes in Publisher present you with several options. Once you have chosen the appropriate option(s) (by pointing and clicking at them), you choose the OK button to tell the program to carry out the command or commands you've picked. If you want to leave the dialog box without doing anything, choose the Cancel button or press Esc.

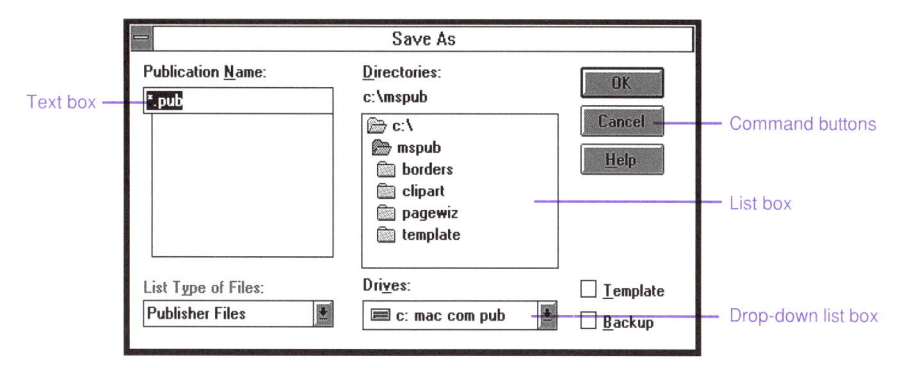

Figure 1.13 Publisher's Save As dialog box gives you a number of choices that will let you save the file under another name and/or directory.

Like other types of windows on your electronic desktop, you can move dialog boxes around—a handy feature if the box is obscuring part of your work that you need to see in order to choose the correct option.

At the top of the box is the title bar, just as in the application windows described earlier. The bar might have a title something like File Open or Print, indicating the function of the box. To move the box, move the mouse pointer inside the title bar, hold down the left mouse button, and drag the box where you want it to appear. As long as you keep the button pressed, the dialog box will follow the mouse pointer like a dog on a leash.

The same conventions detailed for commands in the previous section apply to commands in dialog boxes. So if you see a command followed by our old friend, the ellipsis (...), it means that another dialog box with more commands will pop up if you choose that command.

An additional convention applies to commands buttons. If you see a command button marked with two greater than signs >>, it means that if you press the button, the current dialog box will expand. For example, the Color dialog box in the Windows Control Panel contains the button Color Palette>>. Clicking on this button expands the Color dialog box to display options for changing the colors of various elements of the desktop.

Command Buttons

Every dialog box contains *command buttons* (see Figure 1.13). These screen buttons operate the same way as physical buttons such as your doorbell. You press them by pointing and clicking with your mouse, or by using the Tab key to select the button and hitting the Enter key. If your computer has a VGA-quality graphics adapter, these buttons will have a three-dimensional look to show that they are buttons. Some buttons, such as Cancel and OK have no underlined character, so you cannot use a shortcut key to press the button.

Three command buttons are in almost every dialog box in Publisher—OK, Cancel, and Help. Pressing the OK button tells Publisher that, okay, you've done everything you wanted to do in this dialog box and it can now proceed. The Cancel button tells Publisher, "Whoa, back up!" It cancels the actions of the dialog box and returns you to your previous situation on the screen. Choosing Help accesses Publisher's on-line help system.

Using List Boxes

Many dialog boxes contain one or more *list boxes*, which provide a list of choices. To activate a list, press Alt plus the underlined letter in the list's name or click inside the list with your mouse. Often, the entire list is not shown due to lack of space; in such cases, the box will have a scroll bar that lets you view the remaining choices. You can use the scroll bar or arrow keys to scroll through the list. To select an item in the list, click on the item or highlight it and press Enter. To unselect a selected item, click on it again or highlight it and press Enter.

Drop-Down Lists

A *drop-down list box* (see Figure 1.13) is a modified version of the list box. An example in Publisher is the Font list in the Character dialog box. This list box initially shows only the currently selected font. To the right of the box is a down-pointing arrow. By clicking on this arrow or pressing Alt+↓ when the list box is selected, you can view the rest of the items in this list; the list drops down as does a pull-down menu. To cancel the list, press Alt+↑ or Tab, or click outside the list.

Using Text Boxes

A *text box* (see Figure 1.13) is a box within a dialog box. Unlike list boxes, text boxes do not allow you to select from a list of choices. Instead, they require you to type an entry, such as the name under which you want a file saved. To type information in a text box, click on the text box with your mouse or press the Tab key to activate the box. A flashing vertical cursor within the box indicates where you will start typing.

Sometimes the box contains information that you must replace. You can simply start typing the new text if you need to completely replace what was already there (the old text will disappear). To edit the existing text, move the cursor in the box to the information you want to change. You can use the Backspace key or Del to delete existing text. You can then type the required information.

Using Check Boxes

Many dialog boxes also contain a list of options with *check boxes* (see Figure 1.14). These options allow you to specify how you want a particular command executed; you can select more than one check box at a time. To select a check box, click on the box or press Alt plus the underlined letter in the option's name. With the keyboard, use the spacebar to select an option. An X appears in the check box, indicating that the option is turned on. To remove the X and deactivate the option, select the option again. Any option that is dimmed or grayed out is temporarily unavailable.

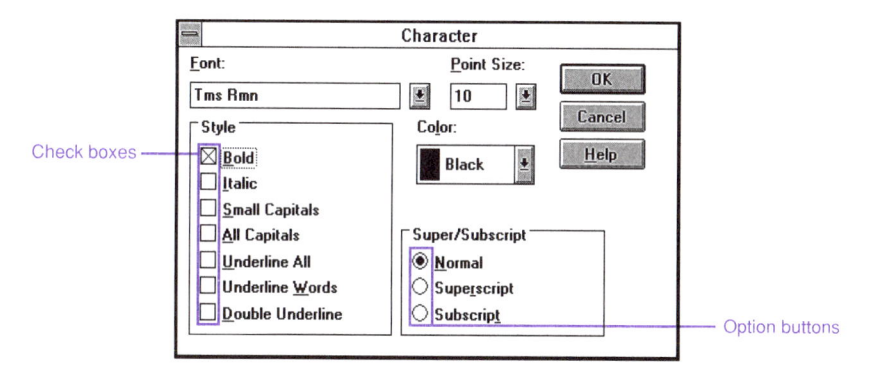

Figure 1.14 You can choose one or more check box options to control how a command is carried out.

Chapter 1

Option Buttons

Option buttons are similar to check boxes, in that they allow you to select options that control the way a command is carried out. However, they differ from check box options in that you can select only one option button in any group. You have already seen a type of option button earlier in this chapter: the PageWizards, Templates, Blank Page, and Open buttons on Publisher's opening screen. There, you selected an option button to specify your choice and then selected a command button to carry out the command.

Option buttons in dialog boxes look a little different (see Figure 1.14). The buttons usually look like circles. When you select a button, a dot appears inside the circle, indicating that the button is selected. To select a different option, click on the option's button or use the arrow keys to highlight the option.

The Publisher Mouse Pointer

You've already learned a little about the mouse pointer—the on-screen arrow which lets you point and select. But the mouse pointer can take on other forms as well, depending on the task you are currently performing:

- *Arrow:* A hollow arrow that slants to the left is the most common. You use it to point at and select items.
- *Cross hair:* When you select any of the several tools in Publisher that draw a box or an area to insert text or graphics, the mouse pointer changes to a cross hair. Move the cross hair where you want to start the box, hold down the left mouse button, and drag the cross hair to the diagonally-opposite corner. As you drag the mouse, a dotted line appears to show the shape and position of the object. When you release the mouse button, the dotted line becomes solid, showing the object as it will appear.
- *Selection cursor:* The *selection cursor* is where text you type will be entered. It is a small, blinking vertical bar. It is not to be confused with the I-beam mouse pointer described next. Whenever you create or select a text frame, the selection cursor appears. Whatever you type

will be inserted at this point. You can move this cursor with the arrow keys or with the I-beam cursor, as explained next.

The I-beam symbol is used to select the text insertion point. If you define a text area with the cross-hair cursor as described earlier, an I-beam pointer appears, because Publisher assumes you want to enter text in the box. The selection cursor also appears, indicating where the text you type will appear. Once you've typed some text, you can move the selection cursor by moving the I-beam where you want the bar to appear and clicking with your mouse.

Moving van: Whenever you attempt to move an object on-screen, the mouse pointer turns into a truck. To move an object, you first select it (click on it). Eight small black squares, called *handles*, appear around the object to show that it has been selected. When you move the mouse cursor inside the object, the truck appears, indicating you can move the object. Hold down the left mouse button and drag the object to its new location.

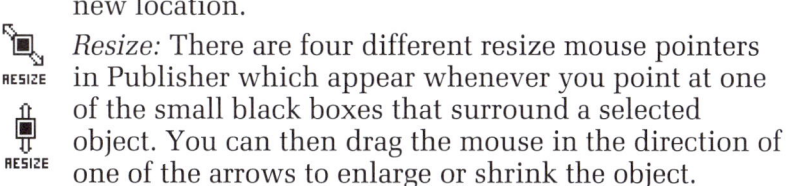

Resize: There are four different resize mouse pointers in Publisher which appear whenever you point at one of the small black boxes that surround a selected object. You can then drag the mouse in the direction of one of the arrows to enlarge or shrink the object.

Crop: If the object selected is a piece of clip art or a photograph, you can crop the image to use only a portion of it. If you've selected an object that can be cropped, a crop tool button appears on the Toolbar. It has a small square on it that has the lines continuing out on two corners. Click once on this button, then move to one of the small black squares which surround the selected object. The mouse pointer turns into the *cropper*. Use the cropper to snip off parts of the image you don't want to use.

If you would like to use simpler, less graphic cursors, you can change the appearance of the cursors. For example, you can change the move cursor so it appears as a cross with arrowheads instead of as a moving van. Pull down the Options menu and select Settings. A dialog box appears, as show in Figure 1.15. The Helpful Pointers check box is selected. To use less graphic pointers, select the Helpful Pointers option to turn it off. Then press the OK button.

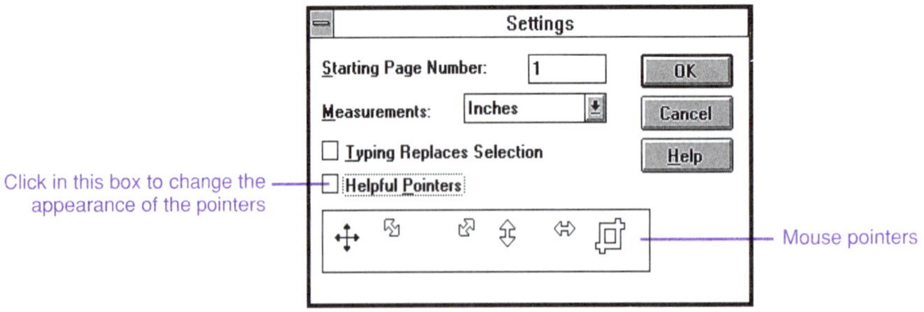

Figure 1.15 The Settings dialog box on Publisher's Option menu lets you change six of the nine mouse pointers used in Publisher.

On-line Help

Publisher offers you an *on-line* help facility. The term on-line means that you can access help from within Publisher. A help window will appear offering information to help you use and understand Publisher. This Help window can be moved, resized, iconized, or expanded to cover the entire screen just as any application window.

Publisher's help comes in two forms: *context-sensitive help* and a *help index*. Context-sensitive help displays a help window that contains information related to what you are doing. The program "knows" the task you are trying to perform and offers the information it thinks you need. The help index provides a list of topics about which users commonly need help. Although the index requires a little more thinking on your part, it allows you to select the help you need.

The Save and Save As dialog boxes provide good examples of context-sensitive help. In the upper right corner of these boxes are three command buttons—OK, Cancel, and Help. Clicking on the Help button or pressing Alt+H displays a Help window that contains information about the Save or Save As command. This saves you the trouble of looking through the help index to find these command listings. If this window contains the information you need, you can exit the window and return to the dialog box. If the window does not contain the information you need, you can access the rest of Publisher's on-line help system. If you are performing an operation and there is no Help button, you can access context-sensitive help by pressing the F1 key.

You will definitely want to play with the Help window and become familiar with its operation. Once you have mastered the basics of Publisher through this book, you'll find that the on-line help is very useful for refreshing your memory about procedures you may know but rarely use.

Maneuvering in the Help System

When the Help window pops up, you'll see five option buttons just below the Help window's menu bar. These provide an easy way to maneuver through the help system to find the information you need:

- ▶ Index provides a lengthy index of all topics available. To scroll through the list of topics, use the vertical and horizontal scroll bars or the cursor keys: PgUp, PgDn, and the arrow keys. To select a topic, click on it or highlight it and press Enter. A help window appears, displaying information about the selected topic.
- ▶ Back has a slanted series of little footprints on it. Clicking on this button takes you back one topic at a time until you return to the Help index. This button is dimmed or grayed out until you access information on a help topic. In other words, you can't go back until you've gone forward.
- ▶ Browse and Browse let you move backward and forward through topics related to the one that you started with. If one or the other of these buttons is grayed out, you cannot browse in the direction of that button; there is simply no information to browse to in that direction.
- ▶ Search allows you to search for topics using *keywords*. Keywords are entries unique to a topic. For example, if you need to know about printing, you would type print to display a list of topics about printing. You can then click on one of the topics in the list. The following Quick Steps lead you through the search process.

Searching for a Help Topic

1. Click on the Search button or press S.   The Search dialog box appears, as shown in Figure 1.16.
2. Start typing the keyword that pertains to the topic about which you want help.   As you type the keyword, the list of topics in the list box below the keyword changes.

3. When you see the topic you want, stop typing.
4. Click on one of the topics in the list box and then press the Search button, or tab to the list of topics, highlight the topic, and press Enter.

   The line below the topics list changes to show the number of topics found. The box below this line displays a list of topics found.

5. Click on a topic in the list and press the Go To button, or tab to the list, highlight the topic, and press G.

   A help screen appears, displaying information about the selected topic.

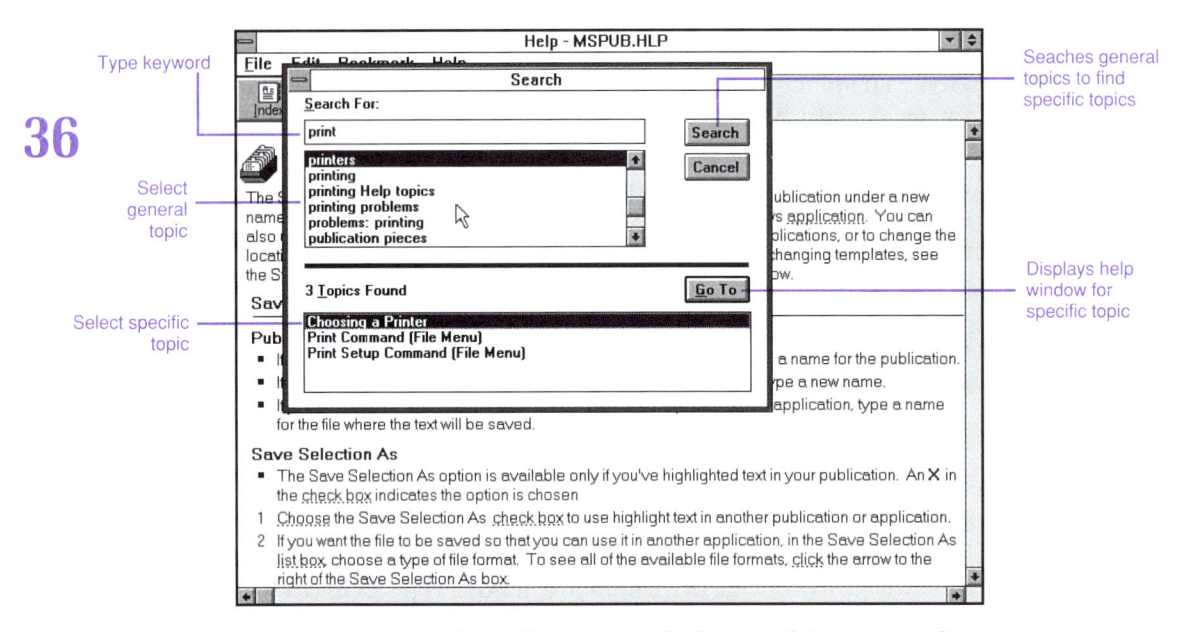

   □

Figure 1.16 Finding all topics with the word "print" in them.

The Help Menu

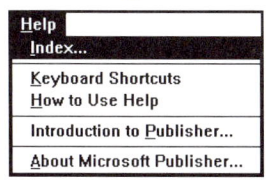

With many operations, you may not want context-sensitive help. For example, you may not have a clear idea of what you need to do—you want more general help. In such cases, you can use Publisher's Help menu. To access the menu, select Help from the menu bar; either click on it or press Alt+H. This menu offers general help features plus access to the Help index and the search features.

To select an option on the Help menu, click on it or press the underlined letter in the option's name. The Help menu has the following options:

Index	The index of on-line help topics.
Keyboard Shortcuts	The keyboard shortcuts available in both Publisher and Windows.
How to Use Help	A description of the procedures used to obtain on-line help.
Introduction to Publisher	A subprogram showing how documents are built.
About Microsoft Publisher...	A title screen showing version and serial number.

Exiting Publisher

To exit Publisher, pull down the File menu and select Exit Publisher, or press the F3 key. If the document you are currently working on has not been saved, a dialog box appears, asking if you want to save your changes. Otherwise, you are returned to the Windows desktop. To reopen Publisher, double-click on its icon.

What You Have Learned

Microsoft Publisher is a powerful program that allows you to produce professional-quality documents such as newsletters, letterhead, business cards, greeting cards, brochures, and much more. In this chapter, you learned,

- ▶ The basics of using the popular graphical user interface, Windows. You learned how to move and select items using both the mouse and the keyboard, how to resize windows, shuffle them around, under, and over other items on your electronic desktop, how to shrink application windows down to icons and restore them, and how to have more than one copy of an application running at the same time.
- ▶ How to start Publisher by selecting and clicking on its icon, and how to select an initial page layout or file.
- ▶ The parts of the Publisher application window including the menu bar, Toolbar, work area, status line, menus, dialog boxes, text boxes, list boxes, check boxes, the scroll bars, and paging control.
- ▶ How to use Publisher's on-line Help feature and search for topics.
- ▶ How to leave Publisher by choosing the Exit command from the File menu.

Chapter 2

A Quick Start to Publishing with PageWizards

In This Chapter

- Using Publisher right out of the box to create publications right away
- Tapping the power of PageWizards
- The types of publications you can create with PageWizards
- Sample PageWizard publications
- A quick method for printing your publications
- Saving your publication files to disk

Desktop Publishing Right Out of the Box

We all want to get a quick start on learning a new program. This chapter is for those of us who just can't wait; those who like to play with a program before diving into the manuals to learn the advanced moves. Yep, those of us who want to see what Microsoft Publisher can do right away. With this chapter and Publisher's PageWizards, you can get that quick start and produce some useful publications at the same time.

What is PageWizards? It's a collection of *smart templates*, a publishing consultant that leads you through the process of designing various types of publications. It's a subprogram that performs the difficult, tedious calculations and measurements, the repetitive layout tasks, and other such busy work for you. In fact, knowing nothing about desktop publishing, you'll be able to *immediately* create useful documents. Today. Right now.

What PageWizards Is Not

Many desktop publishing programs have *templates*—things like labels, brochures, letterheads, and a variety of documents all set up so you can create a publication simply by inserting your own text and graphics. Publisher itself comes with several such templates, which are explained in Chapter 3.

Now, how does a PageWizard differ from a template? A template is a document that someone else has already designed and created; you edit it to fit your needs. With PageWizards, you watch as the program *builds* the document from scratch. During the creation process, PageWizards asks you various design questions, allowing you to interact with the program to customize the design. A template is static; that is, you load it, and it sits there waiting for you to make your move. PageWizards, however, is dynamic; it works *with* you to customize designs for newsletters, calendars, invoices, greeting cards, and so on.

As the PageWizard builds the document, it presents you with a list of choices for design elements such as overall design style (classic, modern, jazzy, etc.), borders, room for artwork, and so on. You simply point and click at the option of your choice, and PageWizards implements the design.

But that doesn't mean you're stuck with PageWizard's final creation. Once the document is built, it appears in the work area, waiting for any further changes. You can then edit and save it as any other Publisher document. Change the border art, add new pieces of clip art, drop in more text boxes—whatever you want to do to further customize the document.

A Real Time Saver

PageWizard's subprograms save you hours of tedious work, while still giving you complete control of the finished document. For example, say you need an invoice form. Notorious for their excessive detail, these forms consist of many small text boxes which are arranged in a grid pattern and require detailed labeling. You could create such a form from scratch, putting together the scores of elements that make it up, but why waste all that time over something so mundane as an invoice form?

Instead, you can have PageWizards create the form for you. Simply press the PageWizards button in the Start Up dialog box and select Seven Business Forms from the list box. The Forms PageWizards dialog box appears, as shown in Figure 2.1. As you can see, this PageWizard can help you create seven widely-used business forms.

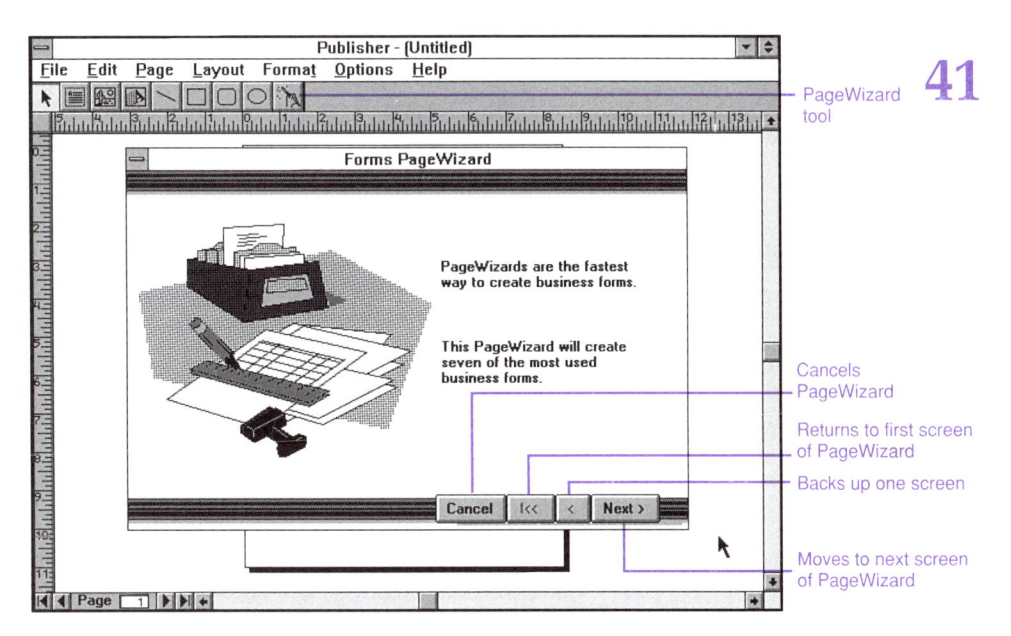

Figure 2.1 The Forms PageWizard dialog box appears, telling you what this PageWizard can do.

Using PageWizards within Other Publications

The Forms PageWizard, shown in Figure 2.1, and the other PageWizards in the list box build entire documents for you. However, some of the PageWizards listed and others that are not listed let you create mini-publications which you can use as *parts* of another document, as shown in Figure 2.2.

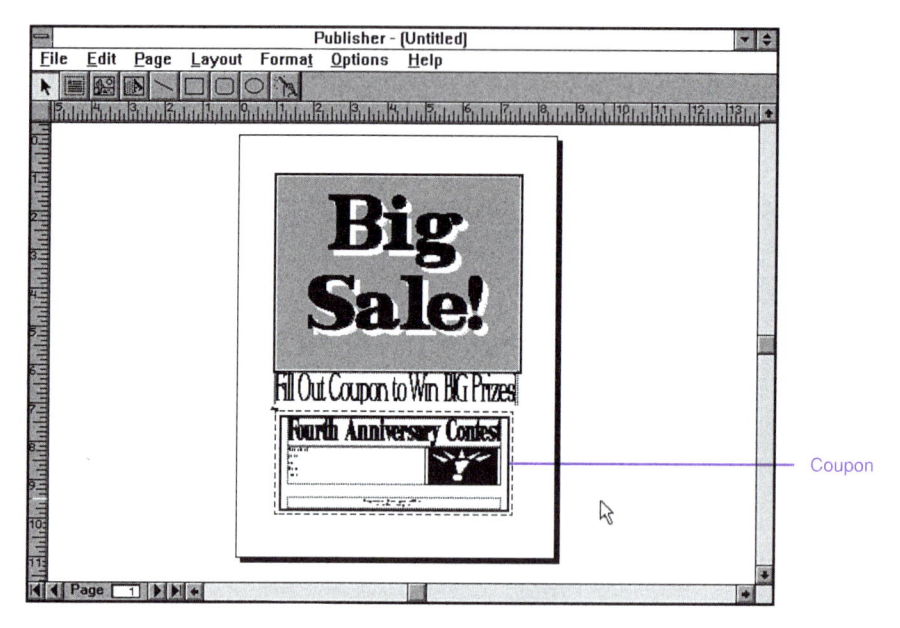

Figure 2.2   You can include a coupon in a sale flyer to generate business and check the effectiveness of the flyer.

The Coupon PageWizard, shown in the figure, lets you create a wide variety of coupons. If you were building a flyer to advertise your business, you might want to include a coupon, saying "Ten Percent off on all Widgets When This Coupon Is Presented." Instead of closing the flyer file and creating a new file for the coupon, you could use the Coupon PageWizard to create a coupon and paste it into the flyer displayed on-screen.

> **FYIdea:** If you create newsletters, use the Calendar PageWizard to add a small calendar for the month on the front page of the newsletter. This adds a nice touch. If the newsletter is for a club or other organization, you can use the Coupon PageWizard to make a nice subscription coupon or membership renewal form. Church newsletters could include a tithe coupon.

To create these mini-publications, you do not access PageWizards from the Create New Publication dialog box. Instead, you use the PageWizard tool from the Toolbar (the bar just under the menu bar); it's the button that has a picture of a hand holding a wand:

You'll learn how to use the PageWizards tool later in this chapter.

Available PageWizards

In the current version of Publisher, the Start Up and Create New Publication dialog boxes list six PageWizards from which to choose; eight more are available with the PageWizards tool. Table 2.1 lists and describes the available PageWizards.

Table 2.1 Microsoft Publisher's PageWizards.

PageWizard	What It Does
Full-Page PageWizards	
Newsletter	Creates a basic newsletter layout allowing you to place text in columns and leaving room for pictures or artwork.
Seven Business Forms	Makes seven basic business forms: Customer Refund, Expense Report, Fax Cover Sheet, Invoice, Purchase Order, Statement, and Quote.

continues

Table 2.1   continued

PageWizard	What It Does
Three-Fold Brochure	Creates various brochure layouts you can use for advertising your business or presenting information.
Greeting Card & Invitation	Creates custom greeting cards and invitations, allowing you to add your own personal touch.
Calendar	Creates a wide range of calendars from the year 1800 A.D. through the distant future. The calendars cover a full year or just one month, and you can have PageWizards translate the days and months into any of eleven different languages.
Paper Aeroplane	A wonderful way of beating stress! The Paper Aeroplane PageWizard lets you create paper airplanes of three main styles, plus whirligigs! You have the option of printing out a sheet of folding instructions for each style also.

PageWizards Tools

Ad	Lets you create camera ready advertisements for use in newsletters or other publications.
Calendar	Allows you to include calendars as a part of a document.
Fancy First Letter	Allows you to create oversized letters for use in starting your publications or chapters, just like the monks used to do back in the middle ages.
Newsletter Banner	Allows you to create a banner for your newsletter without having to use all the options offered in the full-page Newsletter PageWizard.
Note-It	The electronic equivalent of those little yellow Post-It notes. Use this PageWizard to create notes to yourself or to others who might be using or modifying the document.

PageWizard	What It Does
Coupon	A coupon is exactly what you would expect it to be—something to be clipped out and used for discounts, for ordering products or services, or for the reader to communicate in some other way to the creator of the publication.
Table	Creates a grid of columns and rows like those used in most business forms. A handy and easy way to build forms not included in the Forms PageWizard.
Paper Aeroplane	Same as the full-page PageWizards option.

Starting a PageWizard

If Publisher is not running, start Publisher as explained in Chapter 1. If Publisher is already running, pull down the File menu and select Create New Publication. If you just started Publisher, its application window appears, with the Start Up dialog box in the center of the screen (see Figure 2.3). If you selected Create New Publication, the Create New Publication dialog box appears; this dialog box is similar to the Start Up dialog box, except that its title differs and it has no Open option.

Because PageWizards is the default selection, the PageWizard button is pressed, as you can tell by looking at the screen in Figure 2.3. On a VGA or EGA screen, the three-dimensional effect shows this button depressed, while the three next to it are raised. If you have lower resolution graphics, the selected button appears in a different color or shade.

The list box in the bottom of the dialog box displays the available PageWizards. Choosing a PageWizard and clicking on the OK button starts the selected PageWizard. If you are using a keyboard, tab to the list box, highlight the PageWizard you want to run, and press Enter.

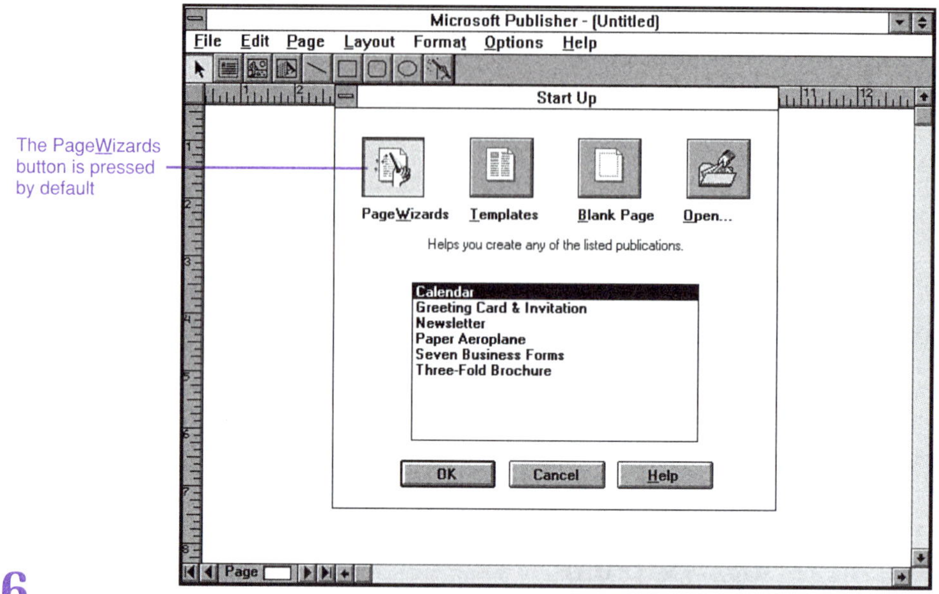

Chapter 2

Figure 2.3 When you start Publisher, the Start Up dialog box appears with the PageWizards button selected.

The following Quick Steps summarize how to start a PageWizard:

Starting a PageWizard

1. Start Publisher from Windows or select Create New Publication from the File menu if Publisher is already running.

   Either the Start Up dialog box or the Create New Publication dialog box appears.

2. Press the PageWizards button by clicking on it or pressing Alt+P.

   The list box under the buttons shows the available PageWizards.

3. Click on a PageWizards option in the list box, or Tab to the box and use the arrow keys to highlight an option.

   The selected option appears in reverse video.

4. Click on the OK button or Tab to the button and press Enter.

   The selected PageWizard starts running.

Maneuvering a PageWizard

During the creation process, PageWizards presents a series of dialog boxes which lead you through the process. One such box is shown in Figure 2.4. On the left side of the box is a graphic representation of the page. On the right are the options available for one design element in the publication. If you choose a different option on the right, the graphic image (on the left) changes to *show* you how the selected option will modify the appearance of the page. After you select an option for this design element, you can tell PageWizards to display the *next* dialog box in the series.

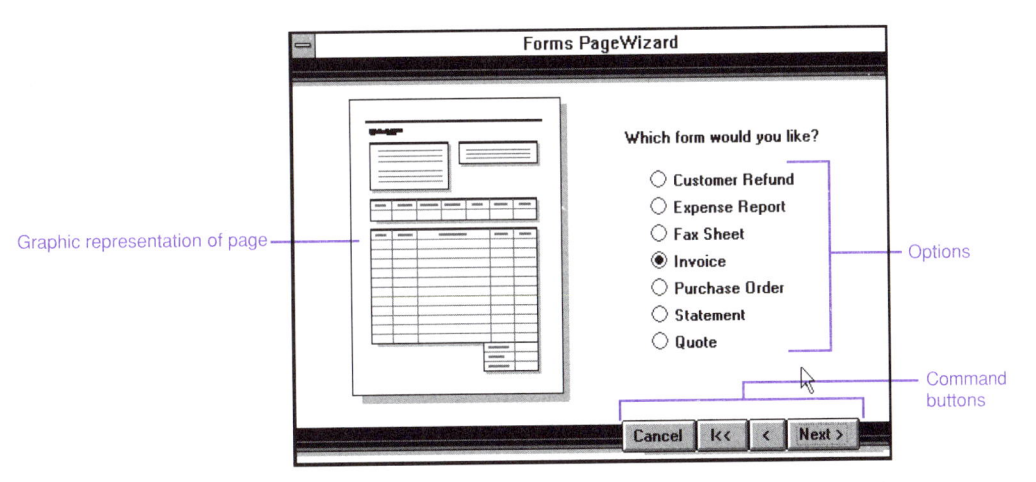

Figure 2.4 PageWizards leads you through the creation process by presenting a series of dialog boxes.

At the bottom right of each dialog box are four command buttons, as shown in Figure 2.4. The leftmost button, Cancel, allows you to terminate the current PageWizard; simply click on the button. The rightmost button, Next, allows you to move to the next dialog box in the series. The two middle buttons allow you to move back to previous dialog boxes, in case you change your mind. The button on the left (¦<<) takes you to the first dialog box in the series; the button on the right (<) takes you to the previous dialog box.

For example, Figure 2.4 shows the dialog box that appears after you press the Next button at the bottom of the Forms PageWizard dialog box you saw in Figure 2.1. This box allows you to choose any of the seven available forms. If you select a different form, the picture on the left side of the box changes to show the overall appearance of the selected form.

Your First Project: Creating a Fax Cover Sheet

For speed and convenience, businesses and individuals often send faxes instead of letters or order forms. Almost every copy shop now offers a fax service, both for sending and receiving faxes. So, even if you don't own a fax machine, someone somewhere is likely to ask you to "just fax it to me." No matter how you send your faxes, having your own personalized fax cover sheet allows you to add a personal touch to all your electronic correspondence.

Of course, you could go to an office supply store and buy some generic prefab cover sheets made by some well-known company. All you have to do is write your name and your company's name in the blanks. But anyone who receives any volume of faxes will see the same cover sheets over and over; yours might get lost in the stack.

Publisher offers a better way. Using the Forms PageWizard, you can create a *personalized* fax cover sheet that commands attention and reflects the professional interest you have in the current transaction or correspondence. So, here's your first project in Publisher—it's going to be fun!

Start Publisher or, if Publisher is already running, select Create New Publication from the File menu. In either case, a dialog box appears, which allows you to run PageWizards. If the PageWizards button is not selected, press the button. The available PageWizards appear in the list box beneath the option buttons.

Select Seven Business Forms from the list box. Following is a list of ways you can select and run a PageWizard that appears in the list box:

- ▶ Double-click on the PageWizard you want to run. This is the fastest way.
- ▶ Click on the PageWizard and press Enter.
- ▶ Tab to the list box, use the arrow keys to highlight the PageWizard you want to run, and press Enter.
- ▶ Highlight the PageWizard you want to run using the keyboard or mouse, and then press the OK button; either click on it or Tab to it and press Enter.

No matter how you select the option, the Forms PageWizard dialog box appears as you saw in Figure 2.1. Press the Next button in the lower right corner of the dialog box to display the seven available forms.

The Seven Business Forms

As shown in Figure 2.4, the second Forms PageWizard dialog box shows the seven business forms it can create for you: Customer Refund, Expense Report, Fax Sheet, Invoice, Purchase Order, Statement, and Quote. The sample form on the left shows what the selected form type looks like.

You select a form by clicking on the circle preceding its name or on the name itself. A dot appears in the circle, and a box appears around the name to show that the option is selected. The sample form on the left side of the dialog box changes to show the general appearance of the selected form. You won't see a lot of detail. Click through the various options now to see what the other forms look like.

When you are finished looking at the other six forms, select Fax Sheet. Click on the Next button to accept your choice and move to the next dialog box in the series. The keyboard is useless in maneuvering in these dialog boxes, so you *must* have a mouse. However, you will use the keyboard occasionally to fill in a text box (for example, to type a title for a newsletter).

Portrait and Landscape

When you select the Next button, a dialog box appears prompting you to select the *orientation* of the form. (If your printer does not support landscape orientation, Publisher will skip this step.) The orientation option tells PageWizards how you want the form positioned on the page. You have two choices: portrait or landscape. *Portrait* prints the form as you would print a letter on a page—the form is longer than it is wide. *Landscape* prints the form sideways, making it wider than it is long.

A standard sheet of typewriter paper in the U.S. and Canada is 8.5 inches wide by 11 inches high. The size is slightly different in Europe and is called A4 (it is 8.27 inches wide by 11.70 inches high).

The most common orientation of either paper type is portrait; that is, the page is longer than it is wide. If you turn the page on its side, it is now in landscape orientation.

To your system's printer, portrait and landscape have a more precise meaning. Portrait means your printer prints the page normally, whereas landscape means it prints everything sideways.

> **Caution:** To have Publisher print in landscape orientation, your printer must support landscape orientation. Refer to your printer manual to find out. The printer must also be properly installed in Windows (using the Printers option in the Control Panel). If your printer does not support landscape orientation or if it is not installed properly, you will not be able to print properly in landscape orientation.

Because most fax pages are printed in portrait orientation, this is the most logical choice. It saves the person on the other end of the fax from having to rotate the page in order to read it. However, you can choose to print in landscape mode. Select the orientation and then press the Next button.

A Matter of Style

The next dialog box in your fax sheet design asks

```
Which style would you like?
```

You have three styles from which to choose: Classic, Traditional, and Modern. A sample form appears on the left side of the dialog box—this time, it represents the appearance of the fax cover sheet in the currently selected style. Click on each of the three style choices to see how the various options affect the look of the cover sheet. Figure 2.5 shows the Traditional look.

When you are satisfied with the style selection, click on the Next button to continue.

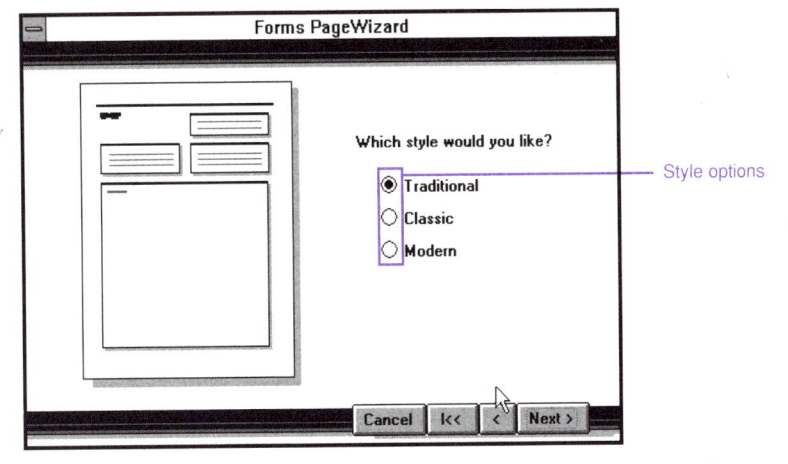

Figure 2.5 You can select any of three style options to control the overall look of your fax cover sheet.

Filling Out Forms in Publisher

After you select a style, a dialog box appears asking if you want empty text frames added so you can fill the form out in Publisher. You can answer Yes or No; No is the default.

This is a significant design decision for you, not just in fax cover sheets but in most forms you will be creating. A *text frame* is a box in which you can import or enter text. You can move this box on-screen, change its dimensions, or format the text it contains quickly and easily. For now, it's enough to know that text frames allow you to type text in a document. Chapter 4 covers text frames in greater detail.

If you let a PageWizard create text frames as part of the document, the PageWizard positions the frame in the correct place and sets the text in a usable size and style. You can then click on a text box and start typing the appropriate text in each box. This allows you to create a neatly typed fax cover sheet for each fax you send. The disadvantage is that every time you want to send a fax, you have to load this fax file, type the required information, and then print the cover sheet.

On the other hand, you can design the sheet to be filled out by hand, and then print out only one sheet. Take that sheet and run off a hundred copies, and now everyone in your company can use the same snazzy fax cover sheet for all the company's fax messages. When the forms run low, anyone can just pull the master from the file and run off a new supply of fax cover sheets.

> **FYIdea:** Fax sheets, letterheads, invoices, and all the other documents that customers or potential customers might see are *great* places for subtle ads. Be sure to customize your documents to reflect what your business does, adding an appropriate graphic from Publisher's extensive file of clip art to call attention to your firm's name and specialty.

The best choice is Yes; let the PageWizard insert the text frames. These frames are invisible on the printed page, so they won't appear on the printed form. This gives you the best of both worlds. You can have a standard fax sheet for your office, *and* you can call up the document and fill out the cover sheet whenever you want to send an especially neat and professional-looking fax.

For the purpose of this exercise, choose Yes, and then click on the Next button.

Languages

The next dialog box asks you which language you want to use for the cover sheet. In today's international business environment, it's nice to be able to send fax cover sheets overseas with the labels in the appropriate language. Even if the rest of the fax is in English, this is a nice gesture on your part. This dialog box appears in other PageWizards as well. For example, in the Calendar PageWizard, the days and names of the months will be in the language selected.

At this time, you have the choice of the following languages: Danish, Dutch, English Finnish, French, German, Italian, Norwegian, Portuguese, Spanish, and Swedish. The default selection is English, as shown in Figure 2.6; you can accept this setting simply by clicking on the Next button.

Building Your Fax Sheet

The next dialog box displays a message telling you that you have answered all the questions and PageWizards is about to create the specified form. You have two options here: You can press the Create It button to give PageWizards the ok to create the form, or you can press either of the backup buttons (¦<< or <) to change the settings you selected.

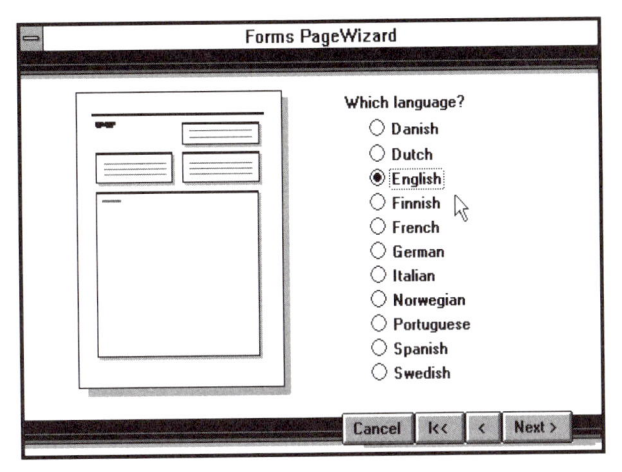

Figure 2.6 PageWizards can label forms in several different languages.

If you go back to change settings, keep in mind that PageWizards remembers your settings. If you return to a dialog box that contains a setting you do not want to change, you can skip the box without changing your selection by pressing the Next button or one of the backup buttons.

As an exercise, click on the double-less-than button to go back to the first dialog box, and step through the Seven Business Forms PageWizard pages, noting whether the dots in the circles and the boxes around the names (indicating selected options) are the options you chose during your first trip through the PageWizard.

When you are satisfied that your selections are correct, go to the last dialog box and click on the Create It button. The PageWizard window disappears and a smaller one, titled Forms PageWizard, appears as shown in Figure 2.7. This box steps you through the creation process; it displays each step in the process and explains the procedures needed to accomplish each step.

In the bottom of this box is a horizontal "scroll bar" that serves as a speed control. You can use this bar to change the speed at which PageWizards constructs the page:

▶ *Click on either arrow* to change the speed incrementally. Click the left arrow to slow the process or the right arrow to speed it up.

▶ *Hold down the mouse button* on either arrow to change the speed continuously.

▶ *Drag the scroll box* to the left to decrease the speed or to the right to increase the speed.

▶ *Click in the scroll bar* on either side of the scroll box to increase the speed in greater increments than by clicking on the arrows.

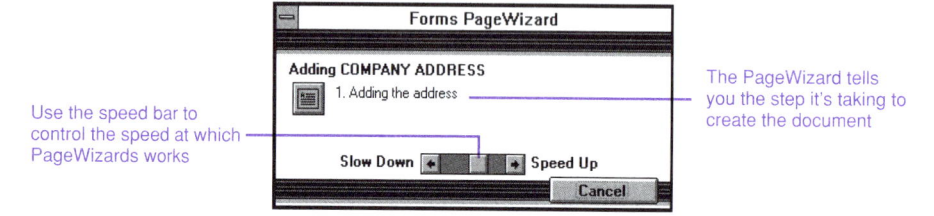

Figure 2.7 PageWizards show and tell you how they construct documents as they create the document.

If you move the speed control all the way up, the PageWizard tells you, Full speed ahead, Captain..., and runs at the fastest speed your computer allows it. At first, set PageWizards to slow, so you can see how PageWizards constructs the various publications. This will give you some idea of how to assemble your own publications. As you get more experienced, you may want to crank up the speed.

The Completed Form

When the document is finished, the small dialog box disappears, and a larger one with a checkered flag pops up to tell you that the PageWizard is done. You are also reminded to put your name or your company's name and address on the form before printing it, and you are reminded that help is available from the Help menu.

Click on the OK button to return to the Publisher work area. Your newly created fax cover sheet appears. To take a closer look at your fax sheet, pull down the Page menu and select the Actual Size option. This makes the page the same size it will appear in print so you can read the text easily. However, because it's larger, you'll need to use the horizontal and vertical scrolls bars described in Chapter 1 to see different parts of the page. You can also switch between views by using the F9 function key, which toggles from a full page view to an actual size view.

You can now customize your fax cover sheet to meet your specific needs and desires. The techniques needed to customize your fax sheet begin in Chapter 4, "Adding Text to a Document," and continue through Chapter 9, "Creating Special Text Effects."

For the moment, there are two things you might want to do. The first is to save this fax cover sheet to a file on your hard disk so that you don't have to use the Seven Business Forms PageWizard to create it again. The other is to print it out and see what it looks like on paper. Both procedures are covered in the next two sections.

The following Quick Steps summarize the process of using a PageWizard.

Creating a Document with PageWizards

1. Start Publisher, or if it is already running, pull down the File menu and select Create New Publication.

   The Start Up dialog box or the Create New Publication dialog box appears.

2. Press the PageWizards button, select a PageWizard from the list box, and press the OK button.

   The first screen of the PageWizard appears.

3. Click on the Next button.

   The next screen in the series appears.

4. Respond to each dialog box as the PageWizard leads you through the creation process. Press the Next button after selecting your options.

   You define how the document is to be built by the PageWizard.

5. On the last screen, if all is okay, press the Create It button; otherwise use the arrow buttons to go back though the screens and make changes.

   The document is created and you are returned to Publisher's application window.

   □

Saving Your Files

A newly created document, such as the fax cover sheet you just made, exists only in your computer's electronic memory (Random Access Memory, or RAM). This memory is purged each time the computer is turned off, so even a blip in the electrical circuit can wipe out the document. This is why you need to save all your documents to a more stable storage location—to disk. And you must do this often, to prevent losing any changes you made to a document.

To save a file, pull down the File menu. This menu contains two options for saving files: Save and Save As (see Figure 2.8).

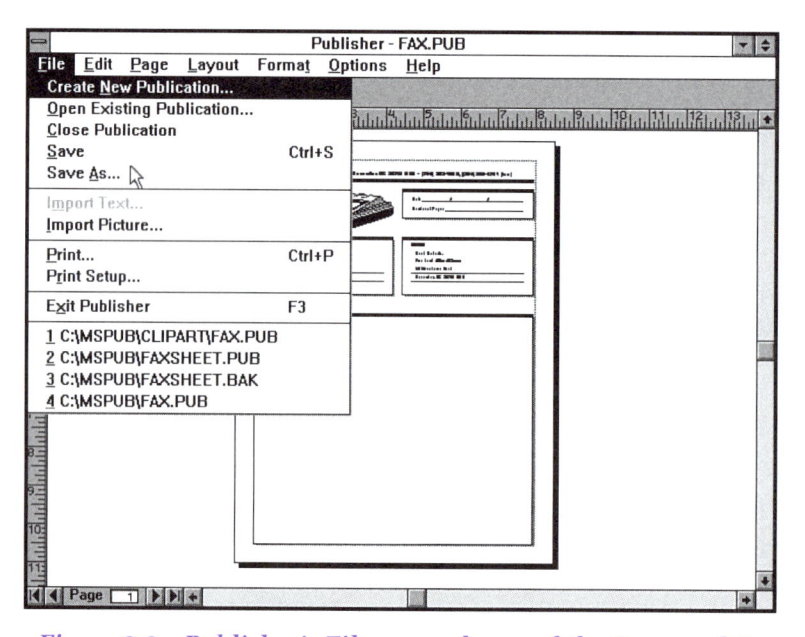

Figure 2.8   Publisher's File menu, home of the Save and Save As commands.

The Save option is for saving new or existing documents. The fax sheet you just created is a new document. You can tell by looking at the title bar; (Untitled) indicates that the file has never been named, and hence has never been saved to disk. It also indicates that the file exists *only in RAM*; it can disappear forever in the blink of your office lights.

If the document has already been saved, the title bar would include the name of the file, for example, FAXSHEET.PUB. If you've already saved the file and named it, Publisher knows in which file to save the document. When you select Save, Publisher saves the document immediately to disk, without asking for any more information.

The Save As option is used primarily for creating copies of a document. If you have already saved a document to a disk file, you can use the Save As option to save it under another name or in a different directory on disk, creating an exact duplicate of the file. You can then modify the duplicate file without affecting the original.

Saving a New File

Because your fax cover sheet has not been saved yet, selecting either option, Save or Save As, displays the Save As dialog box, as shown in Figure 2.9. Publisher wants to know what name you want to give the file and where you want to put it. Select either option now to display this box on your screen.

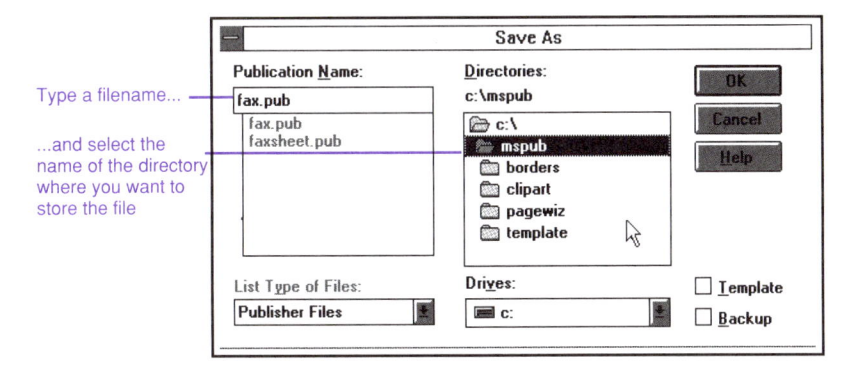

Figure 2.9 Publisher's Save As dialog box prompts you to name the file and specify a directory in which to store it.

Filenames in Publisher

The first step is to name the file. In the upper left corner of the dialog box is the Publication Name text box with the text *.pub in reverse video and a blinking cursor. You can type a name in this box or edit the current entry, but first you need to know about the DOS filename conventions.

Because of the limitations of the DOS operating system, imposed on both Windows and Publisher, you are limited to using a name of up to eight characters with an extension of up to three characters; the name and extension must be separated by a period. Neither the name nor the extension can contain any of the following characters:

" . / \ [ ] : * < > | + ; , ?

Also, in Publisher, it's a good idea to use the .PUB extension for any files you create. That way, you can tell by looking at a list of files which ones are Publisher documents. The extension, .PUB, stands for *publication*.

To name the file, you can type a name for the file from scratch or edit the current entry in the text box. To replace what's in the text box, start typing. The `*.pub` disappears, and the characters you type appear in the box. To edit the current entry, in this case `*.pub`, click inside the text box or use the arrow keys to move the cursor to the text you want to change. Use the Del or Backspace key to delete text, and then type your change. You can type upper- or lowercase letters; it doesn't matter here.

When you're done naming the file, don't do anything else. You still have to tell Publisher where to store the file, as explained in the next section.

Saving to the Right Location

To the right of the Publication Name text box is the Directories option. Below that is the path to the current directory; it might be something like `c:\mspub`, meaning that drive C: is the current drive, and MSPUB (the Microsoft Publisher directory) is the current directory. If you don't select a different directory, Publisher will save the file you just named to the current drive and directory.

For now, the best policy is to save all your document files to the MSPUB directory, so that both you and Publisher can find them easily. Later, you may want to create a separate directory for storing your publication files, to keep those files separate from Publisher's program files.

To specify a different location for saving a file, you must select the drive and directory where you want the file saved. To save the file to a different drive, click on the Drives drop-down list box or press Alt+V. You can pull down the list by clicking on the down arrow to the right of the list box or pressing Alt+↓. A list of available drives appears. To select a different drive, click on one of the drives or highlight it.

Once you've selected a drive, the Directories list box shows the names of the directories on that drive (see Figure 2.9). To activate this list box, click on it or press Alt+D. Each directory name is preceded by a small file folder (directory) icon. At the top of the box is the letter of the current drive, for example c:\. To the left of the drive letter is an open folder, indicating the drive is currently active. If the drive contains one or more directories, you'll see folders directly below the drive letter and slightly indented. If a folder is open and shaded inside, it is the currently active directory.

Once the Directories list box is active, you can move through the directory tree of the current drive. To move to the top of the directory tree (the root directory of the current drive), double-click on the drive letter or highlight it and press Enter. To activate any of the directories in the list, double-click on the directory's name or highlight it and press Enter. You will see no files at this point because Publisher is looking only for document files—those ending with the .PUB extension.

Protecting Your Files by Making Backups

In the lower right corner of the Save As dialog box are two check box options: Template and Backup. The Template option allows you to save the file as a template; you will learn more about templates in Chapter 12. The Backup option allows you to save a duplicate copy of the file to disk. If you select this option (putting an X in its check box), Publisher will save two files to disk—the file you named and a duplicate file with the same name but with the extension .BAK. This backup file protects you in the event that you accidently delete or damage the original file. You can use the backup file to get back most of your work.

If you select the Backup option, Publisher updates the backup file each time you save the document. Publisher saves the document that's displayed on-screen in the file that contained the original document. This bumps the original document out of its file and into the backup file. The old backup file is then bumped off the disk.

Chapter 2

> **Tip:** Keep this process in mind when making major changes to a document. As long as you don't save the document to disk, you can return to the original file by selecting Close Publication from the File menu and answering No when asked if you want to save your changes. If you make a change and save the file to disk, you can recover the original file by closing the current publication, opening the backup file, and then saving the file under its original name (with the .PUB extension instead of the .BAK extension).

Completing the Save Operation

To execute the Save command, click the OK button. Publisher saves the file to the specified drive and directory under the name you gave it. The following Quick Steps summarize the Save File operation.

Saving a Document

1. Pull down the File menu and select Save.

   If this is the first time you've saved the file, the Save As dialog box appears, otherwise the file is saved and you are returned to the document.

2. If the Save As dialog box appears, type a name for the file in the Publication Name text box.

   Follow the DOS filename conventions explained earlier, and use the extension .PUB, so you will know in the future that this file was created in Publisher.

3. To save the file to a different disk or directory than the one displayed, use the Drives and Directory options to specify where you want the file saved.

   The path to the directory where the file will be saved is displayed under the Directory option.

4. Select the Backup option to put an X in the check box.

   Creating a backup file protects your hard work from getting destroyed.

5. Press the OK button. Publisher saves the document to disk under the specified filename. ☐

Quick Printing

Although printing is covered in detail in Chapter 11, you are probably anxious to print out the fax cover sheet you just created and saved. This section provides a bare-bones approach to printing a file. If the document does not print, then refer to Chapter 11 for more about printers and how they work with Publisher. The following Quick Steps lead you through the printing process. To print even more quickly, simply press Ctrl+P.

Q Printing a File

1. Pull down the File menu and select Print. The Print dialog box appears.
2. Ignore all the options and click on the OK button. The Printing dialog box appears, telling you that printing is in progress. ☐

If your printer can handle graphics and is properly installed in Windows, then your fax sheet will print out shortly, depending on the speed of the printer. You can cancel printing by clicking on the Cancel button.

Using the Other PageWizards

Now that you've seen a PageWizard in action, you'll probably want to see how some of the other PageWizards operate. Because they all use a series of dialog boxes to lead you through the creation process, once you've learned one, the others are a snap. Following are explanations of what each of the currently available PageWizards do, and helpful notes about the choices they present you.

The Newsletter PageWizard

You receive newsletters in the mail often—they can be anywhere from one page, front and back, to several pages in length. They can be from a club, a company, a school, your church, or almost any other organization.

Newsletters are an effective way to keep an interested group of people informed, whether they are members of your club, customers who are interested in your products, or employees who want to know what's going on in their company.

> **FYIdea:** This holiday season, instead of sending Christmas cards full of cliches, do a newsletter full of family happenings for the past year. It will look professional and certainly be cheaper than cards. Print out a master copy and take the pages to your local quick copy shop. Specify colored paper for that added extra touch. Leave a small box to put Christmas Seals or some other colorful holiday sticker to jazz it up even more.

Start the Newsletter PageWizard as explained earlier in this chapter. The first dialog box presents a title screen, telling you what the Newsletter PageWizard will do. It will create a standard newsletter layout for you with places for such elements as text stories, pictures, headlines, and a table of contents.

Click on the Next button (remember, the keyboard does not work for maneuvering in PageWizards, although you will use it to fill in text boxes when asked). A dialog box appears, presenting three style options: Classic, Modern, and Jazzy. Click on the style you want to use. The graphic on the left side of the screen changes to show the overall appearance of the selected style. You can look at all three styles before choosing the one you like best. Press the Next button when you're done.

The next dialog box prompts you to specify the number of columns in the newsletter: one to four columns. Select the various options, one at a time, and keep your eye on the picture of the page to see how the various layouts will appear in print. Below the options is a small box that presents a design tip. For example, when you select three columns, the design tip tells you that this is the most popular format for newsletters. Select an option and press the Next button.

You are now prompted to type a title for the newsletter, that big banner name that goes across the top of the front page. It should be eye-catching and distinctive. PageWizards uses a tool called WordArt that designs the title for you. All you have to do is type the text that you want to use. (You'll learn more about WordArt in Chapter 9.) Right now, however, all you can do is type a name for your newsletter. For example, you can type `The Smith Family Chronicles` or `The Lion's Roar` (for a Lion's Club newsletter). When you start typing, the name in the text box disappears, and the characters you type appear. After typing a title, press the Next button.

You have to complete four more dialog boxes to provide the Newsletter PageWizard with the information it needs. Although these dialog boxes are explained in more detail in Chapter 13, here's a quick look at them:

- ▶ *Print on both sides?* If you want your newsletter printed on both sides of a page, select Yes. To print on only one side, select No.
- ▶ *Number of pages?* Type the number of pages you think your newsletter will occupy.
- ▶ *Special elements.* You can select any or all of the following four special elements. *Table of contents* displays a list of topics covered in the newsletter. *Fancy first letter* starts each article with a specially designed letter. *Date* inserts the date of the publication. *Volume and issue* allows you to specify a publication number.
- ▶ *Language?* You can select a foreign language. The Newsletter PageWizard will translate any text that appears on the layout into the selected language.

Make your selections to complete the newsletter, and then press the Create It button in the final dialog box.

The Seven Business Forms PageWizard Revisited

You've already seen that the Seven Business Forms PageWizard creates Customer Refund, Expense Report, Fax Sheet, Invoice, Purchase Order, Statement, and Quote forms—together, some of the most often used forms in business today. If you've been following along on your computer, you've already used this PageWizard to create a fax cover sheet.

To create the other forms, you follow the same basic procedure. However, you will encounter minor variations, depending on the form. For example, in building an invoice, you can include or exclude a number of column headings such as Your #, Our #, Sales Rep, Ship Via, Terms, Tax ID, and so on. You must then select which headings you *don't* want to use by clicking on them. Table 2.2 provides a list of the seven business forms and a description of each.

Table 2.2   The seven business forms.

Form	Function
Customer Refund	Used to record items returned by customers and the credit or payment given for the returned merchandise.
Expense Report	Used for listing the work-related expenses incurred by an employee.
Fax Sheet	A cover sheet that must be sent as the first page of a fax package.
Invoice	A form that accompanies a shipment of goods to a customer. Includes places for information such as quantity shipped, date shipped, amount due, date due, and so on.
Purchase Order	A form sent to a vendor, requesting certain merchandise be sent or services performed. Includes places for information such as product name and code.
Statement	Totals the invoices for a given period, usually a month, tells the customer how much they owe and for which invoices, and requests payment.
Quote	Useful for showing prospective customers the merchandise or services you can offer and how much you charge.

The Three-Fold Brochure PageWizard

Three-fold brochures consist of a single sheet of paper, folded twice. The paper is folded in much the same way you would fold a letter to put in a envelope. You make one fold about a third of the way from the top, and the second about a third of the way from the bottom. This creates a narrow form that's suitable for mailing or distributing in some other way. You have probably received three-fold brochures in the mail or seen them at the doctor's office.

The areas on the page defined by the fold, may be thought of as *mini-pages*. Thus, you now have three mini-pages on the front of the paper and three more on the back, for a total of six.

The Three-Fold Brochure PageWizard guides you through the creation of your brochure's basic layout. You'll be able to choose the orientation (portrait or landscape), a variety of stylistic effects, and whether this brochure is to be handed out or mailed, in which case it includes a place for a stamp. The document will be laid out so that when you make the folds, the mini-pages will read correctly.

For more information about creating brochures, refer to Chapter 13, "Professional Techniques: Newsletters, Brochures, and Other Long Documents."

> **FYIdea:** While three-fold brochures fit neatly in a regular business envelope, consider sending them without an envelope. Just fold the brochure and seal it with a small piece of tape or a staple. Add the customer's address and a stamp, and drop it into the mail. This technique saves money and eliminates the tiresome job of stuffing brochures into envelopes. Also, for a slight additional charge, the copy shop where you have your master reproduced can give you the copies already folded, so all you have to do is address, seal, and stamp them.

The Greeting Card & Invitation PageWizard

While store-bought greeting cards might be slicker than the homespun variety, nothing can compare with the personal intimacy conveyed by a homemade card. This PageWizard lets *you* decide what goes on the front of the card, and lets you compose a personal message to go inside.

Like the Brochure PageWizard, the Greeting Card PageWizard divides a sheet of paper into mini-pages and prints the publication so that when you fold the sheet, the mini pages form a greeting card. The PageWizard lays out the card for you, leaving spaces for your messages and for your pictures or artwork. You can then go back and edit the card to change the greeting, message, or artwork inserted during the card's creation. For details on modifying the artwork, refer to Chapter 7, "Adding Pictures to a Document."

The Calendar PageWizard

Calendars are useful in many ways. You can keep one on hand for jotting down appointments and reminders, or you can use calendars to spiff up your newsletters and keep club members informed of important dates. You can also add a sense of urgency to sales flyers or ads where you want to encourage customers to buy before a certain date. Whatever the purpose, PageWizards can help you create the calendars you need.

The Calendar PageWizard creates calendars from the year 1800 A.D. through the distant future. You may create calendars for a full year or for just one month, and you can have the days and months automatically translated into any of eleven different languages: Danish, Dutch, English, Finnish, French, German, Italian, Norwegian, Portuguese, Spanish, and Swedish.

Even more than the other PageWizards discussed in this chapter, the Calendar PageWizard allows you to create and print the finished product in just a few minutes at the most. Unlike our fax sheet—which we will finish later, you can churn out as many totally completed calendars as you like right now!

You can run this PageWizard from the Start Up dialog box (to create a full-page calendar), or by choosing the PageWizard tool on the Toolbar. If you run it from the Start Up dialog box, just step through the various dialog boxes to specify your preferences. When you reach the last page, click on the Create It button and your calendar will appear on-screen, as shown in Figure 2.10. You may then print it out as described earlier.

You can also run the Calendar PageWizard from the Toolbar, to create a mini-calendar for another publication. The following Quick Steps lead you through the process.

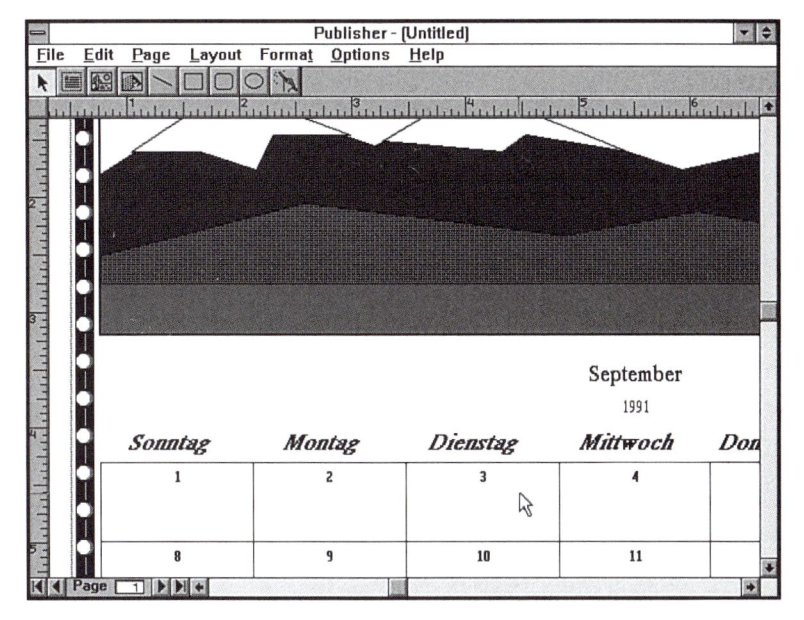

Figure 2.10 Part of a one-month calendar in German as created by the Calendar PageWizard.

ℚ Running the Calendar PageWizard Tool

1. Click on the PageWizard button in the Toolbar.

    The button appears to be pressed.

2. Move the mouse pointer where you want one corner of the calender to appear.

    As you move the mouse pointer to the work area, the pointer turns into a cross hair.

3. Hold down the left mouse button and drag the mouse pointer to the diagonally opposite corner.

    A dotted box appears, showing the location and dimensions of the calendar.

4. Release the mouse button.

    The PageWizard dialog box appears, prompting you to select a PageWizard.

5. Click on Calendar and then click on the OK button.

   The first Calendar PageWizard dialog box appears, telling you what it can do.

6. Work your way through the dialog boxes until the calendar is finished.

   □

The Note-It PageWizard

The Note-It PageWizard is the *only* one that does not create something you can print on paper. Instead, it makes notes that you insert into document files as reminders to yourself or others. These notes convey helpful hints to the next person using or editing the publication. If you think of anywhere you might want to use a yellow Post-It note, you can use Note-It to create the note electronically.

Note-It inserts a graphic symbol of your choice in the document file. When you or another user double-clicks on the symbol, a message box appears, displaying the message you typed (see Figure 2.11). You can resize the symbol at any time or move it out of your way while you work.

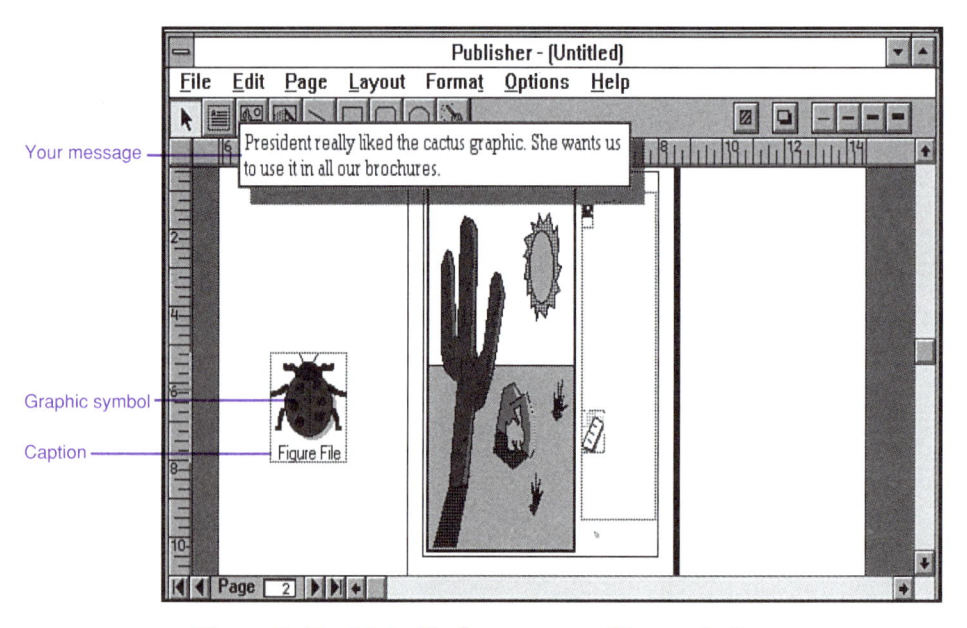

Figure 2.11 Note-It places a graphic symbol on your screen. Double-click on the symbol to read the note.

The Note-It PageWizard first lets you pick the attention-graphic to paste on your document. They include folders, stop signs, a hand with a string tied around one finger, a palm tree, a globe, pencils, a paper clip, and much more. You then type a brief caption for the note; this caption explains the general nature of the note. You then type the complete text of the note; this is what you'll see when you double-click on the graphic symbol.

When you press the Create It button, Note-It creates the note and inserts the specified graphic symbol on the page. You can change any part of the note at any time by clicking on the note, pulling down the Edit menu, and selecting EDIT Note-It Object.

> **FYIdea:** Notes like this are very useful in helping you remember how you created a snazzy effect in one of your publications. Six months later, just open the document file where you produced the effect and read the note on how it was done. You can then either reproduce the effect in another document or edit this one and copy it using the Save As command. Building a library of tricks and templates is one of the secrets to achieving an awesome reputation in desktop publishing.

The Coupon PageWizard

As consumers, we often deal with coupons. We clip them out for discounts on peanut butter or cans of beans. Or we fill them out and send them in to subscribe to a magazine or to order a product.

If you have your own business, you may have a different view of coupons. To you, coupons may be a quick and easy way to add power to flyers, newsletters, ads, and anything else that might bring in customers and generate sales. People are much more likely to clip and fill out a coupon than they are to take a sheet of blank paper and generate something from scratch. It's simple human nature, and it's also why you see so many coupons. They work!

To use the Coupon PageWizard, click on the PageWizard tool. The mouse pointer changes to a cross hair. Move the cross hair where you want any corner of the coupon to be, and hold down the left mouse button. Drag the pointer to the diagonally opposite corner. A box outlined in dashes appears, showing the location and dimensions of the coupon. When the box is the desired size and dimensions, release the mouse button.

A dialog box appears asking which PageWizard you want to use: Ad, Calendar, Coupon, Fancy First Letter, Newsletter Banner, Note-It, Paper Aeroplane, or Table. Click on Coupon and press the OK button or Tab to the list box, use the arrow keys to highlight Coupon, and press Enter. PageWizard then leads you through the process of creating the coupon. When the PageWizard is finished, the coupon appears in the area you outlined. You can, of course, edit and change it as much as you like. Chapter 4, "Adding Text to a Document," gives the procedures you will use most in editing the words needed on a coupon.

The Table PageWizard

A table is a grid made up of intersecting rows and columns, labeled to fit your particular needs. The Table PageWizard lets you specify the style and number of columns you want in the table, and whether the columns should be the same width or variable width (under your control). PageWizards determines the number of rows by how tall you drew the box for the table. You also can have Table PageWizard insert text frames so you can enter information into the table from within Publisher.

You create a table in much the same way as you create a coupon. After selecting the PageWizards tool, you move the mouse pointer where you want one corner of the table to appear. Hold down the left mouse button, drag the mouse pointer to the diagonally opposite corner, and release the mouse button. The PageWizard dialog box appears, showing the available PageWizards. Choose Table, and then work through the series of dialog boxes to enter your preferences. When you're done, select the Create It button.

The table is created with numbers as column headings (along the top). If you chose the Traditional or Classic style, you can change the column headings from numbers to names by editing the contents of each heading's text box. Just click on the text box, use the Backspace key to delete the number, and then type a name for the column heading.

If you chose Modern style, the process is a little more complicated, because PageWizards uses WordArt objects (instead of text boxes) to style the column headings. This gives the headings a fancier look, setting the headings in white on black. To edit a WordArt object, select the object, pull down the Edit menu, and select EDIT WordArt Object. A dialog box appears as in Figure 2.12. You can then press the Backspace key to delete the number and then type a name for the column heading. Press the OK button when you're done. Chapter 9, "Creating Special Text Effects," covers WordArt in greater depth.

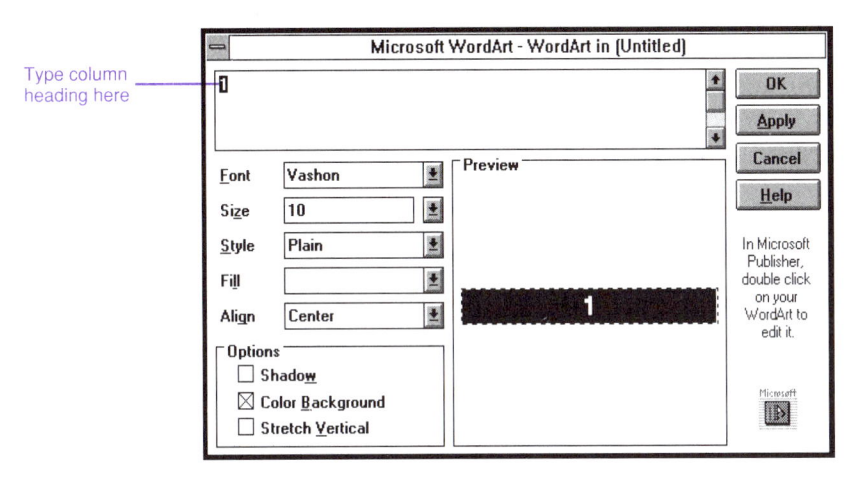

Figure 2.12 You can edit the text in a WordArt object at any time.

If you told PageWizard to include text frames, you can easily add row names to your table. Simply click on the leftmost text box in each row and type a name.

What You Have Learned

With Publisher's PageWizards, you can use Publisher right out of the box to create professional-looking publications. PageWizards leads you through the creation process, allowing you to select from a series of finely crafted designs. In this chapter, you learned a lot about Publisher, simply by using PageWizards:

▶ PageWizards are smart templates that create commonly used publications for you. They allow you to create useful, well-crafted publications simply by answering a few questions.

- ▶ You can use PageWizards from the Start Up dialog box or from the Create New Publication dialog box to create full-page publications consisting of one or more pages.
- ▶ You can use PageWizards to create mini-publications (including calendars, tables, and coupons), by selecting the PageWizards tool from the Toolbar. You must then use your mouse to specify the location and dimensions of the mini-publications.
- ▶ After you create a publication in PageWizards, you can use Publisher to further customize the publication.
- ▶ You can use the Seven Business Forms PageWizard to create various useful business forms, including a custom fax cover sheet.
- ▶ To save files, you select either the Save or the Save As command from the File menu. The Save command saves a new or modified file to disk under the name you specify. Save As lets you save an existing file under another name to create a copy of the file.
- ▶ To print a document you select the Print command from the File menu, or press Ctrl+P.

Chapter 3

Setting Up a Document from Scratch

In This Chapter

- Setting up a printer and page for page layout
- Selecting a paper size on which to print
- Choosing a general page layout
- Understanding units of measurement
- How to create documents of more than one page
- Using layout guides and rulers to position and size objects more precisely
- Changing the page view from bird's-eye-view to close-up

Starting a New Document

If you were going to build a birdhouse, you would need some sort of plan, no matter how sketchy. You would calculate beforehand how much wood you needed, the type of hardware required for attaching the birdhouse to the old elm tree in the backyard, the color of paint you wanted (nobody ever seems to consult the birds on that), and the other materials and tools necessary. Building a birdhouse without any prior planning can result in failure or, at best, some darn funny looking birdhouses.

The same is true when you decide to design and lay out a document in Publisher. Before you begin the process of electronically pasting together the elements of text and pictures that will make up the document, you must make a few informed decisions—decisions that will make the job easy, efficient, and enjoyable. After all, that's what Publisher is all about.

The best way to learn is by doing, so you might want to follow along on your computer as this chapter leads you through the process of starting a document from scratch. In each section, you'll see the decisions you need to make when constructing your own documents.

Setting Up Your Printer

Before you create a publication in Publisher, you should make sure your printer is set up properly. That is, you must check to see that Windows is using the correct printer, that it is set up to use the paper that's loaded in the printer, and that the printer is going to print in the proper orientation.

If only one printer is connected to your computer, and if you print documents exclusively on one size paper in one orientation, you have little to worry about. However, if you are connected to more than one printer or if you print on various sizes of paper, you should at least check your printer setup to make sure it's correct. To check the setup, pull down the File menu and select Print Setup. The Print Setup dialog box appears, as shown in Figure 3.1.

Selecting a Printer

In the upper left corner of the Print Setup dialog box is the Printer box. The first option, Default Printer, tells Publisher to use the printer that Windows uses as the default. Under this option is the name of the default printer. If that's the printer you want to use, and the Default Printer option is already selected, leave it alone.

Setting Up a Document from Scratch

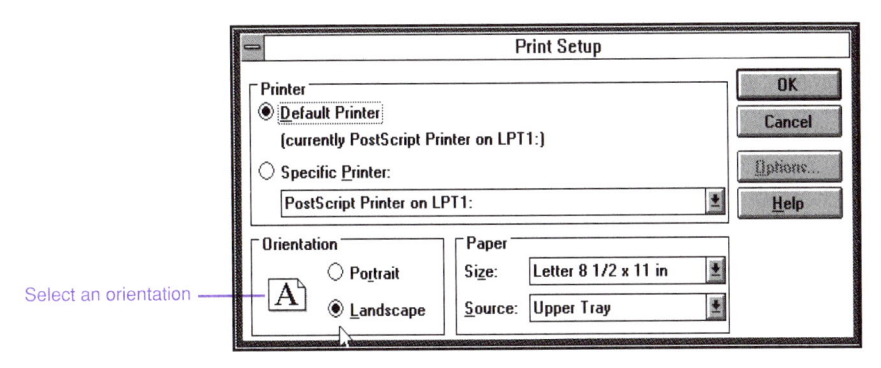

Figure 3.1   Use the Print Setup dialog box to select a printer and type of paper on which to print.

If you want to select a different printer, select the Specific Printer option. Under this option is a drop-down list box, which lists the printers installed in Windows. Click on the arrow to the right of the box or press Alt+↓ to view the list of printers. To select a printer, click on its name and press the OK button. Remember that by doing this you are changing the printer selection for all other Windows applications, so you might want to change it back to the default after you've finished to avoid confusion and wasted paper.

> **Caution:** If you have a printer whose name does not appear in the list box described above, then that printer is not installed in Windows. To install a printer, you must switch to the Main program group, double-click on the Control icon, select the Printer icon, and then install the printer. You'll need the Windows program diskettes to complete the installation.

If you use two printers on the same port (you plug in one or the other or flip a switch to change printers), keep in mind that Windows allows only one active printer per port. To switch printers, you'll have to physically connect the one you want to activate to the printer port, and then use the Windows Control Panel to activate the other printer. Because this is such a hassle, you should consider installing another printer port; they're fairly inexpensive.

Chapter 3

Changing the Physical Paper Size

If you print on different sizes of paper—for example, letter size and legal size, you should make sure Windows is telling your printer to use the correct paper for this print job. For example, if you want to create a publication to print on legal size paper, and the printer is set up to use letter size paper, the publication will not be printed correctly.

You can check the paper size in the Print Setup dialog box. To the right of the orientation options is a box labeled Paper. In this box are two drop-down list boxes: Si*z*e and *S*ource. The Size box lists the paper sizes which the currently selected printer can use. To view the sizes on this list, as shown in Figure 3.2, click on the down arrow to the right of the box or press Alt+↓. The Source box displays the available paper feeders. If your printer uses paper trays, for example, upper and lower, you may have a different size of paper in each tray. This list allows you to choose the paper feeder or tray you want to use.

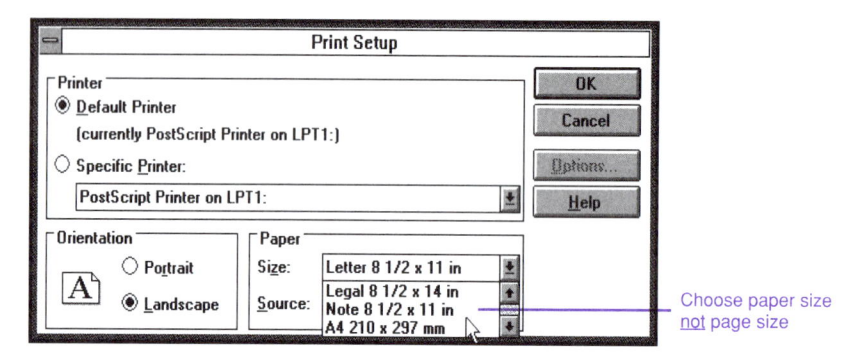

Figure 3.2 To view a list of available paper sizes, click on the arrow to the right of the Size drop-down list box.

Choose paper size
not page size

The following Quick Steps lead you through the process of setting up your printer.

Q Setting Up a Printer

1. Pull down the File menu and select Print Setup.   The Print Setup dialog box appears.

Setting Up a Document from Scratch

2. Select **D**efault Printer to use the Windows default printer, or select Specific **P**rinter and then select a printer from the drop-down list box.

   A dot appears in the circle next to the selected option, and the name of the current printer is shown below the selected option.

3. Select an orientation, Po**r**trait or **L**andscape.

   A dot appears in the circle next to the selected option.

4. Click on the arrow to the right of the Si**z**e drop-down list box, and select the paper size you want to print on.

   Make sure the selected paper size is actually loaded in the printer.

5. Click on the arrow to the right of the **S**ource drop-down list box, and select the paper source which holds the paper you want to use.

   Make sure the paper you want to use is in the specified source on the printer.

6. Press the OK button to accept your selections and return to the work area.

   The new printer is in effect and you are returned to Publisher's work area.

   □

Creating a Blank Page

Before you can begin creating a publication, you need a surface on which to paste your text and graphics; you need a page. The following Quick Steps lead you through the process of creating a blank page.

Q Creating a Blank Page

1. Start Publisher or pull down the **F**ile menu and select Create **N**ew Publication.

   The Start Up or Create New Publication dialog box appears.

2. Click on the **B**lank Page button or press Alt+B.

   The selected button appears pressed.

77

3. Press the OK button at the bottom of the dialog box.

The dialog box disappears and a blank page appears in the middle of the work area. ☐

Changing Page Orientation

By default, Publisher displays the page as a standard 8.5-by-11 inch sheet. However, the orientation of the page may vary; that is, the page may be standing tall (portrait) or lying on its side (landscape). The orientation depends on the orientation of the last page printed from Windows. Remember, Publisher runs on top of Windows and shares many of its facilities with other applications. So if you changed the printer setup in Publisher or in some other Windows application, those changes remain in effect until you change them back. It's always a good idea to check printer settings before printing anything.

If you create a blank page and it appears in landscape orientation when you wanted portrait, or vice versa, you can change the orientation. However, your printer must support landscape orientation, or Publisher will not give you the option to change orientations. If your printer supports both orientations, you can take the following Quick Steps to change orientations.

Q Changing the Page Orientation

1. Pull down the File menu and select Print Setup.

The Print Setup dialog box appears, as shown in Figure 3.1. In the lower left corner of this box is the Orientation box. If the orientation options are dimmed, the currently selected printer does not support landscape orientation.

2. Select Portrait or Landscape by clicking on the option or by typing the underlined letter in the option's name.

A black dot appears in the circle next to the selected orientation.

3. Press the OK button in the upper right of the dialog box.

You are returned to the work area and the page is flipped 90 degrees to reflect the change in orientation. □

Setting Up a Page

In the previous section, you selected a *paper* orientation for your printer. The information you supplied tells your printer how to print the publication on paper. However, a publication can be printed in any number of ways on a sheet of paper. For example, you can divide the paper into 4 *pages* in order to print a greeting card. Just as you set up your printer for printing on paper, you must now set up a page.

To set up a page, you must define the *page layout* and *page size*. You define the page layout and size using the Page Setup dialog box shown in Figure 3.3. To display this dialog box, pull down the Page menu and select Page Setup.

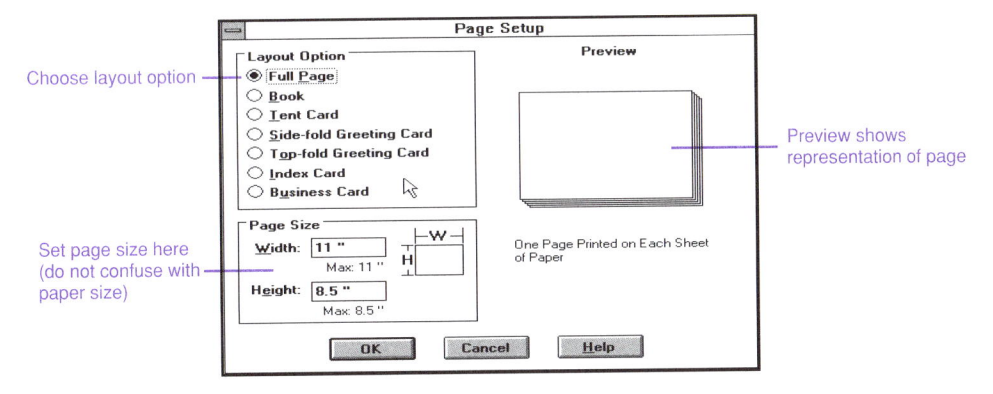

Figure 3.3   The Page Setup dialog box lets you select a page layout and size.

On the left of the Page Setup dialog box is the Layout Option box. This box contains seven page layout settings from which to choose. The page layout setting tells Publisher how to divide the paper into pages. For example, if you select one of the Greeting Card options, Publisher divides the paper into four equal pages.

Chapter 3

In the lower left corner of the Page Setup dialog box is the Page Size box. This box contains two text boxes, which specify the *width* and *height* of each page. When you select a different page layout in the Layout Options box, the dimensions change to show the default dimensions for the selected layout type. For example, if you select the Business card option, the dimensions change to show the default dimensions for a business card (2-by-3.5 inches). You can then change the settings as desired to change the dimensions of the page.

> **Tip:** The height and width dimensions you see may vary, depending on how your printer is set up in Windows.

On the right side of the Page Setup dialog box is a Preview area. In this area is a graphic representation of the page. When you select a different page layout in the Layout Options box, this graphic image changes to show how the *page* will look on a sheet of *paper*.

The following Quick Steps tell you how to select a page layout and size. For more information about the various page layouts, refer to the section called "Deciding on a Page Layout." For information on page sizes, refer to the section called "Adjusting the Page Size."

Setting Up a Page

1. Pull down the Page menu and select Page Setup.

   The Page Setup dialog box appears, as shown in Figure 3.3.

2. Select the layout option you want to use by clicking on it or typing the underlined letter in the option's name.

   A black dot appears in the circle to the left of the selected option. On the right, the graphic representation of the page changes to show how the page(s) will appear on a sheet of paper.

3. To change the page width, type W or click in the Width text box, and then type a width for the page.

   What you type appears in the text box.

4. To change the page height, type E or click in the Height text box, and then type a height for the page.	What you type appears in the text box.
5. Press the OK button to accept the selected layout option and page size.	Publisher returns you to the work area. □

These settings provide a starting point; they don't lock you into a rigid framework. Once you have an overall layout and page size, you can modify them as you can modify any other element in Publisher.

Deciding on a Page Layout

Unlike PageWizards, which lead you through the process of creating a publication, the Page Setup dialog box allows you to set up a page for a particular type of document. Publisher provides a list of seven page layout options from which to choose. The following sections describe each option to help you make the correct choice for your publication.

Full Page

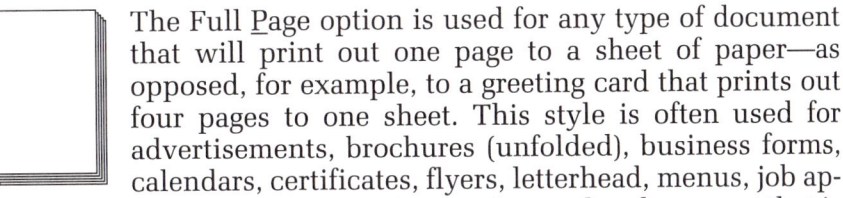

The Full Page option is used for any type of document that will print out one page to a sheet of paper—as opposed, for example, to a greeting card that prints out four pages to one sheet. This style is often used for advertisements, brochures (unfolded), business forms, calendars, certificates, flyers, letterhead, menus, job applications, resumes, questionnaires, and any other document that is made up of full, unfolded sheets of paper.

You can also use the Full Page option for mailing labels, VCR or cassette labels, Christmas present stickers, sale tags, or any small document that you can print several of on a sheet of paper. In the case of labels, you can print them on sheets of peel-off, stick-on labels, as explained later in this chapter.

The full page style would also be the correct choice for newsletters, reports, or other long documents where you plan to use both sides of the page.

Book

The Book option prints two pages on one side of a sheet of paper so that the sheet can be folded vertically. This option is commonly used for books and booklets, folded brochures, manuals, magazines, folded newsletters, and pamphlets.

Tent Card

The Tent Card option divides a page in half horizontally. This creates a free-standing card like the place cards used at formal dinners. Publisher prints right-side-up on one half of the card and upside-down on the other half, so that when you fold the card, the text appears right-side-up on both sides. This layout is useful for creating place cards, sale signs, and other cards that may be set on a table.

When you create a tent card, Publisher creates one page that's half as tall as an 8.5-by-11 inch sheet of paper (if you are in portrait mode). To create the flip side of the tent card, you must insert another page that's the same size (8.5-by-5.5 inches). To insert a second page, pull down the Page menu and select Insert Pages. The Insert Pages dialog box appears; if you don't change any options, Publisher will insert a page of the same dimensions after the page that's displayed. Press the OK button. (A quicker way to insert a page is to press Ctrl+N; this bypasses the dialog box and inserts a page immediately.)

The second page will appear normal as you work on it, but the text you type will print upside-down on the top half of the paper. This assumes your printer supports graphics and is properly installed and selected in Windows—more about that in the "Choosing a Printer" section later in this chapter.

> **FYIdea:** If your business has products or services that visitors from out of town might need, make a deal with the local motels to put tent cards on top of the TVs in all the rooms. If you have products or services to sell, work a trade with local restaurants to put tent cards on their tables and counters. You can also use tent cards as sales tags; use WordArt to set large letters saying things like RENT ME or ON SALE or TAKE ME HOME, and put them on appropriate items in your business. WordArt is explained in detail in Chapter 9.

Side-Fold and Top-Fold Greeting Cards

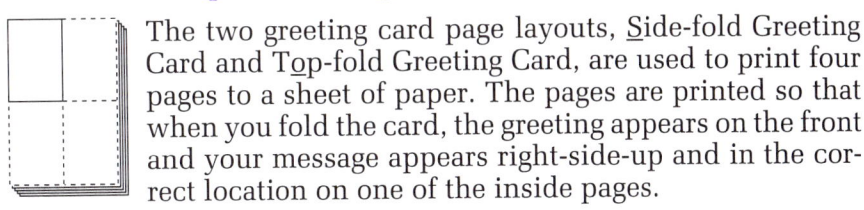

The two greeting card page layouts, Side-fold Greeting Card and Top-fold Greeting Card, are used to print four pages to a sheet of paper. The pages are printed so that when you fold the card, the greeting appears on the front and your message appears right-side-up and in the correct location on one of the inside pages.

As with the tent card, Publisher creates only the first page of the document. To create the greeting card, you have to insert the other three pages. To do that, pull down the Page menu and select Insert Pages. The Insert Pages dialog box appears with the cursor in the Number of New Pages text box. Type 3 to insert three pages and press the OK button. To bypass the Insert Pages dialog box, simply press Ctrl+N three times.

Three new pages are inserted and you are returned to the work area. The first of the new pages (page 2) is the current page. To change pages, use the paging buttons in the lower left corner of the Publisher application window. The page number of the current page also appears there.

Index Card

The Index Card layout option creates a 3-by-5 inch index card. You can create a larger or smaller card by changing the dimensions in the Page Setup dialog box. This type of layout is commonly used to create index cards for card catalogues or note cards for speeches. You can also use this layout to create small advertisements to put in newspapers or phone books, bookplates ("This book stolen from..."), small invitations, recipe cards, Rolodex cards, and more.

If you are creating standard index cards, and if your printer has a tractor-feed mechanism, you can print a series of index cards one-per-sheet. (A tractor-feed mechanism consists of wheels with pins that engage the perforated strips on the edges of tractor-feed computer forms.) Most office supply stores carry tractor-feed index cards.

> **FYIdea:** You can buy a dot matrix printer with a tractor-feed mechanism from almost any dealer for under two hundred dollars. If you do a lot of index cards or labels, consider adding a dot matrix printer to your system to handle these jobs.

If you have a high end printer, such as a laser printer, you won't be able to print on 3-by-5 inch cards. Such printers simply are not set up to properly feed the index cards. In this case, you'll have to print one card per sheet of paper and cut off any excess. To help you cut the excess from each sheet, you can have Publisher print *crop marks* on each page during printing. These crop marks appear at the outer corners of the sheet to provide a guide for cropping (cutting) the excess. To print the crop marks, you select the Print command from the File menu to display the Print dialog box. Select the Print Crop Marks option to put an X in the check box (this turns the Crop Marks option on). You can then proceed with the printing as usual.

Crop marks are also useful if you create a document that you want to send to a print shop or to a newspaper or magazine. By printing crop marks on the sheet, you give the printer a guide for placing the publication more precisely. For example, if the printer needs to take a photograph of the page as a step in preparing it for publication, the crop marks allow the printer to align the page for the camera.

Business Cards

Business cards are one of the most effective ways of advertising and one of the most efficient ways of letting people know how to contact you. And now that you can design your own business cards, they can be one of the least expensive ways to do both.

You can print business cards in either of two ways. The first way is to use the Page Setup dialog box to create a business card that will print in the middle of a page, one per page. This is useful if you want to take the card to a print shop to have many copies of it printed on card stock (a heavier paper). You can then print a single copy of the card and have Publisher print crop marks on the sheet to help the local printer position your card correctly for printing.

The second way to print business cards is to do it yourself. You can purchase card stock from an office supply store and print your cards directly on the card stock, as long as your printer can handle the heavy stock. If you decide to produce the cards this way, you won't want to print one card per sheet. Instead, select the Full Page layout option and define as many standard business cards (size 2-by-3.5 inches) as will fit on one sheet of paper (10 work nicely). You can then build your business card in one box and copy it to the other nine. After that, you can print out cards as needed and cut them apart with a paper cutter. You could have a number of different kinds of cards this way, and test their effectiveness before committing to a large and expensive order of them from a print shop.

For more information about designing business cards, refer to Chapter 13, "Professional Techniques: Newsletters, Brochures, and Business Forms."

Adjusting the Page Size

When you select a page layout, the dimensions of the page appear in the Page Size box (below the Layout Options box). For example, if you select Index Card, the width of the card is shown as 5", and the height of the card is 3". Keep in mind that a page is smaller than a sheet of paper.

You can modify the page size by typing in your own dimensions. For example, you can create larger index cards by increasing the width and height of the cards. To change the width, press Alt+W or click on the Width box. You can use the arrow keys to move the cursor and the Del or Backspace keys to delete characters in the text box. Edit the entry so it displays the desired width. To change the height, press Alt+E or click on the Height box. You can then edit the height setting the same way you edited the width.

Once you've selected a page layout and specified the dimensions of the page, press the OK button to accept your selections and return to the work area. Publisher displays a page in the work area that represents the page you defined.

Using Guides on a Page

Once you've set up your page, it appears in the work area, as shown in Figure 3.4. You'll see two boxes. The outside box (the one with the drop shadow) represents the physical sheet of paper. The inside box (the one shown with a dotted line) represents the page on the paper. Although these dotted lines appear fixed in position, they're not; you can move them to change the size of the page. In short, these lines act as *guides* to help you position various objects on the page, but are flexible enough so they don't restrict you. The guides show you the position of the left and right margins, column margins, top and bottom margins, and so on.

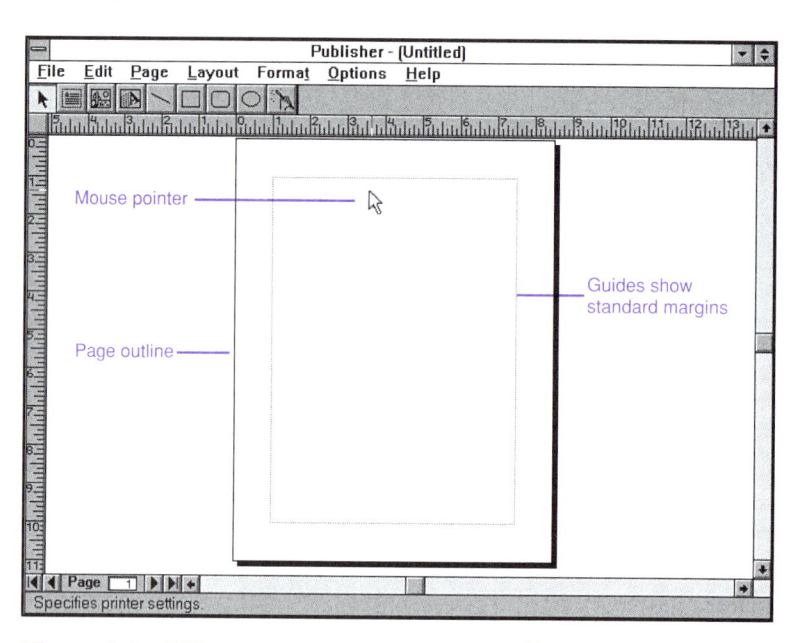

Figure 3.4 When you set up a page, you'll see a sheet of paper with a page, whose dimensions are defined by guides.

If you've ever done conventional layout with standard *layout boards*, then you know that layout boards define the margins and columns with blue lines. Blue is used because it is not picked up by the copy cameras that make plates for printing presses. The guides in Publisher are simply the electronic equivalent of these blue lines. They help you align text and graphic objects correctly on a page.

It is important to understand that guides are only guides. Although they show you where the margins are located, they are not margin settings, such as those you use in a word-processing document. If you place a block of text to the left of the left guide, Publisher will not reformat the text to make it fit within the guide. It is the text frames, picture frames, WordArt frames, and the other objects that determine what area the object covers on the page, and these frames may or may not align with the guides.

Moving the Guides

Before you start laying out any publication, you should make sure the guides are where you want them. This will help you and any others working on the project lay out the pages consistently. The following Quick Steps lead you through the process of checking the position of the guides and repositioning them.

Q Changing the Layout Guides

1. Pull down the Layout menu and select Layout Guides.

   The Layout Guides dialog box appears, as shown in Figure 3.5. In the Layout Guides box on the left are the layout guide settings.

2. Click inside the text box that contains the layout guide setting you want to change or press Alt plus the underlined letter in the layout guide's name.

   The setting is displayed in reverse video.

3. You can delete the setting by pressing the Backspace or Delete key. To edit the setting, click next to the number you want to change or use the arrow keys.

   If you click next to a number or press the ← or → key, a bar cursor appears in the box, allowing you to edit the entry.

Chapter 3

4. Type your change. — Any number you type is inserted at the bar cursor.

5. If you want to change another guide setting, move to its text box. — If you move to a different text box, the Preview box shows how the setting you just changed affects the layout guide on the page.

6. When you've changed all the settings as desired, press the OK button. — You are returned to the work area, and the layout guides appear in their new positions. □

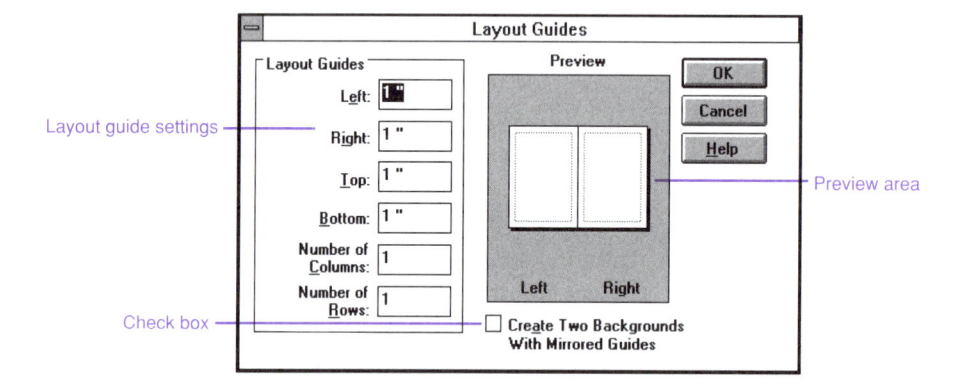

Figure 3.5 The Layout Guides dialog box allows you to change the positions of the layout guides.

Caution: If you change the positions of the guides for pages on which you've already placed text or graphics objects, the change has no affect on the position of these objects. To align those objects according to the new guides, you must return to those pages to reposition the objects.

Creating Mirrored Guides

The Layout Guides dialog box contains two other important items: the Preview area and the check box below it. The Preview area shows two pages labeled Left and Right. These pages represent *facing pages*. For example, in this book, the left and right pages are facing pages; they face each other. This preview helps you visualize how two facing pages will look together, an important consideration when putting together a book.

Below the Preview box is a check box, which allows you to create a mirrored background for your publication. This option is commonly used to set a *binding margin*, which inserts more space on the edge of the paper that is to be bound. This ensures that all the text is readable and that no text is hidden in the valley where the pages are bound.

To set the binding margin, click on the check box. In the Layout Options box on the left, note that the options labeled Left and Right are now labeled Inside and Outside. The Inside setting controls the binding margin. The Outside setting controls the margin on the outside edge of the page. To see the effects of the binding margin, type `1.5` in the Inside text box and then click on one of the other text boxes. The Preview box now shows the binding margin inserted on the right side of the left page and on the left side of the right page.

There are other advantages to creating mirrored guides in the background. For more information, refer to Chapter 13.

Using Snap-to Guides

You have already learned that layout guides are passive lines that help you align objects on a page. To further help you align objects, Publisher offers a more active tool called *snap-to guides*. Instead of just sitting there indicating the position of each margin, these guides reach out and grab the object when it gets close to a precise location, and then snap the object into place.

You can turn snap-to Guides on or off by selecting Snap to Guides from the Options menu. A check mark next to the option indicates that it's on; no check mark means it's off. When on, this option makes layout guides *magnetic*. When you move an object or the cross-hair cursor close to a guide line, the object or cursor *snaps* to the line. You have to *jerk* the object or cursor to pull it off the line.

To get a feel for snap-to guides, try using them now. Pull down the Options menu and select Snap to Guides to put a check mark next to the option, or press Ctrl+W. Select one of the drawing tools from the Toolbar, and then move the mouse back to the work area. Notice that it has changed to a cross hair. Move the cross hair slowly near a guide, and you'll find that the guide is now quite sticky. The cross hair will jump to the guide and not come away easily.

Hiding Layout Guides

Although layout guides are an essential tool for positioning objects on a page, you may want to hide them in order to see what the page looks like without the guides. To hide the guides, pull down the Options menu and select Hide Layout Guides, or press Ctrl+G. The dotted lines that indicate the positions of the guides disappear. This has no effect on objects you've already placed in the document; they remain undisturbed. And if the Snap-to Guides option is on, your cursor will still snap to the guide.

To reveal the guides, pull down the Options menu and select Show Layout Guides, or press Ctrl+G. The guides will reappear in their original locations on-screen.

Using the On-Screen Rulers

In addition to layout guides, Publisher provides two *rulers* to help you position objects precisely on a page. A vertical ruler is displayed on the left side of the window, and a horizontal ruler appears just below the Toolbar. The default unit of measurement for these rulers is inches, but you can change the unit as explained later in this chapter. Keep in mind that the rulers don't always represent *real* inches. If you display a page in full-page view, the rulers are scaled down to match the scaled-down sheet of paper.

Publisher's two on-screen rulers are used for exactly the same purposes you would use physical rulers on real paper—to measure the positions and sizes of objects. Their use is beautifully simple. Just move your mouse pointer around in the work area and watch the rulers. On each, you will see a line that follows the pointer's movement, indicating the exact location of the cursor at all times.

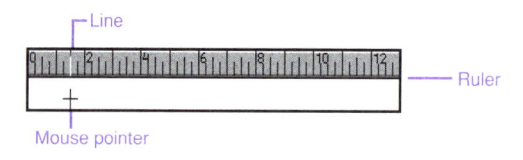

Using Rulers to Draw Objects

The two rulers together act as a coordinate system. The upper left corner of the sheet is the zero point. Whenever you move out from this point, the rulers show the vertical and horizontal distance of the cursor from the zero point. This allows you to reference all points on the page exactly.

For example, say you want to draw a 4-inch long horizontal line halfway down an 8.5-by-11 inch page beginning at the left margin. You would perform the following steps:

1. Click on the line tool (the button with a diagonal line on it).
2. Move the mouse pointer (now a cross hair) until the line on the vertical ruler is at 5.5 inches (halfway down the page).
3. Move the mouse pointer until the line on the horizontal ruler is at 1 inch. The default margin is 1 inch; that is, one inch from the edge of the paper. Keep the line on the vertical ruler at 5.5.
4. Hold down the left mouse button and drag the mouse right until the horizontal ruler shows 5 inches (5 inches minus the 1-inch margin gives a line length of 4 inches).
5. Release the mouse button. You now have a four-inch line halfway down the page and beginning at the left margin, as shown in Figure 3.6.

As you can see, whenever you use the rulers you need to keep an eye on *both* rulers at the same time. This takes some practice, but once you get used to it, you'll find that rulers are an essential tool in drawing objects on a page.

Using Snap-to Rulers

If you performed the line-draw exercise in the previous section, you know how difficult it is to place the line in the ruler at a precise location and how hard it is to keep the line there when you move the mouse in another direction. To help, Publisher offers a snap-to feature for rulers. This is similar to the snap-to guides discussed earlier. However, you cannot use both snap-to guides and snap-to rulers at the same time; Publisher allows you to choose only one.

Chapter 3

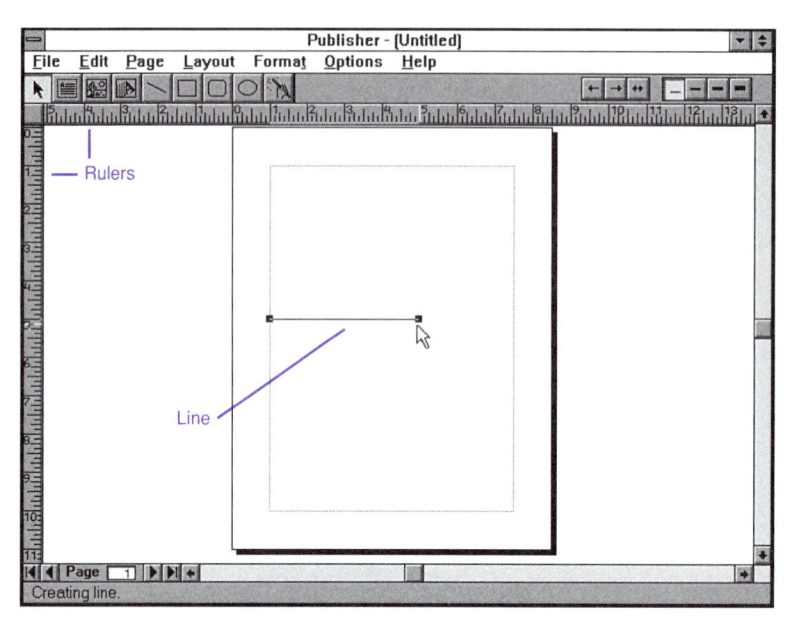

Figure 3.6 You can use the rulers to draw lines a precise length at a precise location on the page.

To use snap-to rulers, pull down the Options menu and select Snap to Ruler Marks. A check mark next to the option indicates that it's on; no check mark means it's off. When on, this option makes the mouse pointer snap to the nearest division marker on the ruler. This helps you move to a specific location on the ruler and stay there.

Using Rulers to Size Objects

Although rulers will help you create the right-sized objects when you first draw them, rulers also help you change the size of an object you've already drawn or placed on the page. Also, remember to use the Snap to Ruler Marks option if you're using the rulers more than the guides to size and place objects. The following Quick Steps lead you through the process of drawing a correctly sized object using the rulers.

Drawing a Box Using the Rulers

1. Click on the Rectangle tool (the button that has a box on it).

    The button appears pressed.

2. Move the mouse cursor back to the work area. The mouse cursor appears as a cross hair.

3. Move the cross hair where you want one corner of the box to be. The lines on the rulers show the exact position of the center of the cross hair.

4. Hold down the left mouse button and drag the cross hair to the diagonally opposite corner. The lines on the rulers show the exact position of cross hair, indicating the position of this corner of the box. A box appears surrounded by a dashed line, showing what the box will look like.

5. Release the mouse button. Publisher draws the box, and the dashed line changes to a solid line. ☐

Hiding the Rulers

If you don't use the rulers or if you are not currently using them, you can turn them off so they won't take up valuable screen space. To hide the rulers, pull down the Options menu and select Hide Rulers. The two rulers disappear from the screen. To turn the rulers back on, pull down the Options menu and select Show Rulers. An even faster way to toggle the rulers on and off is to press Ctrl+K. If the rulers are displayed, this hides them; if the rulers are hidden, this displays them.

> **Tip:** If you need a closer measurement, you can grab the rulers with your mouse and drag them wherever needed. They don't have to stay at the sides of the windows.

Changing the Page View

When you first set up a page, Publisher displays the page in full-page mode. You will see the entire sheet of paper on your screen, but it will look small. Although this provides an excellent overall view of how the page will look in print, it shows very few details. If you want to see how the type looks or how a graphic image appears, you must increase the size of the page.

To change the size of the page view, pull down the Page menu and select one of the many view options. Table 3.1 summarizes these options.

Table 3.1   Page views available in Publisher.

View	Displays
Full Page	Shows the full page on the screen, regardless of its actual size. A tabloid (11-by-17 inch) page will appear approximately the same size as a 3-by-5 inch index card.
25% Size	Displays the page as a quarter of its actual size.
33% Size	Displays the page as a third of its actual size.
50% Size	Displays the page as half of its actual size.
66% Size	Displays the page as two thirds of its actual size.
75% Size	Displays the page as three quarters of its actual size.
Actual Size	Actual size, as Publisher has proportioned real world measurements to screen measurements.
200% Size	Close-up view. Use this view for making precise adjustments.

In the views that show only a part of the document, use the scroll bars on the right and bottom edges of the window to view different portions of the publication, as explained in Chapter 1.

> **Tip:** You can quickly toggle between Full Page and Actual Size by pressing the F9 function key.

If you want to zoom in to see a specific portion of the screen close up, consider selecting the object you want to view *before* zooming in. By doing this, you won't have to use the scroll bars to find the object after zooming in. The following Quick Steps lead you through the process of zooming in on part of the screen.

Zooming In

1. Click on an area of the screen or on an object you want to view close up.

    The cursor appears in that area of the screen, or the object you want to view is selected.

2. Pull down the Page menu and select 200%.

    Publisher displays the selected object or area of the screen in close-up view, as shown in Figure 3.7. □

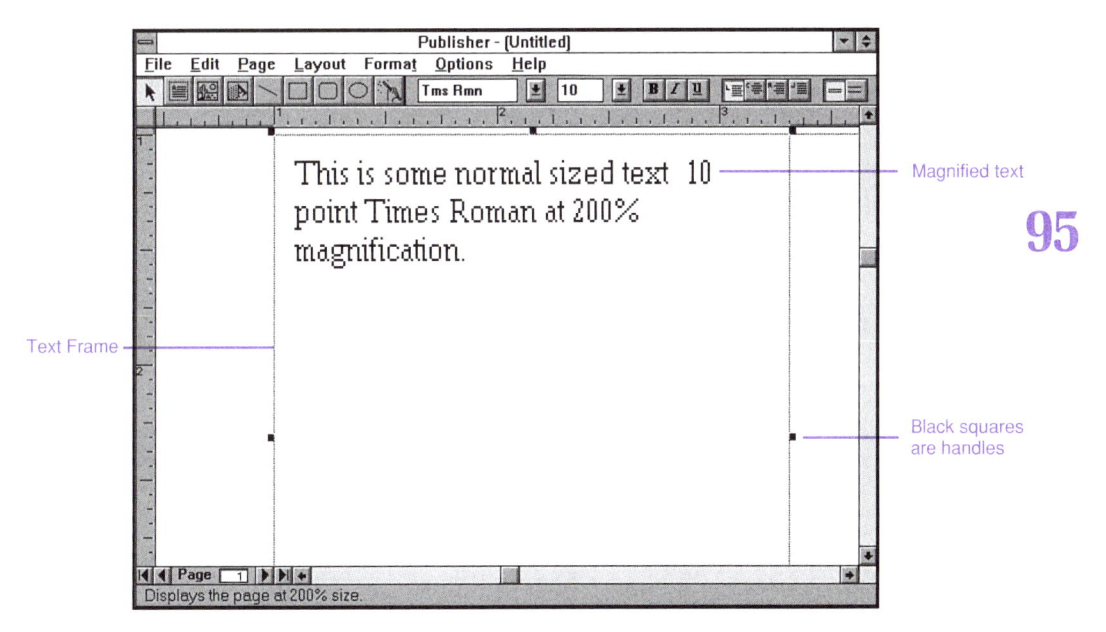

Figure 3.7 A close-up view of normal text at 200% magnification.

Specifying Units of Measurement

Desktop publishing requires a great deal of precision and, hence, a great deal of measuring. You start with measurements of paper size and page size, and then you have to measure everything you set on the page, from text boxes to graphic images and lines, to make sure each object is the correct size and is in the correct position on the page. As you probably know, you can measure in different units (for example, inches or centimeters) depending on what you're accustomed to and how precise you want to be.

Publisher allows you to select the unit of measurement you want to use. Inches is the default. To select a different unit, pull down the Options menu and select Settings. The Settings dialog box appears, as shown in Figure 3.8. Click on the arrow to the right of the Measurements drop-down list box or select Measurements and press Alt+↓ to view the measurements options:

- ▶ *Inches.* Inches are standard in the United States. Because of this, most computer users in the States are able to visualize an inch more clearly than other units and may find this option the easiest.
- ▶ *Centimeters.* The metric system is becoming more popular, especially among people who have a background in science and math. Centimeters is a metric unit of measurement that is much more precise. And because all metric units are in multiples of ten (for example, a millimeter is a tenth of a centimeter), centimeters are much easier to work with (once you get used to them).
- ▶ *Picas.* Picas and points are commonly used by professional printers and publishers. A point is approximately 1/72 of an inch, and there are 12 points in a pica. Picas are commonly used for measuring areas of a document or objects in a publication. If you are unfamiliar with this unit of measurement, it will take you a while to learn it. So why use it? Two reasons. First, because the unit is smaller than an inch, it's more precise. Second, type sizes are commonly specified in terms of points. By using picas and points as your standard unit of measure, you get a clear idea of the relative size and position of all the elements on the page.
- ▶ *Points:* Points allow you to measure small objects with more precision and, hence, are used more often in measuring type size or the leading (space) between lines of text. The standard typewriter for years was called the pica or *10 pitch* because the size of the letters it typed were one pica high (12 points) and 10 characters per inch horizontally (10-pitch). This carried over into computer printers, so that usually the default size of characters printed is twelve points or one pica in height.

> **FYIdea:** Many office supply or art supply stores have rulers that contain measurements in picas, points, inches, and centimeters. Consider getting one of these to check the size, position, and alignment of various elements on the printed page. You may notice something on a printout that's not obvious on screen. By measuring with a pica or point ruler, you can get a clear idea of just how much you'll have to adjust each element.

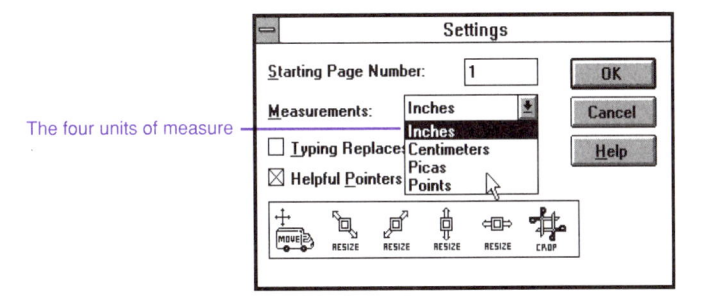

Figure 3.8 The Measurements drop-down list box allows you to select from four units of measure.

Using the Background

If you've ever worked with a word processor that allows you to create a header or footer to appear on every page of a document, you know what a time saver it is. Publisher's background works the same way, but offers a lot more power and flexibility, allowing you to insert both text and graphics on every page of a document. For example, say you have a hundred-page report and you want a border on each page. You could, of course, draw the border on each page or copy it to each page, but either way, you're looking at a long and boring process. With Publisher's background, however, you draw the border once, and it appears on all 100 pages!

What is the background? It's an area in which you put any objects that you want inserted on all pages in your document. (For more information on objects, refer to Chapters 4 and 10.) If the document is to have page numbers, a header (information at the top of each page), a footer (information at the bottom of each page), or any logo or graphic image, it goes in the background once. Publisher takes care of the rest. In addition, if you show Publisher where to put a page number in the background, it will calculate and place the correct page number on each page and recalculate the page numbers if they change. (For more information on page numbering and the background, see Chapter 10.)

To switch to the background, pull down the Page menu and select Go to Background, or press Ctrl+M. At the lower left of the Publisher window, where the page number usually is, you'll see two rectangles, one superimposed on the other, to show that you are now in the background. Figure 3.9 shows a sample background setup which prints a page number and heading on each page of a newsletter.

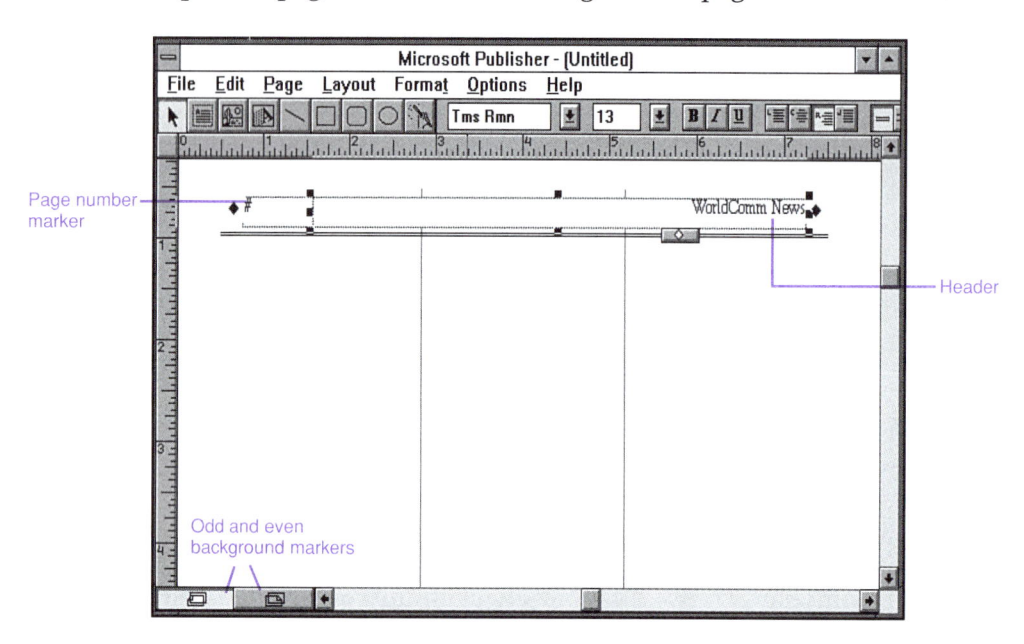

Figure 3.9 You can use the Background to print a heading and page number on every page of your publication.

Whatever objects you create or place here will appear on every page of the document, even those not yet created. If you are working with a layout that has facing pages (for example, a book that has pages 2 and 3 facing each other), the background will also have two pages. Putting an object in the page on the right will cause that object to appear on all odd-numbered pages, while putting an object on the left means it will be on all even-numbered pages. You can then, for example, place a chapter number on all left-hand pages and place a chapter title on all right-hand pages.

To return to your document, either pull down the Page menu again and select Go to Foreground, or simply press Ctrl+M again. The page number will reappear in the lower left of the application window.

For more information about using the Background to create headers and footers and to add page numbers to your publication, refer to Chapter 10.

What You Have Learned

In this chapter, you learned that you have to prepare a page before you can start building a document. Specifically, you learned the following:

- ▶ Before you begin creating pages, you must select a printer, orientation, and page size that matches the paper on which you intend to print.
- ▶ Layout options allow you to divide a sheet of paper into one or more *pages* and control the dimensions of the page(s).
- ▶ On-screen layout guides and rulers help you position and size objects more precisely.
- ▶ Both layout guides and rulers offer a snap-to feature which helps you position the cursor and any objects in exact locations on the page.
- ▶ You can hide layout guides and rulers at any time to prevent them from getting in your way.
- ▶ You can change the page view to view the overall look of the document or to zoom in for more detailed work.
- ▶ Publisher allows you to select from four different units of measurement: inches, centimeters, picas, and points. Although inches is most common, the other units offer greater precision.
- ▶ The background lets you place text, pictures, and other objects once and have them appear on every page of a document.
- ▶ The paging controls in the lower left corner of the Publisher window allow you to flip pages in your document.

Chapter 4

Adding Text to a Document

In This Chapter

101

- *The seven basic objects used to construct Publisher documents*
- *Creating text frames on a page*
- *How to import text generated by other applications*
- *How to connect text frames*
- *Typing text directly into your documents*
- *Editing text in a text frame*
- *Moving, resizing, and reshaping text frames*
- *Deleting text frames*

Assembling a Page

In Chapter 3, you learned how to set up your printer and your overall page layout to prepare for creating a publication. Once you have a surface to work on (a page), you can begin placing text and graphics on the pages.

This chapter presents some general information about the seven basic objects you can place on a page. The chapter then explains in detail how to work with text objects. Subsequent chapters will discuss the other objects in greater detail.

The Seven Basic Objects

Whenever you paste text or pictures on a page, Publisher places the text or graphic image in a *frame* and treats it as an independent object. These objects are equivalent to pieces of paper you would physically paste down on a layout board. Each piece of paper would hold a section of text or a graphic image. You could then arrange the pieces of paper individually on a page. The same holds true in Publisher, except that the objects are electronic; and in addition to changing their location, you can change their dimensions, as well.

In Publisher, you work with seven basic objects. Publisher has a tool for working with each object. You select these tools from the Toolbar as shown below. Table 4.1 provides a brief description of each tool.

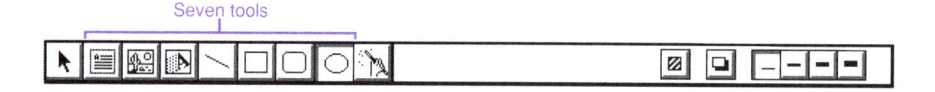

Table 4.1 Publisher's seven basic tools.

Tool	Function
Text Frame	Creates a rectangular frame which allows you to enter text or import text you typed in a word processing program. The frame lets you move the text and change the width and height of the text column.
Picture Frame	Creates a rectangular frame which allows you to import a graphic image created in a paint or draw program. The frame lets you move the image and change its dimensions.
WordArt Frame	Creates a rectangular frame which allows you to create special, graphic text effects. This tool runs the WordArt subprogram, which works like a PageWizard to lead you through the creation of a WordArt object.

Adding Text to a Document

Tool	Function
Line	Allows you to draw a straight line on a page. You can then change the length, thickness, or position of the line at any time.
Rectangle	Allows you to draw a rectangle of any size or dimension on the page. You can then change the line thickness, position, or dimensions of the box at any time.
Rounded Rectangle	Functions like the Rectangle tool, but the rectangle has rounded corners instead of square corners.
Ovals	Allows you to draw ovals and circles. You can then change the line thickness and position of the oval, or stretch the oval to change its dimensions.

Publisher's on-line help facility also has an explanation of the seven basic objects, one screen of which is shown in Figure 4.1. To access this help feature, pull down the Help menu, select Introduction to Publisher, and press the Next button a few times.

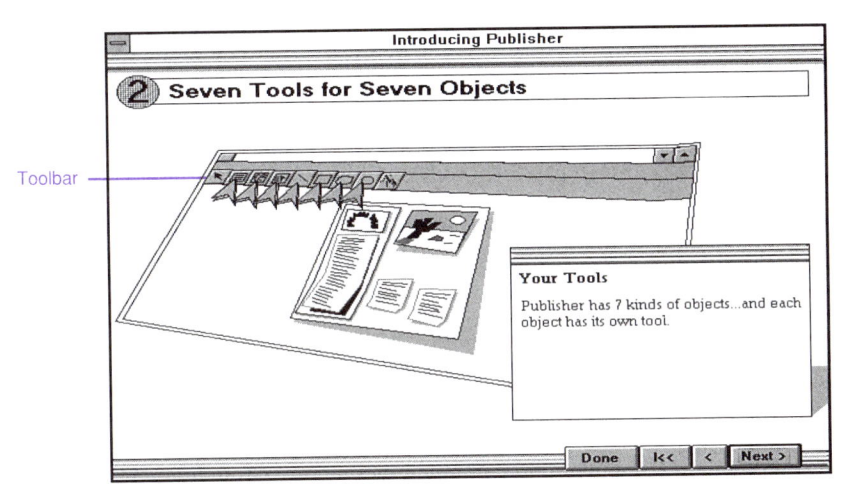

103

Figure 4.1 You can get more general information about the seven basic tools from the Help menu.

Using Text Frames

One picture may indeed be worth a thousand words, but you still need words, no matter what you intend to print. If you are printing a book, you'll need to manage several pages of text, running from one page to the next. If you are assembling a newsletter, you'll need columns of text, running from one column to another. Even if you intend to fill your publication with fancy graphics, you'll need at least a few words to explain the graphic images or to focus on important areas of the image. At the very least, you'll need to add captions or label your pictures.

When you work with text in Publisher, Publisher places the text in a *text frame*, which keeps that text separate from the other objects on the page. You can then move the text frame anywhere on the page, change the width of the frame to change the width of the column, or change the height of the frame. Text frames also give you more control over the style of text in that frame. For example, if you want to change the size of text in the frame, you enter a single command, which affects all the text and only the text in that frame.

If you are following along on your computer, open Publisher now by double-clicking on its icon in the MS Solution Series program group. In the Start Up dialog box, press the Blank Page button and press the OK button. A blank page appears in the work area.

Creating Text Frames

Adding text to a document requires you to perform a two-step process: you create the text frame and then import or type text into the frame. Creating the text frame is simple; you draw a frame (a box) approximately where you want the text to appear. The frame should be about the size and dimensions needed for the text you want to import, but you can move and resize the frame at any time. And if there is too much text for the frame on the current page, you can link frames on following pages and *spill* the excess text over into them.

Take the following Quick Steps to create a text frame.

Creating a Text Frame

1. Click on the Text Frame tool and move the mouse pointer into the work area.

    The mouse pointer turns into a cross hair.

2. Move the mouse pointer where you want one corner of the text frame to appear. You can start with any corner.

    You can use the rulers or guides to place the pointer more precisely.

3. Hold down the left mouse button and drag the mouse pointer to the diagonally opposite corner.

    A box appears with one corner anchored at the original position of the mouse pointer. As you move the mouse away from this point, the box becomes larger.

4. When the box is the desired size and dimensions, release the mouse button.

    An empty text frame appears with a dotted line defining it, as shown in Figure 4.2.

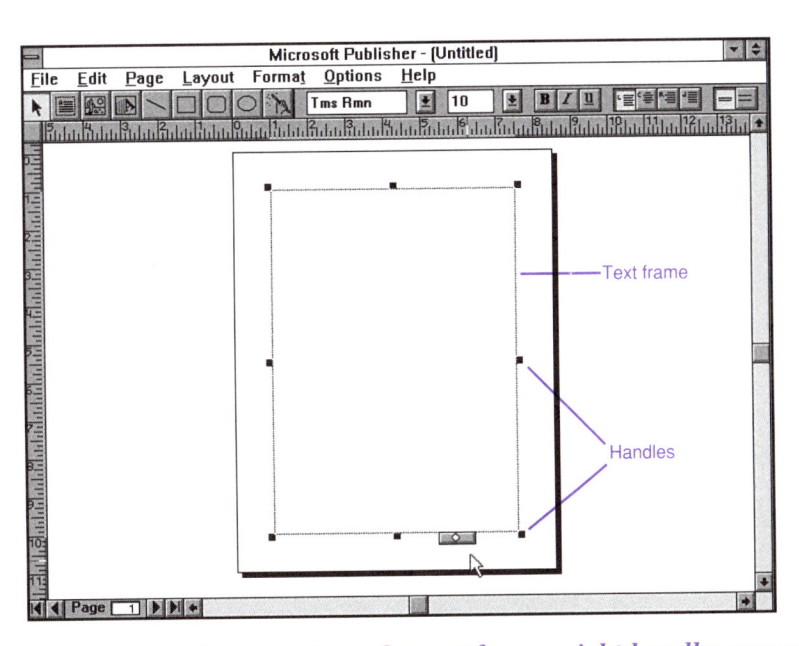

Figure 4.2 After you draw the text frame, eight handles appear around it to show that it's selected.

Unless you specify otherwise, the text frame you create does not print. To have a text frame appear in print, press one of the line-thickness buttons shown here:

These buttons are located on the right end of the Toolbar. Press the button once to activate it; press it again to deactivate it. To draw a frame that appears in print, press one of the buttons *before* you start drawing the frame. To add a printing frame to an existing frame, select the frame and then pull down the Layout menu and select Border. This opens the Border dialog box, which allows you to add a border. This dialog box also lets you change the line thickness of a border at any time or remove the border. You'll learn more about borders in Chapter 8.

As the previous Quick Steps explained, you create a text frame by anchoring one corner of the frame and stretching the frame out from this anchor point. This gives you complete control over the dimensions of the box. However, you may not always want complete control. If you want to create a perfectly square text frame, getting the sides the same length could take some doing. But Publisher can help, as you'll see in the following Quick Steps.

Creating a *Square* Text Frame

1. Click on the Text Frame tool and move the mouse pointer to the work area.

    The mouse pointer turns into a cross hair.

2. Move the mouse pointer where you want one corner of the text frame to appear. You can start with any corner.

    You can use the rulers or guides to place the pointer more precisely.

3. Press and hold down the Shift key. Keep holding it down until you're done drawing the text frame.

    This tells Publisher that you want to create a square text frame.

4. Hold down the left mouse button and drag the mouse pointer to the diagonally opposite corner.

A square box appears with one corner anchored at the original position of the mouse pointer. As you move the mouse away from this point, the box becomes larger.

5. When the box is the desired size, release first the mouse button, and then the Shift key.

An empty text frame appears with a solid line defining it.

☐

The preceding Quick Steps showed how to anchor one corner of a text frame and stretch the text frame out from that corner. However, you also can anchor the *center*, rather than the corner, of a text frame. You can then stretch the text frame out from this center point. To center a text frame, move the mouse pointer where you want the center of the text frame to appear, hold down the Ctrl key, and drag the mouse until the frame is the desired dimensions. When you're done, release the mouse button first and then the Ctrl key. To draw a square, centered text frame, use the same technique, only hold down both the Ctrl and Shift keys. Remember to release the mouse button *before* releasing the keys.

> **Tip:** If you need to create several text frames one after the other, you can *lock* the Text Frame tool on. To lock a tool, click on it with the left mouse button and then click on it again with the right mouse button (reverse this if you have a mouse set up for left-handed use). The selected tool remains selected until you are finished drawing your series of frames. To unlock, just click anywhere without dragging the mouse or click on another tool or on a menu.

In Chapter 8, you'll learn a number of things you can do to really jazz up text frames, such as adding shading and patterns behind the text, creating a three dimensional effect by *shadowing*, putting on fancy borders, and so forth. These operations are all done from the Layout menu using the Border, BorderArt, Shading, and Shadow options. You can try the options now on one of the frames you just created or wait for the more detailed discussions in Chapter 8.

Selecting a Text Frame

When you first create a text frame, that frame is *selected*. Eight little squares, called *handles*, appear around the selected frame, as shown in Figure 4.3. These handles allow you to change the dimensions of the frame. The button at the bottom of the text frame (the *connect* button) indicates whether the frame contains more text than is shown. You'll learn more about this button later in this chapter.

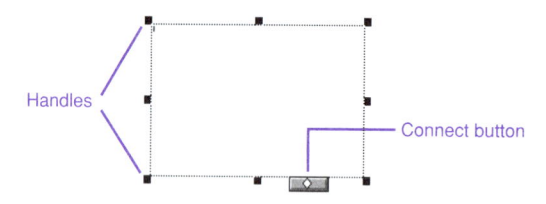

Figure 4.3   A selected text frame.

For now, it's enough to know that the selected text frame is the currently active one. If you perform any text-based operation, such as typing, importing, or editing text, the operation affects the selected text frame. To deselect the text frame, click anywhere outside the frame. The handles that surrounded the frame disappear. To select a frame, simply click anywhere inside the frame.

If you click in a frame to select it, and no handles appear, the frame is probably in Publisher's background. (The background was explained in Chapter 3.) The text in this text frame will be printed on every page of your document. To select a text frame that's in the background, pull down the Page menu and select Go to Background. You can then click on the text frame to select it.

Selecting Multiple Frames

As you paste more frames on a page, you'll find that you often need to work with several frames at once. For example, if you carefully aligned ten separate frames with each other, and you need to move them a quarter inch down on the page, you don't want to have to move each one separately and realign them. In such cases, it's useful to be able to work with a group of frames.

You can select any group of frames; the frames need not be the same type. For example, you can select a group of frames that consist of text frames, picture frames, and WordArt frames. You select a group of frames in either of two ways:

- ▶ *Individually.* If the frames are scattered around the screen, it's best to select each frame individually. Hold down the Ctrl key and click on each frame you want to include in the group.
- ▶ *As a group.* If the frames are in the same general area, you may find it more convenient to draw a box around the frames. Click on the arrow tool on the left end of the Toolbar. Draw a box around the group of frames the same way you drew a frame. A dashed box appears around the group. When you release the mouse button, all the frames appear selected.

If you selected a frame by mistake, or if you want to exclude a single frame from the selected group, you can deselect the frame while leaving the others selected. To deselect a frame, hold down the Ctrl key and click on the frame to deselect it.

Once you've selected multiple frames, you can perform many of the operations you would perform on a single frame, such as moving, cutting, copying, or deleting the objects. To move the frames as a group, place the mouse pointer inside any of the selected frames; the pointer turns into the move pointer. Hold down the mouse button and drag the frame. As you drag one frame, all the selected frames move, as shown in Figure 4.4. If you make a mistake, *immediately* pull down the Edit menu and select Undo. If you've done no other operation since making the mistake, the original state of the selected frames is restored.

Entering Text in a Text Frame

When you create a text frame, Publisher displays an empty text frame on-screen. If the text frame is selected, all that appears in the frame is a blinking vertical bar cursor. Because a text frame isn't much of a text frame without text, the first thing you'll want to do is place some text (a *story*) in the frame. You can do that in either of two ways: import the text created in a word processing program, or start typing.

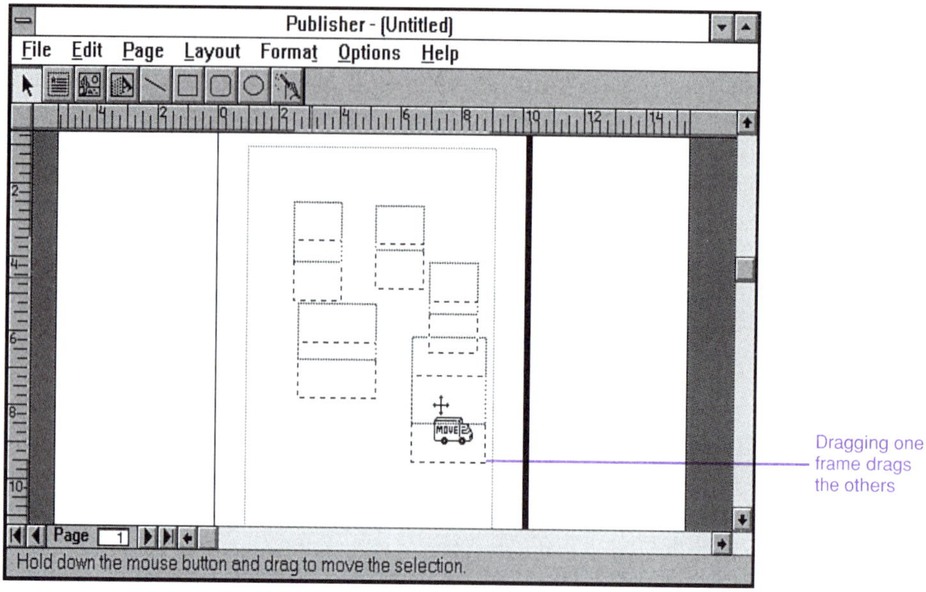

Figure 4.4 To move a group of selected frames, move one frame; the others will follow.

Although Publisher offers some powerful text editing features, including a spell checker, Publisher is not a word processing program. It simply cannot do all that a word processor does and still have the desktop publishing power you bought it for. Because of that, you'll probably want to type most of your text in a devoted word processing program and then *import* the text into a Publisher text frame.

You can import text in either of two ways: you can cut and paste the text from your word processing application into a text frame in Publisher, or you can import an entire file created in another word processing program.

Importing Text Using the Windows Clipboard

If you want to import a short block of text (a page or two) created in another Windows application, you can use the Windows Clipboard to import text. You copy the text from the other application to the Clipboard, and then paste the text from the Clipboard into a text frame.

Adding Text to a Document

The following Quick Steps lead you through the process of cutting and pasting text with the Clipboard. These steps assume that Publisher is running and that you've created a text frame in Publisher. You may have to reduce application windows to icons or resize windows during the process to switch from one program to another. If you need help with this, refer to Chapter 1.

Q Cutting and Pasting with the Clipboard

1. Run the word processing program you used to enter the text you want to import. — The application's window appears.

2. Open the file that contains the text you want to import and scroll down to the beginning of that text.

3. Highlight the text. — The text is selected.

4. Select the command you use to copy data to the Windows Clipboard. This is usually the Copy command on the Edit menu. — The selected text is copied to the Windows Clipboard.

5. Switch back to the Publisher window.

6. Select the text frame into which you want to paste the text. — Eight handles appear around the selected frame.

7. Pull down the Edit menu and select Paste Text. — The text on the Clipboard is pasted into the selected frame. If the text does not fit in this frame, a dialog box appears, as in Figure 4.5, telling you that the text won't fit.

8. Press the No button. — A button appears at the bottom of the text frame, indicating that the frame contains more text than can be shown.

Chapter 4

If the imported text was too long for the frame, you have several options for dealing with the problem. These options are explained in the section called "Too Much Text in a Frame?" later in this chapter.

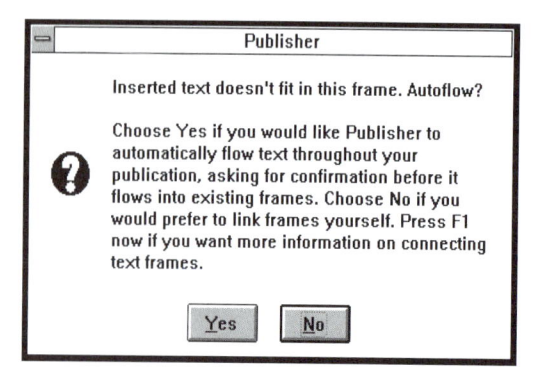

Figure 4.5 If the imported text is too much for the selected frame, Publisher asks if you want to autoflow the text into another frame.

> **Tip:** If a portion of text in a frame needs an extensive rewrite, consider cutting the text from the frame and pasting it into your word processing program. You can then use the advanced text-editing features of that program to enter your changes. When you're done, simply cut and paste the text back into Publisher.

Importing an Entire Text File

The second way to import text is to import a complete file created by another word processing application. Although the word processing program need not be compatible with Windows, it does need to create and save files in a format which Publisher recognizes.

What's a Format? Any file you create in any application program contains two elements: the text you type and any codes the program uses to enhance that text. Although the text is handled uniformly in most programs, the codes used for enhancing (formatting) the text and performing other functions vary a great deal among programs. Whenever you save a file, the file saves both the text and these *formatting codes*. The file is then said to be saved in a specific format, say WordPerfect 5.1. The variations in formats make it difficult to transfer files between different applications.

Is the File in a Compatible Format?

Although Publisher can handle many of the more common word processing formats, there are some formats it cannot handle. Before you import a file created in another word processing program, make sure Publisher can handle the format. The current version of Publisher can handle the following formats:

Publisher (text from other Publisher .PUB documents)	WordPerfect 5.1
Plain Text	Word for Windows 1.x
Plain Text (DOS)	Windows Write
MS Word for DOS	WordStar 3.3
MS Works	WordStar 3.45
MS Works for Windows	WordStar 4.0
RTF	WordStar 5.0
WordPerfect 5.0	WordStar 5.5

If your word processing program is not among those listed, don't despair. Many programs allow you to save your files in a format that's compatible with one of the word processing programs listed or in ASCII (ASSkey) format. An ASCII file contains none of the special formatting codes specific to the application; it contains only characters. If ASCII is not specifically listed as an option, look for an option that lets you save the file as a *DOS Text File* or as a *Text File*.

> **Tip:** If your word processing program does not allow you to save the file in a compatible format or as a text file (this is not likely), then you may need to purchase a *file conversion* program, such as Software Bridge.

Importing the File

To import a text file, first select the frame into which you want to import the text. Pull down the File menu and select Import Text. The

Import Text dialog box appears, as shown in Figure 4.6. This box prompts you to enter the following information about the file you want to import. Work through the options in the order they are listed:

- ▶ *List Type of Files.* By default, Publisher assumes you are going to import a file created in Publisher. If you created the file in another program, click on the arrow to the right of this drop-down list box, and select the format in which the file was saved. If you select the wrong format, Publisher may not be able to import the file, or the file conversion may not be completely successful.
- ▶ *Text Name.* This list box displays a list of files that have the filename extension used most often for the type of file you selected. To view a list of files having a different extension, type `*.ext` where *ext* is the extension of the file you want to import and press Enter. You can type a filename (if you know the entire name of the file), or you can type a wild-card entry to view a list of files.

  A *wild-card* entry uses wild-card characters in place of actual letters. An asterisk (*) stands in for any group of characters, whereas a question mark (?) stands in for a single character. For example, *.doc will find all files with the .DOC extension; le??er.doc will find files with names such as LETTER.DOC, LEDGER.DOC, and LESSER.DOC.
- ▶ *Drives.* Publisher displays the letter of the currently active drive. If the file is saved on another drive, click on the arrow to the right of the Drives box and select the letter of the drive.
- ▶ *Directories.* Under the Directories option is the path to the current drive and directory. If the file is stored in another directory on the current drive, use the directory tree that's displayed under the path to move to the directory that contains the file.

As you move through the directory tree, the list displayed in the Text Name box changes to display the names of those files in the currently selected directory which match the filename entry you typed. Double-click on the file you want to import or highlight it and press Enter. A dialog box will appear, indicating that the conversion is in process. If the file contains more text than the selected text frame can display, you'll see the dialog box you saw in Figure 4.4. Press the No button.

Adding Text to a Document

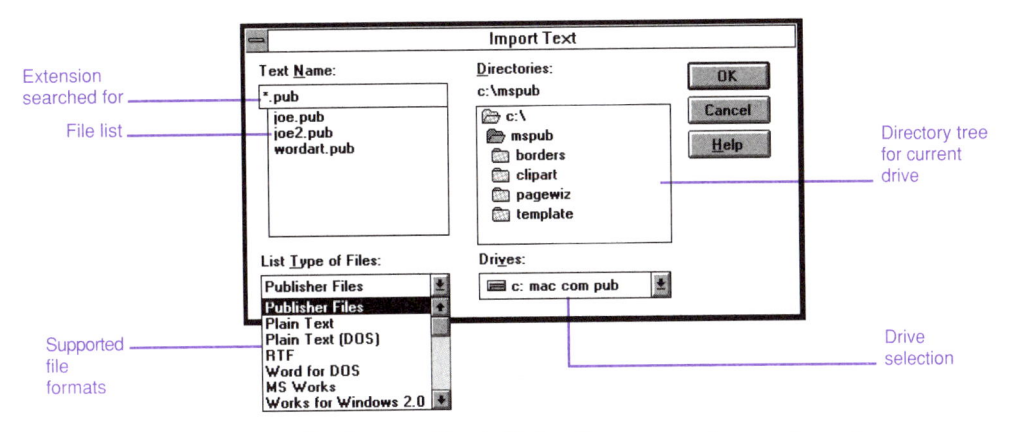

Figure 4.6 *The Import Text dialog box prompts you to enter the name and location of the file you want to import.*

(Callouts: Extension searched for; File list; Supported file formats; Directory tree for current drive; Drive selection)

The following Quick Steps summarize how to import a text file.

115

Importing a Text File

1. Select the text frame into which you want to import the file.

2. Pull down the File menu and select Import Text.

   The Import Text dialog box appears.

3. Select the format in which the file was saved from the List Type of Files drop-down list.

   The format appears in the List Type of Files box.

4. Edit the filename entry in the Text Name box, if needed, and press Enter.

   If any files in the current directory match your entry, the names of those files appear in the list.

5. Select the drive where the file is stored from the Drives drop-down list.

   The directory tree above the Drives box changes to show the directories on the selected drive.

6. Use the directory tree to select the directory in which the file was saved.

   The Text Name list changes to show a list of files in the the selected directory which match the filename entry you typed.

7. Select the name of the file you want to import from the Text Name list.

    A dialog box appears, telling you the conversion is in progress. If the text does not fit in this frame, a dialog box appears, telling you that the text won't fit.

8. Press the No button.

    A button appears at the bottom of the text frame, indicating that the frame contains more text than can be shown. ☐

Typing Text in a Text Frame

If you don't have a text file you want to import, you can type text directly in the text frame. Just select the text frame and start typing. When you select the frame, a vertical bar cursor appears. Any text you type is inserted at this cursor. When the cursor reaches the right side of the frame, it automatically drops down to the next line and starts inserting text there.

If the text is too small for you to see, press the F9 key or select a closer view from the Page menu. If you are in full page view, you won't be able to read the text.

Because the text automatically wraps from one line to the next, don't press the Enter key except at the end of a paragraph. or when you want to insert blank lines between lines of text. If you press Enter at the end of every line and then change the width of the text frame later, you'll see some strange line breaks, as those shown in Figure 4.7.

Too Much Text in a Text Frame?

You saw earlier that text frames can display a limited amount of text. If you import more text into a text frame than it can display, any text that doesn't fit is not displayed. How do you know if a text frame contains more text than is displayed? Look at the bottom of the frame. You'll see one of the three following *connect* buttons:

	The *end mark* indicates that the text frame displays all the text it contains.
	The *ellipses* indicates that the text frame contains additional text that is not displayed.
	The *arrows* indicate that this text frame is linked to another frame. Any text that can't fit in this frame automatically spills over into the frame that it is connected to.

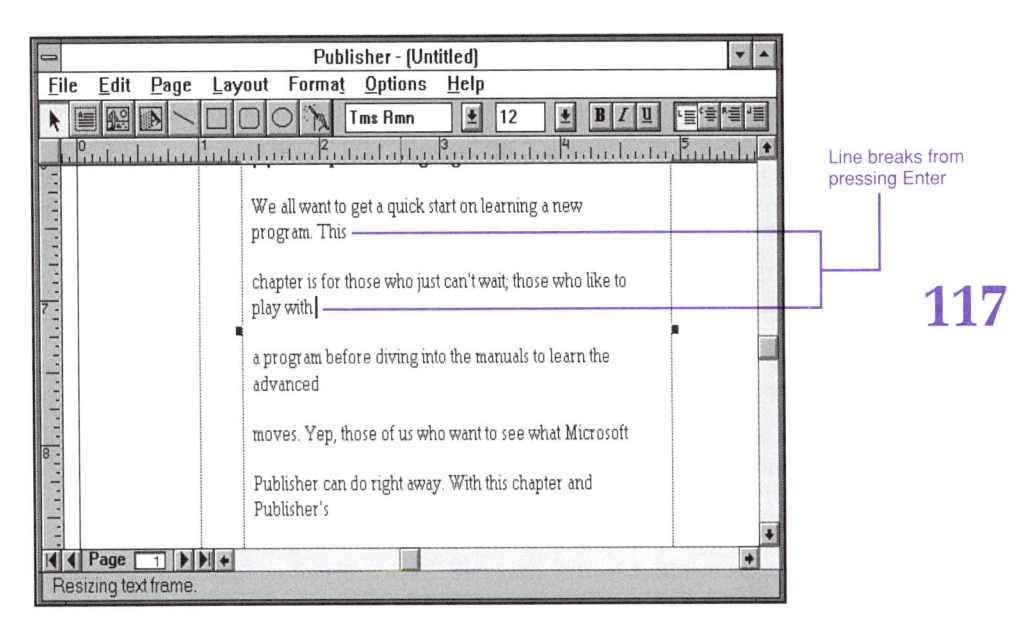

Figure 4.7 If you press Enter at the end of each line and then change the width of the frame, you'll get strange line breaks.

You can view the remaining text in either of two ways. If you know that only a small portion of text is hidden, you can enlarge the text frame (assuming you have room in your publication to accommodate a longer or wider frame). If, however, you imported more than a page of text, or if enlarging the text frame will mar your publication, you'll need to link the current frame to another frame, either on the same page or on another page. This is similar to the way newspapers often start an article on one page and spill it over onto another page.

Linking Text Frames

Before you can link two frames, the two frames must exist. One of the frames may already contain text. The other frame must be empty; you cannot spill text from one frame into another frame that already contains text.

Once you have the two frames, click on the connect button at the bottom of the first frame. The cursor turns into a pitcher, as shown here:

If necessary, flip to the page on which the other text frame is located (use the page control in the lower left corner of the window). Move the pitcher into the frame you want to link, and click the left mouse button. Text appears in this frame. If the end of the text is still not visible, enlarge this text frame or link it to another text frame.

> **FYIdea:** If you are working on a newsletter, you may want to link frames *before* importing text. That way, when you import the text (say on page one), you can have Publisher automatically spill any text that won't fit in the frame into a linked frame on another page. This saves you the trouble of having to flow the text later.

Moving Through Linked Frames

Once you've linked two or more frames, you'll need to get from one frame to another in order to read or edit the text in that story. To move from frame to frame, click on the first linked frame in the series. To move to the next frame, press Ctrl+Tab. Press Ctrl+Tab to continue to move to subsequent frames in the series. To backtrack through the frames, press Ctrl+Shift+Tab.

> **Tip:** To quickly move to the last frame in a series of linked frames, press the F8 function key and then the → key.

Disconnecting Linked Frames

You can disconnect linked frames at any time without losing any text from the story. To disconnect linked frames, select the text frame that precedes the frame you want to disconnect. Click on the connect button at the bottom of the frame (the button should have three arrows in it, showing that it's linked). The pointer turns into a pitcher; click anywhere outside a text frame. The arrows in the button change to dots, indicating that the frame now contains more text than can be displayed. (You didn't lose any text; it was moved from the linked frame into this one.) You can now link the frame to a different frame.

Editing Text

Whether you import text or type text directly in a text frame, you may need to edit the text to improve it or to correct errors. Although you could export the file into your word processing program, edit it, and then import it back into Publisher, that is very inconvenient. Besides, with Publisher, you have a number of advanced text-editing tools at your fingertips.

You'll find most of Publisher's edit commands on either the Edit or Options menu. These commands let you cut and copy text and paste the cut or copied text to a new location in the current document or into another document. Publisher also has two features you won't find in most low-end DTP programs: a spell-checker and a search and replace feature. The search and replace feature helps you find text and allows you to replace any specified word or phrase with a word or phrase of your choice, automatically.

The following sections explain the various editing tools in more detail. The first few sections explain basic text-editing features. Subsequent sections explain the more advanced features.

Editing One Character at a Time

Most of the editing you'll do in Publisher consists of deleting and inserting text one character at a time. You may need to correct a typo, insert or delete a word, or insert a sentence. Publisher offers the basic tools you need to complete these tasks.

To edit the text in a text frame, select the frame by clicking anywhere in it. A vertical bar cursor appears at the point where you clicked. If you were to start typing, text would be inserted at this point. To move the cursor to a different point, click on that point. You can also use the arrow keys to move the cursor.

To delete characters or spaces, move the cursor before the character or space you want to delete and press the Del key. Or move the cursor to the right of the character or space and press the Backspace key. To insert text, simply start typing. Whenever you delete or insert text, Publisher automatically rewraps the text to accommodate the change.

Highlighting Blocks of Text

Although editing character-by-character is sufficient for making minor changes, you need some more powerful tools when it comes to working with sentences, paragraphs, and larger chunks of text. For working with these *blocks* of text, Publisher offers several tools, which allow you to cut, copy, and paste a block of text or change character formatting for a selected block. Working with blocks consists of a two-step process: you *mark* the block (highlight it), and then enter a *block command*, such as Copy or Cut.

The easiest way to highlight a block of text is to use the mouse. The following Quick Steps lead you through the process.

Highlighting Text

1. Click inside the text frame that contains the block of text you want to highlight.

   A selection box appears around the frame, indicating it has been selected.

2. Move the I-beam pointer before the first letter of the block you want to highlight or after the last letter.

   This point becomes the anchor point. You will *stretch* the highlight out from this point.

3. Hold down the mouse button and drag the I-beam pointer to the opposite end of the block.

   As you drag the mouse, you stretch the highlight from the original I-beam location to its current location, as shown in Figure 4.8.

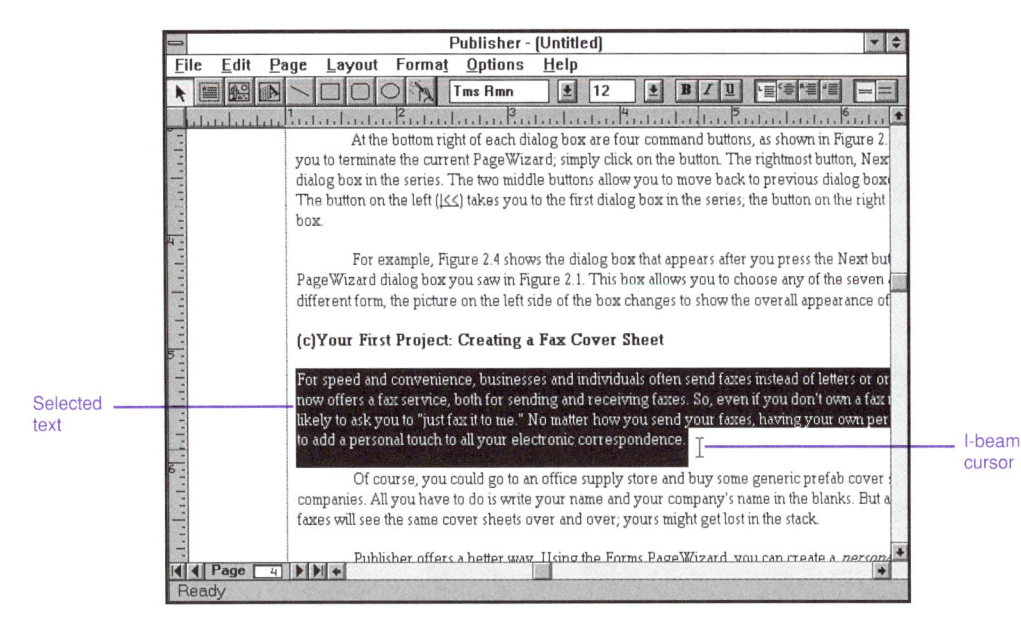

4. Release the mouse button.   The text you highlighted is now selected.   ☐

Figure 4.8   A highlighted block of text.

> **Tip:** If you want to modify an entire story, for example to change the type size of all the characters, you can highlight the whole story with a single command. Select the text frame, pull down the Edit menu, and select Highlight Story. This highlights all text in this frame and in any frame it's linked to. An even faster way to highlight an entire story is to select the text frame and press Ctrl+A or F8.

Although the mouse is the most intuitive way to highlight text, the keyboard offers a few shortcuts. Many users prefer to use the keyboard to highlight text, because they can keep their fingers on the keyboard during the editing process. They don't have to switch back and forth between keyboard and mouse. Table 4.1 provides a list of keyboard shortcuts.

Table 4.1 Keyboard shortcuts for highlighting text.

Keystroke	Function
F8 or Ctrl+A	Highlights the entire story.
Shift+← or →	Anchors cursor at current position and stretches highlight in direction of the arrows.
Shift+↑ or ↓	Anchors the highlight at the current position, stretches the highlight left or right to the beginning or end of the current line, and then up or down one line at a time.
Shift+Home	Stretches the highlight from the current position to the beginning of the current line.
Shift+End	Stretches the highlight from the current position to the end of the current line.
Ctrl+Shift+←	Stretches the highlight left one word at a time.
Ctrl+Shift+→	Stretches the highlight right one word at a time.
Ctrl+Shift+↑	Anchors the highlight at the current position and stretches it to the beginning of the paragraph.
Ctrl+Shift+↓	Anchors the highlight at the current position and stretches it to the end of the paragraph.
Ctrl+Shift+Home	Anchors the highlight at the current position and stretches it to the beginning of the frame.
Ctrl+Shift+End	Anchors the highlight at the current position and stretches it to the end of the frame.

If the text you want to highlight is in more than one text frame, you can carry the highlighting over into the next linked frame. The following steps explain the procedure.

1. Anchor the cursor at the beginning of the block you want to highlight.
2. Stretch the highlight to the right of the last character in the current frame.
3. Hold down the Shift key (if you don't, what you've selected will be deselected), and press the → key once. Publisher stretches the highlight into the next linked frame.
4. Hold down the Shift key and stretch the highlight over the remaining text you want to select.
5. If there is another linked frame, repeat the steps to stretch the highlight into the next frame.

Working with Highlighted Blocks of Text

Once you've selected a block of text, you can then cut, copy, or delete the block, or change the formatting of the block. You simply select the appropriate command from a menu or press a keystroke shortcut.

Copying and Pasting a Block of Text

Many times, you'll need to copy a sentence or paragraph from one part of a text frame to another part or from one frame to another. You can then modify the text as needed instead of retyping it. For such instances, Publisher offers the Copy command.

To copy a highlighted block, you perform two basic operations. First you *copy* the block to the Windows Clipboard, a temporary holding area in your computer's memory. Then, you *paste* the block from the Clipboard into the text frame in which you want the copy to appear. Because the clipboard continues to store the block even after you paste it, you can paste as many copies of the block as you like. You can even paste the copied block into a document you created in another Windows application. The following Quick Steps lead you through the process.

> **Caution:** The Windows Clipboard is a *temporary* storage area, which can hold only one item at a time. If you copy another block to the clipboard, the new block replaces the old block. Also, if you exit Windows or turn off your computer, the block is removed from the Clipboard.

Copying Text

1. Select the text frame that contains the text you want to copy.
2. Select the block of text you want to copy. — The selected block appears highlighted.
3. Pull down the Edit menu and select Copy Text, or press Ctrl+C. — The selected block is copied to the Windows Clipboard.

Chapter 4

4. Create or select a text frame to hold the copied text, and move the cursor where you want to insert the copied block.

   The text will be inserted at the cursor location.

5. Pull down the Edit menu and select Paste Text, or press Ctrl+V.

   The block from the Clipboard is inserted at the cursor, and Publisher rewraps the surrounding text to accommodate the inserted text. ☐

Moving a Block of Text

Although you can move a block of text by copying it to another location and then deleting it from its original location, such a process is inefficient. A better way is to *cut* the text from the original location and then *paste* it into the new location. The following Quick Steps lead you through the process.

Cutting and Pasting Text

1. Select the text frame that contains the text you want to move.

2. Select the block of text you want to move.

   The selected block appears highlighted.

3. Pull down the Edit menu and select Cut Text, or press Ctrl+X.

   The selected block is removed from its original location and is stored on the Windows Clipboard.

4. Create or select a text frame where you want to move the cut text, and place the cursor where you want to move the text.

   The text will be inserted at the cursor location.

5. Pull down the Edit menu and select Paste Text, or press Ctrl+V.

   The block from the Clipboard is inserted at the cursor, and Publisher rewraps the surrounding text to accommodate the change. ☐

> **FYIdea:** Keep in mind that Windows is a *multitasking environment*. This means you can have more than one program running at the same time and switch between programs. All your Windows programs share the same clipboard, so you can paste the block from the clipboard into a file created in another Windows-compatible program.
>
> You can even move and resize the application windows for each program to place the windows side-by-side. You can then switch from window to window with the click of a mouse.

Deleting a Block of Text

The safest way to delete a block of text is to highlight the block and then enter the Cut Text (Ctrl+X) command. This way, the deleted block is stored on the Clipboard, and you can get it back (as long as you don't cut or copy another block to the Clipboard).

However, if you're sure you don't need the text and you don't want to take the time to enter the Cut command, you can delete the block. Simply press the Del key, or pull down the Edit menu and select Delete Text.

Although the text is not sent to the Clipboard, it is sent to a temporary buffer where it is stored until you perform some other operation. As long as you don't delete any more text, perform any operation, or exit Windows, you can restore the deleted text. To restore the text, pull down the Edit menu and select Undo Delete Text. You'll find the Undo command useful for many operations, but it is much more risky than using the Clipboard.

Deleting Text by Replacing It

Occasionally, you'll want to replace a block of text with a different block or simply type something in place of an existing block of text. Of course, you could delete the original block and then cut and paste a new block in its place, but there's a faster way. Publisher offers a feature which allows you to replace a highlighted block of text with text that's stored on the Clipboard by entering a single command.

To turn this feature on, pull down the Options menu and select Settings. The Settings dialog box appears, as shown in Figure 4.9. Select the Typing Replaces Selection option to put an X in the check box; an X means the option is on. This option will remain on until you display the Settings dialog box and select the option again.

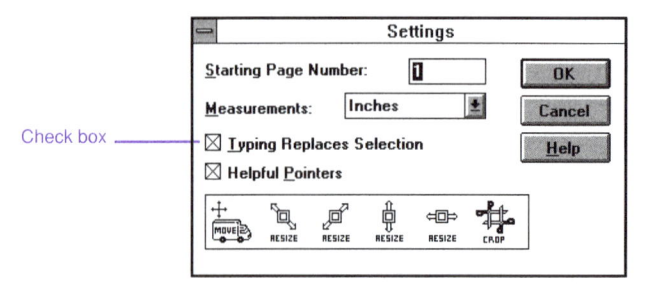

Figure 4.9 The Settings dialog box allows you to replace highlighted text with other text.

When the option is on, you can replace a highlighted block of text much more quickly. To replace a highlighted block with what you type, simply highlight the block and start typing. As soon as you start typing, the highlighted block disappears, and what you type appears in its place. To replace a block with another block of text, take the following Quick Steps.

Replacing One Block of Text with Another

1. Cut or Copy the block of text you want to use to the Clipboard.

   This text will replace the text you want to delete.

2. Highlight the block of text you want to replace.

3. Pull down the Edit menu and select Paste Text, or press Ctrl+V.

   The highlighted text is removed from the text frame, and is replaced by the text from the Clipboard.

Adding Text to a Document

Searching for Text

When editing a story, you may realize that you have used the wrong word or name in the story or that a certain part of the story (you can't remember where), needs some revision. Whatever the reason, you need to find the location of some text.

To help, Publisher offers a search feature, which allows you to specify a word, phrase, punctuation mark, or any character to search for. Publisher then carries out the search and stops at the first entry it finds that matches your description.

If your word processing program has a search feature, you are probably familiar with the process. The following Quick Steps summarize the basic procedure.

Performing a Search

1. Click on a point where you want the search to start or use the arrow keys to move the cursor to this point.

   Publisher will start the search from this point and will proceed up or down as you choose.

2. Pull down the Edit menu and select Find.

   The Find dialog box appears as shown in Figure 4.10.

3. Select Find What and then type the word, phrase, or character you want to find.

4. Select the Up or Down option button to specify the direction of the search.

   Down tells Publisher to search from the cursor to the end of the story. Up tells Publisher to search to the beginning of the story.

5. Select the Find Next option to start the search.

   Publisher searches in the specified direction and stops on the first item that matches your description and highlights it.

If the Find dialog box blocks your view of the highlighted item, move the box. If the highlighted item is what you were searching for, press the Cancel button to return to the text frame; the highlighted item remains highlighted. If the highlighted item is not the one you were looking for, press the Find Next button. Publisher will continue searching for the next occurrence of the item that matches your entry.

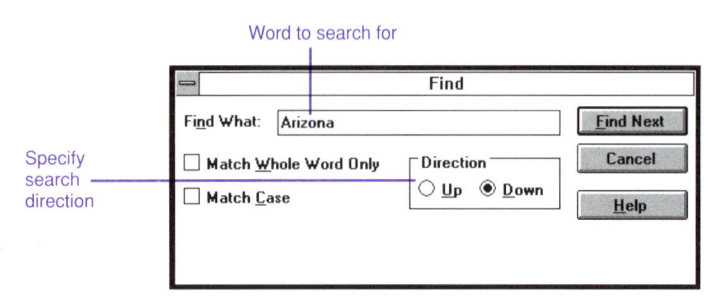

Figure 4.10   The Find dialog box prompts you to describe what you want to search for.

> **Tip:** You can use wild-card entries to perform a more general search. Use question marks in place of single characters or an asterisk in place of a group of characters.

The Find dialog box contains a couple options that we haven't yet discussed: Match Whole Word Only and Match Case. Use the Match Whole Word Only option to find exact entries. For example, if you want to find all occurrences of the word *book*, but not *books*, *bookkeeper*, or *cookbook*, select this option to put an X in its check box. The Match Case option tells Publisher to find only the text that's typed *exactly* as you typed it, paying attention to uppercase and lowercase characters. For example, if you wanted to find all occurrences of *Publisher*, but not *publisher*, you would select the Match Case option.

Searching and Replacing Text

Although finding individual words or phrases is helpful, you'll often find that you need to replace all occurrences of a word or phrase with another word or phrase. For example, you used the word *gadget* throughout your training manual, and the company has now decided to call them *widgets*. Of course, you could use the Find feature to search for the word or phrase and then type a replacement yourself, but why? With Publisher's Find and Replace feature, you can have Publisher do it for you, and much more quickly.

To find and replace text, select a text frame and click on the point where you want the operation to begin. Publisher will search and replace from this point down to the end of the story; you won't have the option of searching up. Pull down the Edit menu and select Replace. The Replace dialog box appears, as shown in Figure 4.11. Here's what you need to enter to respond to the box:

▶ Find What: Select Find What and type the word, phrase, or character you want to replace.
▶ Replace With: Select Replace With, and type the word, phrase, or character you want to use for the replacement.
▶ Whole Word Only: Select Match Whole Word Only to replace only those items that match your entry exactly.
▶ Match Case: Select Match Case to have Publisher pay attention to uppercase and lowercase characters during the search.

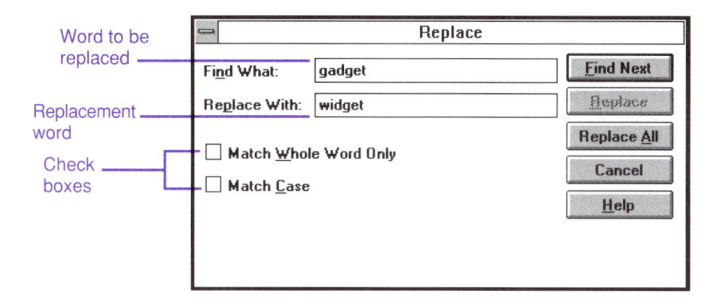

Figure 4.11 The Replace dialog box prompts you to specify what you want to replace and what you want to replace it with.

When you're done entering the search and replace text and specifying the search options, press the Find Next button. Publisher stops on the first occurrence of the item that matches your description. If the dialog box is in your way, move it to view the highlighted word or phrase. To replace the word or phrase, press the Replace button. To replace all occurrences of the word or phrase without having Publisher ask for your confirmation, press the Replace All button. Publisher replaces all occurrences in this text frame and all the text frames to which it is linked. To cancel Search and Replace without replacing the word or phrase, press the Cancel button.

At the end of the text, Publisher asks if you would like to start from the beginning, which is nice if your insertion point was in the middle of the file somewhere. This makes up for not being able to search and replace backwards.

Checking Your Spelling

Although most low-end publishing programs offer features which allow you to edit text, few of them offer a spell checker. If you edit or type text in one of these programs, and you happen to introduce a typing error, it's up to you to find it. Publisher is the first low-end publishing program to offer a spell-checker. It has a 100,000 word dictionary that helps you proofread your stories to ensure perfection.

To check the spelling of a story, select the text frame that contains the story and move the cursor where you want to start checking. Pull down the Options menu and select Check Spelling. Publisher starts spell checking. If Publisher finds a word that does not match a word in its dictionary, Publisher displays the Check Spelling dialog box, shown in Figure 4.12. In the upper left corner of the box is the Not in dictionary text box which contains the questionable word. You have the following options:

▶ Change To: If the word contains a typo, select this option, edit the entry, and press the Change button.
▶ Suggestions: This list box contains a list of suggestions for the correct spelling. This is useful if you are unsure of the correct spelling. If you select a word from this list, the word appears in the Change To box. You can then select the Change button to replace the misspelling with the selected spelling.
▶ Skip ALL-CAPITAL Words: This check box allows you to skip words that are in all uppercase. This is useful, for example, if you use abbreviations, such as AMA or ACLU, and you don't want the spell checker questioning them.
▶ Check All Stories: This check box tells Publisher to spell check all stories in the current file.

Once you've selected the options that specify how you want the spell checker to proceed, you can select one of the following command buttons to proceed:

- ▶ Ignore or Ignore All: To skip only this occurrence of the word, select Ignore; if Publisher finds the word again, it will display the Check Spelling dialog box. To skip all occurrences of the word, select Ignore All.
- ▶ Change or Change All: To change only this occurrence of the word, select Change. Publisher replaces the misspelled term with the word in the Change To box. To change all occurrences of the word, select Change All.
- ▶ Add: This option adds the word to Publisher's dictionary, so Publisher will not question the word in the future. This is useful if you commonly create publications which use specific terminology.
- ▶ Close: Select this command to exit the spell checker and return to the current story.

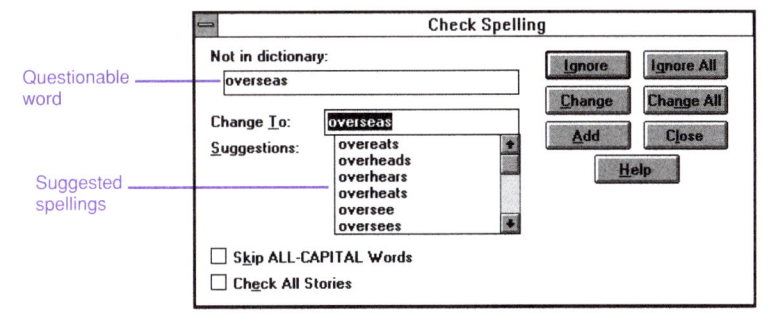

Figure 4.12 Publisher stops on the first word that does not match a word in its dictionary and asks how you want to proceed.

The following Quick Steps summarize how to check the spelling in a story.

Checking Your Spelling

1. Select the text frame that contains the text you want to check.

2. Move the cursor to the place in the story where you want Publisher to start spell checking.

   Publisher will check the spelling from this point to the end of the document.

3. Pull down the Options menu and select Check Spelling.

   Publisher starts checking the spelling of the story. If Publisher finds a word that is not in its dictionary, it displays the Check Spelling dialog box.

4. If the questionable word is okay, press the Ignore or the Ignore All button. Otherwise, go to step 5.

   If you press either Ignore button, Publisher skips the questionable word and continues to check the spelling.

5. To replace the questionable word, edit the word in the Change To box or select a word from the Suggestions list.

   The selected word appears in the Change To box.

6. To add the word to the dictionary, press the Add button.

   The questioned word is added to the dictionary. Publisher will no longer question this word.

7. To replace the misspelled word with the word in the Change To box, select Change or Change All.

   The Change button changes only this occurrence of the word. Change All changes all occurrences. ☐

After Publisher is through checking the currently selected story (text frame or series of linked text frames), you have the option of checking another story.

Adding Text to a Document

Moving, Resizing, and Reshaping Frames

No matter how good you are at estimating the correct location, size, and dimensions of a text frame, you'll probably have to fiddle with the frames after importing text to get them just right. Publisher makes it easy to manipulate text frames. You move the text frame, and Publisher automatically moves the text it contains. Resize the frame or change its dimensions, and Publisher rewraps the text to accommodate the change. The following sections explain how to move and resize text frames.

Moving a Text Frame

To move a text frame, you simply drag it across the screen. Select the frame you want to move. Move the mouse pointer over the selected frame until the pointer turns into a moving van (a van with a four-headed arrow above it). Hold down the mouse button and drag the frame to its new location (see Figure 4.13).

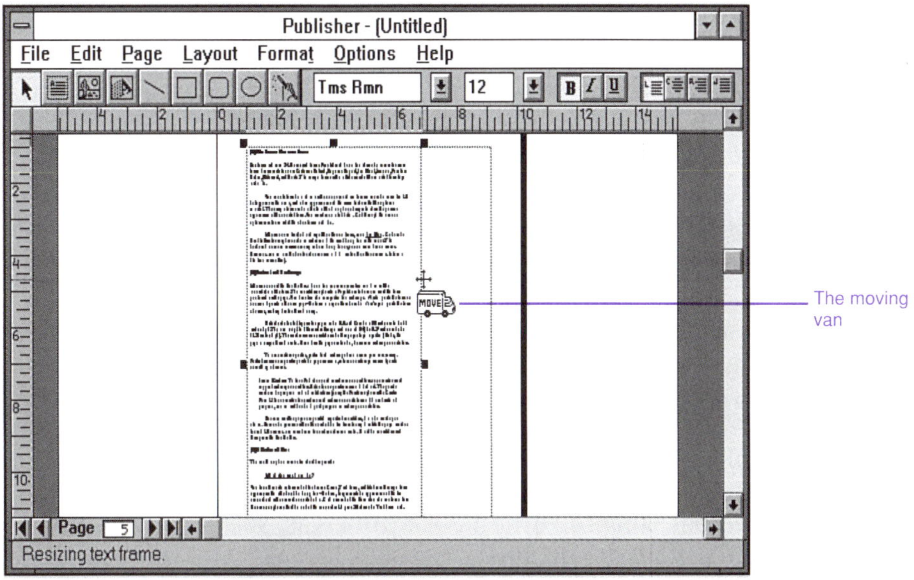

133

Figure 4.13   The moving van pointer allows you to drag an object across the screen.

Changing a Frame's Size or Dimensions

Changing a text frame's size or dimensions is a little trickier than moving the frame. As you know, whenever you select a text frame, eight small handles surround the text frame. Each handle allows you to change the frame's dimensions in a different way:

- *Corner handles* allow you to manipulate two sides at the same time. For example, you can pull the handle in the upper right down and to the left to decrease the height and width of the frame.
- *Side handles* allow you to change the width of the frame without changing its height or depth. For example, if you want a more narrow column, but you want its height to remain the same, you drag one of the side handles inward.
- *Top and bottom handles* allow you to change the height or depth of a frame without changing its width. For example, if you have a frame with excess space at the bottom, but the frame is the correct width, you could drag the bottom of the frame up.

To change the size or dimensions of a frame, move the mouse pointer over one of the handles. The pointer changes to a two-headed Resize pointer, as shown in Figure 4.14. Hold down the left mouse button and drag the pointer in the appropriate direction to change the dimensions of the frame as desired.

Making Frames Transparent

Whenever you create a text frame, the frame's background is solid white. If you layer the frame on top of a picture or another text frame, the frame may block the one below it. In such cases, it is useful to make the frame transparent. To make a frame transparent, you simply remove the background shading entirely. The text, WordArt, or picture is left intact. To restore the shading, you'll have to remember what the original shading was, select the Shading option on the Layout menu, and add it back just as if you were shading it for the first time, which in effect you are. So the hot tip here is to only make objects transparent when there is no other way to see and/or fix something underneath.

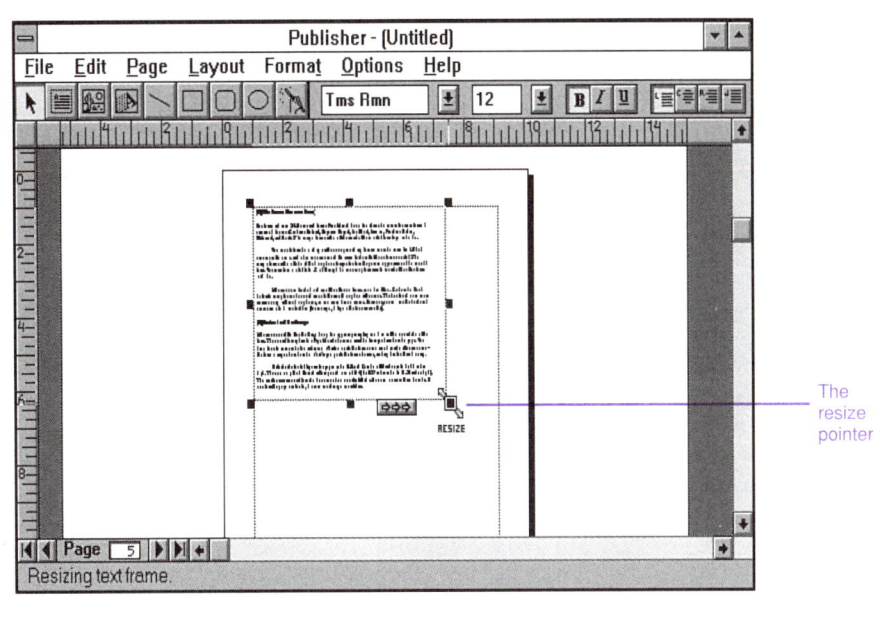

Figure 4.14 When you move the mouse pointer over a handle, it changes into a Resize pointer.

Making Objects Transparent

1. Select the object by clicking on it.
   Eight black handles appear around the object's outline, showing it's selected.

2. Press Ctrl+T.
   The object's shading is changed to clear. □

Deleting Text Frames

You can delete a text frame at any time to remove it from your publication. If you delete a frame that is not linked to another frame, the frame and any text it contains are deleted. If you delete a frame that's linked to one or more other frames, the frame is deleted, but the text it contains is pushed into the next or previous frame. To delete the text in linked frames, you must delete all the linked frames or disconnect the frames (as explained earlier) before deleting them.

Deleting a text frame is simple. Select the frame, pull down the Edit menu, and select Delete Text Frame. If you're using the keyboard, simply press Ctrl+Del. If you accidentally delete a frame, *immediately* pull down the Edit menu and select Undo Delete Object(s).

> **FYIdea:** You can experiment in Publisher without taking risks. If you want to try arranging objects in a different way on the page, simply make your changes without saving the file to disk. If you like the changes, save the file. If you don't like the changes, exit Publisher or select Create New Publication from the File menu, and then answer No when asked if you want to save the changes to disk. Your original file then remains intact.

What You Have Learned

This chapter described how to add text to any Publisher document you create using text frames. In particular, the chapter discussed the following:

- ▶ The seven basic objects that make up Publisher documents are text frames, picture frames, WordArt frames, lines, rectangles, rounded rectangles, and ovals.
- ▶ You create a text frame by drawing the frame on-screen. You can then select the frame by clicking anywhere inside it.
- ▶ You can import text into a text frame by pasting text from the Windows Clipboard or by importing an entire text file created in Publisher or in your word processing program.
- ▶ Another way to add text to a text frame is to type the text directly in the frame.
- ▶ If a text frame contains more text than it can display, you can enlarge the text frame or link it to another frame.
- ▶ You can edit the text you type or import one character at a time.

- ▶ Publisher offers advanced tools, such as a spell checker and a search and replace feature, that help you edit your publications without having to leave Publisher.
- ▶ Publisher offers a series of commands which allow you to cut or copy a selected block of text to the Windows Clipboard and paste the text from the clipboard somewhere else.
- ▶ You can move text frames, change their size or dimensions, or delete the frames at any time.

Chapter 5

Formatting Text

In This Chapter

- *Fonts and type styles: what they are, and how to use them*
- *Enhancing text with bold, italic, underlining, and other attributes*
- *Selecting the right font*
- *Setting margins and tabs*
- *Viewing type as it will appear in print*
- *Manipulating your text by changing fonts, alignment, line spacing, and indents*

Setting Your Own Type

In the past, creating a professional looking document, such as a newsletter, required the services of a typesetter. Only the typesetter could offer high-quality type, various typefaces, and precise spacing and alignment. Now, computer printers offer print-enhancement capabilities that rival the typesetting capacities of a professional print shop. To take full advantage of Publisher, a laser printer is recommended—many very powerful ones now sell for well under

$2,000. However, if you have a good dot-matrix printer or an inkjet printer, you can still create some high-quality publications.

In many cases, the combination of your personal computer, a good laser printer, and Microsoft Publisher equals or *exceeds* what a print shop can do. Technology has been advancing very rapidly in the past few years, and if a print shop has not kept up with the changes, you may have more publishing power on your desktop than the print shop has in its entire building. So, with a little work and creativity, you may be able to create customized camera-ready pages (pages that the print shop can use to create printing plates). You not only save the cost of setting the type and preparing the publication, but you get a high-quality, customized layout as well.

Formatting Text

Desktop publishing documents consist of two major elements: text and graphics. With graphics, you can use a desktop publishing program to change the location, size, and dimensions of the object, but you make most of your changes using the graphics program in which the graphic object was created. With text, however, the desktop publishing program plays a larger role, allowing you to design the text and change its look.

Publisher offers several tools and commands that allow you to manipulate (*format*) the text in your publication. You can change the overall layout of the text by changing line spacing, margins, indents, and other elements that position the text in a text frame. If you use a word processing program, you are probably familiar with such formatting.

Publisher also offers several commands which allow you to change the appearance of the characters. A character's appearance is defined by two elements: *font* and *style*. A font consists of a set of characters which share the same design; for example, Helvetica is a font. A style is any enhancement that is applied to a font, for example, bold or italic. This chapter explores all the ways you can manipulate text to enhance the appearance of your publications.

Controlling Type Style

When you type text in a text frame, Publisher uses the default font to format the text. If you import a text file created in another program, the font used in that program may carry over. In any case, the text is set in a certain font. Later in this chapter, you'll see how to change fonts. In this section, you'll learn how to enhance characters in the existing font by adding attributes, such as bold, italic, and underline. When you enhance the text, the font remains the same; you are changing only its style or appearance.

Publisher offers a variety of type styles for every font. Unless you specify otherwise, text is originally formatted as *normal text* (sometimes called *body text*, because it makes up the bulk of the text). Normal text is how text appears without a style attribute; it's the bare font. You can add a type style or a combination of type styles, or change the type style attributes at any time. Simply highlight the text whose style attributes you want to change, pull down the Format menu, and select Character. The Character dialog box appears, as shown in Figure 5.1. The box labeled Style contains the type style selections described in Table 5.1.

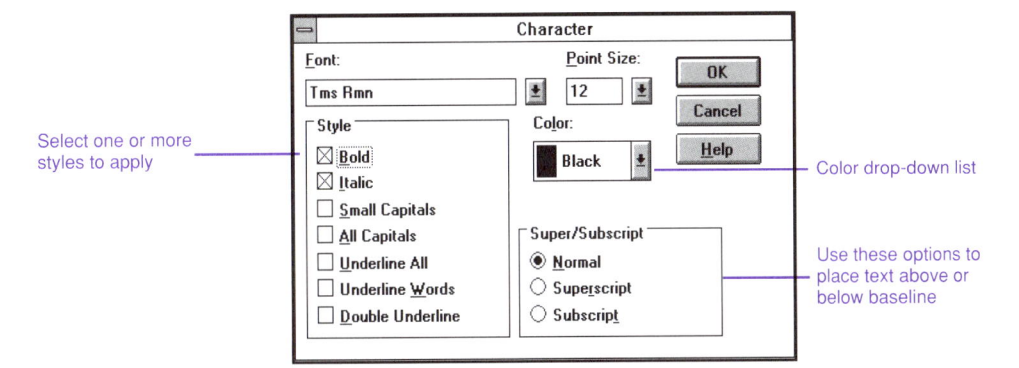

Figure 5.1   The Character dialog box lets you assign type style attributes to a selected block of text.

Chapter 5

Table 5.1 Styles you can assign to characters.

Style	Command	Effect
Bold	Bold	Text appears darker than surrounding text. Used for titles or to emphasize words.
Italic	Italic	Slants the letters and makes them more script-like (effect varies from font to font). Used for titles of books, magazines, and newspapers, and for emphasis.
SMALL CAPITALS	Small Capitals	Sets all characters in uppercase characters that are slightly smaller than regular-sized capitals. Effective for section headings and titles.
ALL CAPITALS	All Capitals	Converts all letters in the selected block of text to uppercase characters. Effective for adding emphasis, such as in "do NOT overuse this style."
Underline All	Underline All	Underscores all characters and spaces in the highlighted area of text. Used to add emphasis and to show the titles of books and magazines when your printer does not have italics.
Underline Words	Underline Words	Underscores only characters, not blanks spaces, so that words are not joined by underlines.
Double Underline	Double Underline	Underscores everything in the selected block of text with a double line.

In the Character dialog box, select the style attributes you want to assign to the highlighted block. An attribute is selected if an X appears in the check box to the left of it. You can select more than one attribute. For example, you might want to style the title of a book in both bold and italic to call attention to it. You can deselect an attribute by selecting it again; this removes the x from the check box. The following Quick Steps summarize how to change the type style for a block of text.

Changing Type Styles

1. Select the text frame that contains the text you want to format.
   Handles appear around the frame, indicating that the frame has been selected.

2. Highlight the character(s) or words whose type style you want to change.

3. Pull down the Format menu and choose Character.
   The Character dialog box appears.

4. In the Style box, select the style attribute(s) you want to apply to the highlighted text.
   An x appears in the check box of each selected type style.

5. Press the OK button.
   You are returned to your document, and the changes take effect. ☐

There are other choices you can make in the Character dialog box (shown in Figure 5.1) which affect the type style of the marked text. In the lower right corner of the Character dialog box is a box labeled Super/Subscript. This box offers three choices—Normal, Superscript, and Subscript; you can select only one.

Superscripts are numbers, characters, or symbols that are raised slightly above the *baseline* (the invisible line on which text sits). For example, you would use a superscript for a registered trademark symbol, such as Microsoft Publisher®. Subscripts are any words, characters, or symbols that go slightly below the baseline. For example, many mathematical publications contain formulae that require subscripts, as in $A_1 + A_2 = A_3$.

Using Publisher's Toolbar To Change Type Style

Although you can change type styles via the Character dialog box, there's an easier way for the more commonly used styles. Whenever you select a text frame, the right side of the tool bar changes to provide a list of text tools. These tools allow you to apply bold, italic, and underline attributes to a selected block of text with the press of a button:

B   This tool allows you to add the bold attribute to the selected text. If the text is already bold, pressing this button removes the attribute. If you press this button without selecting text, it stays pressed until you select it again or move the cursor. Whatever text you type when the button is pressed appears bold.

I   This tool allows you to add the italic attribute to the selected text. If the text is already italic, pressing this button removes the attribute.

U   This tool allows you to underline the selected text. It is equivalent to the Underline All option; that is, words and the spaces between them will be underlined. If the text is already underlined, pressing this button removes the underlining.

Changing Text Color

Also in the Character dialog box is the Color selection drop-down list box. Publisher allows you to choose black, white, red, green, blue, yellow, cyan, or magenta as the color of a block of text.

If you have a color printer, you can see the benefit of setting text in different colors. You can use the different colors to highlight headings, to emphasize your main points, or to improve the overall look of your publication.

If you don't have a color printer, however, what's the point? The point is that you can use the color options to create your publication as you want it to appear. You can then print each color in black-and-white on separate sheets of paper. For example, you would print all the red on one sheet, yellow on another sheet, and so on. This is called creating *color separations*. A print shop can then use your black-and-white printouts to create a separate printing plate for each color. By printing each color separately on a single sheet of paper, the plates create a page with the proper colors in each position. The process is similar to laying transparencies one on top of another. You'll learn more about creating color separations in Chapter 11, "Printing with Publisher."

Again, you can mix color with type styles. For example, you can have text appear in bold with a second color. But be careful not to overdo it. Too many colors and styles can detract from the content of your publication.

Using Fonts to Communicate

As mentioned earlier, a font is a family of characters all having the same design. Common fonts include Times Roman, Courier, and Helvetica, to name only a few. Professional typesetters have thousands of fonts to choose from, using them for different purposes and effects.

The use of fonts on a reader may be likened to the effect that a speaker's voice can have on a listener. Some styles suggest strength, others delicacy. Some styles are formal or legalistic, while others are informal or adventurous. You use fonts in the same way—to give your publication the right look and feel for your purpose. But to use them effectively, you must choose the right font.

Selecting Fonts—Some Guidelines

Fonts are divided into four general classifications—serif, sans serif, script, and black letter, as shown in Figure 5.2.

The serif fonts have finishing strokes (little extensions to the letters). These fonts are the most common, being used for the running text in newsletters, books, and other lengthy, formal publications. Serif fonts provide a professional look and are easy to read. In your publications, you should use a serif font for any body text, including paragraphs, lists, and captions. Commonly used serif fonts include Times Roman (included with most PostScript laser printers), Baskerville, Garamond, Bodoni, Caslon, and Century.

Sans serif fonts, which literally means "without serif," do not have the finishing strokes (serifs) on letters. Use a sans serif font to set off a word or phrase from surrounding text. Sans serif fonts are effective for titles, headlines, or product names in ads. Commonly used sans serif fonts include Helvetica and Futura. Helvetica is an excellent choice for headlines.

> This is Times Roman, a font with serifs.
>
> **Helvetica is a popular sans serif font.**
>
> *Brush is a rather elegant script font.*
>
> 𝕰𝖗𝖑𝖎𝖈𝖍 𝖜𝖆𝖍𝖗 𝕱𝖊𝖙𝖙𝖊 𝕱𝖗𝖆𝖐𝖙𝖚𝖗.

Figure 5.2   The four types of fonts—serif, sans serif, script, and Germanic black letter.

Script type styles look like neat, fancy handwriting with the letters joined together. Script is commonly used for brief, less formal publications such as brochures. The handwritten format gives the publication a friendly, less intimidating look. Because this font is somewhat difficult to read, use it only for titles, headings, small blocks of text, brief publications, or greeting cards. Zapf Chancery, Commercial, and Bank are commonly used script fonts.

The last of the four major classifications, black letter, is like the German manuscript handwriting in Gutenberg's time (Johannes Gutenberg invented movable type around 1440 and made printing possible). Gutenberg's first type was this style. Printers in Germany and other Northern European countries still occasionally use this font, but it is seldom used elsewhere because it is difficult to read. Fraktur and Schwabacher are black letter fonts.

> **FYIdea:** Although fonts are fun to play with, don't get carried away. Using too many fonts in a single document can detract from your message rather than enhance it. The mark of the amateur is a plethora of confusing fonts on the same page. One rule of thumb in the print trade is to use no more than three fonts for an entire publication!

In addition to the four general groups of fonts, fonts are grouped in terms or *proportional* and *nonproportional* fonts. With proportional fonts, each letter is given a specific amount of space depending on its width. A wide character such as *m* is given more space than a narrow character such as *i*. The type appears more even as in professional publications. With nonproportional fonts, each character is given the same amount of space, similar to the way characters are printed on a standard typewriter. Because nonproportional fonts allocate the same amount of space to each character, the size of these fonts is commonly expressed in terms of characters per inch (cpi), rather than points. This difference will become important when you select a size of font later in this chapter.

Changing Fonts

There are two ways to change fonts: use the Character dialog box, or use the Toolbar. The following Quick Steps lead you through the process of changing fonts using the Character dialog box.

Changing Fonts

1. Select the text frame that contains the text you want to format.

   Eight handles appear around the frame, showing it is selected.

2. Highlight the character(s) or words whose font you want to change.

3. Pull down the Format menu and choose Character.

   The Character dialog box appears.

4. Click on the arrow to the right of the Font drop-down list box, or press Alt+F and then Alt+↓.

   The Font list appears, showing the available fonts.

5. Select the name of the font you want to use by clicking on it or highlighting it and pressing Enter.

   The list disappears, and the name of the selected font appears in the drop-down list box.

6. Press the OK button.

   You are returned to your document, and the changes to the marked block of text take effect. □

Font selection works the same way as type style selection. If a text block is marked, the whole block is changed to the new font. If no block is highlighted, all text typed at the cursor will be in the new font. If, however, you move the cursor into a block that's formatted with a different font, the font drop-down list box in the Toolbar will change to show the name of the font used for this text. Any text typed at this point will appear in the font selected for this block of text.

> **Tip:** Remember, you can highlight an entire story by pressing Ctrl+A or F8 or by selecting Highlight Story from the Edit menu. You can then change the font for all the characters in that story in a single step.

An easier way to change fonts is to use the Toolbar. When you select a text frame, the Toolbar changes to display a list of text tools. One of these tools is a drop-down list box that contains the name of the current font. To change the font, click on the down arrow to the right of this box. A list of available fonts appears, as shown in Figure 5.3. You can then select a font from this list.

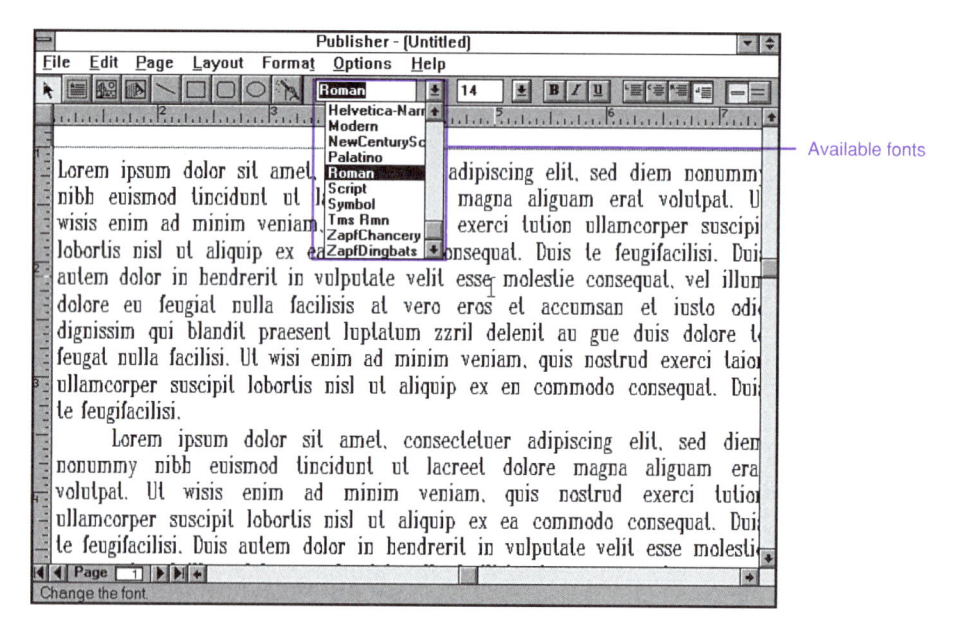

Figure 5.3   The drop-down fonts list from Publisher's Toolbar. Somehow, putting a Latin text in Times Roman seems appropriate.

The following Quick Steps summarize the procedure for changing fonts using the Toolbar.

Changing Fonts Using the Toolbar

1. Select the text frame that contains the text you want to format.
   Eight handles appear around the frame, showing it is selected.

2. Highlight the character(s) or words whose font you want to change.

3. Click on the down arrow to the right of font drop-down list box in the Toolbar.
   The drop-down list appears, showing the available fonts for the currently active printer.

4. Select the font you want to use by clicking on it or highlighting it and pressing Enter.
   You are returned to your document and the highlighted text appears in the selected font. The font's name appears in the font drop-down list. ☐

If you don't like the change in fonts, immediately pull down the Edit menu and click on the Undo Format option. Your document will be restored the way it was before the change. Of course, you can always change back to the original font by highlighting the text again and selecting the original font from the drop-down list.

Using the Right Size Font

In addition to choosing an appropriate font for your publication, you will need to select the appropriate size of font for your particular purpose. For example, you may want to set a chapter title in large print, set headings and subheadings in slightly smaller print, and set the running text in even smaller print.

However you decide to size your type, you will need a system for measuring the type. Font sizes are measured primarily in *points* for proportional fonts, and in *characters per inch* (cpi) for non-proportional fonts. A point is a printer's measurement approximately equivalent to 1/72 of an inch. Type is measured from the top of an *ascender*, such as a lowercase h, to the bottom of a *descender*, such as a lowercase j:

Ascender — hj — Font size
Descender

As a standard for reference, keep in mind that most typewriters use type that is 10 cpi, which is roughly equivalent to 12-point type. Newspapers usually use 8- or 9-point type for text in articles, while using larger print, 36- to 72-point type, for headlines.

Your body text, therefore, should be somewhere in the range of 9 points to about 14 points. Any larger or smaller, and the text becomes difficult to read. Tiny text makes the reader strain to discern the characters, while large text prevents the reader from seeing enough text to read smoothly. Too big or too small, and you trip the reader; the style will detract from the content.

Headings can and should be larger to set them off from the surrounding text. Headings should range in size from 20 to 40 points, depending on the level of the heading. For example, if you have three headings in a book (say a chapter heading, a main heading, and a subheading), you should set the headings in a point size from largest to smallest. For example, set the chapter heading in a large font (40 points), set the main heading in 30-point type, and set the subheading in 20-point type.

You should also consider the number of words generally used in a specific level of heading. For example, if you usually use only one or two words in a heading, a larger font may be appropriate. If the heading takes up two or more lines, however, you'll need to use a smaller point size.

Changing Font Sizes

You change font sizes in either of two ways, depending on whether you are using proportional or nonproportional fonts. For nonproportional fonts, you will select the font size when you select the font; the size, in cpi, is listed next to the font on the font list. For proportional fonts, you select only the font from the font list; you then select the font size from the point size list.

There are two ways to change font sizes: use the Character dialog box, or use the Toolbar. The following Quick Steps lead you through the process of changing font sizes using the Character dialog box.

Changing Font Sizes

1. Select the text frame that contains the text you want to format.

    Eight handles appear around the frame, showing it is selected.

2. Highlight the character(s) or words whose font size you want to change.

3. Pull down the Forma<u>t</u> menu and choose <u>C</u>haracter.

    The Character dialog box appears.

4. To change the size of a nonproportional font, click on the arrow to the right of the <u>F</u>ont drop-down list box, or press Alt+F and then Alt+↓.

    A list of available font sizes appears either in characters per inch (cpi) or in points, as shown in Figure 5.4.

    To change the size of a proportional font, click on the arrow to the right of the <u>P</u>oint Size drop-down list box, or press Alt+P and then Alt+↓.

5. Select the size you want to use by clicking on it or highlighting it and pressing Enter.

    The list disappears, and the selected size appears in the drop-down list box.

6. Press the OK button.

    You are returned to your document, and the changes to the marked block of text take effect. □

Chapter 5

> **Tip:** There's a quicker way to change the font size. After highlighting the block of text, select a font size from the Toolbar. For proportional fonts, click on the down arrow to the right of the point size drop-down list box, and select the desired point size from the list. For nonproportional fonts, click on the down arrow to the right of the fonts drop-down list box, and select the same font with a different size measured in cpi.

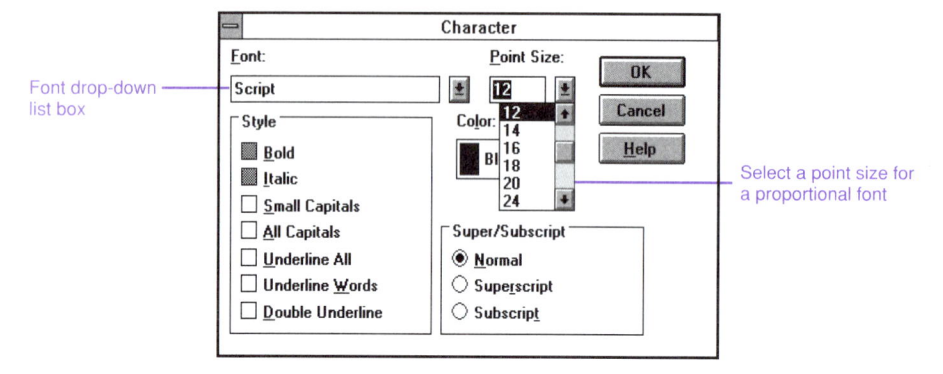

Figure 5.4 The Point Size drop-down list displays the available point sizes for a font.

Experiment with selecting different fonts and point sizes. Try different combinations, using Undo to restore each time, until you find the one that's just right for the effect you want to achieve. You may not have any idea what you want when you begin, but chances are you'll recognize the right font when you see it. So never be afraid to experiment—that's one of the reasons for the Undo feature.

What You See Is What You Get, Maybe

What You See Is What You Get (WYSIWYG, pronounced *wizzy-wig*) is one of those buzzwords so beloved by the jargonheads who write computer manuals. Actually, the acronym *should be* WYSIMCTWYG or What You See Is Maybe Close To What You Get.

First, the bad news. Publisher and other Windows applications try valiantly to show you on the screen what will be printed out. However, there are an incredibly wide range of computer screens and video boards, and not all screens and boards are created equal.

And even if you have a high-resolution monitor, your printer may print a higher quality output than your monitor can display.

In addition, to properly display the printer font as it will appear on paper, Windows must have a corresponding screen font installed. Otherwise, Windows uses some other font for display purposes. Thus, while the font may print correctly, it may not appear on the screen in the same size or format as what you actually get on paper.

Now the good news. When you choose a font in Publisher, Windows tries to match a screen font to the printer font. If a corresponding screen font is not installed, Windows will use an installed screen font that most closely approximates the font and point size you selected. Thus, while you may not have true WYSIWYG (you seldom really do), what you see on the screen will be close enough to the printed page for your design work.

Adding Fonts

All printers have at least one built-in font. (Even those obsolete old manual typewriters gathering dust at flea markets and yard sales have a built-in font.) When a printer is installed in Windows, the printer driver that was copied to your hard disk during installation tells Windows, and thus Publisher, what fonts the printer has. You can then select these fonts from the Character dialog box or from the Toolbar.

However, most printers have a very few fonts, which can limit your control over text. Does that mean you have to go out and buy a new printer? No. You may be able to add fonts to your printer in one of the following ways:

- ▶ *Font cartridges.* Many laser and inkjet printers have plug-in cartridges that contain memory chips that store selected fonts. You purchase a font cartridge from the manufacturer and plug it into your printer. The printer then acts as if the font is built-in.
- ▶ *Soft fonts.* In addition to built-in fonts, many laser printers contain additional memory (similar to RAM) that can temporarily store information about other fonts. You can purchase fonts on disk (soft fonts) that you load into this storage area whenever you want to use a particular font. This is called *downloading* the font to the printer. Because the printer's memory is blanked whenever you turn off the power, you

must download the fonts before printing. While not as convenient as built-in or cartridge fonts, soft fonts offer a wide selection at a low price.

▶ *Font Managers.* The least expensive way to add fonts to your printer is to purchase a font manager program, such as Adobe Type Manager or Publisher's Powerpak for Windows. These programs reside in your computer's memory and feed the necessary font information directly to your printer. Your printer does not need additional memory to store the fonts, and you don't have to download the fonts.

> **FYIdea:** One of the best ways to purchase software is through a mail-order company. You can usually purchase a good font manager program for under $60 from a mail-order software warehouse. Look in a reputable computer magazine for names and addresses of warehouses. Many of these firms offer overnight delivery for under $10; and even when you add this cost to the cost of the software, you still save money.

Regardless of how you add fonts, you must install the font in Windows before you can use it. Installing a new font is a one-time process. If you are adding fonts via font cartridges, you must select the Printers icon from the Windows Control Panel and use the Printer Setup dialog box to reconfigure your printer. The setup dialog box for the selected printer will have a list of cartridges from which to choose.

For soft fonts and font managers, you'll need to install fonts for both the printer (*printer fonts*) and the display (*screen fonts*). The printer fonts send your printer the information it needs to print the selected fonts. The screen fonts tell Windows what it needs to know to display the fonts. If you bought the fonts, chances are an installation program came with them. Follow the installation instructions to install the necessary fonts.

If you don't have an installation program, you'll have to install the fonts using Windows' Control Panel. The following Quick Steps will work in most cases.

Installing a New Font in Windows

1. Go to the Main program group and double-click on the Control Panel icon.

    The Control Panel window appears.

2. Double-click on the Fonts icon.

    The Fonts dialog box appears, as in Figure 5.5, listing the previously installed fonts. At the bottom of the box are samples of how the highlighted font looks.

3. Press the Add command button.

    The Add Font Files dialog box appears, prompting you for the filename of the font set you want to install.

4. In the Font Filename text box, type the name of the font file that contains the font you want to use, and press Enter. You can use a wild-card entry to display a list of fonts.

    For example, Windows uses the default entry *.FON to list all files with the .FON extension. The Font Files list box displays a list of files matching your entry.

5. Use the Directories list box to change to the drive and directory that contains the font file you want to use.

    The Font Files list box changes to show a list of files in the selected directory that match your Font Filename entry.

6. Select the font file(s) you want to add from the Font Files list box by clicking on the file's name or highlighting it and pressing the spacebar.

    You can select more than one font file. To deselect a selected file, select it again.

7. Press the OK button.

    The selected font or fonts are added for the current printer in Windows. □

Chapter 5

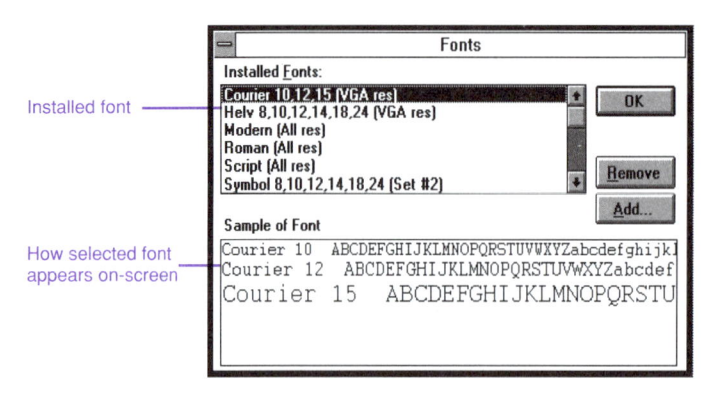

Figure 5.5 The Fonts dialog box lists the installed fonts and allows you to add or remove installed fonts.

Regardless of how much trouble it takes to get a set of downloadable fonts installed in Windows, thus making them available to Publisher, it is definitely worth all the hassle. However, you should keep in mind that installed fonts take up valuable memory. If you find that you never use a font, use the Remove button in Windows' Fonts dialog box to remove the font. (Do NOT remove Helvetica, because Windows uses that font for its help screens.) This removes the font from memory, but keeps the font file on disk, usually in the C:\WINDOWS\SYSTEM subdirectory. If you find later that you need to use the font, you can add it as explained earlier. You should also keep in mind that publications that use a lot of fonts also take longer to print.

> **FYIdea:** You can, however, *use too many fonts at once.* Just because your PostScript printer has 48 fonts does not mean you should use all 48 on the same page. The rule of thumb is to stay within the same type family as much as possible on a page. For instance, you might make up a striking camera-ready ad using Helvetica, Helvetica Black, Helvetica Condensed, and Helvetica Light. You stay within the same type family (Helvetica) but get a wide range of harmonious effects.

Adjusting Letter Spacing

Whenever you type, spaces are inserted between the characters. Sometimes, more or less space is inserted than desired. Usually the problem is that too much space is inserted, giving the text a non-uniform, airy look. Although this is usually not a problem with small type sizes in running text, it often becomes a problem in large type used for headings. The following samples show loose character pairs that often cause problems:

AW To Ya Wa Wo Va

Professional typesetters fix these loose character pairs by *kerning* the pairs—removing the extra space between the characters.

With Publisher, you can adjust the spacing between selected text to kern loose character pairs or to insert space between characters that are too close together. You can use this feature to create special effects or to improve the appearance and readability of the text. The following Quick Steps lead you through the process.

Adjusting Letter Spacing

1. Select the text frame that contains the text you want to adjust.

   Eight handles appear around the frame, showing it is selected.

2. Highlight the letters, word, or block of text.

3. Pull down the Format menu and select Spacing Between Characters.

   The Spacing Between Characters dialog box appears, as shown in Figure 5.6.

4. Select Squeeze Letters Together or Move Letters Apart.

   A black dot appears next to the selected option. A suggested amount appears in the By This Amount text box.

5. In the By This Amount text box, enter the amount you want to adjust the text in points.

   Usually, a one- or two-point adjustment is sufficient.

6. Press the OK button.

   You are returned to your document, and the change takes effect.

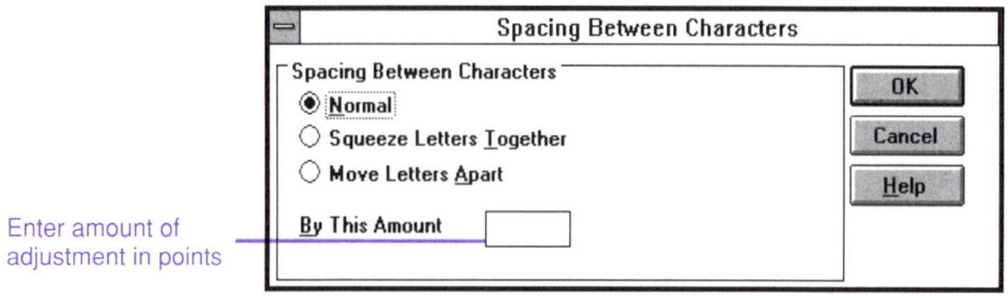

Figure 5.6 The Spacing Between Characters dialog box allows you to loosen or tighten the text.

Indents, Line Spacing, Tabs, and Other Text Formatting

Up to this point, we have discussed character formatting—changing the appearance of characters on-screen and in print. But there are other formatting options that affect text by controlling the position of the text on the page. Of course, you could move and resize text frames to reposition text, but this type of repositioning doesn't accomplish all the formatting you'll need to do. For example, you may want to create an indented list within the frame, change the margins for a block of text, or change the line spacing.

The following sections explain the various formatting options that control the overall layout of text on a page.

Setting Frame Margins

In Chapter 4, you learned how to change the dimensions of a text frame to increase or decrease the *page* margins—the space between the outer edges of the text and the page. You also saw in Chapter 3 that you can use layout guides to help you position a frame at a precise distance from the edge of the page.

However, you can also set the margins *within* a frame. For example, if you want to place a text frame between two columns, as shown in Figure 5.7, you would probably want to increase the space between the text and the frame to prevent the text within the frame from interfering with the surrounding text.

Formatting Text

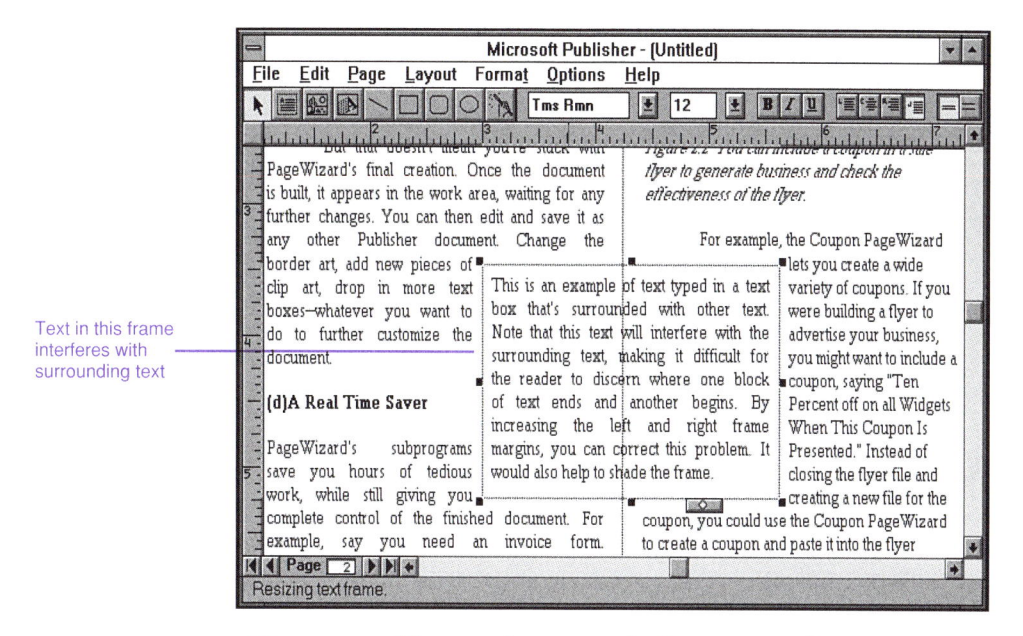

Figure 5.7 You can increase the frame margins to increase space between the frame and the text or other object it contains.

Text in this frame interferes with surrounding text

To set frame margins, pull down the Layout menu and select Frame Columns and Margins. The Frame Columns and Margins dialog box appears, as shown in Figure 5.8. Select Left and Right, and type the setting you want to use for the left and right margins. Select Top and Bottom, and type the setting you want to use for the top and bottom margins. Press the OK button. Publisher reformats the text in the selected frame.

Set the margins for the text frame

Specify the number of columns and the space between them

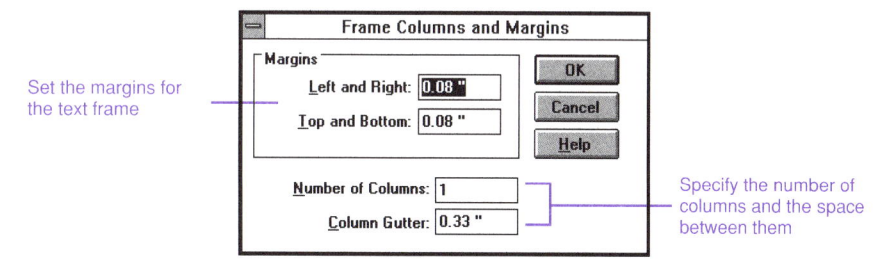

Figure 5.8 The Frame Columns and Margins dialog box allows you to set the margins for text within a frame.

159

Chapter 5

Creating Columns within a Frame

You can create columns of text in either of two ways. One way is to create side-by-side text frames and link the text frames. An easier way is to have Publisher create the columns for you. You specify the number of columns and the space between columns, and Publisher does the rest, creating the specified columns *within* the text frame.

To have Publisher create columns, select the text frame in which you want the columns created. Pull down the Layout menu and select Frame Columns and Margins. You'll see the dialog box shown in Figure 5.8. Select Number of Columns and type the number of columns you want in the frame. Select Column Gutter and type the space you want inserted between each column. Press the OK button when you're done. Publisher reformats the text in columns and displays the result, as shown in Figure 5.9.

Three-column format is common in newsletters

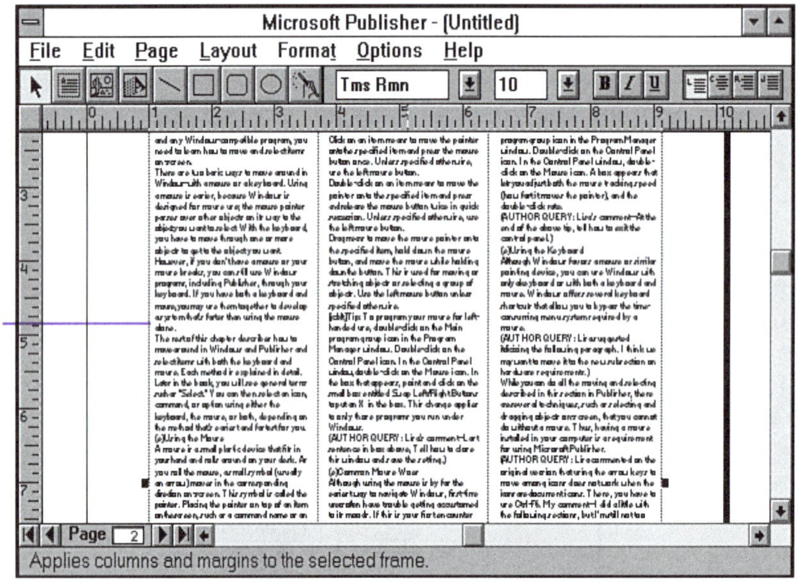

Figure 5.9 Publisher formats the text to create the specified number of columns.

Tabs and Tab Stops

Tab settings are really *stops*. If you press the Tab key on a typewriter, the carriage jumps to the next tab stop. In word processing programs, and in Publisher's text frames, the Tab key on your computer's keyboard does the same thing. This provides an easy way to indent the first line of a paragraph or align entries in a list. You will most often use tabs in setting up *tables*—rows and columns of numbers and other data.

It is *very important* that you use tabs instead of spaces to format a table. The reason is that most fonts are *proportionally spaced*; that is, wide letters like *m* get more space than narrow letters like *i*. Although the table may look okay on-screen, when you print it, the columns may or may not align. Using tabs ensures proper alignment. Another reason for using tabs is that they make it easier to realign columns in a table. Instead of inserting or deleting a bunch of spaces, you simply change the tab stop settings for a block of text.

Publisher has a default tab stop setting every half inch. If you press the Tab key without changing this default, the cursor and any text in front of it will jump to the next half inch mark (indicated in the horizontal ruler at the top of the window). You can continue typing from there. You can change tab stop settings at any time. If you want to change the settings for an existing block of text, highlight the block before setting the tabs; otherwise, the tab settings will affect only the paragraph in which the cursor is located. The following Quick Steps explain how.

Setting Tab Stops

1. To set tab stops for an existing block of text, select the text frame that contains the block and highlight the block.
2. Pull down the Format menu and select Tabs.

   The Tabs dialog box appears, as shown in Figure 5.10.
3. In the Tab Positions text box, type the distance you want the tab stop from the left margin of the frame.
4. Press the Set button.

   The number you typed appears in the list box below the Tab Positions text box.

Chapter 5

5. Continue entering tab stop settings until all the settings you want to use are listed. Press the OK button.

You are returned to your document.

☐

> **Caution:** If you changed tab stops for a highlighted block of text and the changes did not affect the block, you may need to display the Tabs dialog box again and delete old tab settings. You may also run into problems if the tabs you used are not where you think they are. Because tabs are invisible on-screen, it's impossible to tell where the tabs are or how many have been used.

If you add a tab setting to replace an existing setting, you should delete the original setting. To delete a setting, highlight the setting in the list box and press the De_lete button. If you want to reset all tabs, you can delete all the original settings before you begin by pressing the Delete All Ta_bs button.

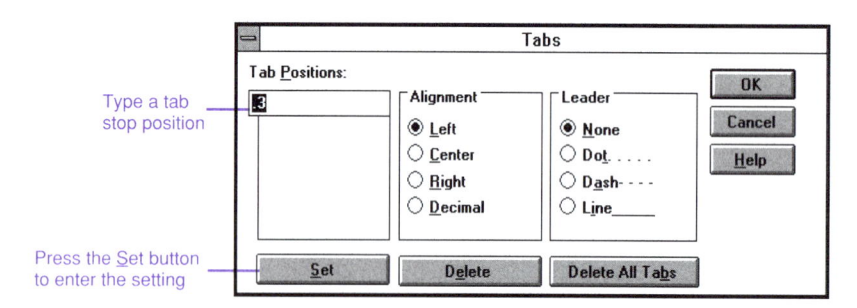

Figure 5.10 The Tabs dialog box allows you to enter and delete tab stop settings.

> **Tip:** If you do not already have the text for the table, it would be better to use PageWizards Tables tool to create the table rather than fiddling with tabs.

You will notice two boxes of options in the Tabs dialog box—these are titled Alignment and Leader. Alignment choices are Left (the default), Right, Center, and Decimal. They refer to how the text will be aligned on the tab stop. For example, Center centers any text you type on the tab stop. For numbers with decimal characters, you can use decimal tab stops to align a column of numbers on the decimal points. This makes it easier to tally the column.

The Leader options box contains several options for inserting leaders up to the tab stop. A leader consists of a line or a series of dots or dashes that extend from the cursor position up to the tab stop. You commonly see leaders in a table of contents:

Chapter 1: Using Leaders........................10

They help the reader follow a line of data across a row. To have Publisher insert a leader, select one of the leader options: Dot, Dash, or Line.

Changing Line Spacing

Line spacing is the space between lines or, as the old print shop folks call it, *leading* (pronounced LEDDing). The term *leading* is used because in the days when type was set manually, typesetters used thin strips of lead to separate lines of type. To increase the leading, they would insert thicker strips of lead. To decrease leading, they used thinner strips.

Most users will choose to either single space or double space the text. In either case, you can change the line spacing quickly using one of the line spacing buttons on the far right end of the Toolbar:

Simply highlight the text whose line spacing you want to change and click on one of the buttons.

> **Tip:** You can change line spacing quickly using the keyboard. Highlight the text whose spacing you want to change. Press Ctrl+1 to single space the text, Ctrl+2 for double spacing, or Ctrl+5 for one and a half line spaces.

You can adjust the leading more precisely by using the Indents and Spacing dialog box, shown in Figure 5.11. To display this box, pull down the Format menu and select Indents and Spacing. At the bottom of this dialog box are text boxes that allow you to set the line spacing and the space before and after paragraphs.

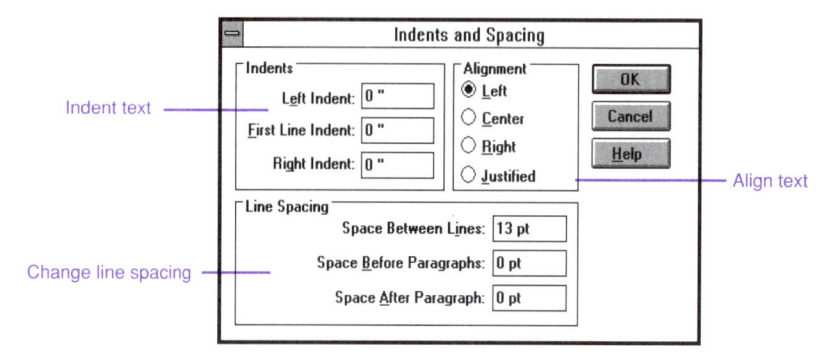

Figure 5.11 The Indents and Spacing dialog box.

In the Space Between Lines text box will probably be an entry something like 1 sp or 2 sp, depending on whether the single space or double space button is pressed on the Toolbar. You can edit this entry to increase the line spacing to three or four lines, but for most purposes, you'll want to adjust the leading in smaller increments—in *points*.

To determine the line spacing in points, you need to know a little about how line spacing is measured. First, you should know that line spacing is measured from the baseline of one line of text to the baseline of the next line of text. (Remember that the baseline is the imaginary line on which the text rests.) To prevent lines of text from overlapping, you need to insert enough space to account for the point size of the font plus additional space to keep descending characters (such as g) from crossing over ascending characters (such as *f*).

To determine the line spacing in points, take the type size (in points) and add to it the number of extra points you want inserted between the lines. For example, if you are using 12-point type and you want an additional point inserted between lines, the line spacing will be 13 points.

FYIdea: Professional printers commonly include a point size and line spacing specification when referring to fonts. In the example just shown, the type would be said to be *12 on 13* or 12/13.

To enter a line spacing setting in points, select Space Between Lines, type the number of points, type `pt`, and press Enter or press the OK button. For example, type

```
13 pt
```

Remember that the line spacing should always be greater than the size of the font. Publisher reformats the selected text according to the new line spacing.

Indenting Text

You will often come across the need to indent a block of text. For example, if you want to set off a long quote from the surrounding text, you may want to indent the left and right sides of the quote. If you want to create a numbered list, you may want to indent the text so it stands apart from the number, as shown in Figure 5.12. Of course you could use tabs to indent the text, but then you have to insert tabs to manually indent each line in the block. An easier way is to use Publisher's Indents and Spacing dialog box, as you saw in Figure 5.11.

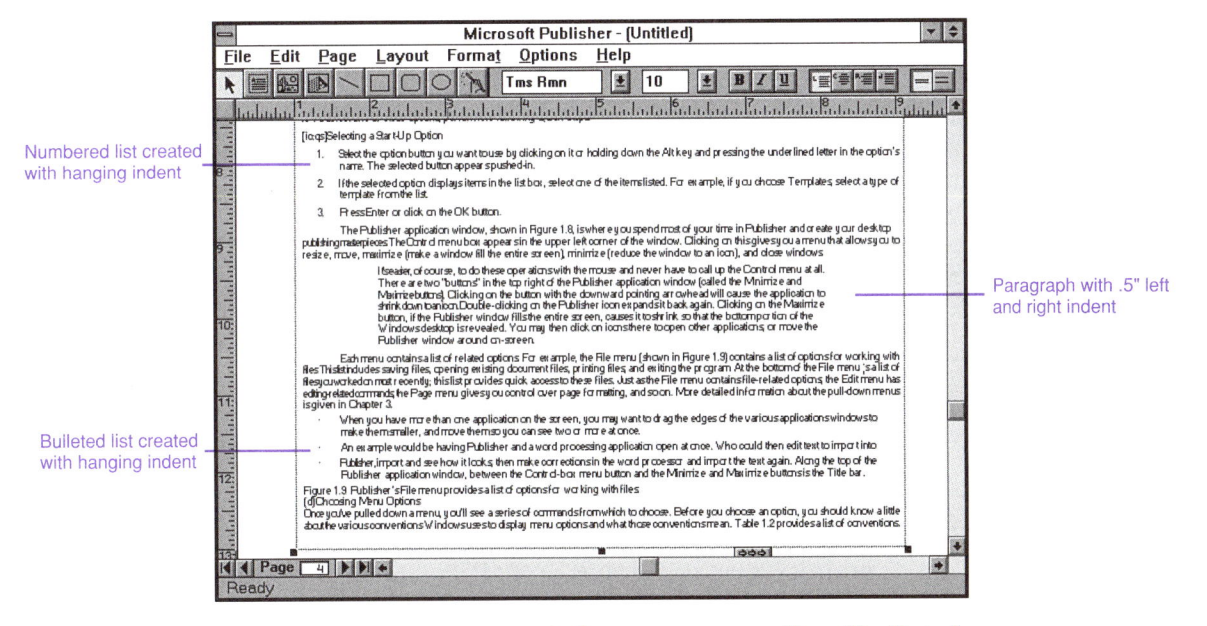

Figure 5.12 You can use indents to create a list of bulleted items, a numbered list, or an indented paragraph.

To indent an entire paragraph, simply type the desired setting for the left and right indents. You can also use the Left Indent setting to indent the first line in a paragraph. That way, you don't have to insert tabs at the beginning of each paragraph.

For a bulleted or numbered list, like the one shown in Figure 5.12, the process is a little more complicated. You need to create what is called a *hanging indent*; that is, the entire paragraph is indented *except* for the first line, which hangs out a little. To create a hanging indent, take the following steps:

1. Type a left indent entry that will indent the entire paragraph the desired distance (the example indented .5").
2. Type a negative First Line Indent setting to bring the first line back to the left (the example used –.3").

In the example, I used a tab between the period following the number and the text. If the left indent setting aligns with a tab stop setting, the text will align properly. (In the example, the left indent and first tab stop are both at .5".) If the text does not align properly, change the tab stop setting (as explained earlier) to match the left indent setting.

Changing the Alignment of Text

In addition to indenting text, you can change the way the text is aligned with respect to the left and right margins. To change text alignment, first highlight the text whose alignment you want to change. You can then press one of the alignment buttons on the right end of the Toolbar, or pull down the Format menu and select Indents and Spacing to use the Indents and Spacing dialog box. You can align the text in any of the following ways:

Left starts all lines flush against the left margin or indent. The right ends of the lines fall wherever they end, giving the right margin a *ragged* look. This is the default option, and is used for most running text.

Center centers all lines between the margins. This option is useful for greeting card messages, letterhead, addresses on envelopes or mailing labels, or for other short blocks of text.

Right starts all lines flush against the right margin or indent. The left ends of the lines fall wherever they end, giving the left margin a ragged look. This option is useful for typing a date at the top of a letter or for aligning colons in a memo. It is not used for large blocks of text.

Justified inserts space between letters and/or words to make the text flush against both the left and right margins. This style is often used in newspapers, magazines, newsletters, and other publications that are laid out in columns.

Hyphenating Words

Whenever you type or import text, Publisher automatically wraps the text to fit within the left and right margins of the frame. If a word is too long to fit on one line, Publisher moves the word to the next line. By default, Publisher does not automatically hyphenate words.

If your publication consists of long, wide paragraphs, and you align all text flush left, you may not want to hyphenate words. The text will probably look okay on the page. However, if you justify the text or set the text in long, narrow columns, you'll need to hyphenate some words to prevent the text from appearing too choppy. Although you can hyphenate the words manually (as you'll see later), it's easier to have Publisher hyphenate for you.

Before you use the hyphenation feature, you should know a little bit about how it works. Publisher uses an invisible *hyphenation zone* to determine whether to hyphenate a word. The zone exists between a left boundary and the right margin. If a word falls in this zone and can be hyphenated, Publisher hyphenates the word automatically. If the word falls in this zone and cannot be hyphenated, Publisher wraps the word to the next line.

You can change the hyphenation zone in the Hyphenate dialog box, shown in Figure 5.13. To display this box, pull down the Options menu and select Hyphenate, or press Ctrl+H. The default hyphenation zone setting is .25 inch, which means that hyphenation, if possible, will occur within a quarter inch of the end of the line. To make the right margin more even (less ragged), decrease the hyphenation zone setting; this increases the frequency of hyphenated words. To reduce hyphenation, increase the setting.

Chapter 5

Decrease setting to increase hyphenation
Increase setting to decrease hyphenation

Figure 5.13 *The Hyphenate dialog box.*

The Hyphenate dialog box also contains two check box options: Check All Stories and Confirm. To have Publisher check the hyphenation in all text frames in the publication, put an X in the Check All Stories check box. To have Publisher prompt you before hyphenating a word, select the Confirm option. With the Confirm option on, Publisher will display a dialog box, shown in Figure 5.14. You must respond before Publisher will hyphenate the word.

Publisher shows where word will be hyphenated

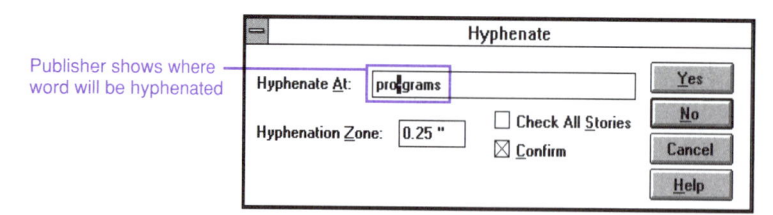

Figure 5.14 *With the Confirm option selected, Publisher asks for your okay before hyphenating a word.*

When you're done setting the hyphenation options, press the OK button to start the hyphenation process. Publisher proceeds according to your instructions. The following Quick Steps summarize the process for using Publisher's automatic hyphenation feature.

Using Automatic Hyphenation

1. Move the cursor where you want to start the hyphenation process.

   Hyphenation will proceed from this point to the end of the story.

2. Pull down the Options menu and select Hyphenate or press Ctrl+H.

   The Hyphenate dialog box appears.

3. To change the hyphenation zone setting, select Hyphenation Zone and type a new setting.

   Increase the setting to decrease hyphenation; decrease the setting to increase hyphenation.

4. Place an X in the Confirm check box to have Publisher ask for your okay before hyphenating a word.

   Turn Confirm off if you want the process to proceed more quickly.

5. Place an X in the Check All Stories check box to have Publisher hyphenate throughout the publication.

6. Press the OK button to begin the process.

   If you placed an X in the Confirm check box. Publisher stops on the first word it thinks requires hyphenation and displays the dialog box you saw in Figure 5.14. Otherwise, Publisher hyphenates as needed and returns you to your document.

7. Respond to any dialog boxes until hyphenation is complete.

There are also three types of hyphens that you can manually insert. The following list explains the three types of hyphens and the keystrokes required to enter each hyphen:

Keystroke	Type of Hyphen
Hyphen key (-)	*Regular hyphen*, for words that require hyphenation according to the dictionary. For example, *hurdy-gurdy*. If the word falls in the hyphenation zone, Publisher may break the word at the hyphen.
Ctrl+hyphen	*Optional hyphen*, to break the word only if it falls in the hyphenation zone. If you rewrap the text so it doesn't fall in the zone, Publisher automatically removes the hyphen.

Ctrl+Alt+hyphen   *Nonbreaking hyphen*, for terms or names that must remain on one line. For example, The Firm of Smythe-Jones. Even if the hyphenated word falls in the hyphenation zone, Publisher will not break the word at the hyphen.

What You Have Learned

This chapter discussed how to manipulate the text within frames to change the character formatting and layout of the text. In particular, you learned the following:

- ▶ A font consists of a family of characters that share the same design.
- ▶ You can change the appearance of a font by applying styles such as bold, italic, small capitals, superscripts, and subscripts.
- ▶ You can change type styles by pulling down the Format menu and selecting Character. For bold, italic, and underline, you can change the style by selecting it from the Toolbar.
- ▶ You should select the proper fonts for the content of your publication, and you should avoid using too many different fonts in the same publication.
- ▶ You can change fonts and point sizes by pulling down the Format menu and selecting Character. You also can change fonts by pulling down the fonts list from the Toolbar.
- ▶ Windows uses two types of fonts: printer fonts and screen fonts. Printer fonts tell your printer how to print the font. Screen fonts tell your monitor how to display the font.
- ▶ You can set text frame margins by pulling down the Layout menu and selecting Frame Columns and Margins. This is useful for inserting space between the text and the frame when the frame is surrounded by other objects.

- You can adjust the spacing between characters by pulling down the Forma*t* menu and selecting Spacing *B*etween Characters. This feature is useful for *kerning* loose character pairs.
- You can single space or double space text quickly by pressing the corresponding button in the Toolbar. To change line spacing (*leading*) in smaller increments, pull down the Forma*t* menu and select *I*ndents and Spacing.
- You can indent text within a text frame by selecting *I*ndents and Spacing from the Forma*t* menu.
- There are four kinds of text alignment—left (ragged right), right (ragged left), center, and justified. You can change the alignment by pressing the appropriate button in the Toolbar or by selecting *I*ndents and Spacing from the Forma*t* menu.
- You can hyphenate words automatically or have Publisher hyphenate for you. In either case, you have control over what words do and do not get hyphenated.

Chapter 6

Creating Objects with the Drawing Tools

In This Chapter

- *How to draw circles, ovals, lines, squares, boxes, arrows, and other objects using the four drawing tools*
- *How to add special effects to basic objects to enhance their look*
- *Changing the thickness and color of the lines that define graphic objects*
- *Moving and resizing drawn objects*
- *Putting shades of colors and patterns in the background of drawn objects*
- *How to create your own illustrations by assembling basic objects*

The Four Drawing Tools

Simple, but elegant and powerful certainly describes Publisher's drawing tools. There are only four but, as you'll see in this chapter, they let you create some great effects that will spice up your documents and add that professional touch. As shown in Figure 6.1, you can use basic objects to accent everyday publications.

Chapter 6

Figure 6.1 Basic graphic objects let you add a professional touch to any publication.

As you learned earlier, on the left end of Publisher's Toolbar is a set of nine tools, which are displayed at all times. Four of the tools allow you to draw basic objects on-screen:

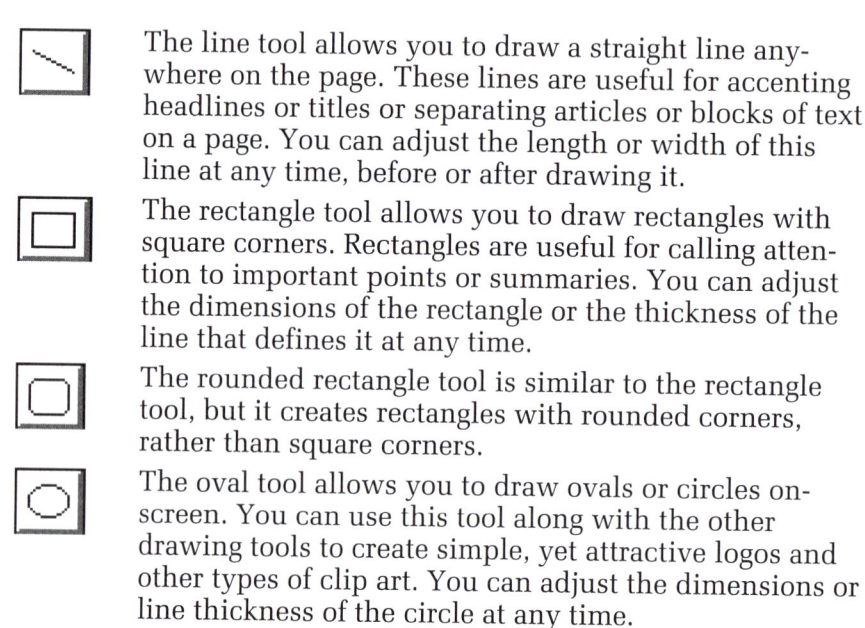

The line tool allows you to draw a straight line anywhere on the page. These lines are useful for accenting headlines or titles or separating articles or blocks of text on a page. You can adjust the length or width of this line at any time, before or after drawing it.

The rectangle tool allows you to draw rectangles with square corners. Rectangles are useful for calling attention to important points or summaries. You can adjust the dimensions of the rectangle or the thickness of the line that defines it at any time.

The rounded rectangle tool is similar to the rectangle tool, but it creates rectangles with rounded corners, rather than square corners.

The oval tool allows you to draw ovals or circles on-screen. You can use this tool along with the other drawing tools to create simple, yet attractive logos and other types of clip art. You can adjust the dimensions or line thickness of the circle at any time.

The procedure for using these tools is basically the same for all the tools. The major difference is the object that results. The following section explains in detail how to use these tools to draw objects.

Drawing Objects

Drawing any of the four objects—lines, rectangles, rounded rectangles, and ovals—is easy. If you already drew some text frames, you'll notice that the procedure is basically the same. You click on the tool for the object you want and then use the cross-hair mouse pointer to stretch the object out from an anchor point. The rulers and on-screen guides are very helpful for sizing and placing the object, but you can always move or resize the object after it is drawn.

Before you begin drawing, click on the line draw tool and take a look at the right end of the tool bar. You'll see the following set of tools:

The three buttons on the left allow you to add various arrowheads to the line before or after you draw it. The four buttons on the right allow you to specify a thickness for the line: 1, 2, 4, or 8 points in width. If no button is pressed, the line is drawn .25 points in width.

If you select one of the rectangle drawing tools or the oval tool, you'll see the following set of tools on the right end of the tool bar:

In place of the arrow tools are two buttons. The first button (the one with the diagonal lines) calls up the Shading dialog box, which allows you to fill an object with a color or shade. The second button puts a *shadow* on your box or oval to give it a three-dimensional look. The line thickness tools on the right give you the same line thickness options as are available for the line draw tool. If no line thickness button is pressed, you get an object without a line. You can shade a lineless object to create some interesting effects.

Chapter 6

After you've specified the line thickness and any other options you want to use when drawing, you can begin. Move the mouse pointer (the cross hair) where you want one end of the object to appear. This will be the anchor point. Hold down the left mouse button, and drag the pointer to the diagonally opposite end. The object is stretched out from the anchor point, as shown in Figure 6.2. When the object is the desired size and dimensions, release the mouse button. The drawn object appears in its finished form, and handles appear around the object showing it is selected.

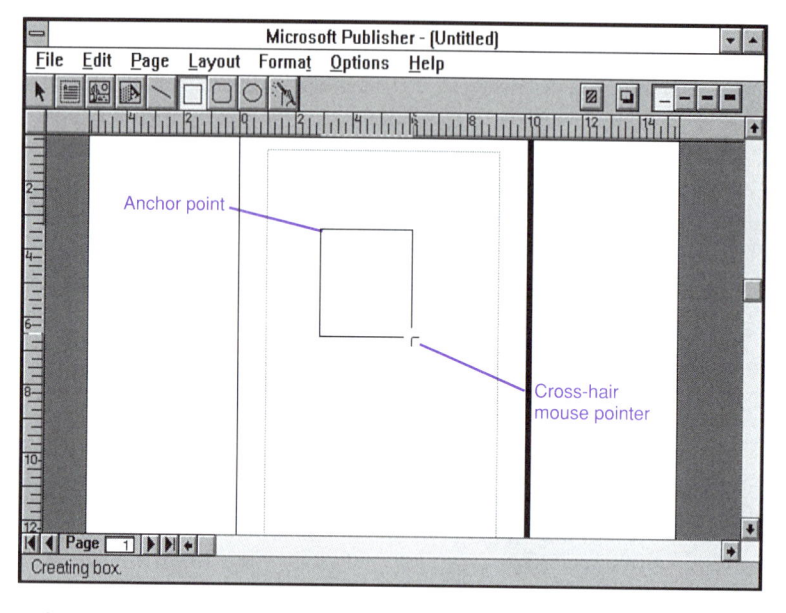

Figure 6.2 To draw any object, you anchor the mouse pointer at one point and drag the pointer away from this point.

The following Quick Steps summarize the procedure for drawing an object.

Drawing an Object

1. Click on the drawing tool for the object you want to draw.

   The button appears pressed.

2. To enhance the object with one of the drawing options, click on the option's button on the right end of the Toolbar.

   The selected button appears depressed. If you don't select an option, a 1-point line (.25-point for a line) will define the object.

3. Move the mouse pointer where you want one end of the object to appear.

   The mouse pointer turns into a cross hair. You can use the rulers or guides to place the pointer more precisely.

4. Hold down the left mouse button and drag the mouse pointer to the diagonally opposite end.

   As you drag the mouse, the selected object is *stretched* out from the anchor point. As you move away from the anchor point, the dimensions of the object increase.

5. When the object is the desired size and dimensions, release the mouse button.

   The object appears on-screen surrounded by eight handles. If you drew a line, the object has two handles.   □

> **Tip:** If you need to draw several boxes, ovals, or lines, you can lock the drawing tool button. Hold down the Ctrl key while clicking on the button in the Toolbar. The tool stays active, allowing you to draw several objects. To unlock the tool, click on it again or click in the work area without dragging the mouse.

The preceding Quick Steps showed how to anchor one end of an object and stretch the object out from that point. However, you also can anchor the *center*, rather than the corner, of an object. You can then stretch the object out from this center point. To center an object, move the mouse pointer where you want the center of the object to appear, hold down the Ctrl key, and drag the mouse until the object is the desired dimensions. When you're done, release the mouse button first and then the Ctrl key.

Although you can stretch an object to any dimensions, there may be times when you want the dimensions to be more controlled. For example, you may want to draw a perfectly round circle, a square instead of an oblong rectangle, or a perfectly straight line. Trying to eyeball the dimensions can be frustrating. Publisher can help, as the following Quick Steps show.

Drawing a Perfect Circle, Square, or Line

1. Click on the drawing tool for the object you want to draw.

   The button appears pressed.

2. To enhance the object with one of the drawing options, click on the option's button on the right end of the Toolbar.

   The selected button appears depressed. If you don't select an option, a 1-point line (.25-point for a line) will define the object.

3. Move the mouse pointer where you want one end of the object to appear.

   The mouse pointer turns into a cross hair. You can use the rulers or guides to place the pointer more precisely.

4. Press and hold down the Shift key. Keep holding it down until you're done drawing the object.

   This tells Publisher that you want the object to have uniform dimensions.

5. Hold down the left mouse button and drag the mouse pointer to the diagonally opposite end.

   As you drag the mouse, the selected object is *stretched* out from the anchor point. If you are drawing a line, You can draw only a horizontal or vertical line, or a line at a 45-degree angle.

6. When the object is the desired size, release the mouse button.

   The object appears on-screen surrounded by eight handles. If you drew a line, two handles appear.

Tip: To draw a perfectly proportioned object that's centered on a point, use the same technique, only hold down both the Ctrl and Shift keys. Remember to release the mouse button *before* releasing the keys.

Selecting Drawn Objects

When you first create an object, that object is *selected*. If the object is a rectangle or oval, eight *handles* appear around it, as shown in Figure 6.3. In the case of a line, two handles appear: one at each end of the line. These handles allow you to change the dimensions of the object. Before you can move, resize, or otherwise modify an existing object, the object must be selected; its handles must be displayed.

To select an object, you use the same basic procedure you used to select text frames—you click on it. But with objects, you cannot click just anywhere on the object. You must click on the edge of the object. To deselect a selected object, click anywhere on the screen.

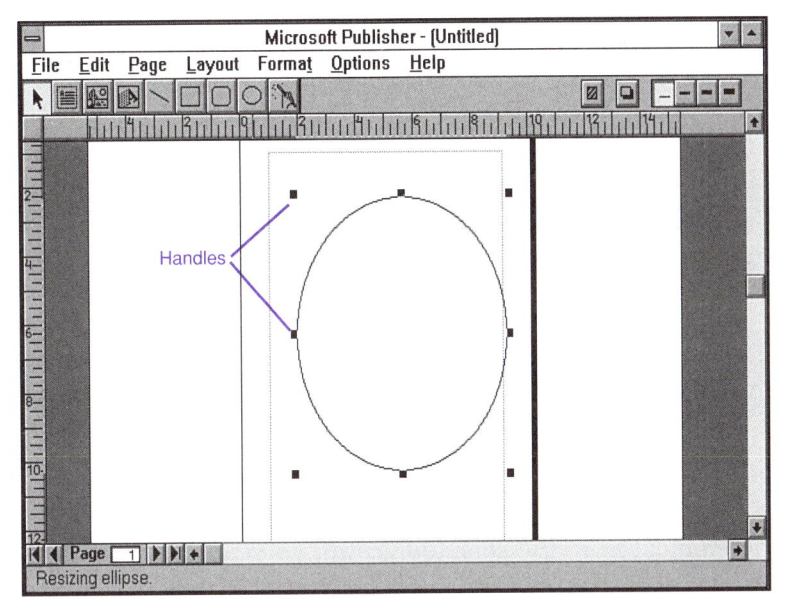

Figure 6.3   Before you can modify an object, you must click on its edge to display its handles.

Selecting Multiple Objects

As you draw and assemble objects on-screen, you'll find that you often need to work with several objects at once. For example, say you assembled several basic objects to create an illustration. You carefully positioned the objects to create the proper effect, but then you find that the entire illustration is in the wrong position. Moving each object separately would be time-consuming and could result in the objects losing the correct alignment. To save time, you could move the objects as a group, keeping them in the proper relative positions.

You can select any group of objects; the objects need not be the same type. For example, you can select a group of objects that consist of shapes or objects you've drawn, text frames, picture frames, and WordArt frames. You can then move or modify the group as a whole. You select a group of objects in either of two ways:

- *Individually.* If the objects are scattered around the screen, it's best to select each object individually. Hold down the Shift key and click on each object you want to include in the group.
- *As a group.* If the objects are in the same general area, you may find it more convenient to draw a box around the objects. Click on the arrow tool on the left end of the Toolbar. Draw a box around the group of objects the same way you draw a rectangle. A dashed box appears around the group. When you release the mouse button, all the objects appear selected.

If you selected an object by mistake, or if you want to exclude a single object from the selected group, you can deselect the object while leaving the others selected. To deselect an object, hold down the Ctrl key and click on the object you want to exclude from the group. To deselect an entire group of selected objects, click anywhere outside the selected group.

Moving Drawn Objects

Once you've selected an object or group of objects, you can move the object or group by dragging it across the screen. The process is the same process you followed for moving text frames. Move the mouse pointer near one of the edges of the selected object until the pointer appears as the moving van. (If you are moving a group of objects, moving any object in the group moves all selected objects.) Hold down the left mouse button and drag the selected object(s) to the desired location. Remember to use the guides and rulers for exact placement. As you drag the pointer, dotted outlines of the objects are moved to indicate the new position of the object(s), as shown in Figure 6.4. When the object or group is where you want it, release the mouse button.

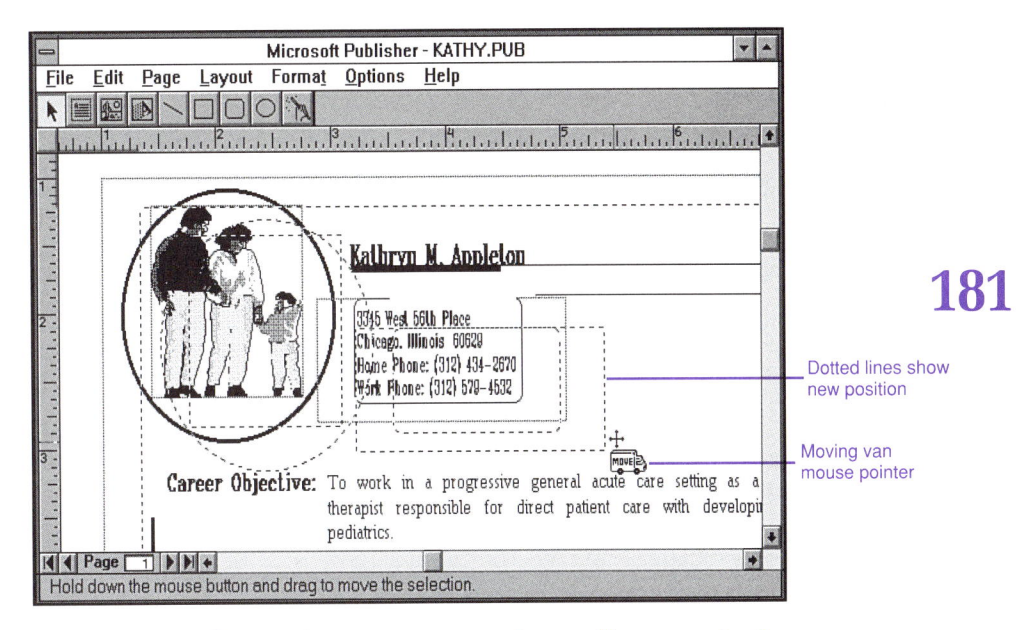

Figure 6.4 The moving van mouse pointer allows you to drag an object or group of objects across the screen.

Resizing Drawn Objects

To resize objects, you perform the same steps as those required for resizing text frames. You first select the object to display the handles surrounding the object. When you move the mouse pointer over any handle, the pointer turns into a double-headed arrow, as shown in Figure 6.5. Hold down the mouse button and drag the pointer to change the dimensions of the object.

Chapter 6

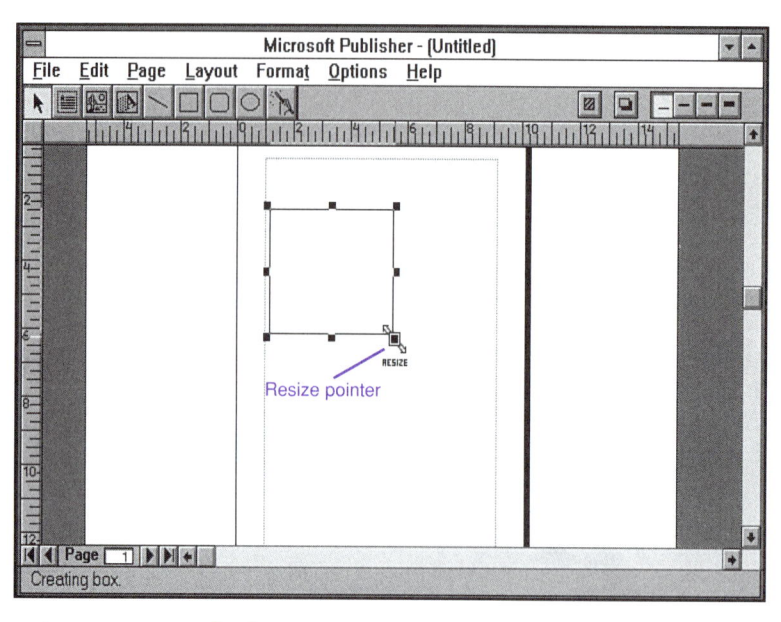

Figure 6.5 With the resize pointer, you can grab a handle and stretch the object to new dimensions.

The two side handles and the top and bottom handles allow you to change only one dimension of the object at a time. That is, you can adjust the height of the object without adjusting its width, and vice versa. The corner handles allow you to change two dimensions at the same time: the height of the object as well as its width.

Changing an Object's Line Thickness and Color

The default line thickness for any object you draw is one point (printers call this a *hair line* because it's so narrow). You can, of course, select a thicker line before you start drawing, but most of us don't know how thick to make the line until we see it on the page. Because of this, Publisher allows you to change the line thickness at any time.

You can change the line thickness for an object in either of two ways. The first way is to select the object and press one of the four buttons in the Toolbar: 1, 2, 4, or 8 points. For a wider range of options, you can select the object, pull down the Layout menu, and select Border or Line. The Border option allows you to change the line thickness for ovals, rectangles, and rounded rectangles. The

Line option is for lines. The Line or Border dialog box will appear (see Figures 6.6 and 6.7).

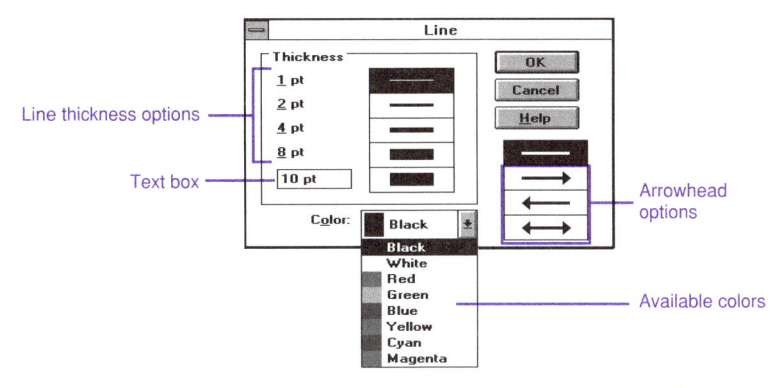

Figure 6.6 The Line dialog box for line objects. The drop-down list box for colors has been dropped down to show the available colors.

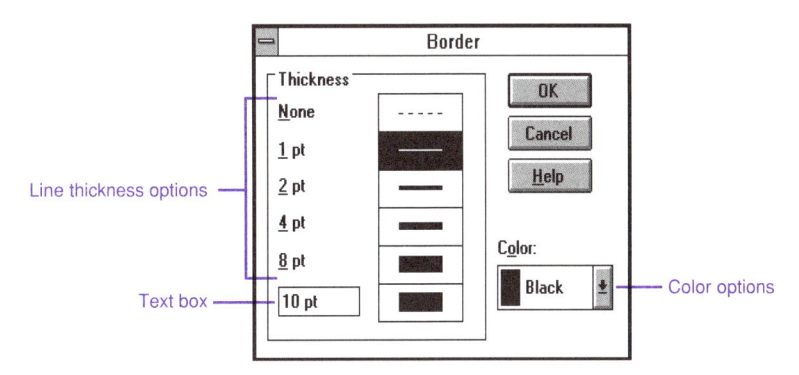

Figure 6.7 The Border dialog box allows you to change the line thickness and color of the line that defines the object.

In the Thickness box, select one of the line thicknesses from the list or click in (or tab to) the text box at the bottom of the list and type the thickness desired in points. For example, for a 3-point line, type **3**.

If you are setting the line thickness for a line, the Line dialog box provides three arrowhead options from which to choose. You can add an arrowhead to either end of the line or to both ends of the line. These are useful if you are using the arrows to point to an area in a picture or illustration.

Chapter 6

If you plan on printing in color, you can change the color of the line as well as its thickness. Simply click on the down arrow to the right of the Color drop-down list box, or press Alt+O and then Alt+↓. Click on the color you want to use or highlight the color and then press Enter.

The following Quick Steps explain how to change the line thickness for an object you've drawn.

Changing Line Thickness for Drawn Objects

1. Select the drawn object.   Handles appear to show that the object is selected.

2. Pull down the Layout menu and select Border or Line.   The Border or Line dialog box appears. (See Figures 6.6 and 6.7).

3. In the box labeled Thickness select a thickness, or type a thickness in the text box at the end of the list.

4. To add an arrowhead to a line, click on one of the arrowhead options or Tab to the options and use the arrow keys to highlight your choice.   The selected arrowhead option is highlighted.

5. To print the line in color, click on the down arrow to the right of the Color drop-down list box, or press Alt+O and then Alt+↓. Then highlight the color you want to use.

6. Press the OK button.   You are returned to the work area, and the line appears with the new options in effect. ☐

Shading an Object

In addition to being able to change the line thickness and color of the line that defines an object, you can add color or shading to the *inside* of the object. You can use shading to create some interesting effects, such as those shown in Figure 6.8. Of course, you cannot shade a line, because the line has no "inside," but you'll learn a trick later for creating shaded lines.

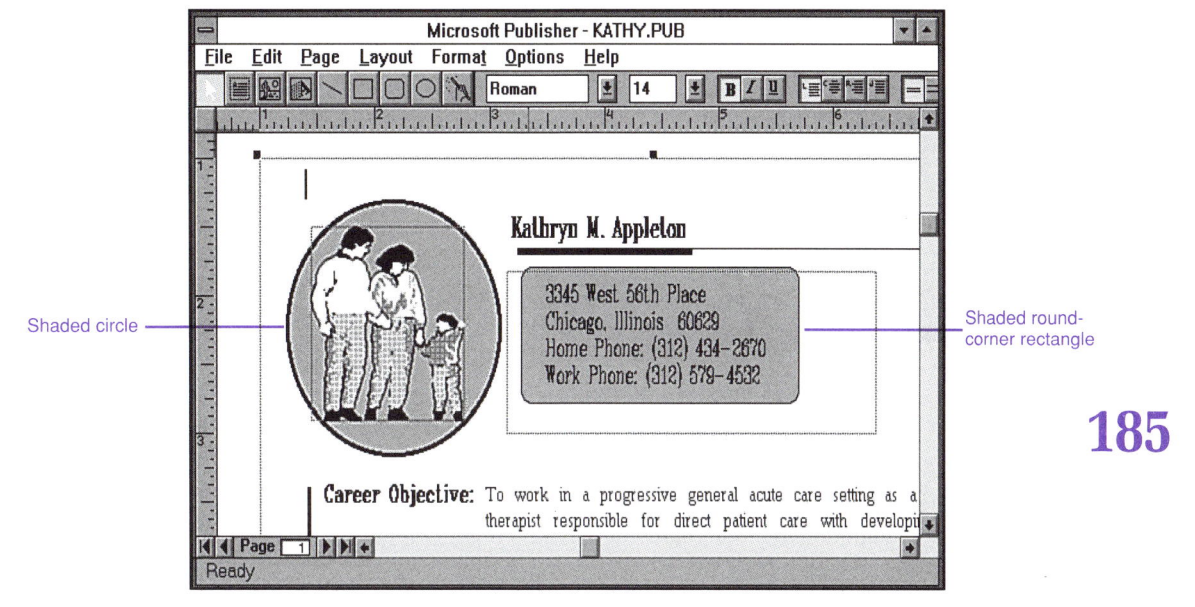

Figure 6.8   You can add color or shading to objects to create some interesting effects.

To change shading, first select an object. Then, click on the shading tool in the Toolbar or pull down the Layout menu and select Shading. The Shading dialog box appears, as shown in Figure 6.9.

In the left side of the box are several shading style options. The top three options are the most common: clear, white, and black. The clear option is the default. A line surrounds the object, but you can see through the object. This allows you to place the object around text or another graphic object. The white option fills the object with a white shade that hides any object that this object may overlap. Black fills the object with solid black. The other options on the screen consist of various amounts of black-on-white in various patterns. To select a shading style click on the style or press Alt+S and then use the arrow keys to highlight a style.

By default, white is the background color and black is the foreground color in the various shading style options. However, you can change the background and foreground colors by using the two

Chapter 6

drop-down lists below the Preview box. For example, you can select blue on a cyan background, or red on a yellow background. To change the colors, click on the down arrow to the right of either the Foreground or Background drop-down list box or press Alt+F or Alt+B and then Alt+↓. The list appears, showing the color options. Select an option from the list by clicking on it or using the arrow keys to highlight it.

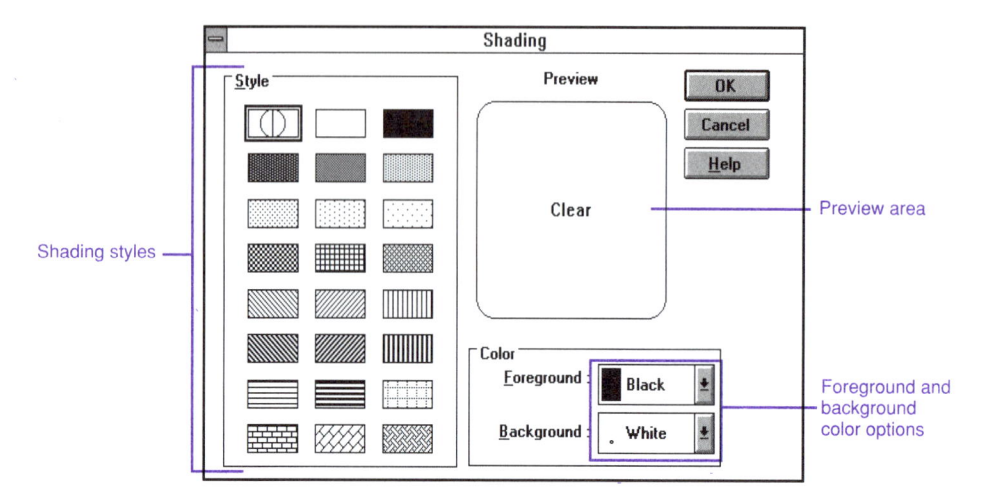

Figure 6.9   The Shading dialog box allows you to add shading and color to your objects.

To the right of the Style box is a box titled Preview. Here you can see what the pattern and/or shade you've selected looks like before clicking the OK command button and returning to your document. When the shading appears as desired, press the OK button.

The following Quick Steps summarize how to add shading to a drawn object.

Shading Objects

1. Select the object you want to shade.
   Handles appear around the selected object.

2. Pull down the Layout menu and select the Shading, or click on the shading button in the Toolbar.
   The Shading dialog box appears.

3. Select a style option by clicking on it or using the arrow keys to highlight it.

   A box appears around your selection, and its pattern or shade is depicted in the Preview box.

4. To change the foreground or background color, pull down the Foreground or Background drop-down list, and select a color from the list.

   The changes are shown in the Preview box.

5. Press the OK button.

   The display is refreshed and you can see the shading and/or pattern change for the selected object. □

Tip: To create a shaded line, create a long, narrow rectangle without a border and then shade the rectangle. To create the borderless rectangle, draw it as you normally would, and then press the line thickness button in the Toolbar that appears pressed. This deselects line thickness and removes the line from around the rectangle.

Adding a Shadow to an Object

Another way to enhance an object is to add a *drop shadow* to the object. A drop shadow is shading that appears along the bottom and right edges of the object, to make the object appear as though it is casting a shadow on the paper below it, as shown in Figure 6.10. This makes the object appear to be raised off the paper. To add a drop shadow, you must first select the object. You can then perform any of the three following actions to add the shadow:

▶ Press Ctrl+D.
▶ Pull down the Layout menu and select Shadow.
▶ Click on the shadow tool in the Toolbar.

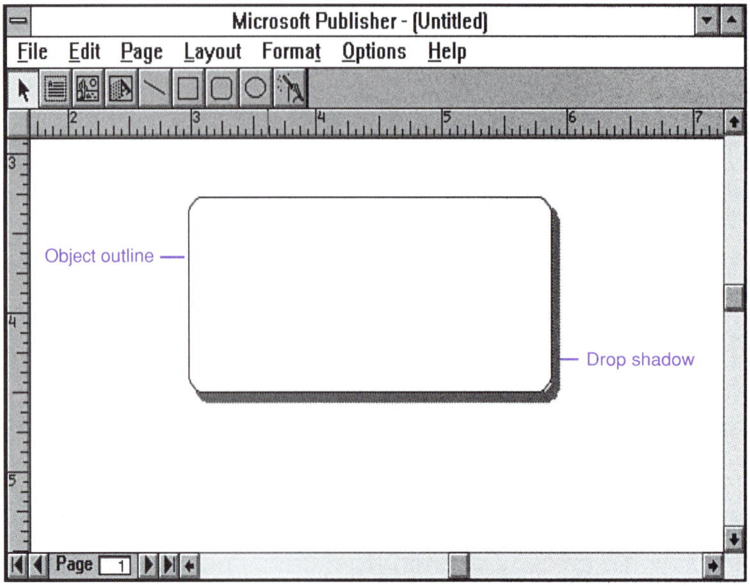

Chapter 6

Figure 6.10 A drop shadow gives an object a three-dimensional look.

Deleting Objects

You can delete any drawn object simply by selecting the object and pressing the Del key. If you delete an object by mistake, you may be able to restore it, as long as you haven't performed any other action in the meantime. To restore a deleted object, pull down the Edit menu and select Undo Delete Object(s).

> **Tip:** A safer way to delete an object is to select the object, and then pull down the Edit menu and select Cut or press Ctrl+X. The selected object is then cut and put on the Windows Clipboard. As long as you don't copy or cut any other material, you can get the object back by pulling down the Edit menu and selecting Paste, or by pressing Ctrl+V.

Combining Drawn Objects

Once you've learned how to draw the four types of objects—lines, rectangles, rounded rectangles, and ovals—you are ready to move on to the wonderful world of *composite shapes*. Composite shapes consist of two or more objects combined to make a symbol, logo, or illustration. The farmer in Figure 6.11 is a good example of what you can do by combining the four basic shapes.

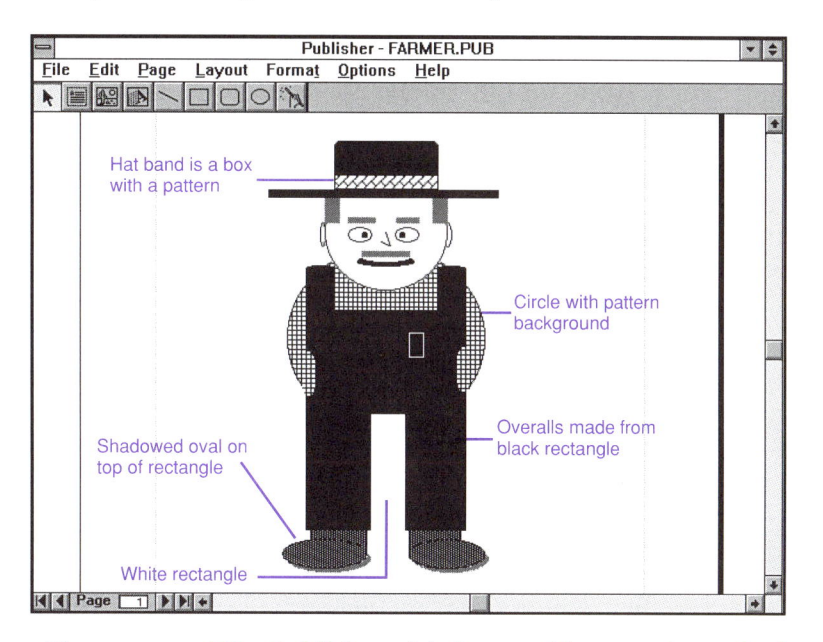

Figure 6.11   Like Publisher, this farmer (drawn using only the four drawn objects) is out standing in his field.

Because Publisher is not a *paint* program, it does not allow you to draw freehand. That is, if you wanted to create a realistic farmer, you would need a paint program, such as PC Paintbrush, that gives you more control over the line drawing and shading. But for geometric illustrations, such as drawings of cities, floor plans, logos, and other designs made up of basic shapes, Publisher is much better than a paint program.

Because you have only basic shapes to work with, You need to learn a few tricks about how to use these shapes to create illustrations. The best way to learn is by doing, so try your hand at drawing the farmer. Start first with a large circle in the middle of the screen; this will be the farmer's shirt. Call up the Shading dialog box and choose the checked pattern to shade the shirt.

Now draw a large rectangle on top of the circle that starts high up on it, is not quite as wide, and extends below the circle. This is going to be our farming buddy's overalls. Shade them black. With a little imagination, you can see how the arms are going down into his pockets.

Okay, trick time. Draw a narrow box starting at the bottom edge of the black box, and going up to make the empty space between the farmer's legs. While the box is still selected, go to the Border dialog box and choose None for line thickness, then to the Shading dialog box and pick White as the shade.

Perform the same trick at the top of the black box to define the area between his overall straps and the top of the bib. Draw a small box there, and then make its lines invisible and shade it to the same pattern as the original large circle.

Try to get the basic objects of the body done as described above, then embellish the figure by adding a head, hat, pocket on the overalls, and so forth. The little details can really turn it into a masterpiece for you!

> **Caution:** When creating an illustration, make it the size you want it to appear in your illustration. You cannot resize a group of drawn objects, so if you combine twenty objects and then decide you want the illustration smaller, you'll have to resize each object separately.

Working with Layered Objects

If a drawn object is behind one it should be in front of, or vice versa, you can move it to the front or to the back as needed. Think of the objects as being painted on transparencies. You can layer transparencies in various ways to create different effects. The same is true with objects. You can move an object to the front to lay it on top of another object, hiding part of that object, as shown in Figure 6.12.

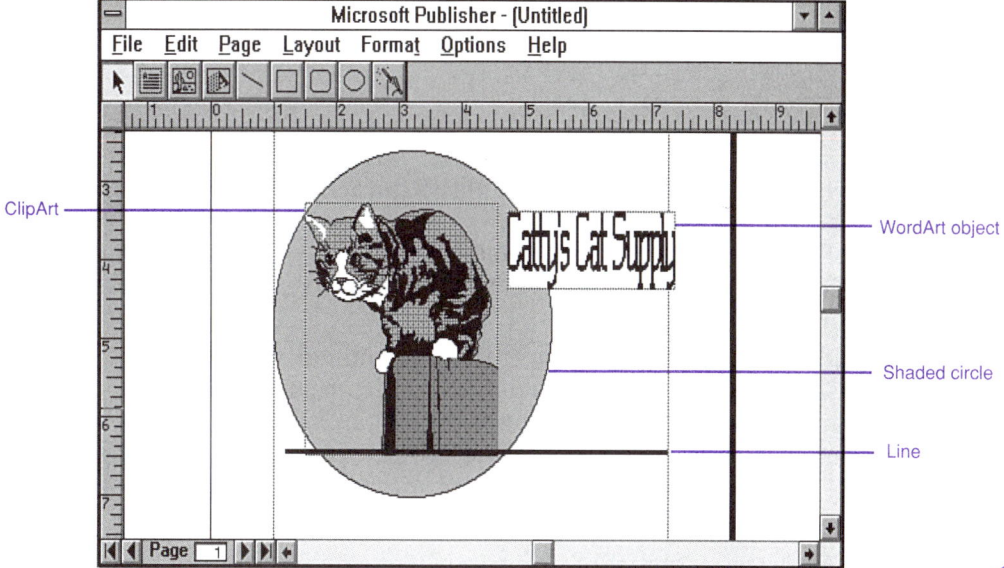

Figure 6.12   You can lay objects on top of each other to create some interesting effects.

To move an object to the front or back, first select the object. Pull down the Layout menu and select Bring to Front or Send to Back. The selected object is moved as requested. A quicker way to move objects to the front or back is to select the object and press one of the following keyboard shortcuts: Ctrl+F to move the object to the front, or Ctrl+Z to move it to the back.

Learning Other Effects

Many more special effects are available in Publisher. For drawn objects these include *BorderArt* which, like the shades and patterns you already met, lets you select from a library of patterns to add fancy lines, exquisite frames, and much more to objects. Chapter 8, "Creating Special Frame Effects," goes into detail about BorderArt.

What You Have Learned

The four drawn objects are the line, the rectangle, the rounded rectangle, and the oval. This chapter taught you how to use these objects. In particular, you learned the following:

- ▶ To draw an object, you select the object's drawing tool, and then stretch the object out from its anchor point using the mouse.
- ▶ You can change the line thickness and color of an object by selecting the Line or Border option from the Layout menu or by pressing one of the line thickness buttons in the Toolbar.
- ▶ To draw several objects of the same type, you can lock down a drawing tool button in the Toolbar by holding down the Ctrl key when clicking on the button.
- ▶ To draw an object of uniform dimensions (such as a perfect square), hold down the Shift key when drawing the object.
- ▶ To stretch an object out from a center point rather than from a corner or end, hold down the Ctrl key when drawing the object.
- ▶ You can move and resize a selected object the same way you move and resize text frames.
- ▶ To select an object, you must click on the edge of the object. You cannot select an object by clicking just anywhere inside it.
- ▶ You can add shading to a rectangle or circle by selecting the Shading option from the Layout menu or by clicking on the shading button in the Toolbar.
- ▶ You can layer basic objects one on top of another to create composite drawings.
- ▶ With layered objects, you can bring one object to the front or send it to the back by selecting the appropriate command from the Layout menu.

Chapter 7

Adding Pictures to a Document

In This Chapter

- *Using graphics in your publications*
- *Creating picture frames for importing pictures*
- *Using Publisher's ClipArt to enhance your publications*
- *Importing pictures and graphics files created in other applications*
- *Moving, resizing, and copying pictures*
- *Combining text and graphics on a page*
- *Cropping a picture to use only part of it*
- *Deleting pictures*

Working with Graphics in Publisher

In case you haven't noticed, over the years publications have gotten more and more graphically oriented. Instead of having page after page of running text, today's publications try to break up the text as much as possible with illustrations, photographs, graphs, icons, and other graphic elements to stimulate the reader. Just page through *USA Today* or *Time* magazine to see what I mean.

With Publisher, you can use the same techniques used in these professional publications to break up your text and give your publications an attractive, enticing look. In this chapter, you will learn how to paste drawings from Publisher's ClipArt library directly into your publications. (During the installation process, Publisher copied a generous selection of ClipArt to your hard disk.) You'll also learn how to import drawings created in other paint and draw programs or scanned in with a scanner. You'll learn how to import graphs and other visuals from programs such as Excel for Windows. And you'll learn how to use Publisher to manipulate these images once you've imported them.

Pictures and Picture Frames

Publisher considers any piece of art (ClipArt, illustration, graph, scanned image) to be a *picture*. Every picture in Publisher is contained in a *picture frame*. Whenever you import a picture, a picture frame appears as a rectangular dotted box surrounding the picture. You can use this frame to move the picture or to change its dimensions without affecting the other objects on the page.

Importing Pictures with and without Picture Frames

You can import a graphics file in either of two ways. The easiest way is to import the file *without* creating a picture frame. Publisher creates a picture frame for you that matches the original dimensions of the image. You can then resize the frame as needed to make it fit. The second way is to create a picture frame first and then import the image. This is useful if you have a limited amount of space for a picture and you've already pasted a picture frame on the page and arranged other elements around the frame. Publisher then sizes the image to fit your frame; this may result in a distorted image.

The following section explains how to create a picture frame for importing a picture. If you want Publisher to create a picture frame that matches the size and dimensions of the original picture, then don't create a frame. When you import the picture, Publisher will create the frame.

Creating Picture Frames

Many users begin a publication by laying out all the elements on a page. For example, the user may envision a page with a headline, three text frames, and a picture frame. Instead of importing the text and graphics and then manipulating them to make them fit the page, the user may prefer to place text and picture frames on the page first and then import the text and graphics. That way, when the user imports the text and graphics, Publisher makes the files fit their frames automatically. If this is how you plan on working with Publisher, you will create picture frames before importing the graphic images.

Although Publisher resizes any graphic image to fit the frame you draw, the image may get distorted in the process. Try to make your picture frames the same relative dimensions as the original graphic image. For example, if the original image is 4-by-6 inches, make the frame 4-by-6 inches (to match the original), 2-by-3 inches (to reduce the original by 50%), or 6-by-9 inches (to enlarge the original by 50%). If you import a 4-by-6 inch original into a 5-by-5 inch frame, the image will be distorted (see Figure 7.1). If you are unsure of the dimensions and you want to prevent the image from getting distorted, import the picture without creating a picture frame, and then resize the frame as explained later.

To create a picture frame, select the picture frame tool from the Toolbar:

Then draw the frame the same way as you drew text boxes or rectangles earlier. The following Quick Steps explain the process.

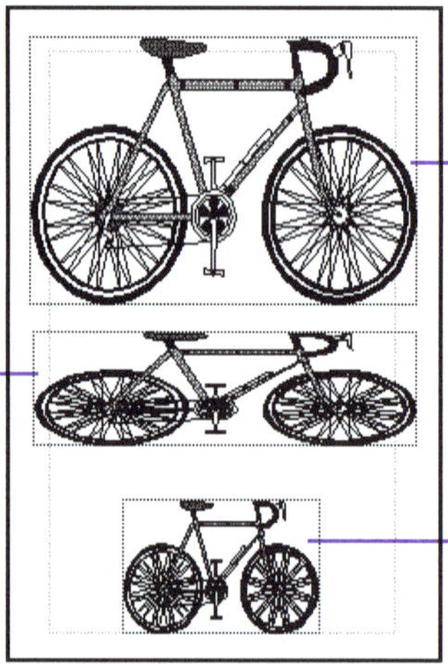

Chapter 7

Figure 7.1 Importing a graphic image into a picture frame that does not match the relative dimensions of the image may cause distortion.

Creating a Picture Frame

1. Click on the picture frame tool and move the mouse pointer into the work area.

   The mouse pointer becomes a cross hair.

2. Using the rulers or guides, move the pointer where you want the upper left corner of the picture frame to be.

   The rulers or guide indicate the precise location of the cross-hair pointer.

3. Hold down the left mouse button and drag the pointer to define the lower right corner of the frame.

   The picture frame's outline appears, enlarging as you drag the pointer.

4. Release the mouse button.

   A picture frame appears, as in Figure 7.2, showing the location and dimensions of the picture. □

Tip: If you need to draw several picture frames, you can lock the picture frame tool button. Hold down the Ctrl key while clicking on the button in the Toolbar. The tool stays active, allowing you to draw several picture frames. To unlock the tool, click on a different tool or click in the work area without dragging the mouse.

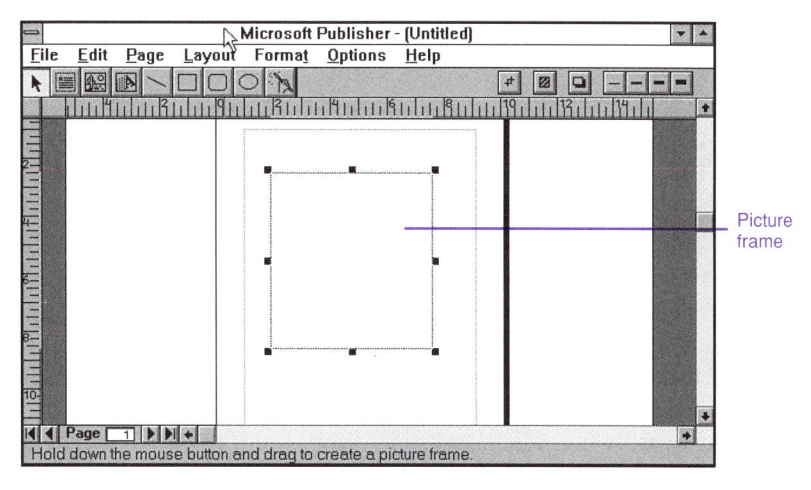

Figure 7.2 An empty picture frame appears, ready for importing a graphic image.

As you've already learned when creating other types of frames, you can drag a frame out from the center and/or create a perfectly square frame by using the Ctrl and Shift keys:

▶ To center a frame, move the mouse pointer where you want the center of the frame to appear, hold down the Ctrl key, hold down the mouse button, and drag the mouse pointer until the frame is the size and dimensions you want. Release the mouse button and then the Ctrl key.

▶ To create a square frame, move the mouse pointer where you want one corner of the frame to appear, hold down the Shift key, hold down the mouse button, and drag the mouse pointer until the frame is the size you want. Release the mouse button first and then the Shift key.

▶ To create a square centered frame, move the mouse pointer where you want to center the frame, hold down the Ctrl and Shift keys, hold down the mouse button, and drag the mouse pointer until the frame is the size you want. Release the mouse button and then the Shift and Ctrl keys.

> **Tip:** The frame you created is invisible. To create a frame with a line, click on one of the line thickness buttons on the right end of the Toolbar before you start drawing. To add a line to an existing frame, select the frame and then press one of the line thickness buttons. Chapter 8 explains more ways you can jazz up picture frames.

Selecting a Picture Frame

As with any other frame, to perform an operation on a picture frame, you must select the frame first. To select a frame, click anywhere inside the frame. Eight handles appear around the frame to show that it is selected. You can use these handles to change the size and dimensions of the frame at any time. To deselect a frame, click anywhere outside the frame.

If you click in a frame to select it, and no handles appear, the frame is probably in Publisher's background. (The background was explained in Chapter 3.) The picture in this frame will be printed on every page of your document. To select a frame that's in the background, pull down the Page menu and select Go to Background, or press Ctrl+M. You can then click on the frame to select it.

Importing Pictures

You can import a picture in any of several ways. The most common way is to import a graphics file from Publisher's ClipArt library or a graphics file created in a graphics program, such as CorelDraw! or Paintbrush. (Paintbrush is included with Windows, so you can create a graphic image in that program, save it in a file on disk, and then import the image into your publication.) You can also import a graph from a Windows program, such as Microsoft Excel.

Keep in mind that you can import a picture into an existing picture frame or have Publisher create the frame for you. To import a picture into an existing frame, select the frame before importing the picture. To have Publisher create a frame for you, make sure no picture frame is selected when you import the picture; otherwise, Publisher imports the picture into the selected frame.

Importing Publisher's ClipArt

Publisher comes with more than 100 pieces of ClipArt—excellent illustrations you can use to spark up brochures, newsletters, and the rest of your publications. Each piece of clip art is stored in a single file. Publisher's installation program copied these files to your hard disk during the installation process. You simply select the file you want to use.

To import a ClipArt file into an existing frame, create and select the frame before you begin. If you want Publisher to create a frame that matches the size and dimensions of the ClipArt picture, make sure no picture frame is selected. Pull down the File menu and select Import Picture. The Import Picture dialog box appears, as shown in Figure 7.3. This box prompts you to enter the following information about the file you want to import. Work through the options in the order they are listed:

- ▶ *Type of File.* By default, Publisher lists all files that have extensions matching the extensions used for the graphics file formats it supports, including the .CGM extension used for all ClipArt files. If you created the file in another graphics program, click on the arrow to the right of this drop-down list box, and select the format in which the file was saved. If you select the wrong format, Publisher may not be able to import the file, or the file conversion may not be completely successful.
- ▶ *Picture Name.* This list box displays a list of files that have the filename extension used most often for the type of file you selected. To view a list of files having a different extension, type `*.ext` where *ext* is the extension of the file you want to import and press Enter. You can type a filename (if you know the entire name of the file), or you can type a wild-card entry to view a list of files.
- ▶ *Drive.* Publisher displays the letter of the currently active drive. If the file is saved on another drive, click on the arrow to the right of the Drives box and select the letter of the drive. All ClipArt files are stored on the drive that contains Publisher's program files.
- ▶ *Directory.* Under the Directories option is the path to the current drive and directory. If the file is stored in another directory on the current drive, use the directory tree that's displayed under the path to move to the directory that contains the file. All ClipArt files are stored in the CLIPART directory under the MSPUB directory.

As you move through the directory tree, the list displayed in the Picture Name box changes to display the names of those files in the currently selected directory which match the filename entry you typed. Click on the file you want to import or highlight it.

Chapter 7

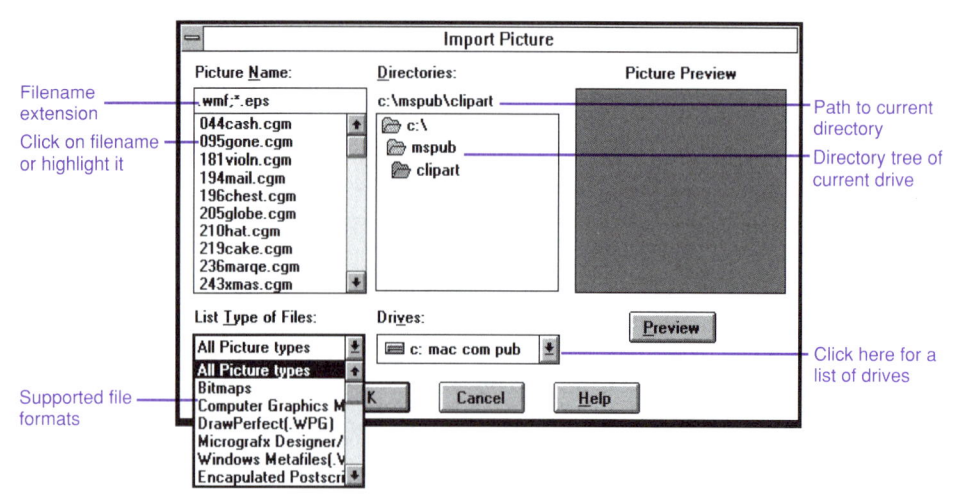

Figure 7.3 The Import Picture dialog box prompts you to select the filename of the picture you want to import.

On the right side of the Import Picture dialog box is a Preview area. You can use this area to see what the selected picture looks like. To view the picture, press the Preview button (below the Preview area). The picture appears in the Preview box. To import the picture, press the OK button. The picture appears in the selected picture frame or in a frame created by Publisher.

The following Quick Steps summarize the process for importing a ClipArt picture.

Importing a ClipArt Picture

1. Draw and select a picture frame, or (to have Publisher create a frame) make sure no picture frame is selected.
2. Pull down the File menu and select Import Picture.

    The Import Picture dialog box appears.
3. Select the drive where Publisher's program files are stored from the Drives drop-down list.

    The directory tree above the Drives box changes to show the directories on the selected drive.

Adding Pictures to a Document

4. Use the directory tree to select the CLIPART directory.

    The Picture Name list changes to show a list of files in the CLIPART directory.

5. Highlight the name of the file you want to import in the Picture Name list.

6. To view the picture, press the Preview button.

    The selected file is displayed in the Preview area, as shown in Figure 7.4.

7. Press the OK button to import the picture.

    The picture is imported into the selected text frame, or (if no text frame was selected) the picture is imported into a text frame created by Publisher. ☐

Name of selected file

Picture in selected file

Press the Preview button to view the picture

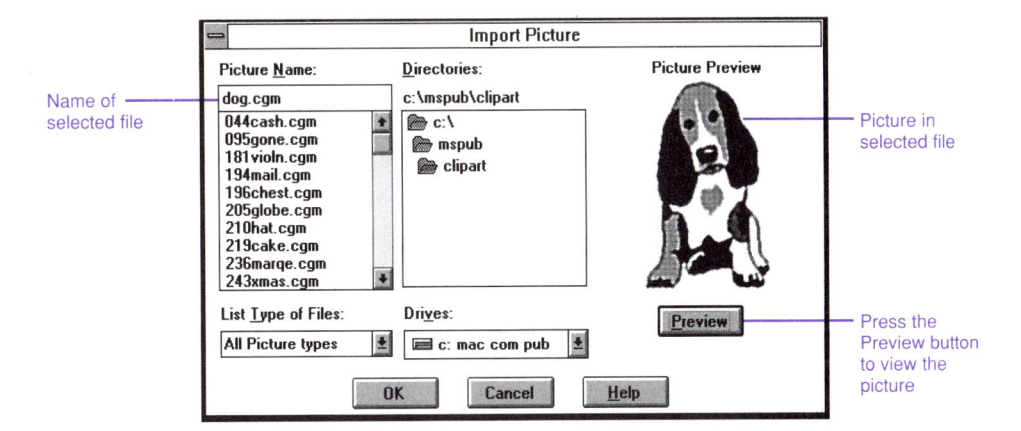

Figure 7.4 To see the picture stored in a selected file, press the Preview button.

Importing Pictures from Other Applications

If you purchase electronic art from an outside vendor or if you create your own electronic art using a scanner and/or paint/draw program, you may be able to import this art into your publications. The reason I say *may* is that the graphics file you purchase or create must be in a format that Publisher recognizes. Otherwise, Publisher cannot display or print the graphics file. Publisher does, however, support a wide range of graphics file formats, as shown in Table 7.1.

Table 7.1 Types of graphics files Publisher recognizes.

Filename Extension	Type of File
.BMP	Bitmapped file created by paint programs, such as Windows Paintbrush and PC Paintbrush.
.CGM	Computer Graphics Metafile used for Publisher's ClipArt. Also created by many drawing programs, such as CorelDraw! and Windows Draw.
.DRW	Draw files. Another type of file created by many drawing programs.
.EPS	Encapsulated PostScript used by many programs to print using a PostScript printer.
.PCX	PC Paintbrush files. A bitmapped file format used by the PC Paintbrush program.
.TIF	Tagged Image File. A bitmapped format used by scanners and paint programs to store bitmapped images.
.WMF	Windows Metafile created by many Windows draw programs, including CorelDraw! and Windows Draw.
.WPG	WordPerfect Graphics used for files created in DrawPerfect and for clipart that comes with WordPerfect.
All Picture Types	All formats listed above.

Tip: Many graphics programs allow you to save the file in more than one format. If the file you want to import is not in a format that Publisher recognizes, open the file in the program you used to create it and try to save it using a format that Publisher supports. If you get the files from an outside vendor, specify a file format when purchasing the art.

To import a file saved in one of these formats, follow the same steps for importing a ClipArt file. The only difference is that you may have to spend a little more time in the Import Picture dialog box. Once the dialog box is displayed, take the following steps to import the picture:

1. Select the format in which the file was saved from the List Type of Files drop-down list. If you are unsure, select All Picture Types.
2. Edit the filename entry in the Picture Name box, if needed, and press Enter.
3. Select the drive where the file is stored from the Drives drop-down list.
4. Use the directory tree to select the directory in which the file is stored. The Picture Name list changes to show a list of files in the selected directory which match the filename entry you typed.
5. Select the name of the file you want to import from the Picture Name list.
6. Press the OK button. The picture is imported in the selected picture frame or into a frame created by Publisher.

Using the Windows Clipboard to Import Drawings

You saw in Chapter 4 how text was copied from a document created in another Windows application to the Windows Clipboard and then pasted from the Clipboard into a Publisher document. Pictures, drawings, and other graphic elements may be copied in the same manner. If you have a Windows paint or draw program, such as Paintbrush or CorelDraw!, you can create complex illustrations, and then use the Clipboard to copy them into your publications.

Here's the procedure you would use to copy a drawing from most other Windows-based graphics programs.

Chapter 7

Q Importing Drawings with the Clipboard

1. In the application window of the graphics program, select the graphic image that you want to import.

    In most Windows graphics applications, you use a selection tool to draw a box around the picture or section of the picture you want to use.

2. Pull down the drawing application's Edit menu and select the command required to copy the selected picture to the Clipboard. (The command may vary from program to program.)

    Figure 7.5 shows an image being copied in CorelDraw! The drawing is now in the Clipboard.

3. Return to Publisher.

    You are now back in your Publisher document.

4. Pull down Publisher's Edit menu and select Paste Picture, or press Ctrl+V.

    The drawing is now inserted into your document, as shown in Figure 7.6. You may resize it and place it where you like.

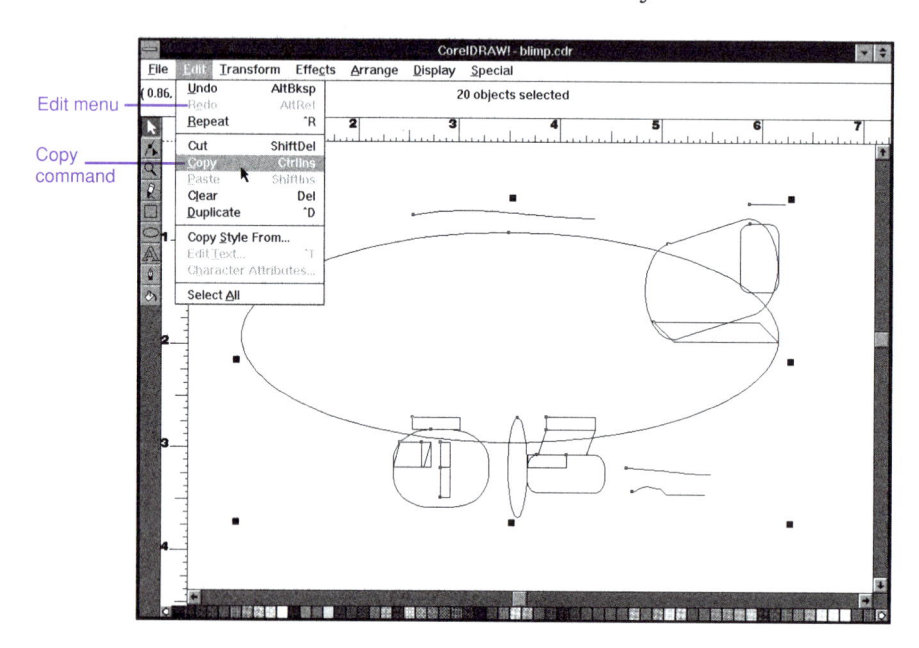

Figure 7.5   Use the other application's Edit menu to copy the selected drawing to the Clipboard.

Adding Pictures to a Document

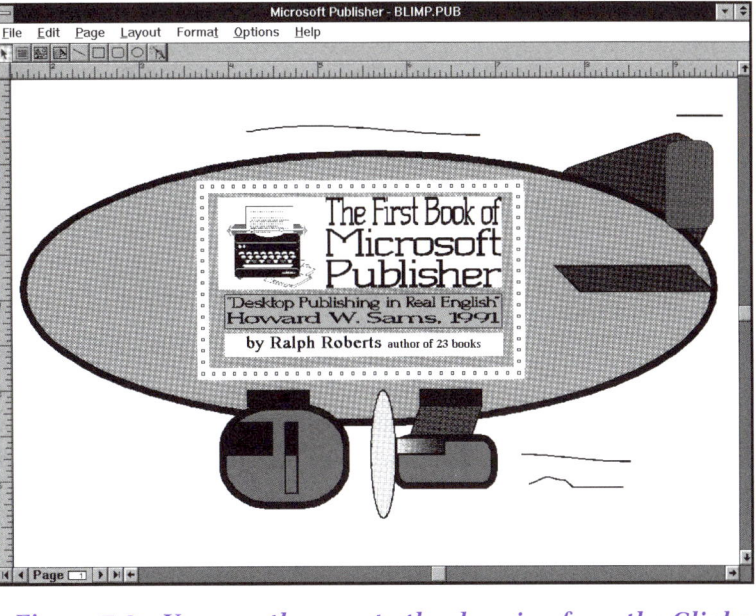

Figure 7.6 You can then paste the drawing from the Clipboard into your Publisher document.

Inserting Objects

In addition to importing drawings created in another application, you can insert drawings that have not yet been created. For example, if you want to include an Excel chart in your publication, and the chart has not been created, you can run Excel from Publisher, create the chart, and insert it into your publication.

To insert an object, draw a picture frame and pull down the Edit menu. You will see that the Insert Object option is now available (solid instead of grayed out). Clicking on this option gives you the Insert Object dialog box, as shown in Figure 7.7. From here, you can run other applications from inside Publisher and use them to create a "picture" within the picture frame. The quotes are around the word *picture* because the program you call might be a spreadsheet program, such as Excel for Windows. The table or chart you might create in Excel for Windows is treated as a *picture* in Publisher.

The Insert Objects dialog box contains a list of the applications you can run. This list is determined by Publisher from the other applications installed in Windows and shows only those that will work with this feature. In Figure 7.7, there are two available Publisher programs (Note-It and WordArt) and two Excel for Windows options (Excel Chart and Excel Worksheet).

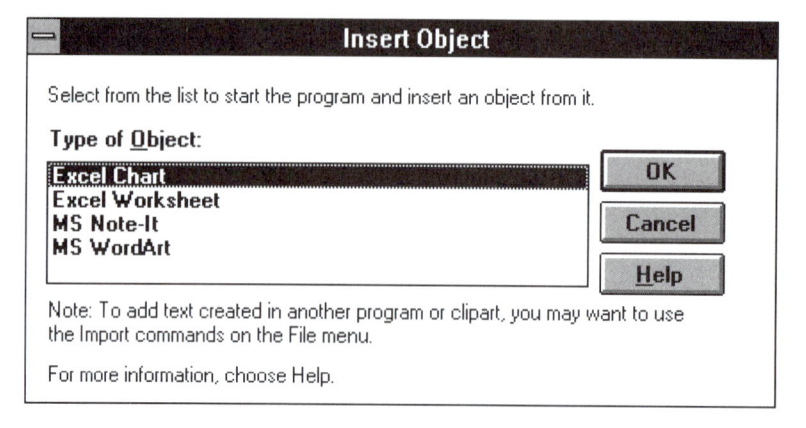

Figure 7.7 *The Insert Object dialog box allows you to run another Windows application from Publisher.*

One nice thing about this feature is that Publisher remembers which application you used to create the object. If you decide to edit the picture, simply select it, pull down the File menu, and select the Edit Object. Publisher will run the application which was used to create the picture, and you can use that application to modify it.

Using the Edit Menu's Paste Special Option

The Paste Special option is similar to Insert Object; it allows you to insert a copy of a picture from another Windows application. The difference is that the picture remains *linked* to the file created by that other application. Thus, whenever you update the file using the other application, the picture in the Publisher file is automatically updated to reflect the changes.

The value of setting up a document like this is obvious. You can build a fancy sales report one time in Publisher, linking its charts to chart files created in Excel. Each month, you simply print out the charts; they will contain all the up-to-date sales figures. It's great!

There are three choices you should be aware of in linking a picture file as described above. You will need to specify your selection in the Paste Special dialog box:

Native	Retains the original format of the picture (that is, the same format used to create the file).
MetaFilePict	Pastes the picture into your document as a *metafile*, which simply means you can crop it and do the other editing operations you can to regular Publisher pictures.
Bitmap	For files that you want to treat as a picture, but the MetaFilePict option does not work on.

Pictures and Text

Once you have a picture on your page, you may be a little concerned about how that picture will affect the surrounding text. Will it hide the text? Will the text overlap the picture? You need not be concerned. Whenever you paste a picture frame on top of some text, Publisher automatically wraps the text around the frame, as shown in Figure 7.8. If the text overlaps the frame, all you have to do is select the text frame and send it to the back (using the Send to Back option from the Layout menu), or select the picture frame and bring it to the front (Bring to Front). You can insert pictures in the middle of brochures, in newsletters, in greeting cards, and in any other publication.

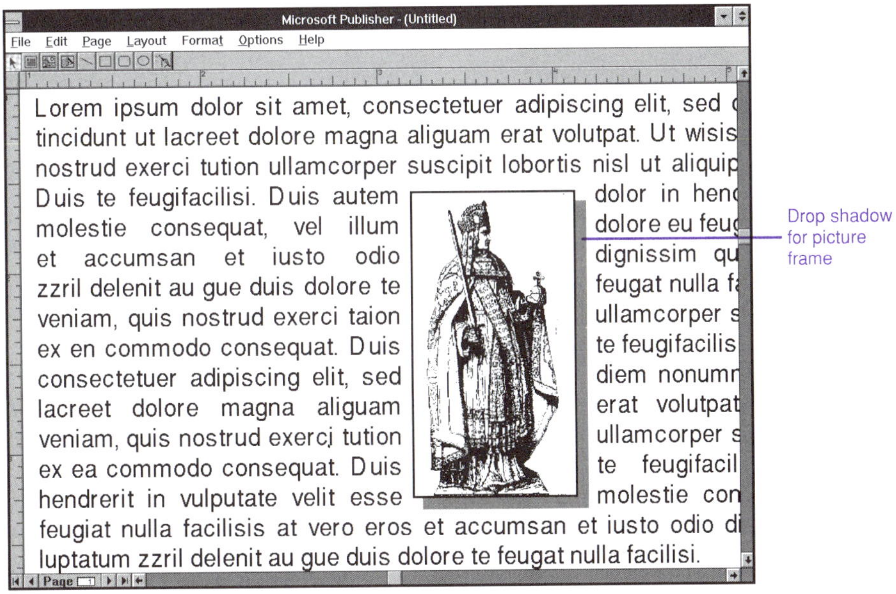

Figure 7.8   If you paste a picture frame over some text, Publisher wraps the text around the frame.

Chapter 7

> **FYIdea:** There's nothing like a pat on the back to perk up employees, to make customers remember you, or to reward someone who has been especially nice to you. Awards are an inexpensive but effective way to do that. You can create awards using Publisher's ClipArt to really jazz it up. Use special paper for awards. A buff-colored, high-rag content paper will give your certificates an expensive-looking parchment effect.
>
> If you are creating and presenting an award to a customer or vendor, add your company logo and a tasteful but subdued advertising message (maybe in the form of a slogan) on the certificate. Consider framing the award; the customer may hang it on a wall, providing you with some inexpensive advertising.

Adding White Space Around a Picture

Although Publisher wraps text around the picture as required, the text can get so close to the edges of the picture that the text and picture may almost touch. To prevent this from happening, you can add extra white space around the picture, as shown in Figure 7.9. To do this, you increase the picture frame margins.

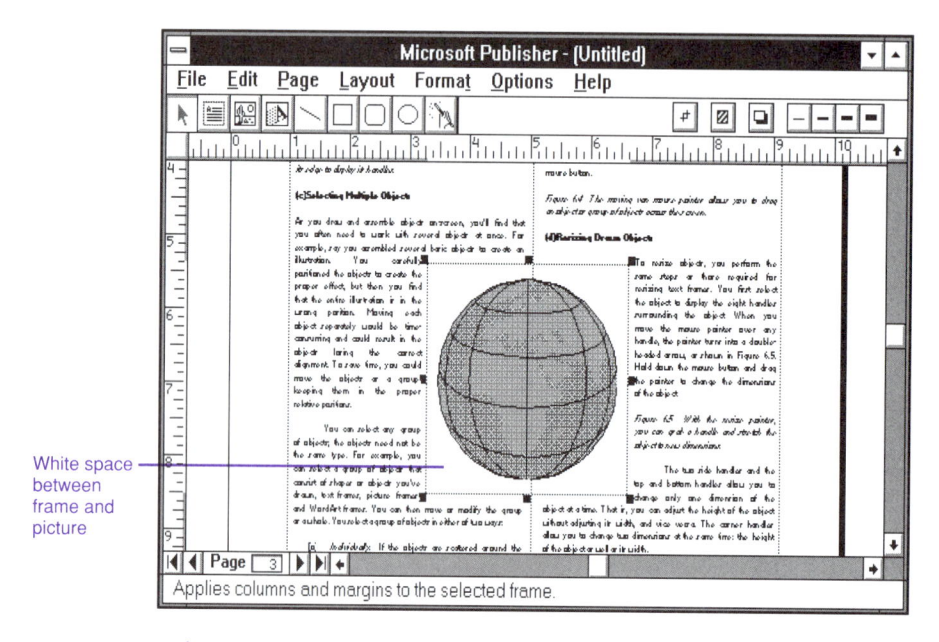

Figure 7.9   You can increase the frame margins to increase space between the frame and the picture it contains.

To set frame margins, pull down the Layout menu and select Frame Margins. The Frame Margins dialog box appears, as shown in Figure 7.10. Select Left and Right and type the setting you want to use for the left and right margins. Select Top and Bottom, and type the setting you want to use for the top and bottom margins. Press the OK button. Publisher keeps the text frame the same size and reduces the size of the picture to increase the margins.

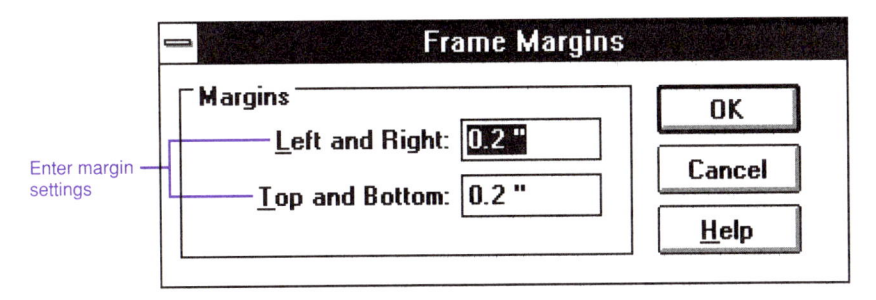

Figure 7.10 The Frame Columns and Margins dialog box allows you to set the margins for a picture frame.

Cropping Images

Many times a picture will include more than you want to show. For example, say you've scanned in a photograph of all the people in a department and you want to show only the employee of the month. If you were working with an actual photograph, you could use scissors to cut away all the other people in the picture. With Publisher, you can do the same thing electronically, by *cropping* the image.

To crop an image, first select the image. Eight handles appear around the picture frame and the crop tool button appears in the Toolbar:

Click once on this button, and then move the mouse pointer to one of the handles. The mouse pointer changes into the cropping pointer. Hold down the mouse button and drag the cropping pointer to cut away sections of the image, as shown in Figure 7.11.

Cropping tool
in action

Figure 7.11 With the cropping tool selected, the author can crop out the rest of the scanned photo to show himself at a book signing.

When you crop an image, you don't lose any of the detail you crop out. The cropped parts remain; they're just hidden. To bring them back into view, select the cropping tool and then move the sides of the frame out to reveal the cropped sections.

Moving, Resizing, and Copying Picture Frames

No matter how good you are at estimating the correct location, size, and dimensions of a picture frame, you'll probably have to fiddle with the frame after importing the picture to get it just right. Publisher makes it easy to manipulate picture frames. You move the picture frame, and Publisher automatically moves the picture it contains and rewraps any surrounding text. Resize the frame or change its dimensions, and Publisher resizes the picture and rewraps any surrounding text to accommodate the change.

Selecting Picture Frames

Before you can move, resize, or copy a picture frame, you have to select it; click anywhere inside the frame. Eight handles appear around the frame to show that it is selected. To deselect the frame, click anywhere outside it.

Although you cannot copy or resize multiple frames with a single command, you can move a group of objects by moving their frames. This keeps the objects in their same relative positions as you move them across the screen. To move a group of objects, you must select them. You can select any group of objects; the objects need not be the same type. For example, you can select a group of objects that consist of shapes or objects you've drawn, text frames, picture frames, and WordArt frames. You select a group of objects in either of two ways:

- ▶ *Individually.* If the objects are scattered around the screen, it's best to select each object individually. Hold down the Ctrl key and click on each object you want to include in the group.
- ▶ *As a group.* If the objects are in the same general area, you may find it more convenient to draw a box around the objects. Click on the arrow tool on the left end of the Toolbar. Draw a box around the group of objects the same way you draw a rectangle. A dashed box appears around the group. When you release the mouse button, all the objects within the box appear selected.

If you selected an object by mistake, or if you want to exclude a single object from the selected group, you can deselect the object while leaving the others selected. To deselect an object, hold down the Ctrl key and click on the object you want to exclude from the group. To deselect an entire group of selected objects, click anywhere outside the selected group.

Moving Selected Objects

Once you've selected an object or group of objects, you can move the object or group by dragging it across the screen. Move the mouse pointer near one of the edges of the selected object until the pointer appears as the moving van. (If you are moving a group of objects, moving any object in the group moves all selected objects.) Hold down the left mouse button and drag the selected object(s) to the desired location. As you drag the pointer, dotted outlines of the objects are moved to indicate the new position of the object(s), as shown in Figure 7.12. When the object or group is where you want it, release the mouse button.

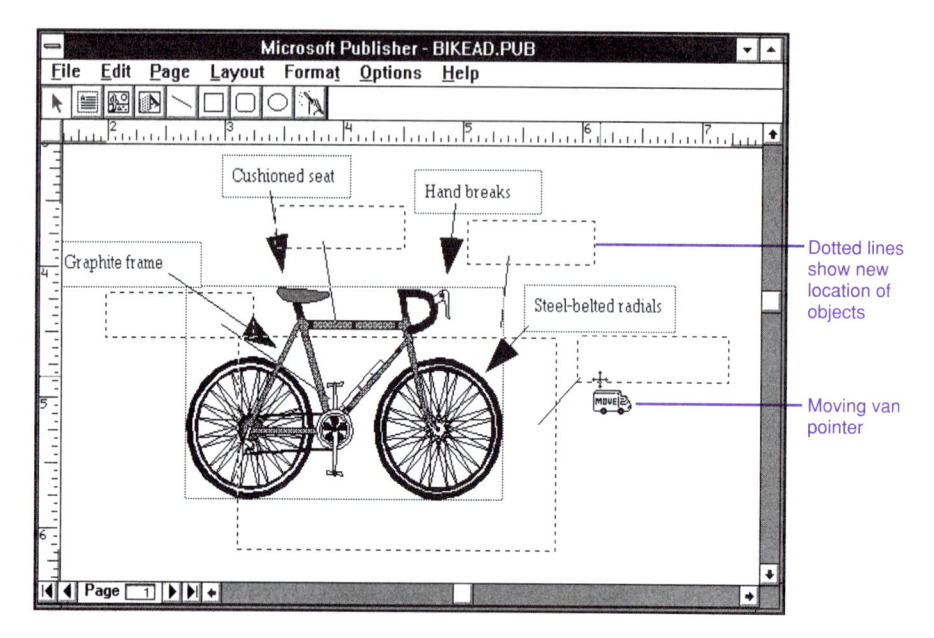

Figure 7.12 The moving van mouse pointer allows you to drag an object or group of objects across the screen.

Resizing Picture Frames

To resize a picture frame, first select the frame to display its handles. When you move the mouse pointer over any handle, the pointer turns into a double-headed arrow, as shown in Figure 7.13. Hold down the mouse button and drag the pointer to change the dimensions of the picture. To maintain the correct proportions of a photograph or other picture, hold down the Shift key as you drag.

The two side handles and the top and bottom handles allow you to change only one dimension of the object at a time. That is, you can adjust the height of the object without adjusting its width, and vice versa. The corner handles allow you to change two dimensions at the same time: the height of the object as well as its width.

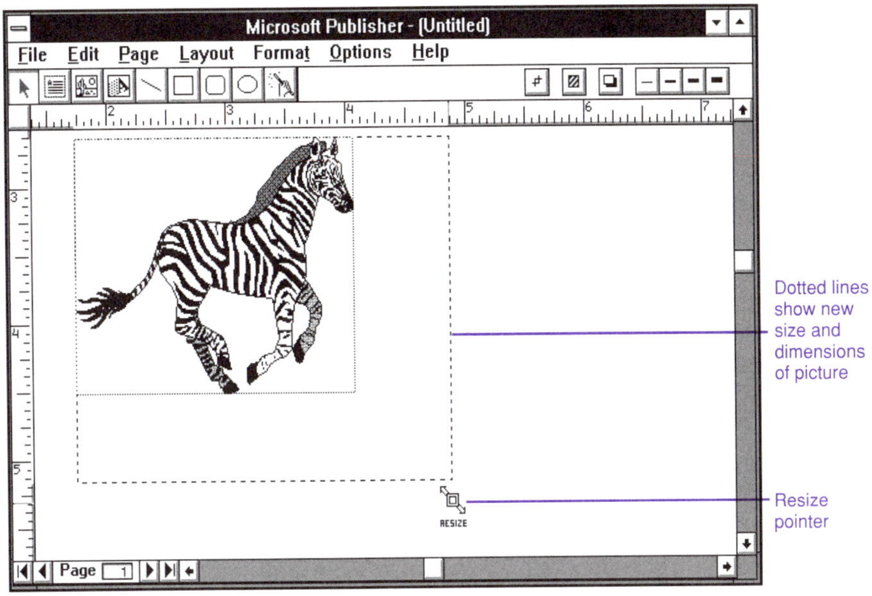

Figure 7.13   With the resize pointer, you can grab a handle and stretch the picture to new dimensions.

> **Tip:** Another way to resize a picture without distorting its dimensions is to select the Scale Picture command from the Format menu. The Scale Picture dialog box appears, as shown in Figure 7.14. To retain the proper proportions of the image, enter the same percentage for both the height and width. You can also use this dialog box to return the image to its original size.

Copying, Cutting, and Pasting Picture Frames

In the previous chapters, you learned how to use the Windows Clipboard to cut and copy blocks of text. You can use the Clipboard to cut and copy pictures as well; the procedure is the same. Whatever you cut or copy is cut or copied to the Clipboard. You can then paste the picture from the Clipboard onto another page, into another publication, or into another document in a Windows compatible program.

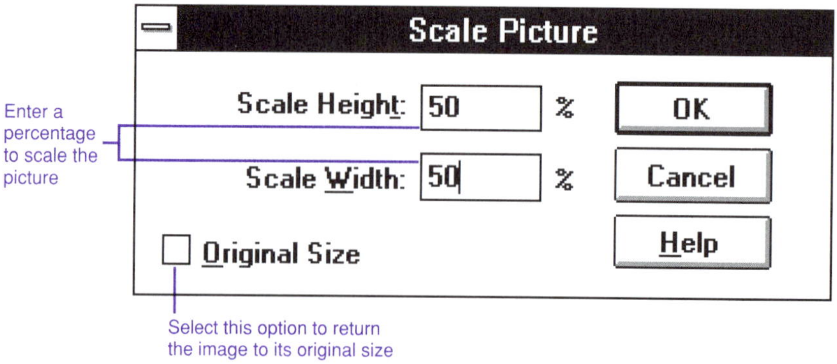

Chapter 7

Enter a percentage to scale the picture

Select this option to return the image to its original size

Figure 7.14 The Scale Picture dialog box allows you to scale an image by entering a scaling percent for the width and height.

To cut a picture, select the picture's frame, pull down the Edit menu, and select Cut Picture Frame. To copy a picture, select the picture, pull down the Edit menu and select Copy Picture Frame. Once the picture is on the Windows Clipboard, you can paste the picture. Move to the page where you want the picture to appear, pull down the Edit menu, and select Paste Object(s).

> **Tip:** Publisher offers keyboard shortcuts that allow you to bypass the Edit menu. To cut a picture frame, press Ctrl+X. To copy a frame, press Ctrl+C. To Paste a frame, press Ctrl+V. These shortcuts work for all frames and objects, not just picture frames.

Deleting Picture Frames

The safest way to delete a picture is to select it and then enter the Cut Picture Frame (Ctrl+X) command. This way, the deleted picture is stored on the Clipboard, and you can get it back (as long as you don't cut or copy anything else to the Clipboard).

However, if you're sure you don't need the picture and you don't want to take the time to enter the Cut command, you can delete the picture. Simply press the Del key, or pull down the Edit menu and select Delete Picture Frame.

Although the picture is not sent to the Clipboard, it is sent to a temporary buffer where it is stored until you perform some other operation. As long as you don't delete anything else, perform any operation, or exit Windows, you can restore the deleted picture. To restore the picture, pull down the Edit menu and select Undo Delete Object(s). You'll find the Undo command useful for many operations, but it is much more risky than using the Clipboard.

> **Tip:** You can also delete a picture by replacing it with another one. To do this, just select the frame that contains the picture you want to replace and then import the new picture.

What You Have Learned 215

In this chapter, you learned how to import graphics into your publications and how to manipulate those graphics using picture frames. In particular, you learned:

- ▶ If you import a picture into a picture frame, Publisher makes the picture fit the frame, possibly distorting the image.
- ▶ If you import a picture without drawing or selecting a picture frame, Publisher creates a frame that matches the dimensions of the original picture. You can move and resize the picture frame to fit the space you have.
- ▶ Pictures are inserted into their frames using the Import Picture option on the File menu.
- ▶ Publisher comes with well over one hundred drawings, which are stored in the CLIPART subdirectory.
- ▶ To view a picture before importing it, highlight the picture's filename in the Import Picture dialog box and press the Preview button.
- ▶ You can increase the white space around a picture by selecting the Frame Margins option from the Layout menu. By increasing the margin settings, you increase the white space between the picture and the frame.

- You can crop a picture in order to use only a portion of it. To crop the image, pull down the Format menu and select Crop Picture, or press the crop tool button in the Toolbar.
- You can move a selected picture frame by dragging it across the screen.
- You can resize a picture frame by dragging one of its handles. To retain the proper proportions of the image, hold down the Shift key while dragging the handle.
- You can resize an image more precisely by selecting the Scale Picture option from the Format menu. By entering the same percentage for the height and width scale percent, you retain the original proportions of the image.
- You can cut or copy a picture using the Windows Clipboard. To cut or copy the picture, select it and then select the appropriate command from the Edit menu. You can then paste the image onto another page or into another publication.
- You can delete a picture by cutting it to the Clipboard or by selecting it and pressing the Del key. If you delete a picture by mistake, pull down the Edit menu and select Undo Delete Object(s).
- You may also delete a picture by selecting its frame and importing another picture into the frame.

Chapter 8

Creating Special Frame Effects

In This Chapter — 217

- Using simple line borders to enhance your publication
- Using BorderArt to add fancy, decorative borders to all types of frames
- Choosing the right sized border for the proper effect
- Using several borders together
- Adding shading to a frame
- Adding a three-dimensional effect with the Shadow option
- Working with overlapping frames

Designing Frames

In the last chapter, you learned how to add pictures to your publications to make them more graphic. In this chapter, you'll learn how to enhance your publications by adding other design touches to the frames you create. You will learn how to add borders to your frames, how to shade the frames, and how to add drop shadows to give the frames a three-dimensional look.

Chapter 8

Working with Borders

Borders consist of lines or designs printed along the edges of a frame or page. You may have seen some fancy borders on greeting cards and invitations. Other, more formal publications, such as magazines and newsletters, may use borders that consist of simple lines. Whatever the purpose, Publisher provides the basic lines and designs you need to accent your publications.

Adding a Simple Line Border

You can add a simple line border around any object: text frame, picture frame, or WordArt frame, or any of the draw objects you create. (In the case of draw objects, the border is the line that defines the object; refer to Chapter 6 for more information.) These simple line borders are useful for setting off text in a text frame, for framing a picture, or for enhancing your publication with a very basic design element. Figure 8.1 shows some uses for simple line borders.

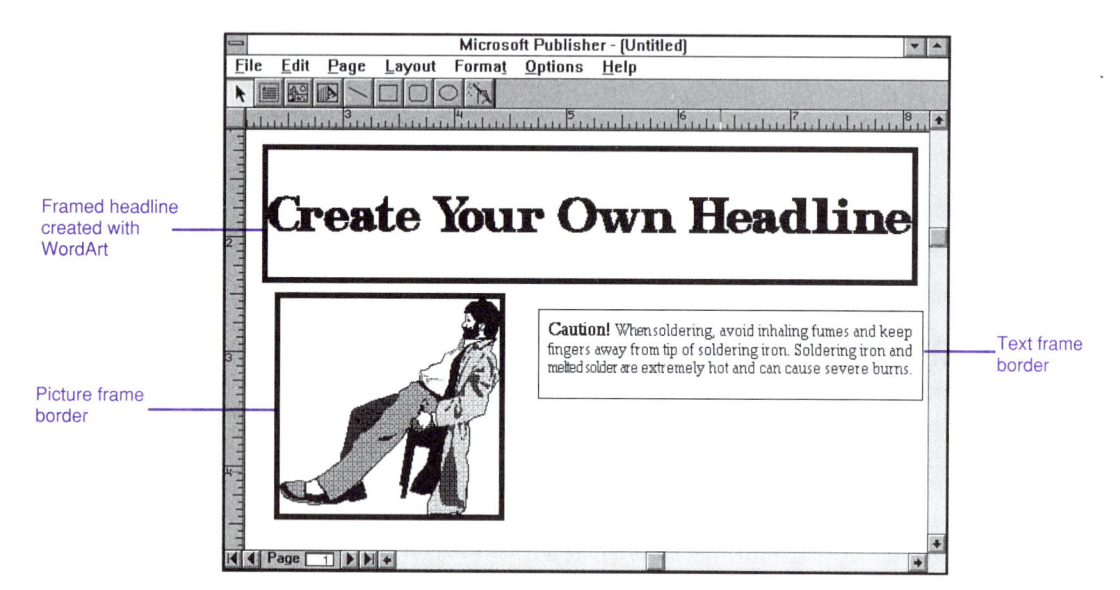

Figure 8.1   Simple line borders can enhance any publication.

You can add a line border to any frame as you draw it. Select the tool for the frame you want to draw and then click on one of the line thickness buttons on the right end of the Toolbar. When you draw the frame, Publisher creates a simple border around it. If none of the line thickness buttons is pressed (as is the default for text frames), no border appears.

To add a border to an existing frame, select the frame and then pull down the Layout menu and select Border. This opens the Border dialog box, shown in Figure 8.2. On the left side of this dialog box is a preview area that shows a graphic representation of the border. By default, any line thickness or color options you change affect all sides of the border. To change the line thickness and/or color of only one side, click on the side that you want your changes to affect. For example, you can select None for the top, left, and right sides to use only the bottom of the border.

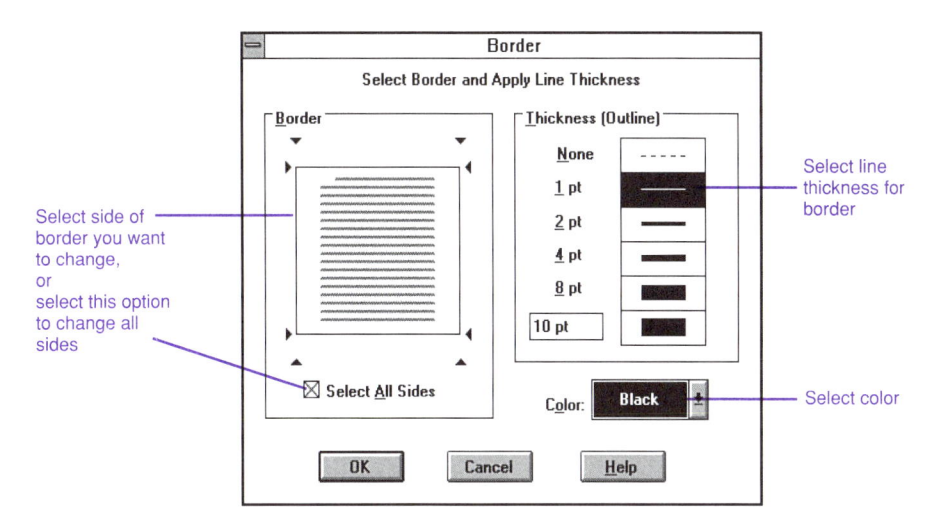

Figure 8.2 The Border dialog box lets you set the color and line thickness for the border.

In the Thickness box, select one of the line thicknesses from the list or click in (or tab to) the text box at the bottom of the list and type the thickness desired in points. For example, for a 3-point line, type **3**. This setting will affect only those sides you selected earlier.

If you plan on printing in color, you can change the color of the border as well as its thickness. Simply click on the down arrow to the right of the Color drop-down list box, or press Alt+O and then Alt+↓. Click on the color you want to use or highlight the color and then press Enter.

The following Quick Steps explain how to add or modify a frame's border.

Adding or Changing a Frame's Border

1. Select the frame. — Handles appear to show that the frame is selected.

2. Pull down the Layout menu and select Border. — The Border dialog box appears.

3. To change a selected side of the border, click on the side you want the change to affect in the Border box. Or, press Alt+B and use the arrow keys to select a side. — Triangles appear to point out which border is selected.

4. In the Thickness box select a thickness, or type a thickness in the text box at the end of the list.

5. To print the line in color, click on the down arrow to the right of the Color drop-down list box, or press Alt+O and then Alt+↓. Then highlight the color you want to use.

6. Press the OK button. — You are returned to the work area, and the border appears with the new options in effect. □

Understanding BorderArt

Although plain, single-line borders are sufficient for formal publications, you may be working on a publication that requires a more eye-catching design. For such publications, you can use Publisher's *BorderArt*. When you installed Publisher, the installation program copied Publisher's BorderArt library to the C:\MSPUB\BORDERS directory on your hard disk. This library contains over 100 border designs for use in your publications. In the following sections, you'll learn how to use these designs in your publications.

With BorderArt, you can add a decorative border made of flowers, cabins, little palm trees, or any other BorderArt design. You control the size of the border simply by specifying a point size; use a large border for announcements, or a dainty, unassuming border for an invitation—the choice is yours. Some examples of BorderArt are shown in Figure 8.3.

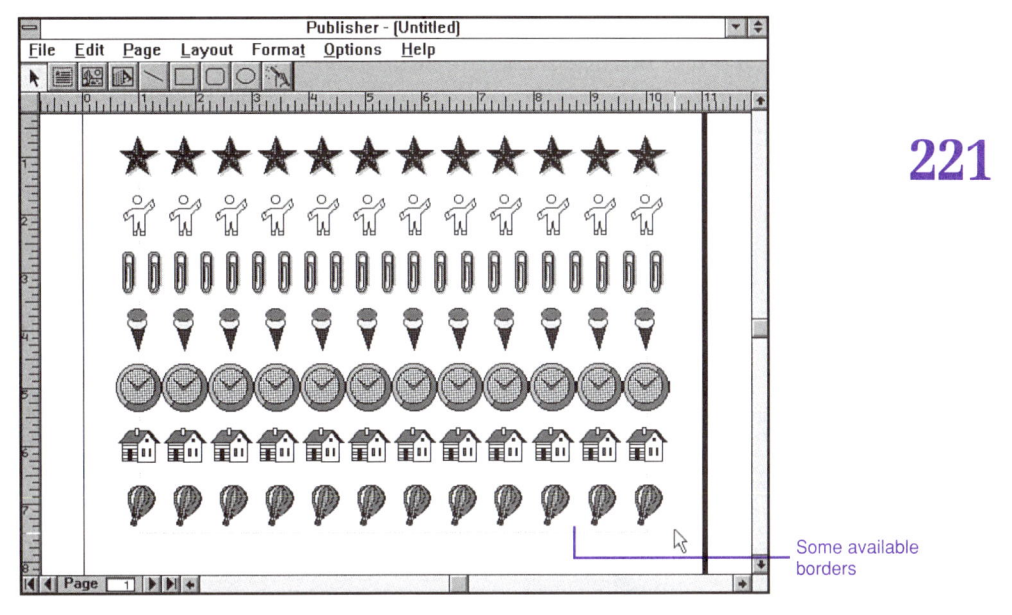

Figure 8.3 Examples of BorderArt.

Where To Use BorderArt

Although you can use BorderArt around almost any object, there are a few limitations. As a general rule, you can use BorderArt around the following objects:

- ▶ Text frames.
- ▶ Picture frames.
- ▶ Rectangles.
- ▶ WordArt objects.

You cannot use BorderArt around ovals or rounded rectangles, because the objects do not have square corners. Also, you cannot use BorderArt around a line, because the line has no border. However, there are ways to get around these limitations.

To use BorderArt around a line, draw a rectangle so narrow that it appears to be a line. If you draw the rectangle without one of the line thickness buttons pressed in the Toolbar, you can use BorderArt by itself, without any other lines appearing.

To use BorderArt with rounded rectangles and ovals, you can use the trick illustrated in Figure 8.4. The inner and outer rounded rectangles were drawn and no BorderArt was used for them. Between the two rounded rectangles is a rectangle with square corners; this rectangle was turned into BorderArt (you'll see how in the next section). The poem itself is done in WordArt, which is covered in Chapter 9. The WordArt, by the way, also has a border and can have BorderArt. In this case, however, its border is invisible.

Figure 8.4 A decorative border using the Roses BorderArt combined with rounded rectangles.

Using BorderArt

You begin the process of adding a decorative border by first selecting the object around which you want the border to appear. To select a text frame, picture frame, or WordArt frame, click anywhere inside the frame. To select a rectangle, click on one of the lines that defines the rectangle. Eight handles appear around the object to show it has been selected.

Next, pull down the Layout menu, as shown in Figure 8.5. You will see two options involving borders: Border and BorderArt. The Border option is used to change the thickness and color of borders for a frame that has a simple line border. The second option, BorderArt, allows you to add a fancy border to the frame. If the frame already has a simple line border, you can use the BorderArt option to replace the line with a border from the BorderArt library.

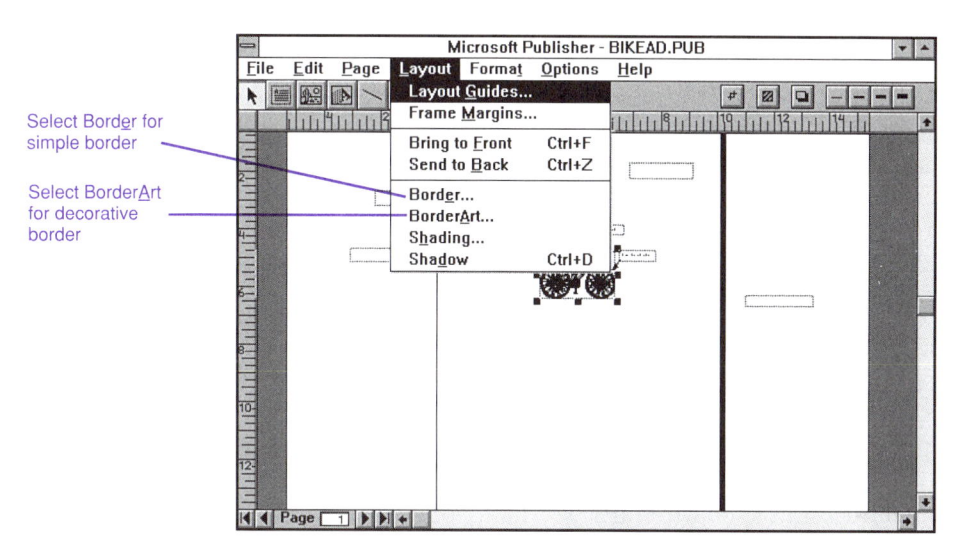

Figure 8.5   The Layout menu contains two options for working with borders.

Select BorderArt from the Layout menu. The BorderArt dialog box appears, as shown in Figure 8.6. On the left is a list of the available borders. Click on one of the borders listed, or press Alt+A and use the arrow keys to highlight the border. You may use the scroll bar at the side of the list box to scroll down through the choices. The selected border appears in the Preview area, as shown in Figure 8.6.

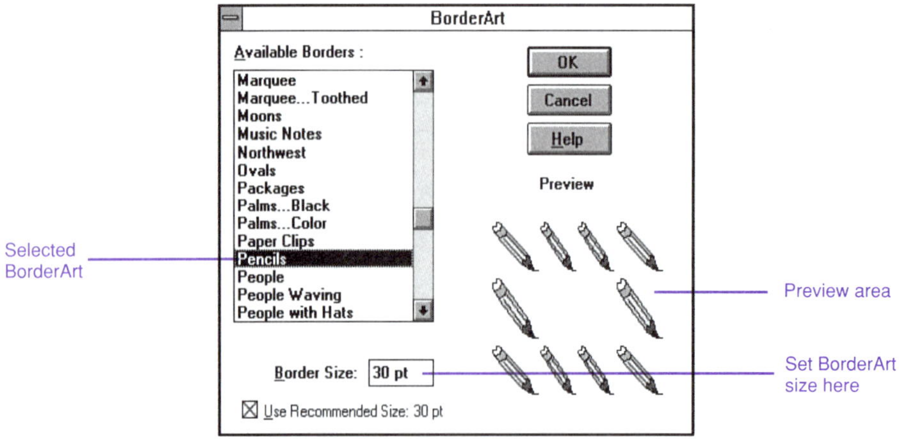

Chapter 8

Figure 8.6 The BorderArt dialog box is used to select and modify the size of BorderArt.

In the lower left corner of the dialog box is the Border Size text box. This box contains the recommended size of the border, in points. Although the border will look best printed in the recommended size, that size may not be appropriate for how you are using the border. To change the size, press Alt+B or click inside the text box and type a size, in points. Press Tab to view the border in its new size. If you decide the original size was best after all, just click on the Use Recommended Size check box, just below the Border Size text box.

> **Tip:** By default, BorderArt is measured in points because points give you more control over the border size. If you prefer to work with another unit of measurement, type the amount followed by the abbreviation for the unit you want to use: `in` for inches, `cm` for centimeters, or `pi` for picas.

If you like the BorderArt you've previewed, then click on the OK command button. Publisher returns you to the work area, where the BorderArt now forms the border of the selected frame. You can call up the BorderArt dialog box any time this frame is selected and change the BorderArt as desired.

> **Tip:** If the border is too close to the text or object in the frame, pull down the <u>L</u>ayout menu and select the Frame <u>M</u>argins option. You can then increase the frame margins to increase the space between the border and the text or object contained in the frame.

The following Quick Steps summarize the process of adding BorderArt to a frame.

Adding BorderArt to a Frame

1. Click on the frame you want to enhance with BorderArt.

   Eight handles appear around the frame to show that it's selected.

2. Pull down the <u>L</u>ayout menu and choose Border<u>A</u>rt.

   The BorderArt dialog box appears.

3. Click on a border in the <u>A</u>vailable Borders list box, or press Alt+A and use the arrow keys to highlight your choice.

   The selected border appears in the Preview area.

4. To change the size of the border, click in the <u>B</u>order Size box or press Alt+B, type the size you want to use, and press the Tab key.

   The Preview area displays the border in its new size.

5. Press the OK button.

   You are returned to your document, and the BorderArt is now in place around the edges of the selected frame. □

> **FYIdea:** A number of the BorderArt designs can be used appropriately and effectively for businesses or organizations. The Cabin design is great for real estate flyers or open house signs. The Flower designs are appropriate for any festive occasion, and the Stars designs can work well around a photograph of an employee of the month or for an award. The Sun BorderArt is great for announcing outdoor activities. The Lightning or Firecrackers BorderArt works for sales or special events. Any memo looks good with the Pencils or PaperClips BorderArt. As you can see, Publisher includes a BorderArt design for almost every occasion.

Enhancing BorderArt

Although a border adds a great deal to a publication by itself, you can often *enhance* a border to make it look even better. For example, you can draw a rectangle outside or inside the border, as in the example in Figure 8.4. Such effects are a matter of artistic choice and taste. Feel free to stop and experiment throughout this chapter to get a taste of the possibilities.

Figure 8.7 shows a practical example of how one user enhanced BorderArt to create a sign. The sign was created by Fred, owner of *Fred's Old Style Clock Repair Service*. For the outside border of the sign, Fred drew a rectangle and then used the Border option on the Layout menu to set the border width to 10 points.

He then drew a slightly smaller rectangle inside the larger one. He used the BorderArt option on the Layout menu to add a more decorative border to this rectangle. Because Fred is in the clock repair business, he selected Clock BorderArt. He enlarged the border to 60 points to emphasize the clocks.

Fred then clicked on the WordArt tool and created a WordArt frame slightly smaller than the inside box. He typed his text into it and selected a font as described in the next chapter. To make the text appear white on a black background, Fred selected white as the fill color for the text and selected the Color Background option, which set the shading for the WordArt frame to black. To create the border of smaller clocks, Fred again used the BorderArt option on the

Layout menu and selected the Clock BorderArt, this time making the clocks a little smaller. The finished sign is shown in Figure 8.7.

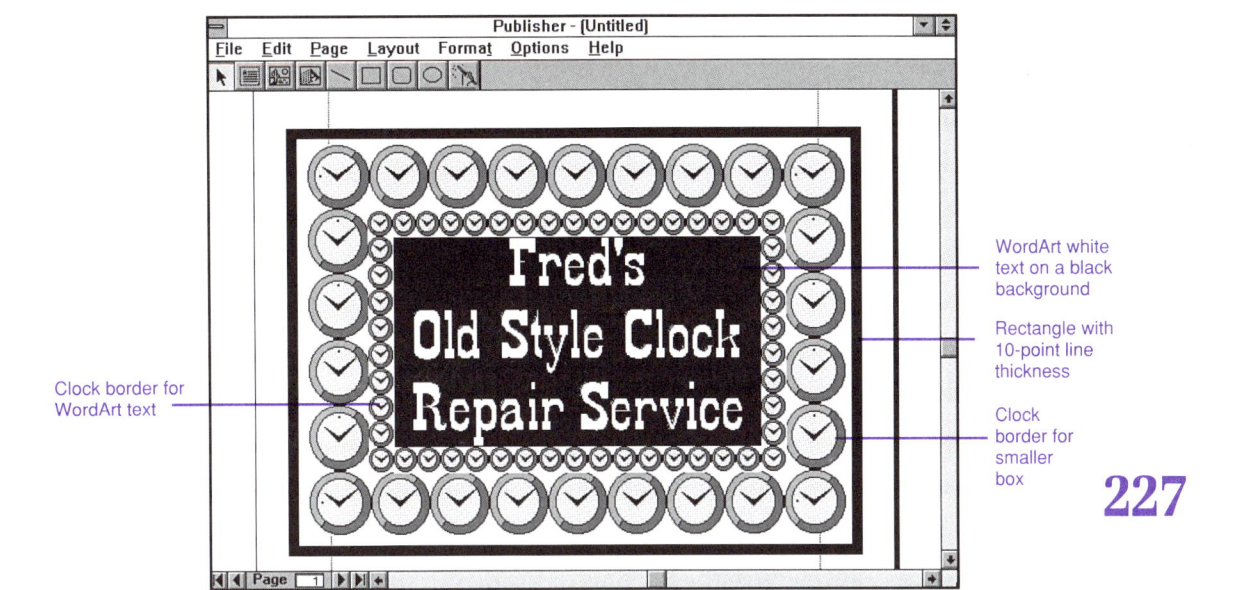

Figure 8.7 Fred enhanced the BorderArt to create a striking sign.

Some BorderArt works very well without any enhancement. Take a look at the Arched Scallops (the first selection in the Available Borders list box). Graphics designers refer to this type of design as a *closed shape*. That is, the shape is continuous; it is not broken by spaces or lines. Such a design needs no inside or outside frame to contain it. In fact, adding additional lines to such a design often results in overkill.

The Roses border used in Figure 8.4, however, is an *open shape*. There are spaces between the roses, which may make the design appear to break up. With open designs, consider framing the design to hold it together. This gives the design a solid feel and makes the border stand out.

Although such enhancements seem minor, these little touches can make or break a design. While your readers may not know why your design is or is not effective, they will know whether it looks good to them or not or whether it detracts from the content of the publication. Whether you are creating the Mona Lisa of publications or a flyer for selling washing machines, these minor touches can make a difference. Here are some rules of thumb for enhancing BorderArt:

▶ If the BorderArt is *open* (does not have solid sides), then drawing a rectangle or rounded rectangle on the outside and/or inside of the Border will enhance it.

▶ Never shadow open BorderArt, it doesn't work. Draw a box on the outside of the BorderArt and then shadow the box.

▶ BorderArt with solid sides can be shadowed. This type of BorderArt works better by itself without enhancement.

▶ Adjust the point size of BorderArt so that it doesn't overpower the material it surrounds. The BorderArt should draw the reader's eye to the message, not to the BorderArt itself.

Removing BorderArt

You can remove BorderArt in either of two ways. If you want to replace the BorderArt with a simple line border, select the frame that has the BorderArt you want to replace, pull down the Layout menu, and select Border. Use the Border dialog box to specify the thickness and color of the border you want to use. If you want to get rid of the BorderArt without replacing it, use the following Quick Steps.

Q Removing BorderArt

1. Click on the frame that has the BorderArt you want to delete.

   Eight handles appear around the frame to show that it is selected.

2. Pull down the Layout menu and choose BorderArt.

   The BorderArt dialog box appears.

3. In the Available Borders list box, click on the first choice, None.

   Nothing should be showing in the Preview area.

4. Press the OK button.

   You are returned to your document and there is now no BorderArt around the edges of the selected frame. □

Overlapping Frames for Special Effects

As you saw in Chapter 6, you can layer drawn objects on-screen to create special effects. But these effects are not limited to drawn objects. You can also overlap text and picture frames to create special effects, as shown in the example in Figure 8.8. Once you get used to thinking of your publications as consisting of *layers*, you'll start designing publications to fully exploit this feature.

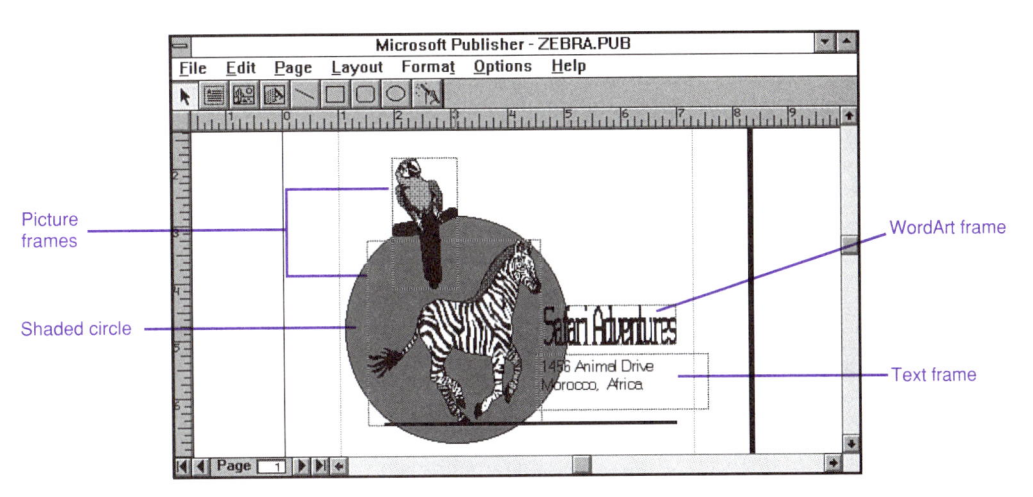

Figure 8.8   You can overlap frames to create special effects.

When overlapping objects on a page, it helps to see the objects' boundaries (the dotted line that defines each frame). These boundaries help you think of each object as being painted on a transparency. However, these boundaries may cause you to misjudge the position of the object in relation to another object. For example, in Figure 8.8, the picture frame holding the zebra is centered inside the circle, but the zebra itself is not centered. To help, you can hide the object boudaries, as shown in Figure 8.9. To hide the boundaries, pull down the Options menu and select Hide Object Boundaries, or press Ctrl+Y.

When you are working with several objects, remember that the object on top covers any object below it. If you want to work with an object at the bottom of the stack, you have to move the other objects off it first or use the Send to Back option on the Layout menu (or press Ctrl+Y) to send the other objects to the bottom of the stack. Figure 8.10 shows the parrot sent to the back to create a new effect.

Figure 8.9 To get a clearer picture of the relative positions of the layered objects, hide the object boundaries. The zebra is now centered.

Parrot sent to back

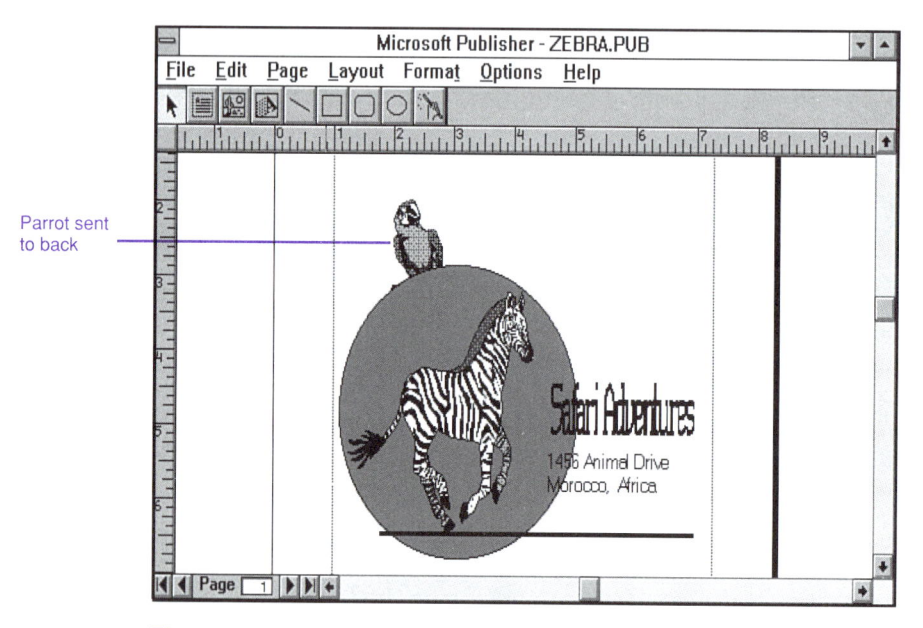

Figure 8.10 You can send objects to the back or bring them to the front to create different effects.

Shading a Frame

In addition to being able to change the border that surrounds the frame, you can add color or shading to the *inside* of the frame. Shading is commonly used for a picture or small text frame to set it apart from the surrounding text, as shown in Figure 8.11.

To add shading to a frame, first select frame. Then, click on the shading tool in the Toolbar

or pull down the Layout menu and select Shading. The Shading dialog box appears, as shown in Figure 8.12.

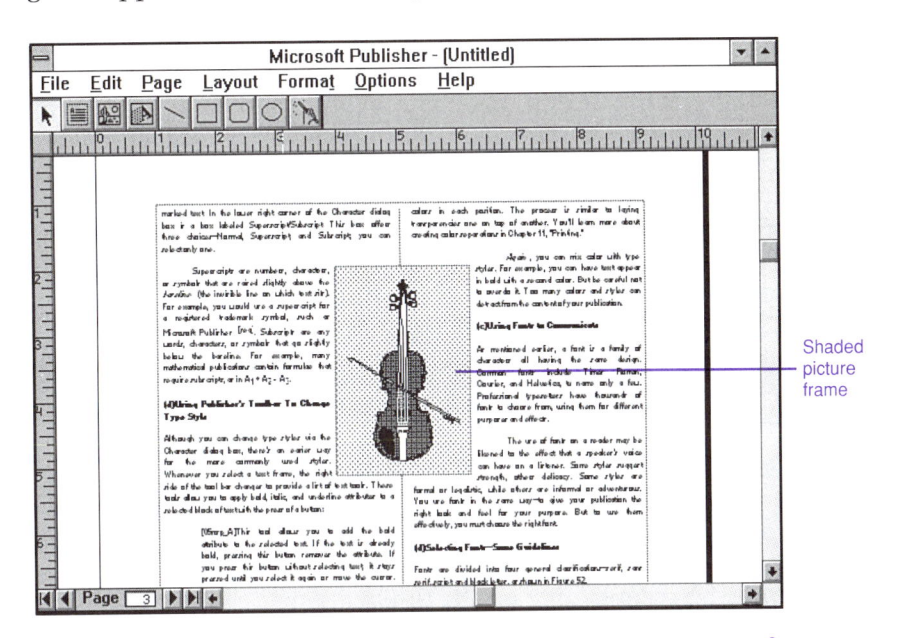

Figure 8.11   You can add shading to a frame to set it apart from the surrounding text.

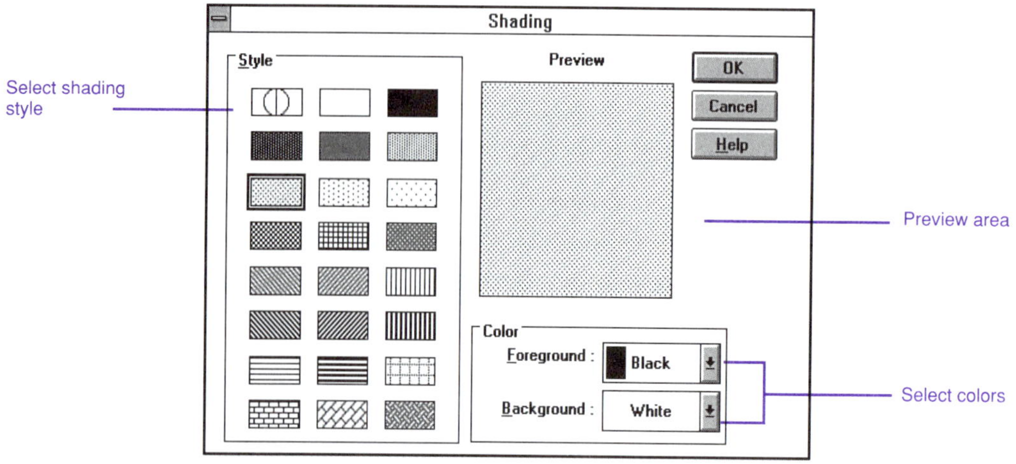

Chapter 8

Figure 8.12 The Shading dialog box allows you to add shading and color to your frames.

In the left side of the box are several shading style options. The top three options are the most common: clear, white, and black. The clear option is the default. A line surrounds the frame, but you can see through the frame. This allows you to place the frame on top of another object. The white option fills the frame with a white shade that hides any object that this frame may overlap. Black fills the frame with solid black. The other options on the screen consist of various amounts of black-on-white in various patterns. To select a shading style, click on the style or press Alt+S and then use the arrow keys to highlight a style.

By default, white is the background color and black is the foreground color in the various shading style options. However, you can change the background and foreground colors by using the two drop-down lists below the Preview box. For example, you can select blue on a cyan background, or red on a yellow background. To change the colors, click on the down arrow to the right of either the Foreground or Background drop-down list box or press Alt+F or Alt+B and then Alt+↓. The list appears, showing the color options. Select an option from the list by clicking on it or using the arrow keys to highlight it.

To the right of the Style box is a box titled Preview. Here you can see what the pattern and/or shade you've selected looks like before clicking the OK command button and returning to your document. When the shading appears as desired, press the OK button.

> **FYIdea:** In many professional publications, you'll see a block of text in a shaded box *without* a line defining the box. To create this same effect in your publications, shade the frame and then display the Border dialog box and choose None for the line thickness.

The following Quick Steps summarize how to add shading to a frame.

Shading Frames

1. Select the frame you want to shade.

   Handles appear around the selected frame.

2. Pull down the Layout menu and select Shading, or click on the shading button in the Toolbar.

   The Shading dialog box appears.

3. Select a style option by clicking on it or using the arrow keys to highlight it.

   A box appears around your selection and its pattern or shade is depicted in the Preview box.

4. To change the foreground or background color, pull down the Foreground or Background drop-down list, and select a color from the list.

   The changes are shown in the Preview box.

5. Press the OK button.

   The display is refreshed and you can see the shading and/or pattern added to the frame. ☐

You can change the shading at any time by selecting the frame and repeating the steps for the shading you want to use. To remove shading, select the clear option.

Adding a Shadow to Any Frame

Another way to enhance a frame is to add a *drop shadow* to the frame. A drop shadow is shading that appears along two edges of the frame, usually the bottom and right edges. The shading makes the frame appear to be raised off the paper, casting a shadow on the page. You can use this technique to call attention to whatever is within the shadowed frame, as in the example shown in Figure 8.13.

You can add shadowing to a frame in either of two ways. The fast way is to select the frame and then click on the shadow button in the Toolbar:

If you want to add a drop shadow to a text frame, you must press this button *before* drawing the frame; if you want to add a drop shadow to an existing text frame, you must use the second method. The second way to add a drop shadow is to pull down the Layout menu and select Sha_d_ow (or press Ctrl+D). Either method adds a drop shadow to the selected frame.

WordArt frame

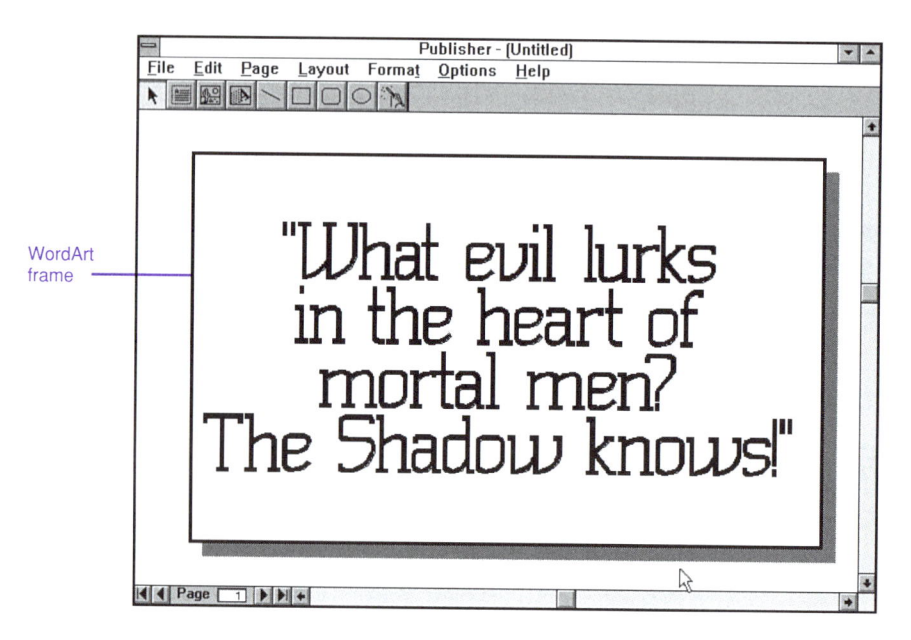

Figure 8.13 Shadowing, as is shown on this box with the quote from Golden Age radio, creates a three-dimensional effect.

> **FYIdea:** For shadowing to be effective, the frame must have a solid border. Don't add a drop shadow to a borderless frame or to one that has an open design type of BorderArt. For example, adding a drop shadow to the roses border will create an awkward design.

To remove a drop shadow from a frame that has one, select the frame and then click on the shadow tool button (or press Ctrl+D) or pull down the Layout menu and select Shadow. In other words, you follow the same procedures to *toggle* the Shadow option on and off.

What You Have Learned

For an effective publication, all the design elements must come together to give the publication a pleasing and striking appearance. In this chapter, you learned about several frame enhancements that can increase a document's impact. In particular, you learned the following:

- Publisher allows you to add simple line borders to any objects except lines. You can use the Border option from the Layout menu to change the thickness and color of the borders.
- You can add fancy borders using Publisher's BorderArt. The BorderArt library contains over one hundred decorative and fancy borders.
- BorderArt can be used with text frames, picture frames, WordArt frames, and rectangles.
- You can enhance a border by framing it with rectangles, rounded rectangles, or ovals. This enhancement is especially effective for use with BorderArt that has an open design.
- You can enhance a frame by shading inside the frame. To shade a frame, you select the Shading option from the Layout menu.
- Adding a drop shadow to a frame makes the frame appear to rise off the page, casting a shadow on the page. You can add a drop shadow by using the shadow tool or by selecting Shadow from the Layout menu.

Chapter 9

Creating Special Text Effects

In This Chapter

- *How to create graphic text using Publisher's WordArt feature*
- *Guidelines for using special effects*
- *Using WordArt for headlines, titles, call outs, product names, and much more*
- *Using WordArt's fonts and styles*
- *Adding background patterns and colors to WordArt frames*
- *Other tricks to enhance text, both WordArt and regular text, including text reverses, call outs, and sidebars*

Breathing Life into Your Text

Although drawings, pictures, and BorderArt allow you to add impressive and professional graphic effects to your publications, your text doesn't just have to lie flat on the page. Publisher offers several options for working with text, allowing you to reverse out the text (print white text on a black background), and create special boxed text to use for callouts and sidebars. Publisher also offers a facility called *WordArt* that you can use to make bits of text jump up off the page.

What Is WordArt?

WordArt allows you to create *graphics-based* text objects that exist independent of other objects. You can then move, resize, and reshape these WordArt objects in much the same way as you manipulate pictures, without affecting surrounding objects. In addition, you can add special effects such as shading and shadowing, and even change the color of the text.

Graphics-based text objects. Isn't that a contradiction in terms? Not quite. Regular text in Publisher is actually handled by Windows. As detailed in Chapter 5, the only text fonts and type styles available in Publisher are the ones installed in Windows. Although these fonts are sufficient for body text, they fall far short when you need a fancy design. You can't create special effects with these fonts like arching a series of words, or slanting words and phrases, or otherwise manipulating the text to create the effects you see in professional ads and brochures.

WordArt gets around Windows' unimaginative handling of text by treating text as *art*. Instead of treating characters as one of the installed fonts, WordArt handles characters as graphic objects. The text performs more like a Publisher ClipArt drawing than it does like normal text. You can then turn, twist, and tilt these WordArt objects to create some interesting effects. Figure 9.1 shows some examples of what you can do.

Knowing When To Use WordArt

Because Publisher provides such a wide range of tools for enhancing publications, it's tempting to use a bunch of tools in a publication. The publication then ends up looking like a teenager who's just started using makeup. Enhancements are meant to be used in moderation, to bring out the beauty of a publication without calling attention to the enhancements themselves. As you work with WordArt, keep the following guidelines in mind:

- *Make the design fit the content.* If the design calls attention to itself or distracts the reader, the design is a failure. The whole idea of using special effects—such as WordArt, pictures, fancy borders, and drawn objects—is to enhance the publication and focus the reader's eye on your message. The end result is to communicate.
- *Use WordArt sparingly.* While you can punch a lot of text into WordArt frames, overkill makes the special effects seem not so special. Use WordArt on small snippets of text, such as titles or headlines.
- *Use special effects consistently.* Just as any essay or article needs to be unified, a publication needs unity of design. Widely differing effects will clash and confuse the reader.

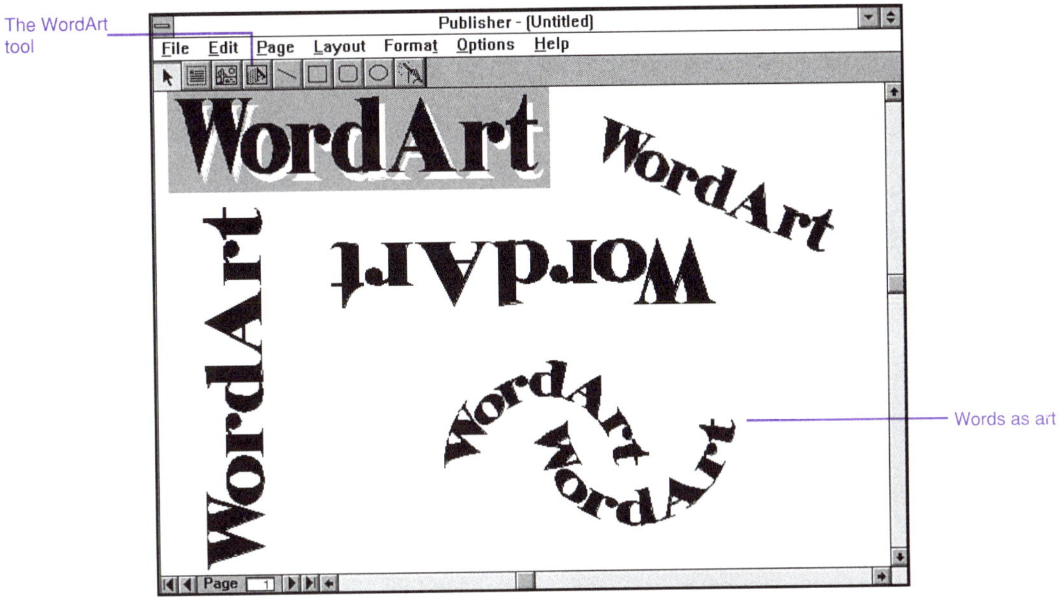

Figure 9.1 Some examples of text turned into art so that it can be slanted, arched, and turned topsy-turvy.

Using WordArt

Although WordArt requires you to type the text you want to use, WordArt creates graphic objects, not text objects. You can't highlight a block of text and then turn it into WordArt, nor can you import text into a WordArt frame. WordArt creations have their own frames—WordArt frames, and they exist as independent WordArt objects.

You create a WordArt frame by clicking on the WordArt tool in the Toolbar:

When you move the mouse pointer into the work area, it turns into a cross hair and you can draw the WordArt frame just as you do a text or picture frame. When you release the mouse button, however, the WordArt dialog box appears, as shown in Figure 9.2. You use this dialog box to create a WordArt object.

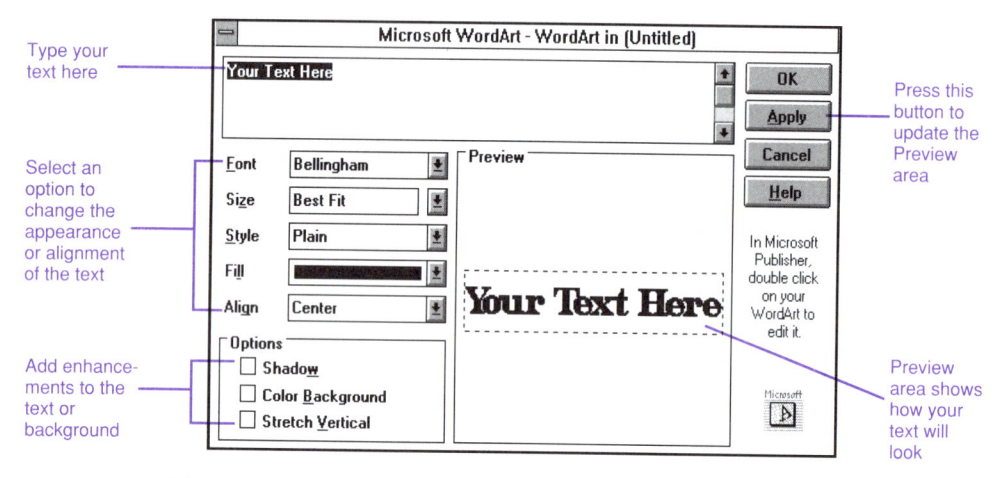

Figure 9.2 The WordArt dialog box.

In the upper left corner of the dialog box is a text box that contains the text `Your Text Here`. Type the text you want to use for your WordArt object. As you type, the `Your Text Here` text disappears and what you type appears in its place. To see how your text will appear in print, press the Apply button. The Preview area at the lower right of the dialog box shows how your text will appear.

Once you've typed the title, headline, or other text you want to use, you can change the appearance of the text by selecting any of the WordArt options. Below the text box are five drop-down list boxes—Font, Size, Style, Fill, and Align—and three check boxes labeled Shadow, Color Background, and Stretch Vertical. These options are explained in more detail later in the chapter.

The following Quick Steps summarize the process of creating a WordArt object.

Creating a WordArt Object

1. Click on the WordArt tool and move the mouse pointer into the work area.

   The mouse pointer changes into a cross hair.

2. Move the cross-hair pointer where you want the upper left corner of the WordArt frame to be.

   Use the rulers or guides if you want to position the corner in a precise location.

3. Hold down the left mouse button and drag the pointer where you want the lower right corner of the frame to be located.

   As you drag, the frame's outline is stretched out from the anchor point.

4. Release the mouse button.

   The WordArt frame appears, and then the WordArt dialog box is displayed on-screen.

5. Type the text you want to use for your WordArt object.

   As you type, the Your Text Here phrase in the upper left corner of the dialog box disappears and what you type appears in its place.

6. To change fonts, pull down the Font list and select a WordArt font.

   As you highlight different fonts in the list, the Preview area shows how your text will appear in the selected font.

7. To change the size of the text, pull down the Si_ze list and select a size, or select Best Fit.	As you highlight different point sizes in the list, the Preview area changes to display the text in the selected size.
8. To make the text slant or to arch it, pull down the _S_tyle list and select a style.	The Preview area displays the text arched, slanted, or flipped according to the selected style.
9. To change the color of the text, pull down the Fi_l_l list and select a color.	Black is the default fill color. You can shade the text with gray, select a color, or use white text against a black background.
10. To change the text alignment, pull down the Align list and select an option.	Center is the default alignment. You can align the text in various ways including flush left, flush right, and fully justified.
11. To have a drop shadow appear around the text, select Shado_w_.	An x appears in the check box to show the option has been selected.
12. To have the text appear on a black or gray background instead of on white, select Color _B_ackground.	The color of the background (black or gray) depends on the fill color you selected in step 9.
13. To increase the height of the text, select Stretch _V_ertical.	The Preview area displays the text as it appears stretched.
14. Press the OK button to create the specified WordArt object.	This closes the dialog box, and the WordArt object appears in its frame. ☐

Now it's time to really use some WordArt power. As you look at the other options in the WordArt dialog box, you'll begin to see some exciting possibilities for adding verve and life to your own documents.

WordArt Fonts

WordArt fonts are fabricated, pseudofonts that are unique to Publisher. In the version of Publisher used during the writing of this book, there are nineteen of these fonts, including Anacortes, Bellingham, Marysville, Tupelo, Vancouver, and WallaWalla. You'll not recognize these names as font names, even if you are well versed in using standard fonts such as Times, Courier, and Helvetica.

To change fonts, click on the arrow to the right of the Font drop-down list box, or press Alt+F and then Alt+↓. The Font list appears, showing the available fonts, as in Figure 9.3. Click on a font in the list, or use the arrow keys to highlight the font. When you highlight a different font, the Preview area changes to show how the text you typed will appear in the selected font. Figure 9.3 shows text with the Touchet font.

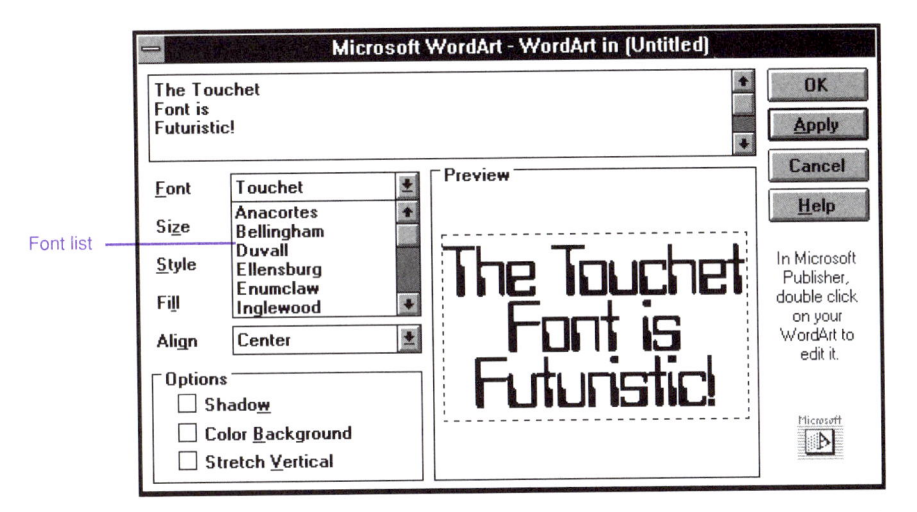

Figure 9.3   Touchet, one of the WordArt fonts included with Publisher provides a futuristic look.

You're going to love this! Even if you have the most basic and inexpensive of printers—perhaps a dot-matrix machine that has only one font—you can *still* print all nineteen WordArt fonts. Because WordArt fonts are graphics, rather than text, any printer that can handle graphics can print WordArt fonts.

If you've ever printed graphics, however, you'll realize that treating text as graphics slows down the printing process. Graphic elements contain much more information than text elements, and all this information must be sent to the printer, which is another reason for using WordArt only for small bits of text such as headlines.

When you begin to work with WordArt, proceed through the entire list of fonts before making your final selection. This will help you learn the fonts and use them more intelligently.

Sizing Your WordArt Object

The *size* of WordArt fonts is specified in points, just like regular fonts. To change the size of the font, click on the arrow to the right of the Size drop-down list or press Alt+Z and then Alt+↓. Click on a size or use the arrow keys to highlight your selection. The default choice is Best Fit, which makes the characters as large as possible for the WordArt frame you drew.

The Best Fit choice is especially useful for headlines. You simply draw a WordArt frame above the text frame or text you want to headline. Make the WordArt frame the width of the text and as tall as you want the headline to be. Typically, you will have a wide but relatively short box. With the Best Fit option, Publisher will fit the headline into that box, as shown in Figure 9.4.

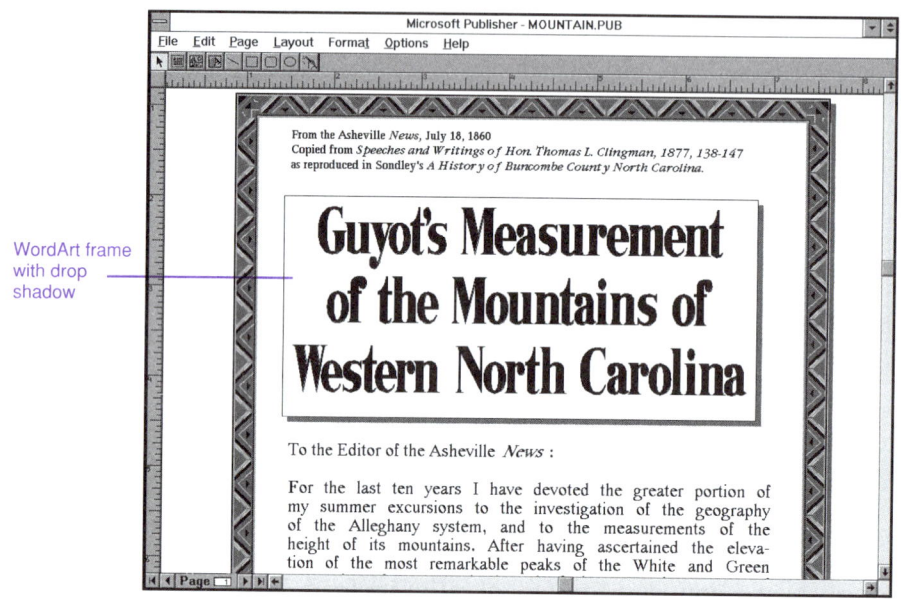

Figure 9.4   The Best Fit choice is excellent for headlines.

Although the Best Fit choice is the easiest to work with, you may need more control over the size of the font. For example, if you have a publication with several headlines, you may want the headlines to be the same size throughout the publication. To set an exact size, click on one of the point sizes in the Size drop-down list box. The Preview area is refreshed to show the change. If the point size you want is not in the list box, then move the cursor to the Size box and type the size you want to use. If you select a size that's too large for the WordArt frame you drew, Publisher will display a warning and ask if you want to resize the WordArt object.

Styling Your WordArt Object

The *style* of WordArt is where the difference between it and regular text really becomes apparent. By clicking on the arrow to the right side of the Style drop-down list box, you'll have the following choices on how the WordArt should look in your document. Experiment with these; they can produce some dazzling effects:

Top to Bottom and Bottom to Top. Rotates the text ninety degrees. Very effective for printing journal or newsletter titles along the left margin of a publication.

Plain. This is the default selection. Prints the text straight across the page just as other text is printed. Effective for headlines.

Upside Down. The name says it all—your text is flipped 180 degrees. Although you probably won't use this style very often, it can be useful for creating special effects in ads.

Arch Up and Arch Down. Causes the text you type to arch up or down. The amount of arch is determined by how wide and how tall you've drawn the WordArt frame. Reshaping the frame will change the steepness of the arch. This is very effective for creative ads and informal publications. Can also be use around art to create some interesting effects.

Button. This style resembles the style used in pin-on buttons, which are especially popular during political campaign years. You can use the style to design your own buttons or to use as part of a publication. You use only three lines of text for this style. The top line arches up, the center line is plain, and the bottom line arches down.

Slant Up (More or Less). Text begins on the left and slants up to the right. The More option makes the text slant up at a steeper angle.

Slant Down (More or Less). Text begins on the left and slants down to the right. The More option makes the text slant down at a steeper angle.

FYIdea: People like buttons. If you have a small business, you can use the Button style to create your own buttons to advertise your goods or services. For $29.95, you can get a Badge-A-Minit starter kit from the following company:

> Badge-A-Minit
> 348 North 30th Road
> LaSalle, Illinois 61301
> 1-800-223-4103

With this kit, you can make buttons out of your Publisher printouts. People don't throw away buttons; your message stays with them, working for years. Any message you can get into a two and a quarter inch circle will work as a badge (a sample button is shown in Figure 9.5). I've used them for years to advertise books, and they generate a great response. You can use buttons to promote your own business or causes, or simply to express your wonderful fun-loving nature!

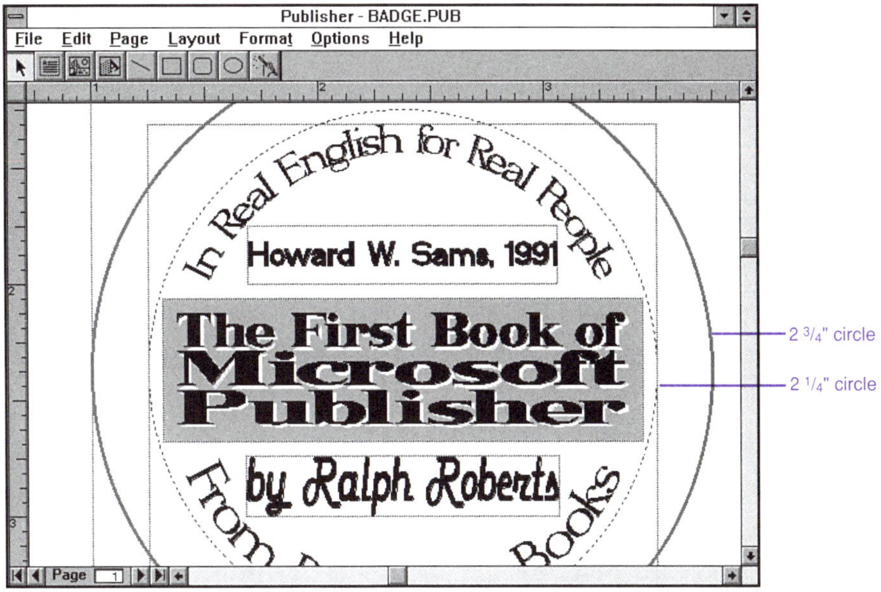

Figure 9.5 An example of a button created with Publisher's WordArt.

Filling Text with Color or Shade

Below the Style drop-down list box is a box labeled Fi<u>l</u>l. This box drops down to show a list of fill options you can use for coloring or shading your text. To pull the list down, click on the arrow to the right of the drop-down list box or press Alt+L and then Alt+↓. When you highlight a color or shade in the list, the Preview area changes to display your text in the selected color or shade.

> **Tip:** Obviously you would need a color printer to print colored text on paper, although you can also use color to print different shades on many printers. In Chapter 11, "Printing with Publisher," you'll learn how to prepare your publications to be printed in color by a print shop.

Above the Black option (the default option on the Fill list), are two shades of gray and a white fill option. If you choose White, a black outline is put around the characters, thus allowing you to have *hollow* letters. To make these white letters really stand out, you can add color behind the letters by using the Shading tool on the tool bar or the S̲hading option on the L̲ayout menu.

Aligning Your WordArt Object

Aligning WordArt text is basically the same as aligning other text in Publisher. You have the same alignment options, including left, right, centered, and justified. Three more choices are added, however, to let you create some interesting effects. The alignment choices for WordArt are:

- ▶ *Left* aligns the text flush against the left margin, leaving the right margin ragged.
- ▶ *Center* centers each line of text regardless of length, leaving both the left and right margins ragged.
- ▶ *Right* aligns the text flush against the right margin, leaving the left margin ragged.
- ▶ *Letter Justify* inserts space between characters to align the text flush against both the left and right margins. Use this option carefully. Because WordArt typically consists of just one or two words per line, character justification can create uneven and unattractive results.
- ▶ *Word Justify* inserts space between words to align text flush against both the left and right margins. This usually works better than character justification for justifying headlines and titles.
- ▶ *Fit Horizontally* changes the size of text on each line to make the text flush against both the left and right margins. You get a much more consistent result in justifying WordArt, but you'll need to have all your lines about the same length. A very short line would wind up in a much larger point size than a long line.

Other WordArt Options

Below the five drop-down list boxes, are three check box options—Shado̲w, Color B̲ackground, and Stretch V̲ertical. Placing an X in the check box next to an option turns it on. Selecting the option again removes the X and turns the option off. You can select more than one option at a time. The Preview area displays your text to show the effects of the selected option.

Shadow adds a drop shadow to the character, giving it a three-dimensional effect; the character appears to cast a shadow on the page. For a few words, such as a title or headline, this works very well, making those few words jump up off the page. An example of a WordArt title with shadowing is shown in Figure 9.6.

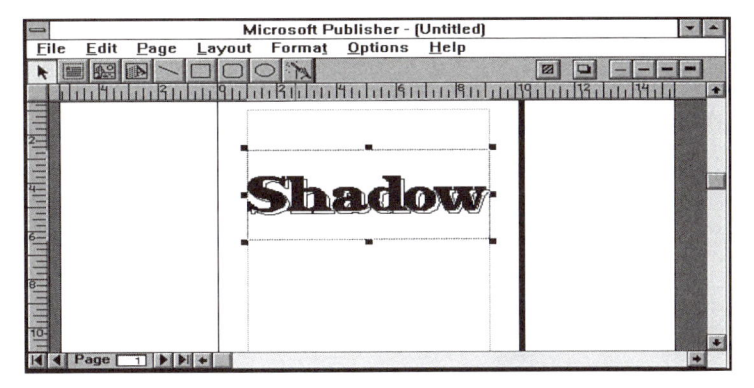

Figure 9.6   The Shadow option adds a drop shadow to the characters, giving them a three-dimensional look.

The *Color Background* option is a little misleading. If you color your text, the "color" background you get is a light gray. If you used white fill or a light gray fill for your text, the background appears black. If you want a true color background, you need to use the shading tool in the Toolbar or select the S̲hading option from the L̲ayout menu after you create the WordArt object.

The *Stretch Vertical* check box allows you to stretch the text vertically to touch the top and bottom edges of your WordArt frame. This is useful if you want to ensure that the text you typed fits the frame you drew without leaving a bunch of white space at the top or bottom. However, this may distort the text.

Editing Your WordArt Objects

All of the options described in the preceding section may be changed. In other words, you can completely reconstruct your

WordArt object by changing the font, editing the text that makes it up, selecting a new style such as Arch Down or Button, adding shadowing to the letters, or any of the other options available in the WordArt dialog box.

To change a WordArt object, select the WordArt frame by clicking on it, then pull down the Edit menu and choose the Edit WordArt Object option. A quicker way to display the WordArt dialog box is to double-click on the WordArt object you want to edit. The following Quick Steps summarize the process.

Editing a WordArt Object

1. Click on the WordArt object you want to edit.

   The eight handles appear around the object to show that it is now selected.

2. Pull down the Edit menu and choose EDIT WordArt Object.

   The WordArt dialog box appears.

3. Make the changes you want, then press the OK button.

   You are returned to your document, and the WordArt object reflects the changes you entered.

Other Text Effects

There are a number of special text effects that you see almost daily in the pages of newspapers and magazines, or in the junk mail that flows through your mailbox like water through the turbines of the Grand Coulee Dam. Now, thanks to Publisher, *you* can reproduce and use many of these text effects in your own documents.

Many of the text effects decribed in the following sections can be done both with regular text and WordArt.

Reversing Text

Page through any magazine, and you are bound to come across at least one or two blocks of text that are *reversed out*; that is, light text is printed on a dark background, usually white-on-black. You can

Creating Special Text Effects

___

create this same effect in your own publications by changing the shading of the text frame and the color of the text.

However, you can create this effect only for a complete text frame; you cannot reverse out a selected block of text within a frame. If you need to reverse out a block of text, you must first cut the text from the text frame and then paste it into its own frame. You can then use the following Quick Steps to reverse out the text.

> **Caution:** A little reversed text goes a long way. Reversed text is harder to read. The eye will naturally pick out a short piece of reversed text—in fact it will stand out from the surrounding text—but will rebel at, say, a whole page of it.

Reversing Out Text

251

1. Select the text frame containing the text you want to reverse out.

   Eight handles appear around the frame, showing it is selected.

2. Press Ctrl+A to highlight all the text in the frame.

   The text appears highlighted. Don't confuse highlighting the text with reversing it out.

3. Pull down the Forma<u>t</u> menu and select <u>C</u>haracter.

   The Character dialog box appears.

4. Pull down the Co<u>l</u>or drop-down list, select White, and then press the OK button.

   Your text disappears and the entire selected area is solid black. Don't worry, you'll get your text back in the next step.

5. Pull down the <u>L</u>ayout menu and select S<u>h</u>ading.

   The Shading dialog box appears.

6. Select the black box in the S<u>t</u>yle area, and then press the OK button.

   You are returned to the work area.

7. Click outside the area of the text frame to deselect the text.

   The selected text appears white on a black background.   ☐

To reverse out WordArt text, set the fill color for the text to white, and then select the Color Background check box option. When text is white, the Color Background option sets the background to black.

> **Tip:** Whenever you reverse out text, use a thick-bodied font. A thin font, like Times Roman, gets choked out by the black background, especially if the ink bleeds even a little during the printing. If you have Helvetica, as PostScript laser printers do, then use that or some other sans serif font. Also consider making the type even thicker by boldfacing it. Figure 9.7 shows text reversed out using the Helvetica Bold font.

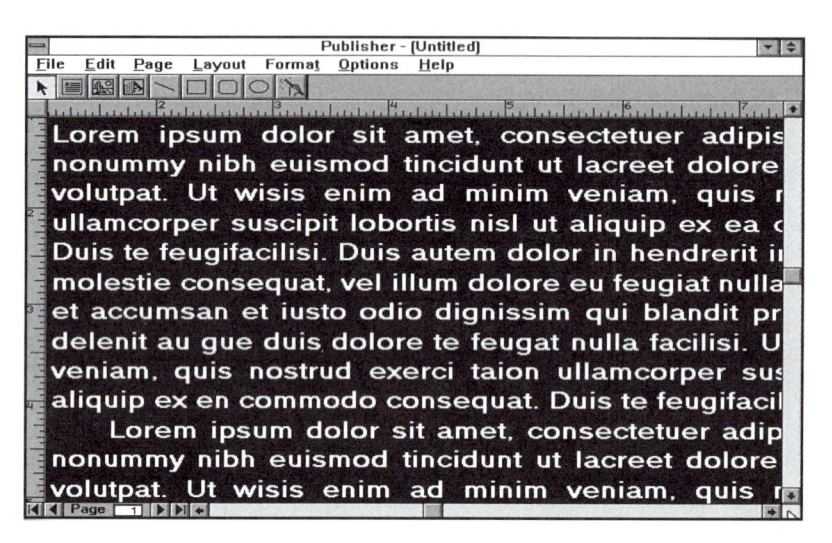

Figure 9.7 White text reversed out of a black background.

Call Outs

Call outs are small quotes or excerpts from a long body of text, set in a larger font size, which are used to entice the reader into reading the text. Call outs are commonly used in magazine articles, where the call out appears in a shaded or unshaded box that sets it off from the rest of the text on the page. To include a call out in your document, follow the Quick Steps below.

Q Making a Call Out

1. Press the text frame button and then press one of the line thickness buttons on the right end of the Toolbar.

    The button appears pressed. This will place a line around the call out text frame.

2. Draw a text frame approximately large enough for your call out, placing it inside the text frame where you want it to appear.

    The call out frame appears, and the text in the surrounding frame reformats itself to accommodate the new frame.

3. Select the text you want to quote in the call out.

    The text appears highlighted.

4. Pull down the Edit menu and choose Copy Text.

    The text is copied to the Windows Clipboard.

5. Click inside the call out text frame.

    The vertical bar cursor appears in the frame.

6. Pull down the Edit menu and select Paste Text.

    The call out quote appears in the new text frame.

7. Select the text in the call out text frame, so you can increase its size.

8. Pull down the Format menu, select Character, and increase the point size by two points. Press the OK button.

    Don't change the font, just change its size. You are returned to the document and your call out quote is in place.

9. Resize and reshape the call out text frame as needed, and move it to its proper location.

    The call out box is now completely finished.

    □

You can further enhance a call out by adding a drop shadow to the frame. To add a drop shadow, select the frame, pull down the Layout menu, and select Shadow. Another way to set off the call out text frame from the surrounding text is to add a light shading to the frame using the Shading option on the Layout menu. You can then remove the frame's border. If the text is too close to the frame's border or to surrounding text, use the Frame Columns and Margins option on the Layout menu to increase the margins. You can even reverse out the text in the call out frame, but if you do, consider boldfacing the text to make it more legible. Figure 9.8 shows one way of doing call outs.

Chapter 9

Figure 9.8 A call out box. While the text on the screen looks to have too much space between words, it prints out fine.

Using Sidebars

Sidebars are mini-articles that shed light on a larger body of text or simply provide an interesting or informative sidelight. Although similar in many ways to call outs, sidebars differ in that they are longer and do not consist of mere abstracts from the main text. Figure 9.9 shows a sample sidebar in action.

To create a sidebar, draw a text frame inside the text frame for which you want to create the sidebar, or place the frame off to one side (if room allows). Import or type the text you want to appear in the sidebar into the text frame. Press Ctrl+A to select all the text; then pull down the Format menu, and select Character. Use the Character dialog box to set the font, color, type styles, and so forth. Then press the OK button to return to your document.

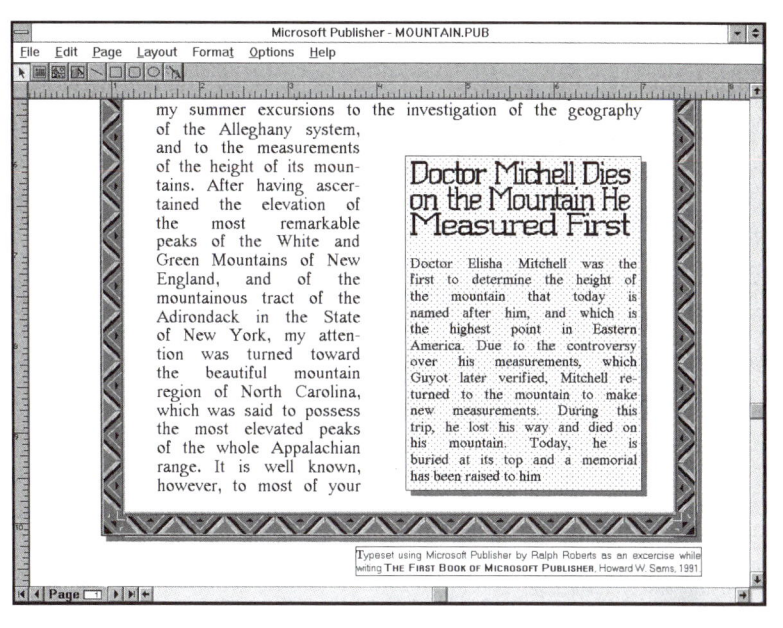

Figure 9.9   Use sidebars to embellish, rather than merely highlight, the main text.

Because sidebars are not main text, you should set them apart from the main text in some way. To see how the pros do it, make mental notes whenever you page through a journal or magazine. You will see that there are usually several ways to create sidebars. Some publications may shade the sidebar by adding a *screen* in color or in light gray. Other publications may use a decorative border around the sidebar or use a simple line and add a drop shadow.

You can create your own screens easily on a noncolor printer by shading the text frame with a light color, which will print as gray. To add shading, pull down the Layout menu and select Shading. In the Shading dialog box, select one of the lighter colors, such as yellow or cyan. On a black-and-white printer, yellow and cyan print as light gray, providing a nice screen for black text. You should experiment with this technique on your own printer to find out which background color gives you the most pleasing contrast.

Adding Lines, Circles, and Rectangles

One of the simplest, yet most effective and commonly used, ways of enhancing text is to add drawn objects to the text. Drawn objects

Chapter 9

differ from pictures in that Publisher does not wrap text around drawn objects. Therefore, you can lay a line or other drawn object over a text frame without affecting the position of the text. Although drawn objects are simple, when combined with text, these simple objects give any publication a professional look, as you can see in Figure 9.10. For more information on using drawn objects, refer to Chapter 6.

Figure 9.10 You can layer drawn objects over text without affecting how the text wraps.

Making Your Own Ads

Every business, large and small, needs to advertise occasionally in magazines, newspapers, or even in the phone book. No matter where you choose to place an advertisement, you must pay not only for the space you rent in that publication, but also for the cost of producing the ad—creating a camera-ready ad that the printer can place in the publication.

Using Publisher To Make a Camera-Ready Ad

What's a *camera-ready ad*? It's an ad that's completely typeset, has the artwork in place, and is *exactly* the right size for the publication. The term comes from the fact that in order for a page to be printed, it must first be photographed and then have a printing plate made from the photo. If you don't supply a publisher with a camera-ready page, the publisher must typeset your text, create the necessary artwork, and paste up the text and graphics in order to make the ad camera-ready. Because this takes time and money, the publisher passes on the costs to you.

To save money, you can use Publisher to create your own camera-ready ads. In addition to saving you money, creating your own ads gives you more control over the finished product, as well. You care much more about your business than some harried, underpaid layout person who's on a tight deadline. You can create the effects you want and see immediately how they will look in the ad. If the effects don't look as good on-screen as you thought they would, you can change them, immediately. You can then print the ad on a laser or inkjet printer for best results, although a high-quality dot matrix machine may be sufficient.

> **FYIdea:** Here's a trick to increase the resolution of an ad. Make the ad slightly oversized (by about 4.2%), then make a 96% reduction of it on a high-quality copy machine. Be sure the reduced ad is exactly the right size as explained below. The reduction process pulls the dots that make up the text and graphics closer together, resulting in a sharper image. If you don't have a high-quality copier, take the ad to a print shop. It should cost no more than fifty cents for a high-quality reduction.

Making Your Ad the Right Size

The ad sales person will tell you the exact size to make the ad. These sizes vary from one publication to another. A quarter-page ad for a tabloid-sized paper is usually something like 5 3/4 inches high by 4 11/16 inches wide (although this varies slightly from paper to paper). Ask the ad person to specify the ad size exactly in inches or picas. Otherwise, they will tell you the size in column inches, which tells them how to charge you but does not help you lay out the ad.

Once you know the size to make the ad, you are ready to begin. The first step is to run Publisher and draw a rectangle the same size as the ad. If you plan on creating a 96% reduction of the ad to increase resolution, multiply each dimension by 1.042; for example, for a 3-by-5 inch ad,

3" x 1.042 = 3.126"
5" x 1.042 = 5.21"

Print the box and measure, then adjust as necessary until you have it *exactly* the right size. Once you have the right size, save a copy of the file to use as a template the next time you need an ad of the same size. This will save you work in the future.

Constructing Your Ad

What you want in an ad (to justify the expense and make it effective), is something that jumps out at the reader. Choose a piece of ClipArt that emphasizes what your business does, or points out some special event such as the Fourth of July or New Year's Day. If you have a scanner, or have access to one, consider scanning in your company logo or some other representative piece of art as either a .PCX or .TIF file. Publisher can import and use either of those formats.

Use a nice bold font from those available to add your company name, and a smaller sized, normal version of the same font to put in the address and phone number.

> **FYIdea:** The cardinal rule in doing an ad is to keep it clean and uncluttered. The most common mistake made in constructing ads is to put in too much. You might have six specials this week, but in a quarter-page ad, there's not a lot of room. Choose the two best and tout those. When people come into your store or office, then trot out the other four.

There are lots of little tricks to make your ad stand out from those around it. For example, you can use the Shadow tool in the Toolbar to add a drop shadow to your rectangle. This will lift your ad off the page to grab the reader's attention. Just be sure that everything fits within the size limitations of the publication. If you add a drop shadow, you'll need to reduce the size of the rectangle to bring the shadow within the boundaries. In ad sizes, you can safely assume that no leeway exists—it *must* fit.

You can also make your ad stand out by adding shading to the rectangle. Although a white background is usually best, a light shading can often be effective. Just make sure the shading is not so dark that it hides your text. The shading may print darker in the publication than it does on your printer. For small ads, you might even consider reversing out the text. But be careful. If the publication in which you are advertising prints on low-quality paper, a lot of ink may bleed, making your ad look like an ink blot test.

Remember also the Coupon PageWizard which, if your ad is large enough, is a very good way to get a response. For a smaller ad, you may consider making the entire ad into a coupon.

Once you have a nice ad, keep it as a template for future ads. Because you can resize it using Publisher, you can use it for other publications simply by resizing the elements used in the original ad. You can also use it in promotional flyers, as you'll see in Chapter 13.

If you are involved in a small business that advertises regularly, Publisher can save you hundreds of dollars in advertising costs over the course of a year.

What You Have Learned

In this chapter, you learned how to enhance text to make it play a more graphic role in your publications. Although you learned mostly about the WordArt tool, you also learned more advanced techniques for working with text frames, shading frames, and adding drop shadows to make your text stand out. Specifically, you learned the following:

- ▶ WordArt allows you to treat small blocks of text as graphic elements. This graphic text can perform desktop publishing gymnastics by slanting up or down, arching, or flipping topsy-turvy.
- ▶ Unlike normal fonts, WordArt fonts are graphic elements which can be printed on any graphic printer regardless of how many or how few fonts that printer has.

- ▶ WordArt has a wide variety of styles; by using the Preview area in the WordArt dialog box, you can experiment with different combinations of options and see the effects immediately.
- ▶ Other text effects include reverses (white on black), call outs (quotes used for emphasis and to entice readers), and sidebars (small articles that embellish a larger article).
- ▶ You can use WordArt and other special text effects along with Publisher's other features to create your own ads. The process is not only easy and fun, but it can save you loads of money, as well.

Chapter 10

Working with Pages

In This Chapter

- Working with multipage documents
- Inserting and deleting pages
- Using the background to add headers, footers, page numbers and other items on every page
- Creating mirrored background pages

Going Beyond the Page

Up to this point, you've worked with publications one page at a time, learning how to use Publisher's tools to paste text, graphics, and other objects on a page. This is fine for single-page publications, such as resumes, flyers, and business cards. But for multipage publications such as books and reports, you'll need tools to create additional pages, to move from page to page, and to control your multipage publications.

This chapter explains the basic tools you'll need to create, insert, and delete pages. You'll also learn how to use Publisher's background to enhance multipage publications by adding page numbers, borders, headers and footers, and other elements that you want to appear on every page of the publication.

Inserting Pages

When a you create a new publication, it is initially only one page—the page you see on-screen. To create a multipage publication, you'll have to insert additional pages. You can insert pages at any time and at any place in a publication. For example, if you have a 15-page publication, you can insert a page between pages 1 and 2. You can also delete pages, as you'll see later. To insert a page, use the following Quick Steps.

Adding Pages

1. Turn to the page you want to insert pages before or after.

   For information on turning pages, refer to Chapters 1 and 3. The page number appears in the page control window in the lower left corner of the Publisher window.

2. Pull down the Page menu and select Insert Pages.

   The Insert Pages dialog box appears, as shown in Figure 10.1.

3. In the Number of New Pages text box, type the number of pages you want to insert.

4. Select Before Current Page or After Current Page to specify where you want the pages inserted.

5. Enter any other options you want, and then press the OK button.

   The specified number of pages are inserted, and Publisher displays the first inserted page. ☐

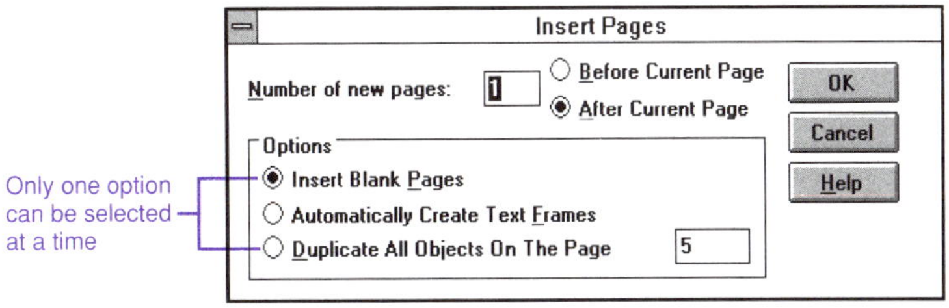

Working with Pages

Figure 10.1 The Insert Pages dialog box lets you add pages to Publisher documents.

> **Tip:** A fast way to insert one additional page, without going through the Insert Pages dialog box, is to use the Ctrl+N shortcut. This key combination will automatically insert one new page *after* the current page.

There are three other choices in the Insert Pages dialog box, all three in the Options box at the lower left. You can choose only one of these three options:

- Insert Blank Pages (the default) inserts blank pages before or after the current page. A blank page is a page without any frames. Although you may see one or more frames on a blank page, these frames are in the background, as you'll see later in this chapter.
- Automatically Create Text Frames creates a text frame on all new pages. These text frames will match the size and dimensions of the layout guides on the current page. You can then resize or reshape the text frames, as needed. If you are going to import several pages of text, you should use this option and insert more pages than you think you'll need. That way, the text will have sufficient room to flow out. You can delete the unused pages later.
- Duplicate All Objects on Page allows you to insert pages that contain all the same objects of another page, but not the contents of the frames. In the text box to the right of this option, type the number of the page whose objects you want duplicated. This makes copying complex groups of objects on one page to another easy. This is a good way to copy elements that you want to appear on other pages but *not* on every page (the background is used for that).

Deleting Pages

You can delete only one page at a time in Publisher. Turn to the page you want to delete, pull down the Page menu, and select Delete Page. The page is removed from the publication. If you delete the wrong page or want to undo the deletion for any other reason, immediately pull down the Edit menu and select Undo Delete Page. The page will be restored if you've done no other operation in the meantime.

> **Tip:** If you plan on making several major changes to a publication, use the Save As command on the File menu to save the publication under another name. This makes a copy of the publication. You can then delete pages and make any other changes you want without worrying. If you decide later that the changes are no good, simply return to the original file.

Working with Publisher's Background

The *background* in Publisher is an interesting and useful concept for any document with two or more pages. Say, for example, you have a hundred-page report in which you want to print a box outlining the page on all 100 pages. You could, of course, draw a box on each page, but such a process would be lengthy and incredibly boring. Or you could go to Publisher's background and draw the box once; it would then appear on all 100 pages!

The background, then, is an area in which you can put any repeating text, pictures, or drawn objects that you want to appear on all pages. This may include page numbers or any other type of header or footer information. (Headers are text that appears on the top of every page; footers are printed at the bottom of every page.) You set the text and graphics once in the background, and Publisher takes care of the rest. If you show Publisher where to put a page number in the background, it will calculate and place the *correct* page number on each page. Insert or delete pages, and Publisher automatically repaginates the publication.

Switching to the Background

Before you can use the background, you must switch to it. Pull down the Page menu and select Go to Background, or press Ctrl+M. At the lower left corner of the Publisher window, you'll see two rectangles, one superimposed on the other, as shown in Figure 10.2. These rectangles show that you are now in the background.

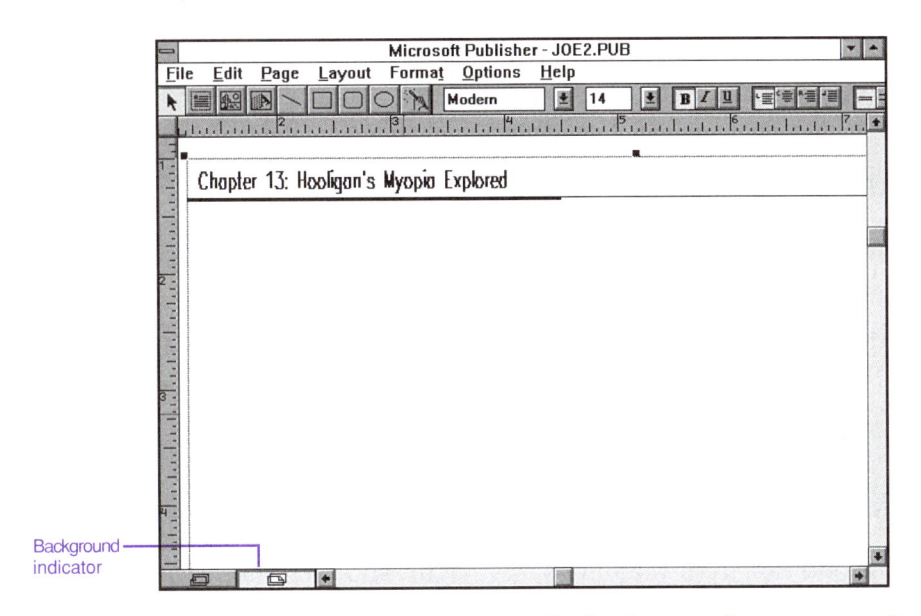

Figure 10.2 When you are in the background, two rectangles appear, one superimposed on the other.

Whatever objects you create or place here will appear on every page of the document, even pages not yet created. If you are working with a facing page format such as the Book publication type (where you have two pages on the screen such as page two and page three), then the background will also have two pages. Putting an object on the left page makes that object appear on all even-number pages, whereas putting an object on the right makes it appear on all odd-numbered pages.

To return to your document, either pull down the Page menu and select Go to Foreground, or press Ctrl+M again. The superimposed rectangles disappear, and the page number reappears in the lower left corner of the application window.

Hiding the Background

To hide the background for just one page, pull down the Page menu and select Ignore Background. This hides the background only for the selected page. For example, most reports contain a title page which rarely requires a header or footer. You can use the Ignore Background option to prevent the headers or footers from printing on these pages.

You can also hide just one background object, as explained in the following Quick Steps.

Hiding a Background Object

1. Select the Rectangle tool from the Toolbar and draw a box around the object.

   A box appears around the object.

2. Pull down the Layout menu and select Shading.

   The Shading dialog box appears. Clear is the default selection. This means that you can see any object that's under the box you drew.

3. In the Style box, press the → key or click on the second box from the left in the top row; this is the White option.

   The word `Clear` disappears from the Preview box on the right, showing that white shading has been selected.

4. Press the OK button.

   You are returned to the background page. White shading fills the box you drew, hiding any object behind it. However, you can still see the outline of the box you drew.

5. Pull down the Layout menu and select Border.

   The Border dialog box appears.

6. Select None and press the OK button.

   You are returned to the work area. The box you drew now appears with a dotted border, indicating that the border is invisible.   □

Inserting Page Numbers into the Background

Even if you choose not to have Publisher print fancy borders or graphics on each page of your publication, you will probably want to number the pages. Page numbers are especially important in publications you will copy; page numbers help ensure that all the pages are included in each copy and that the pages are collated correctly.

Although you could number the pages in a publication separately, it's more efficient to put Publisher's background in control of page numbering. That way, with just one entry, you can be assured that each and every page is correctly numbered, no matter how many pages are inserted or deleted during the course of page layout. If there is a page, such as the first page or pages between chapters, that you do not want a page number to appear on, you can hide the page number. Refer to the tip in the previous section.

To have the background automatically paginate your publication, use the following Quick Steps.

Q Numbering Pages Automatically

1. Pull down the Page menu and select Go to Background, or press Ctrl+M.

   The background appears, as is shown by the two small overlapping rectangles.

2. Create a small text frame where you want the page number to be. (You can move or resize the text frame at any time.)

   The text frame appears.

3. Pull down the Page menu and select Insert Page Numbers.

   A page number *marker* (#) appears in the text frame, as in Figure 10.3. When you go to the foreground, this marker will change to the correct page number for the current page.

4. To add any text to the page number, such as the word *Page*, move the cursor where you want the text to appear and type the text.

   The text appears where you've typed it.

5. Use the text formatting options to change the character formatting, and/or alignment of the text as desired.

6. Change the size and/or position of the text box as needed.

7. To return to the foreground, pull down the Page menu and select Go to Foreground.

Refer to Chapter 5 for information on formatting text.

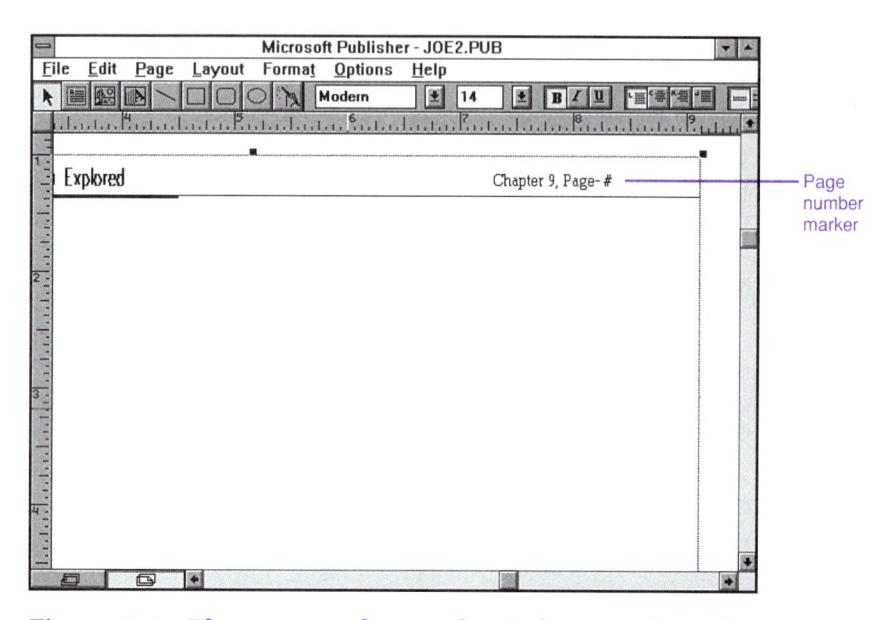

Figure 10.3 The page number marker indicates where the page number will be inserted.

Automatic page numbers in Publisher appear in standard Arabic numerals—as in 1, 2, 3, 4, 185, etc. If you want the numbers in some other system, such as Roman numerals, you have to enter those manually.

Creating Document Headers and Footers

Headers are any information that appears at the top of every page. These can include such things as document titles, chapter names and numbers, and page numbers. These are set up the same way in the background that page numbers were set up in the preceding section. That is, you enter the background by using the Ctrl+M shortcut, create the appropriate text frames, and enter the information you want. Headers may be mirrored as described in the following section "Setting Up Mirrored Backgrounds."

Footers contain information that appears at the bottom of every page. Footers contain the same type of information as headers. They are created in the same manner as headers, except at the bottom of the background, and they can be mirrored also.

Setting Up Mirrored Backgrounds

If you examine this book, or most other long documents, you'll see that the page numbers on even and odd-numbered pages are not in the same place. On even numbered pages, the page number is against the left margin; on odd numbered pages, it's against the right margin. In other words, the pages are *mirrored* to put the page numbers, and any other header or footer text, on the edge of the page, where the reader can find it more easily.

If you want your document to have two mirrored backgrounds, pull down the Layout menu and select Layout Guides. The Layout Guides dialog box appears. Select Create Two Backgrounds With Mirrored Guides to put an X in the check box. In the Preview area above the check box, you'll see two pages depicted instead of one, as shown in Figure 10.4. (The Layout Guides box also changes to give the options Inside and Outside instead of Left and Right. You can use these options to set the inside margin of the mirrored pages.) Press the OK button to create the two background pages.

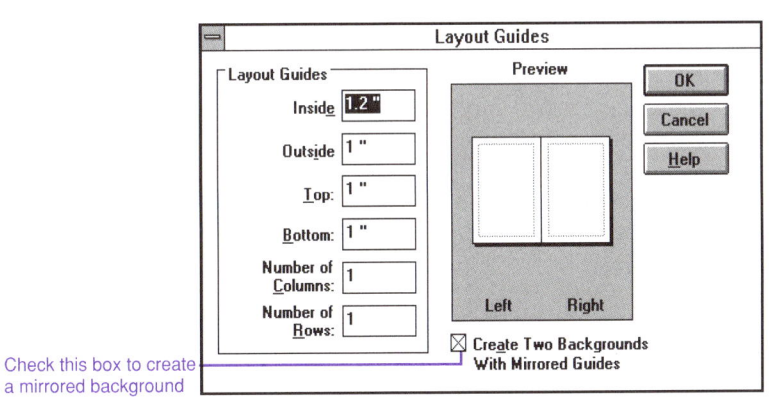

Figure 10.4 Use the Layout Guides dialog box to create a mirrored background.

Once the mirrored background pages are created, you can use them to layout your background material—for example, your headers, footers, and page numbers. To switch to the background, press Ctrl+M or pull down the Page menu and select Go to Background. The background page buttons appear in the lower left corner of the window:

To set up background pages for the left-hand, even number pages, click on the left background page button. To set up background pages for right-hand, odd numbered pages, click on the right page button.

The following steps lead you through the process for creating mirrored background pages which will automatically number the pages in your document:

1. Pull down the Layout menu and select Layout Guides.
2. Select Create Two Backgrounds with Mirrored Guides to put an X in its check box, and then press the OK button.
3. Press Ctrl+M, or pull down the Page menu and select Go To Background.
4. Press the left background page button.
5. Use the left background page to set up the background for the left-hand, even numbered pages. Most elements on this page should be aligned flush left so the elements will appear on the outer edge of the page. To include page numbers, put the page number code flush against the left guide at the top or bottom of the page.
6. Press the right background page button to turn to the right-hand page.
7. Use the right background page to set up the background for the right-hand, odd numbered pages. Most elements on this page should be aligned flush right so the elements will appear on the outer edge of the page. To include page numbers, put the page number code flush against the right guide at the top or bottom of the page.
8. Press Ctrl+M, or pull down the Page menu and select Go To Foreground. This returns you to your document.

Other Background Items

You can put any other items in the background that you feel appropriate. You are limited only by your imagination. For example, a company report might look very nice with a grayed out copy of the company logo behind the text (grayed out so that the text is still readable). If you have a scanned in copy of the company logo, import it as a picture into the background and use the Shading dialog box to change its *foreground* shading to a light color (yellow or cyan) that will show up as a light gray on a noncolor printer. An example is shown in Figure 10.5.

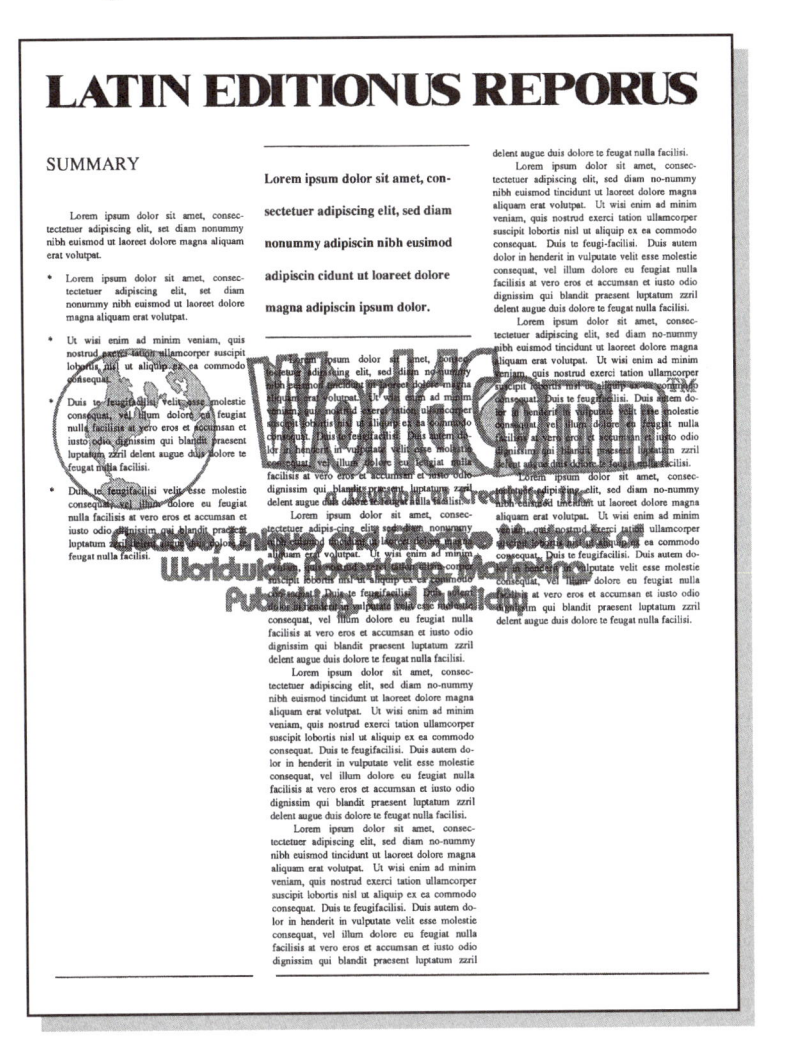

Figure 10.5   *You can add a grayed-out copy of your company logo in the background of any publication.*

> **Tip:** Don't forget that you can use BorderArt in this way also. Do one striking border in the background instead of having to do one for each page.

Or, staying with the company report for a moment, if it's something that really has the company president's dander up (and you may be that president), you might want to put an initial box on each page. The initial box would require each person on the distribution list to initial each and every page after reading it. This technique would also be useful on various types of legal documents.

In general, anything you want to appear on every page goes in the background. You can enter the background and edit, delete, or add objects at any time. Simply press Ctrl+M to move to the background, and then enter your changes. To move back to the foreground, press Ctrl+M again.

What You Have Learned

In this chapter, you learned about working with multipage documents. You learned how to create new pages and place items in the background so they'll appear on every page. Specifically, you learned:

- ▶ You can add pages anywhere in a publication using the Page menu's Insert Pages command, or you can insert single pages by pressing Ctrl+N.
- ▶ Using the Insert Pages dialog box, you can specify that text frames be created on each new page, or that something on one page be copied to as many pages as you specify.
- ▶ Only one page can be deleted at a time, and this is done through the Page menu by clicking on the Delete Page option.
- ▶ The background is where you put page numbers, headers, footers, and any other information that will appear on every page. You enter the background by using the Ctrl+M shortcut. You can then add text, pictures, WordArt, or drawn objects to the background pages.

▶ For a book style publication, the Cre_a_te Two Backgrounds With Mirrored Guides check box (in the Page Setup dialog box) will mirror the objects on each page for greater readability.

Chapter 11

Printing with Publisher

In This Chapter

- Selecting a printer
- Checking your printer setup
- Making the best use of the printer you have
- Aligning the paper in your printer to correspond to the pages on-screen
- Understanding print shop color printing
- Preparing camera-ready copy to be printed in color

The Importance of Printing

Never lose sight of the end result of all the wondrous work you do in Publisher—a printed publication. Whether you print the publication yourself, or take camera-ready copy to a print shop, the printed publication is the goal of all your work. Most people will never see your fancy computer system, or how great your Super VGA display makes the pages look on-screen, but perhaps hundreds or thousands of people will see the publication on paper.

How the publication is printed, then, should be your most important consideration. Take the time to think it out, to choose the right paper for your documents, and to make sure that the printer you are using will do an acceptable job. A great document printed on a cheap printer will impress no one, whereas an average document printed on a laser printer will look pretty impressive.

Selecting a Printer

Although you can use a dot-matrix printer to print your pages, most dot-matrix printers simply cannot provide high-quality output. If you don't want the quality of your publications lost in the printing, get a laser printer.

You can buy two types of laser printers—a PostScript or a non-PostScript. PostScript is a page-description language that Publisher can use to control printing. This language gives the printer much more control over fonts and graphics. With non-PostScript printers you have access to a limited number of fonts. You may be able to install additional fonts by purchasing a cartridge or a font library for the printer. With PostScript printers, you have complete control over fonts and graphics; you can print any font or graphic that the desktop publishing program supports. You can also *scale fonts*; that is, you can change the size of the font in increments of a single point, giving you full control over the size of the font. In addition, PostScript offers a wide range of compatibility with other printers and programs.

If you can't afford a laser printer, consider purchasing an inkjet printer. You can get an HP Deskjet 500 for under $500, about half the cost of a laser printer. The inkjet printer offers high-quality output, but may print more slowly than a laser printer. Another solution is to use a low-quality printer in house to create drafts and then send the files to an outside vendor for high-quality output. Later in this chapter, you will learn how to print a file to disk so it may be printed using another computer connected to a high-quality printer.

> **Tip:** An inkjet printer sprays ink on the page. If you have an inkjet printer, don't use paper that will sop up the ink. Try to find paper that has a glossier finish. With this type of paper, the ink usually takes more time to dry, so be careful when first removing the printed pages from the printer.

Checking Your Printer Setup

Before you print your publication, you should check the printer setup to make sure the publication is printed on the correct printer using the correct printer settings. To check the printer setup, pull down the File menu and select P_rint Setup. This displays the Print Setup dialog box shown in Figure 11.1. Check the following settings to make sure they're correct. For more information on these settings, refer to Chapter 3.

- *Printer.* The two options in the upper left corner of the Print Setup dialog box allow you to select a printer. Select _D_efault Printer to use the default printer or select Specific P_rinter to use a different printer. Use the drop-down list under the Specific Printer option to select a specific printer.

- *Orientation.* Po_r_trait orientation prints the page higher than it is wide. _L_andscape prints the page wider than it is high. Make sure the proper orientation is selected.

- *Paper.* Check the paper in your printer and make sure the paper Si_z_e and _S_ource settings match the paper size and source your printer is using. Use the _S_ource drop-down list to select a paper source if your printer has two or more trays or bins that feed paper into it.

When you are done checking the settings, press the OK button to return to Publisher's work area.

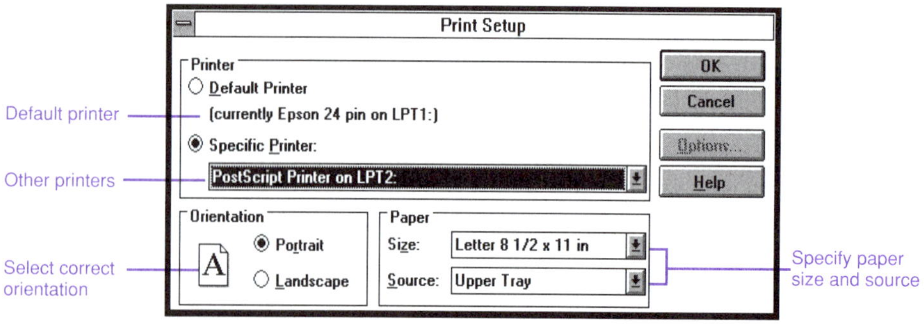

Chapter 11

Figure 11.1 Check the Print Setup dialog box to make sure you are printing the publication on the correct printer.

Calibrating Your Printer

Because Publisher is so precise in formatting a page, you should make sure your printer corresponds as closely as possible with the specified page layout. If you position a line to print 60 points from the top of the page on-screen, you want that line to appear 60 points from the top of the page on paper as well. In order to achieve this corresponding alignment, you may have to make a few minor adjustments to properly position the paper in your printer. By making the proper adjustments, you will be able to create precise page layouts which will transfer consistently to paper.

   Those people lucky enough to have laser printers usually have no worries—all paper positioning is done automatically. If you run into problems, however, consult your printer manual. Some laser printers allow you to print a test sheet with crop marks to check for calibration. You can then use the printer's built-in facilities to tweak the paper alignment to match up with Publisher's on-screen rulers.

   Next easiest to calibrate are printers that have a tractor feed mechanism or a sheet feeder device. A *tractor feed* mechanism is an attachment that fits above a printer's carriage. The mechanism pulls special *fan-fold* paper into the printer. (Fan-fold paper consists of sheets of paper joined at perforations; holes along the left and right edges engage with the pulling devices on the tractor.) For most uses, you'll buy 9.5-by-11 inch fan-fold paper. The extra inch in width accounts for the tear-off tractor holes on the edges of the paper.

When you tear off the holes, the pages are 8.5-by-11 inches—Publisher's default standard.

> **FYIdea:** When shopping for paper, buy 20-pound paper. The 20-pound paper doesn't cost much more than the lightweight 16-pound, and 20-pound paper is much easier to handle, looks better, and lasts longer. If you are purchasing tractor-feed paper, get paper with *micro* perforations. These perforations make tractor-feed paper tear more easily and more evenly, making your final product look more like the single sheet-fed paper you would use in a laser or dot-matrix printer.

Regardless of whether you have a tractor-feed device or a sheet feeder, you need to calibrate it. This is easy enough to do. You simply print a test page at Publisher's default page layout settings and make any necessary changes. Your goal is to get the printed page to match the measurements displayed on-screen. Here is a very short, easy procedure to accomplish this:

1. Start Publisher or pull down the File menu and select Create New Publication.
2. Press the Blank Page button and then press OK. Publisher creates a blank 8.5-by-11 inch page. By default, this page will have one-inch margins all around.
3. Click on the line tool on the Toolbar, and draw a line from the left margin guide line along the top guide to the right margin guide line. Be exact! If necessary, use the Snap to Guides option (Ctrl+W) to position the pointer precisely on the guideline.
4. Do the same thing along the bottom guideline, and then press Ctrl+P to print the page. You will get a page with a line at the top and one at the bottom.
5. Take a ruler and measure the distance from the left end of each line to the left edge of the paper. Each line should start exactly one inch from the left edge of the paper. If they don't, adjust the tractor-feed mechanism and reprint the page.
6. Measure the length of each line—they should measure exactly 6.5 inches. If they don't, select Layout Guides from the Layout menu, and check to make sure the Left and Right layout guides are each set to 1 inch. If that's not the cause, check your printer installation in Windows. If that doesn't correct the problem, refer to your printer manual.

Chapter 11

7. Measure the distance between the top edge of the paper and the top line and from the bottom edge of the paper to the bottom line. This distance should be one inch in each case. If this is not so, use the feed adjustments on your printer to adjust the position of the print head in relation to the top of the page. If you manually feed the paper into your printer, note the exact location of the print head in relation to the top edge of the paper for future reference.

Once the printer is calibrated, you have a *consistent starting point*; you know that what you see on screen is what you will get on paper. You can then experiment with various page layout options and be confident that your changes will be reflected on the printed page.

Printing Your Publications

Once your printer is calibrated, you should not need to adjust it again. You can begin printing the publications you created. The actual process of printing a Publisher document is done via the Print dialog box. To access it, pull down the File menu and select Print. The Print dialog box appears, as shown in Figure 11.2.

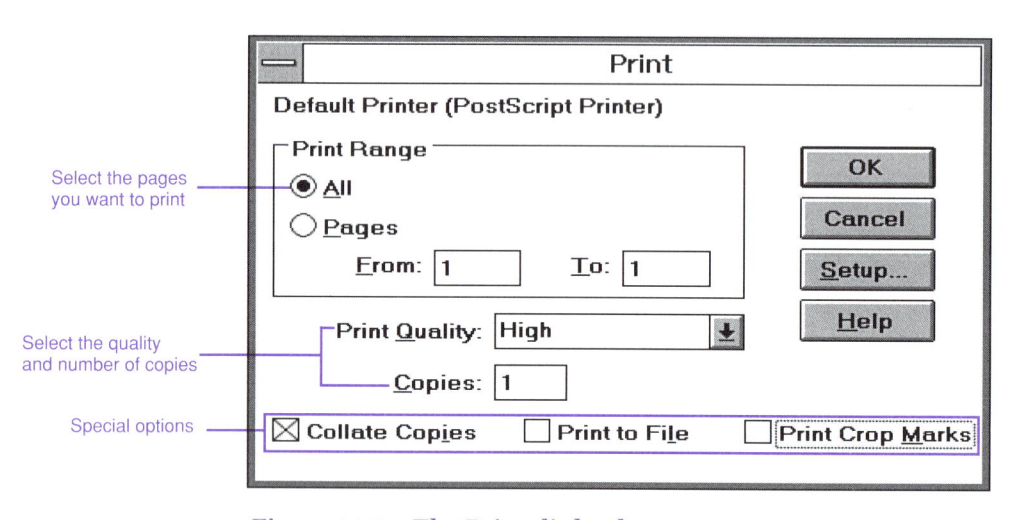

Figure 11.2   The Print dialog box prompts you to enter your printing instructions.

In the upper left corner of the box is the name of the selected printer. In the figure, the author's default printer is an NEC 890 printer, which uses the PostScript page description language. If you have two or more printers installed in Windows, using them for different purposes, you should check this line every time, just in case another Windows application had changed the current printer to an inappropriate one for the document you are now printing. If the right printer is not selected, click on the Setup button. This will give you the Print Setup dialog box, which you can use to select the right printer.

Directly below the line on which the current printer is given, you'll see the Print Range box. If you click on All (the default option), a black dot appears in the circle. This indicates that every page in your document will be printed. If you want to print only a *range* of pages, such as page 1 to page 3, then click on the Pages option and edit the From and To text boxes to reflect the pages you want printed.

Below the Print Range box is the Print Quality drop-down list box. There are three choices—high, medium, and low. Low is useful for quick draft copies to get a general idea of how the page will look in print. (Because ribbons and ink cartridges cost so much money, you should never print a high-quality draft until you are ready to print the final draft.) High, of course, is what you want to use for the final draft. Medium is an intermediate setting that is useful if Low does not give you all the detail you need.

The Copies text box determines how many copies of your document Publisher will print. Usually, it is more efficient to print one high-quality copy and then use a copy machine (or take the original to a copy shop) to make the additional copies.

Finally, at the bottom of the Print dialog box are three check boxes, which give you more advanced options:

▶ Collate Copies. If you are printing more than one copy of a multipage document, place an x in this box to have Publisher print the pages in order for each copy of the document. For example, if you are printing three copies of a three-page document, Publisher would print pages 1, 2, 3; pages 1, 2, 3; and pages 1, 2, 3 instead of three copies of page 1, three copies of page 2, and three copies of page 3.

▶ Print to File. This feature is very useful if you have access to a system that is connected to a higher-quality printer than the one you're using. If you select this option and then press the OK button to print the document, a dialog box will appear asking for a filename. The procedure is explained in the following section.

▶ Print Crop Marks. If the document is to be printed by a print shop on smaller paper than the paper used by your printer, place an X in this box to print crop marks on the page. Crop marks help the print shop people line up your pages accurately. An example of this is when you design your own business card (as explained in Chapter 13). The print shop will need those crop marks on the master camera-ready copy you give them.

When you are done selecting your printing options, press the OK button to start printing. Publisher displays a dialog box, telling you that printing is currently in progress. Keep in mind that because Publisher prints through the Windows Print Manager, the file is printed first to your hard disk and then sent to your printer. Once Windows has completed writing the print file information to disk, you can continue working in Windows. Windows completes the printing process in the background.

Printing to a File on Disk

If you don't have a laser printer but you know someone who does, you can print your Publisher file to disk and then print the file using the other system, even if Publisher is not installed on that system. Find someone with a PostScript machine if possible; that way you will have access to the standard 35 PostScript fonts.

First, use the Printer Setup option in Windows to set up Windows to print to the high-quality printer. Even though your system is not connected to this printer, you can set up the printer in Windows. Once the printer is set up, run Publisher and select the Print Setup command from the File menu. Use the Print Setup dialog box to select the new printer.

When you are ready to print your publication, use the Print to File option in Publisher's Print dialog box to print the publication file to disk. When you click the OK button to print the publication, Publisher will display the dialog box, shown in Figure 11.3, prompting you to type a name and specify a location for the file. Type the name (using the .PRN extension) and select a drive and directory where you want the file stored. If you are printing to a file on a floppy disk, insert a floppy disk in the drive you specified. Press the OK button. Publisher prints the file to disk, creating a .PRN file which contains a print file formatted specifically for the printer set up in Windows.

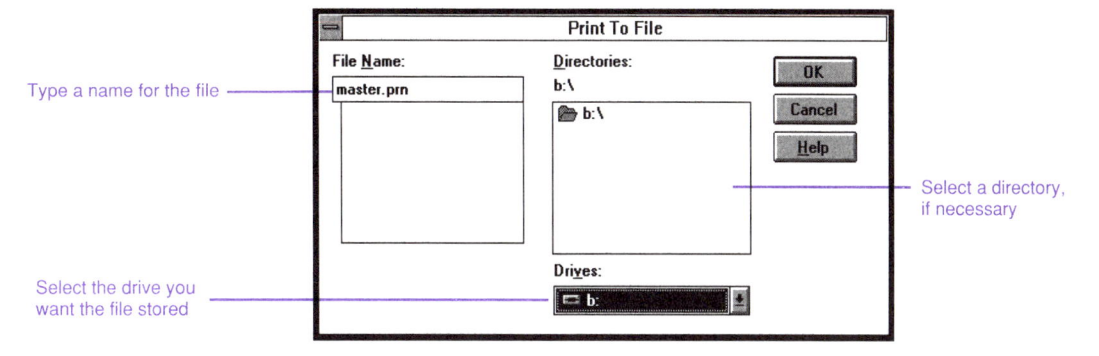

Figure 11.3 Use the Print To File dialog box to give the print file a name and location.

The disk file can then be taken to the computer that has the better printer and printed out. To print the file, insert the floppy disk that contains the file into one of the disk drives on the computer you are using to print the publication. Change to the drive that contains the file, and enter the DOS COPY command in the following form:

```
copy filename.ext >prn
```

For example, to print a file named MASTER.PRN to a printer connected to the LPT1 port, you would enter

```
copy master.prn >prn
```

DOS prints the file as requested.

Printing for Color Reproduction

If you have a color printer, you can print in color simply by including color objects in your publication. Many of Publisher's dialog boxes (including Border, Shading, and Character) contain a Color drop-down list box that allows you to set the color of the selected object.

Also, many of the ClipArt pictures included with Publisher are in color. Of course, if you have a monochrome monitor, you won't be able to see on-screen how your document will print, but as long as you have a color printer, your publications will print just fine in color.

But what if you don't have a color printer? Are you doomed to create colorless publications? Not quite. You have two options. First, you could print your publication to disk and take it to a printer who has an IBM-compatible computer connected to a high-quality color printer, and pay the printer to print your files for you. Good luck; you may spend half your life looking for such a print shop.

The other alternative is to prepare camera-ready pages and take them to a print shop. These camera-ready pages consist of black-and-white pages that the print shop can use to create printing plates. The print shop can then use the printing plates with color ink to print your publication in color.

The Two Methods of Printing in Color

There are two methods of printing color—*spot* and *process*. Spot color allows you to print various elements on a page in different colors. This book, for example, was printed in two colors using the spot color process. Most of the text appears black, while some headings and other special items appear in a *second color*.

How was this done? Each page of this book was originally printed as two pages using a high-quality black-and-white printer. One page contained all the black elements, and a second page contained all the color elements (printed in black-and-white). Although all the elements on both pages were printed in black-and-white, the color objects were on one page and the black-and-white objects were on another page. In other words, the black and color objects were *separated*. The print shop used these pages to create two separate printing plates, one to apply the black ink to the page and the other to apply the color ink. (If you look very closely, you may see some places where the two inks did not align properly on the page.)

The spot color process is useful for creating business cards and brochures on which you want to add color as a decorative element or to highlight important items. Although the spot color process can be used to print as many different colors as you like on a page, the two-color scheme is often used because it is a fairly inexpensive way to enhance a publication. Besides, you don't want to overdo it by using too many colors.

Process color is the method used to print such things as color photographs. It is also referred to as the *four-color process*. This does not mean that four separate colors are printed one at a time, but that the four colors are blended to produce all the different colors in the photograph. You often see this process used in magazines. Because you cannot do process color using Publisher, I won't explain it in detail. The closest you can come is to create your publication and then have the print shop paste in the four-color elements for you.

Creating the Color Separations for Spot Color

Creating the camera-ready pages for using the spot color process is fairly simple. First, as you should already be doing, you must visualize each page in layers. Up to this point, the layers concerned objects that were on top of or under others. Now, you need to think of the layers in terms of layers of different colored inks. The objects on each page of your publication will need to be *separated out*. That is, all objects on a page that are to appear in one color must be printed on a single sheet of paper. All objects that must appear in another color must be printed on another sheet of paper, and so on. To create the camera-ready pages to send to the printer, you must make these *color separations*.

To create the necessary color separations, you must create two or more additional pages for each page in your publication. You then select and cut all objects that you want to appear in one color from the original page of your publication and paste them onto another page. One color will be your *base color*, or the color that most of the document is to be printed in. This is usually, but does not have to be, black. All base color objects need to be printed on the first color separation page, because the larger areas of color have to be printed first to prevent them from covering up the smaller areas.

The example shown in Figures 11.4 to 11.6 illustrates the process you must follow to create the necessary color separations. Figure 11.4 shows the business card layout for one of this author's other books. The title of the book and the author's name are to be green, so those objects were selected and cut from the first page and pasted onto the second page, as shown in Figure 11.6. Figure 11.5 shows the objects left on the first page; these items are to be printed black.

Chapter 11

Figure 11.4   A business card layout before color separations.

Figure 11.5   The first color separation contains the elements that are to be printed black.

> **FYIdea:** When creating color separations, keep in mind that the print shop will print the colors only as bold as the blacks on your printout. If you want an object to appear in a good, solid color, then print it 100% black. If you want the color to appear more pale, then print it in a shade of gray.

Master Ultima

by **Ralph Roberts**
author of 23 books

Figure 11.6   The second color separation contains those elements that are to be printed green.

The following Quick Steps lead you through the process for creating color separations in Publisher. These steps cover the process for a single page. If you have a multipage document, repeat the steps for each page that requires color separations.

> **Tip:** Before you create your color separations, pull down the File menu and use the Save As option to save the file under another name. If you damage the publication while making the color separations, you can then return to the original file.

Making Color Separations

1. Turn to the page for which you want to make the color separations.

2. Pull down the Page menu and select Insert Pages.

   The Insert Pages dialog box appears.

3. In the Number of New Pages text box, type the number of pages you'll need for your color separations minus one page.

   For example, if you plan on printing in two colors, you will need one additional page.

4. Press the OK button.

   The new pages are inserted and you are returned to the document on the first page inserted.

5. Turn back one page to the page that contains the objects you want to separate out.

6. Select all the objects that are to be printed in the topmost spot color (hold down the Ctrl key to select more than object at a time).

   The base color objects will remain on the first page. Other colors should be separated out. As a general rule, put the smallest patch of color on the topmost color separation page.

7. Pull down the Edit menu and select Cut, or press Ctrl+X.

   The selected objects are removed from the page and placed in the Windows Clipboard.

8. Turn to the last page you inserted for the current color separations.

9. Pull down the Edit menu and select Paste, or press Ctrl+V.

   The objects from the Windows Clipboard are pasted in the same locations on the current page. This is the top color separation.

10. Repeat the process as needed to create the other color separations. Remember to paste objects onto pages starting at the last page and working backward. The first page will then contain all objects to be printed in the base color.

11. Pull down the File menu and select Print.

12. Select the Print Crop Marks option to put an X in the check box, and then press the OK button to print the publication.

    The crop marks allow the print shop people to align the colors on the page.

    ☐

> **Tip:** To get crop marks to print, the page you are printing must be smaller than the paper on which you are printing. If you are printing an 8.5-by-11 inch page on 8.5-by-11 inch paper, the crop marks will not print, even though you've selected that option.

> **FYIdea:** If you want to get fancy and you have a laser printer, print the first page of your color separations (the base color) on regular paper and print the remaining pages on transparencies (available at most office supply stores). Place the transparencies over the base color page in order (topmost color on the top); use the crop marks to align the separations. Staple or tape them together. You now can see the complete document again and flip through the color *overlays* (another term for color separations).

What You Have Learned

Although you do most of your page layout work on-screen, what really matters is how your publication looks in print. In this chapter, you learned how to choose a printer and print your publications for your own use or for use by a print shop. Specifically, you learned the following:

- ▶ Choosing the right printer for the job is important. A PostScript laser printer is the best choice by far, but the ink jet and better dot-matrix machines give good results also.
- ▶ The printer must be installed in Windows, because Publisher prints all publications through the Windows Print Manager.
- ▶ You can have more than one printer installed in Windows, choosing the one most appropriate for the job. Just be sure the new printer selected is physically connected to the system.

► Calibrating your printer consists of adjusting the paper in your printer so the output matches the on-screen version. You should calibrate your printer before you begin printing publications.

► To print a document, you pull down the File menu and select Print. The Print dialog box lets you enter your printing instructions.

► To create camera-ready pages for a print shop to print your publication in color, you must create color separations for each page of your publication.

► To create color separations, you must print all the objects that appear in a different color on a separate page.

Chapter 12

Working with Publication Files and Templates

In This Chapter

- *Opening files you've created and saved*
- *Getting to know Publisher's templates*
- *How Publisher's templates differ from PageWizards*
- *Using Publisher's templates to create mailing labels, business cards, brochures, and other publications*
- *Saving your own publication file as a template*
- *Managing directories and files in Windows*

Working with Existing Files

Once you've created and saved a publication, that publication is stored in a file on disk. You can then open the file at any time to modify your publication. But the files you created and saved are not the only files you can use. Publisher comes with several *templates*, which contain predesigned page layouts for mailing labels, business cards, memos, reports, resumes, and other commonly used publications. You can use any of these templates to create customized publications to fit your needs.

In this chapter, you will learn how to open your publication files and use Publisher's template files. You'll also learn how to save your own publication files as templates and how to keep your files organized.

Opening an Existing File

Once you've saved a file to disk, you can open that file at any time to view its contents, print it, or modify it. To open a file, pull down the File menu and select Open Existing Publication. The Open Existing Publication dialog box appears, as shown in Figure 12.1. You will recognize most of its features, because this dialog box is almost identical to the Import Text dialog box you saw in Chapter 4.

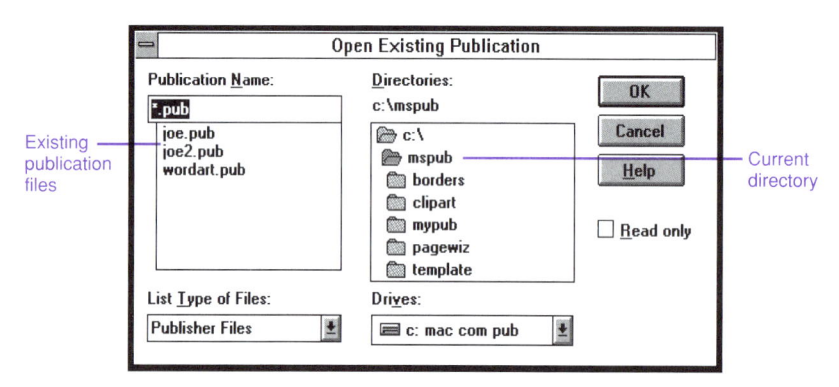

Figure 12.1 *The Open Existing Publication dialog box allows you to open one of your publication files.*

This box prompts you to enter the following information about the publication file you want to open. Work through the options in the order they are listed:

▶ *Type of File.* By default, Publisher assumes you are going to import a file created in Publisher. If you created the file in another program, click on the arrow to the right of this drop-down list box, and select the format in which the file was saved. If you select a file created in another program, Publisher imports the text as if you had chosen the Import Text option, creating the necessary text frames.

▶ *Publication Name.* This list box displays a list of files that have the filename extension used most often for the type of file you selected. To view a list of files having a different extension, type `*.ext` where *ext* is the extension of the file you want to import and press Enter. You can type a filename (if you know the entire name of the file), or you can type a wild-card entry to view a list of files.

▶ *Drive.* Publisher displays the letter of the currently active drive. If the file is saved on another drive, pull down the Drives list and select the letter of the drive.

▶ *Directory.* Under the Directories option is the path to the current drive and directory. If the file is stored in another directory on the current drive, use the directory tree that's displayed under the path to move to the directory that contains the file.

As you move through the directory tree, the list displayed in the Publication Name box changes to display the names of those files in the currently selected directory which match the filename entry you typed. Double-click on the file you want to open or highlight it and press Enter. If the file is a Publisher file, it appears on-screen. If the file is in some other format, a dialog box will appear, indicating that the conversion is in process.

The following Quick Steps summarize how to open a publication file.

Opening a Publication File

1. Pull down the File menu and select Open Existing Publication.

   The Open Existing Publication dialog box appears.

2. Select the format in which the file was saved from the List Type of Files drop-down list.

   The format appears in the List Type of Files box.

3. Edit the filename entry in the Publication Name box, if needed, and press Enter.

   If any files in the current directory match your entry, the names of those files appear in the list.

4. Select the drive where the file is stored from the Drives drop-down list.

   The directory tree above the Drives box changes to show the directories on the selected drive.

5. Use the Directory tree to select the directory in which the file was saved.

The Publication Name list changes to show a list of files in the selected directory which match the filename entry you typed.

6. Select the name of the file you want to import from the Publication Name list.

The file is open, and the publication appears on-screen. □

You can now modify the publication in any way or print the publication. If you modify the publication, be sure to save the file to disk to preserve your changes.

Understanding Templates

As you've seen earlier in this book, Publisher is much more than a basic desktop publishing program. It comes complete with a ClipArt library, a collection of decorative borders, and a PageWizards feature, which leads you through the process of creating customized publications. But that's not all. Publisher also comes with a set of *templates*, which you can use to create your own customized resumes, brochures, and other publications.

What are templates? They are predesigned page layouts that show you where to insert text and pictures. When you select a template, you see a finished publication on-screen, complete with text and graphics. You can then replace the text and pictures with any text and pictures you want to use for your publication. Unlike PageWizards, templates do not lead you through the process of creating the publication. They simply appear in their complete form, allowing you to make your changes. Table 12.1 provides a list of Publisher's templates.

Table 2.1 Microsoft Publisher's templates.

Template	What It Does
Aver 5260-5263	Mailing label template allows you to print a sheet of mailing labels.
Bizcard 1 & 2 and Bizcards	Business card templates. Bizcard 1 & 2 allow you to create a single business card. Bizcards provides a sheet of various business card layouts.

Template	What It Does
Brochure	Allows you to create a three-fold brochure.
Catalog	Provides two pages of catalog entries which you can customize to create your own catalog.
Envelop 1 & 2	Use this template to print your return address in the upper left corner of a letter-size envelope. You may want to modify this template as explained later to include a place for the mailing address of the recipient.
Flyer	Presents a garage sale announcement flyer. You can customize the flyer for any occasion.
Label 1 & 2	Presents a layout for a stick-on label. You can use these labels for addresses, file folders, or VCR tapes. (See Figure 12.2.)
Ltrhead 1 & 2	Provides two types of letterhead, one that prints centered and another that prints in the upper left corner.
Memo and Memoz	Two types of memos. You can print the memos as is and then write your message on the memo, or type the information before printing.
Pricelst	Allows you to create a price list, including a picture of each product, its order number, a price, and a description of the product. (See Figure 12.3.)
Prodinfo	Presents a product information sheet that contains a picture of the product, a description of it, a list of its top selling points, and a number to call to order.
Report and Reportz	Allows you to create your own reports and summaries.
Resume	Provides a basic resume outline on which you can model your own resume.
Roster	Provides a table structure you can use to keep a list of names, addresses, and phone numbers. (See Figure 12.4.)

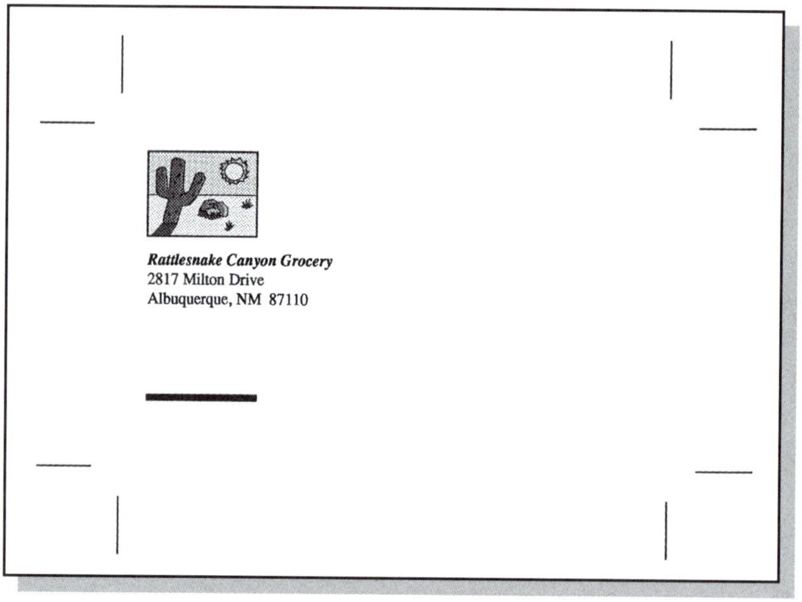

Chapter 12

Figure 12.2 Use the Label 1 template to create mailing labels, labels for file folders, or even labels for your VCR tapes.

> **FYIdea:** You may have noticed that many of Publisher's templates use Latin text as placeholders. Why? Because an unfamiliar language will cause the user to focus on the *design* of the publication rather than its *content*. Greek text is often used in professional publications for the same purpose, and hence has given rise to the term *Greeking the text*. So, if this concept is Greek to you, it should be.

In the following sections, you will learn how to use Publisher's templates to create publications, how to create your own templates from publications you've created, and how to modify templates.

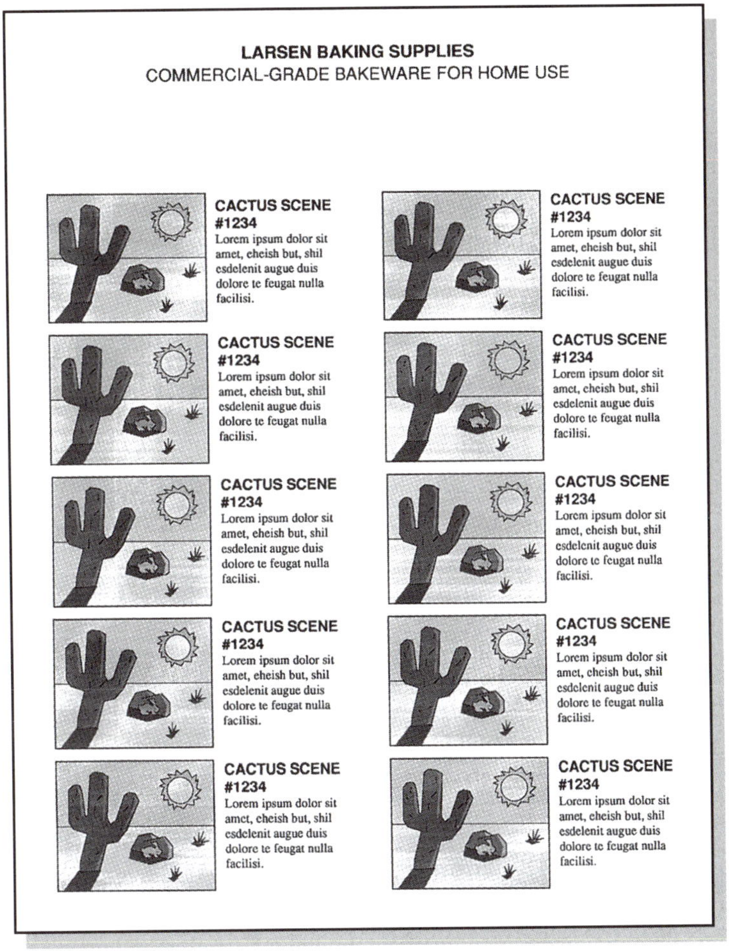

Figure 12.3   A price list can be effective for advertising; you may want to add a phone number to the list.

Opening and Using a Template

To use one of Publisher's templates to create a publication, start Publisher or pull down the File menu and select Create New Publication. The Start Up or Create New Publication dialog box appears, as shown in Figure 12.5. Press the Templates button to view a list of Publisher's templates.

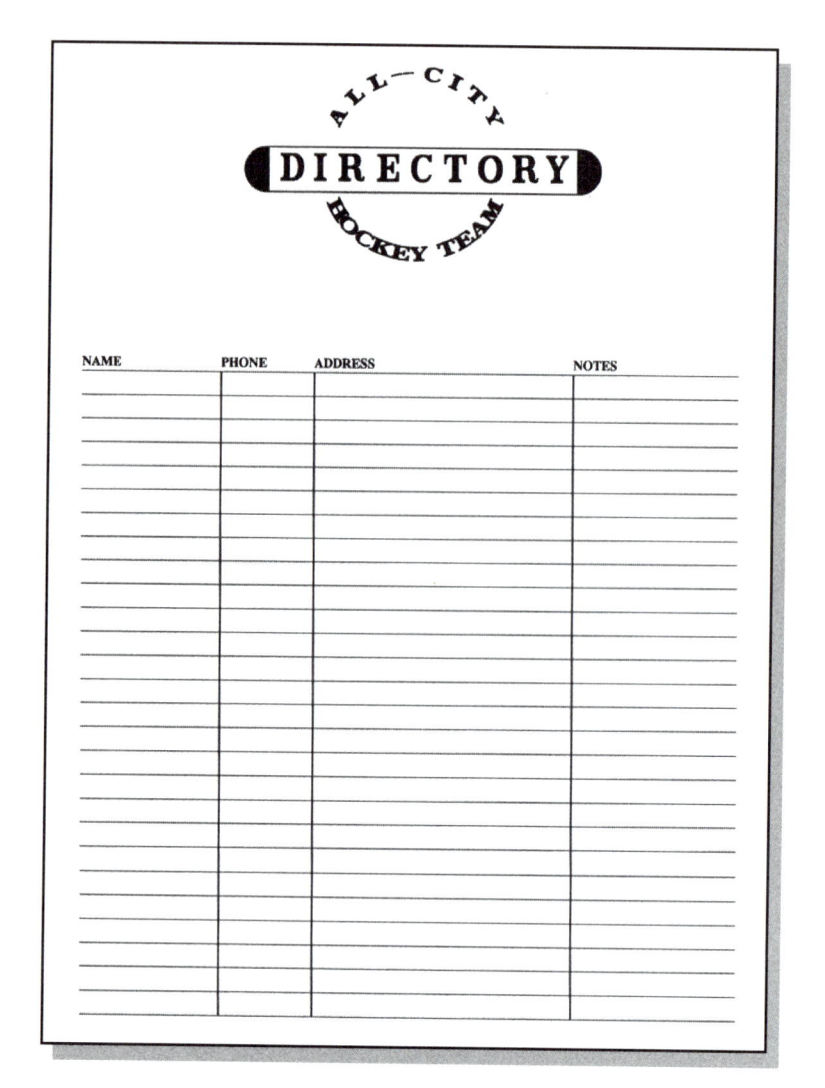

Figure 12.4 Use the roster template to create a phone and address list.

Select a template from the list, and press the OK button. Publisher opens a *copy* of the template and displays it on-screen, as shown in Figure 12.6. It is important to realize that the template you see on-screen is only a copy of the original. As you make your changes, you will change only this copy, not the original, so you can use the template over and over to create as many customized publications as you want. The original template is never changed.

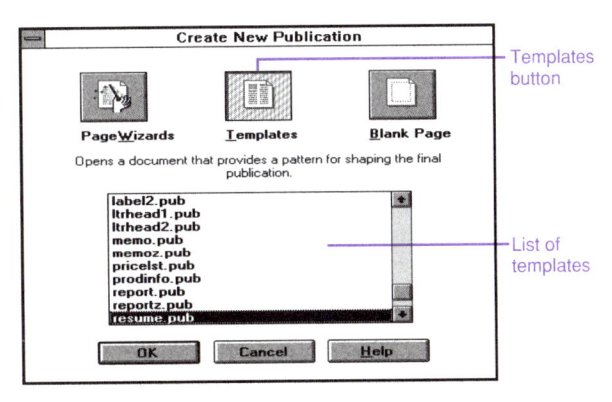

Figure 12.5   The Create New Publication dialog box allows you to use a template for creating your new publication.

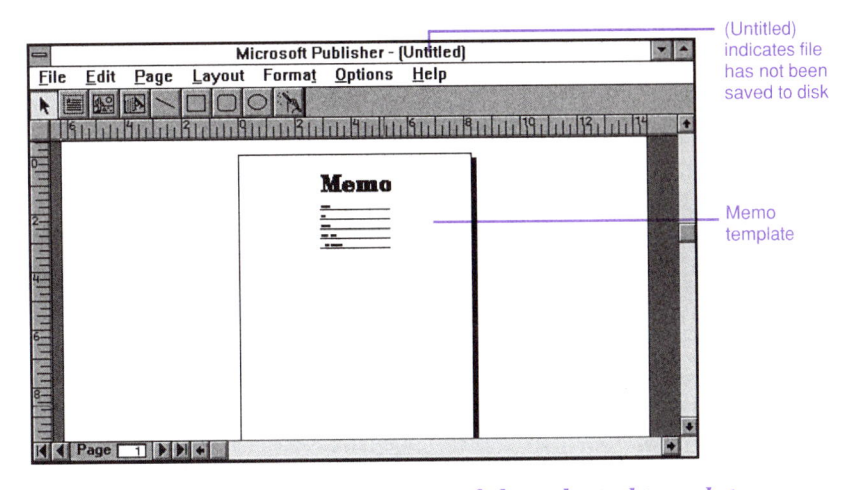

Figure 12.6   Publisher opens a copy of the selected template, allowing you to add your changes and enhancements.

Once you've modified the template, you should save it to disk. Pull down the File menu and select the Save command. The first time you save the file, Publisher displays the Save As dialog box. You must then specify a location and name for the new file you've created. Refer to Chapter 2 for more information about saving a file using the Save As dialog box.

Creating Your Own Templates

Creating an effective design for a publication takes a great deal of work. You may spend hours arranging and rearranging the elements on each page before the resulting design is acceptable. So once you've developed an effective page layout, you will probably want to use that layout for more than one publication. To use the layout over and over, you can save the publication to disk as a *template*. You can then use this template just as you use any of the templates that came with Publisher.

To save an existing publication as a template, open the publication file, so the file appears on-screen. Pull down the File menu and select Save As. The Save As dialog box appears, as shown in Figure 12.7. Press Alt+T or click on the Template option to put an X in its check box. A message appears above the option, indicating all templates will be saved to the TEMPLATE directory.

If you don't change the name of the file, the file will be saved under the same name but in the TEMPLATE directory rather than in the directory in which it was originally saved. You can, however, change the name of the file if you wish. To complete the Save operation, press the OK button. If a file of the same name already exists in the TEMPLATE directory, Publisher displays a warning box asking if you want to overwrite the file with the new one.

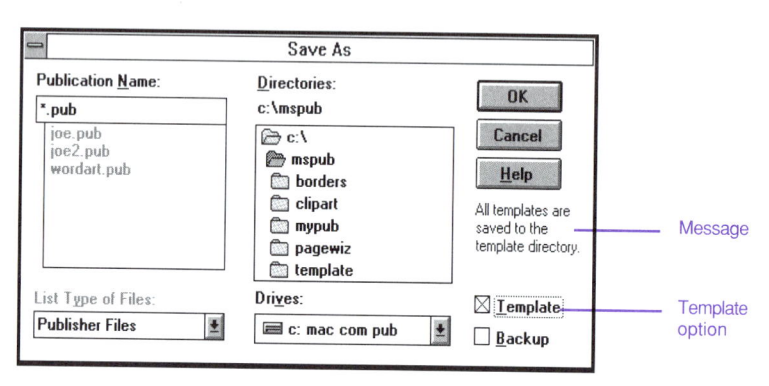

Figure 12.7 Use the Template option to save an existing publication as a template.

The following Quick Steps summarize the process for saving a publication as a template.

Saving a Publication as a Template

1. Open the publication you want to save as a template. — The publication appears on-screen.
2. Pull down the File menu and select Save As. — The Save As dialog box appears.
3. To change the name of the file, type a name in the Publication Name text box. This step is optional. — Follow the DOS filename conventions explained in Chapter 2, and use the extension .PUB, so you will know in the future that this file was created in Publisher.
4. Select the Template option to put an X in the check box. — A message appears above the option indicating that the template file will be saved in the TEMPLATE directory.
5. Press the OK button. — Publisher saves the publication as a template to the TEMPLATE directory. □

Now, whenever you press the Templates button on the Start Up or Create New Publication screen, your template will be listed along with all the others.

Customizing Templates

Whenever you tell Publisher that you want to use a template to create a publication, Publisher displays a copy of the template on-screen. You then modify the copy to suit your needs and save the copy to disk. In other words, you are not changing the template itself; you are changing only a copy of the template.

But what if you want to change the template itself? Say you like the Memo template, but you don't like the fact that the template centers everything; you'd rather have the memo appear flush left. You have two options:

▶ You can keep the original template unchanged and use it to create your own customized memo template. To do this, you would have to use the template to create your own memo as explained earlier, and then save the file as a template using a filename other than MEMO.PUB.

▶ You can edit the MEMO.PUB template and save it to disk, making your changes permanently affect the template.

To change the template permanently, pull down the File menu and select Open Existing Publication. The Open Existing Publication dialog box appears, as shown in Figure 12.8. Use the directory tree to change to the TEMPLATE directory, which is a subdirectory of the MSPUB directory. A list of templates appears, all having the .PUB filename extension. Select the template you want to modify and press the OK button. The template appears on-screen, awaiting your changes.

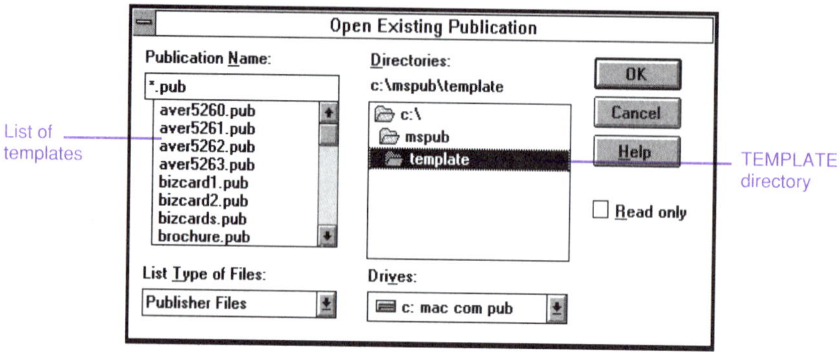

Figure 12.8 To change a template permanently, open the template as a publication file.

Caution: The template is now open as a publication file rather than as a template file. Any changes you make to the template become permanent when you save the file to disk.

Modify the template as desired. When you are done, pull down the File menu and select Save. The template is saved to disk, overwriting the original template file.

Working with Publication Files and Templates

Managing Your Directories and Files

Throughout this chapter and throughout much of this book, you have seen that many of Publisher's program files and the files you create and use are stored in separate directories on your hard disk. For example, Publisher's ClipArt is stored in the CLIPART directory, and templates are stored in the TEMPLATE directory.

As you get more involved in Publisher, and as you create more and more publication and template files, you'll find that you need some way to organize these files on disk. The following sections explain how to use the Windows File Manager to manage files and directories without ever having to leave Windows.

To run the File Manager, select the Directory icon:

from the Main program window. If the Main window is not shown, pull down the Windows menu and select Main. Then double-click on the Directory icon, or use the arrow keys to highlight it and press Enter. The File Manager window appears, as shown in Figure 12.9. Note that some directories in the list have plus signs; these directories contain subdirectories.

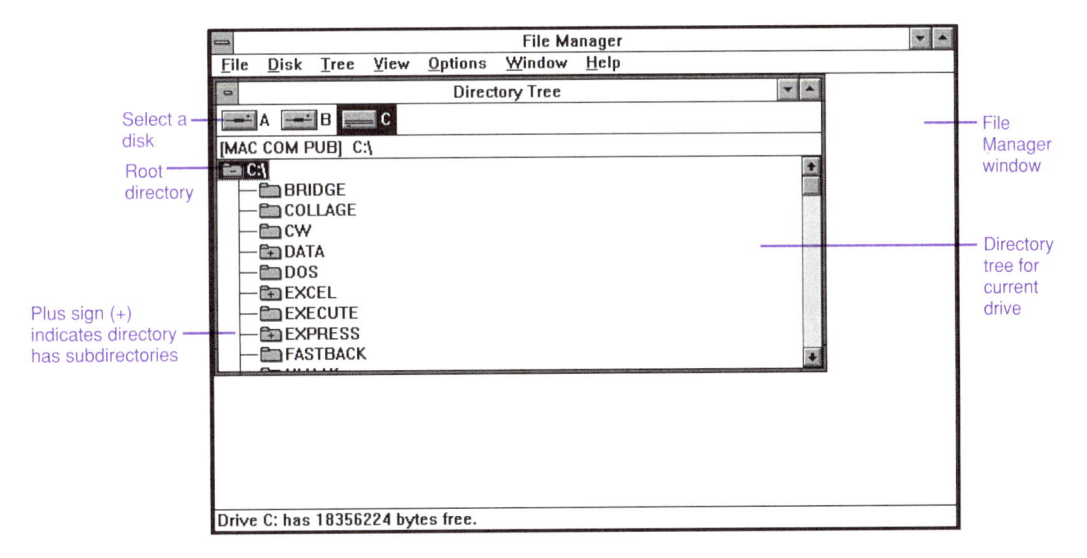

Figure 12.9 Use Windows File Manager to manage your Publisher files and directories.

Before you can manage your files and directories in the File Manager, you should know a few techniques for moving around in the Manager. The following list provides the basics:

- ▶ To change drives, click on the drive letter at the top of the Directory Tree window. If you are using the keyboard, press the Tab key to move up to the drive list, use the arrow keys to highlight a drive letter, and press Enter.
- ▶ To change directories, click on the directory you want to activate, or use the arrow keys to highlight the directory. You can use the scroll bar on the right of the window or press ↓ to move through the directory tree.
- ▶ To display the subdirectories of a directory, click on the plus sign to the left of the directory's name, or highlight the directory and press the + key. The subdirectories are displayed and a minus sign replaces the plus sign. To reverse the process, press the hyphen (-) key or click on the minus sign.
- ▶ To open a directory (to work with the files it contains), double-click on the directory or highlight it and press Enter. A directory window opens showing the files and subdirectories (if any) contained in the selected directory. You can open more than one directory window at a time.
- ▶ To activate a directory window, click anywhere on the window or use the Control menu to switch windows.
- ▶ To close the File Manager, pull down the File menu and select Exit or double-click on the Control Menu box in the upper left corner of the screen.

Now that you know how to move around in the File Manager, you can move on to the more practical tasks of reorganizing your Publisher files.

Creating Directories in Windows

During the installation process, Publisher created several directories on your hard disk, including a directory called MSPUB which contains all of Publisher's program files, and several subdirectories: BORDERS, CLIPART, PAGEWIZ, and TEMPLATE. These directories help organize the files by placing them in logical groups. As you create files, you may want to add directories to organize your own files.

Working with Publication Files and Templates

For example, earlier in this book, we suggested that you save all the files you create in the MSPUB directory. This groups the files in the same directory that contains all of Publisher's program files. A more efficient way to organize the files would be to place them in their own directory, for example, in a directory called MYPUB. You can create this directory as a subdirectory to MSPUB by performing the following Quick Steps.

Making a Directory

1. Highlight the directory under which you want the new subdirectory to appear by clicking on it or using the arrow keys to highlight it.

    For example, to create a subdirectory MYPUB under the MSPUB directory, you would click on the MSPUB directory name.

2. Pull down the File menu and select Create Directory.

    The Create Directory dialog box appears, as shown in Figure 12.10.

3. Type a name for the new subdirectory. For example, type **mypub**.

4. Press the OK button.

    The new subdirectory is added under the current directory.

5. If the directory is not visible because the current directory is collapsed, click on the plus sign next to the directory name or press the + key.

Figure 12.10 *The Create Directory dialog box prompts you to type a name for the new subdirectory.*

Moving Files from One Directory to Another

Once you have a separate directory for your publication files, you can move your publication files from the MSPUB directory to the MYPUB directory. The process consists of two basic steps: selecting the files you want to move and entering the move command. To select files, activate the directory window that contains the files you want to move, and then use either of the following two techniques:

- To select a group of files, hold down the Shift key and click on the first and last files in the group of files you want to move.
- To select several individual files, hold down the Ctrl key and click on each file you want to move. To deselect a file, click on it again.

Once the files are selected, pull down the File menu and select Move, or press F7. The Move dialog box appears, as shown in Figure 12.11. This box prompts you to specify a destination—a directory where you want the files moved. Type a complete path to the directory (for example, type `c:\mspub\mypub`), and then press the Move button.

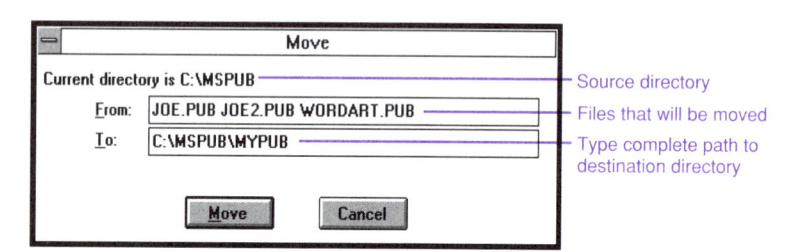

Figure 12.11 The Move dialog box prompts you to enter a path telling the File Manager where to move the files.

The following Quick Steps summarize the process for moving files in Windows.

Moving Files

1. Activate the directory window for the directory that contains the files you want to move.

2. Select the file(s) you want to move. — The selected filenames appear highlighted.
3. Pull down the File menu and select Move, or press F7. — The Move dialog box appears, prompting you to specify a destination directory for the selected files.
4. Type a complete path to the destination directory, and then press the Move button. — The selected files are moved to the destination directory you specified. ☐

You can use a similar procedure to copy files from one directory or drive to another. Follow the same procedure, but instead of selecting the Move command, select the Copy command or press F8.

> **Tip:** A quicker way to copy or move files is to display one directory window for the source directory and another for the destination directory. (You can move and resize the windows as needed to work with both windows.) Use the mouse to drag the files from the source window to the destination window. To move files this way, point to one of the selected files in the source directory window, hold down the Alt key, drag the files to the destination directory window, and release the mouse button. To copy files, point to one of the selected files, hold down the Ctrl key, drag the files to the destination window, and release the mouse button.

Other File Manager Techniques

Although the preceding sections discussed several important uses for the Windows File Manager, File Manager contains several other features not mentioned. For example, you can create, copy, and move entire directories, delete files, search for files, rename files and directories, and more. Refer to the Windows documentation that came with your Windows program for more information on using the File Manager to organize your files, directories, and disks.

What You Have Learned

As you work with your publications and templates, you'll discover the real time-saving feature of all computers—they prevent you from having to start from scratch. You can use the files on disk and modify those files to create new designs and customized publications without having to start from the beginning. In specific, you learned the following:

- ▶ To work with a publication you saved to disk, you must open the file by selecting the Open Existing Publication command from the File menu.
- ▶ Publisher comes with a number of templates, which you can use to create commonly used publications. When you use a template, Publisher opens a copy of the template. You modify the copy, leaving the original intact.
- ▶ To use a template, select Create New Publication from the File menu. Press the Templates button, select a template from the list, and press the OK button.
- ▶ You can create your own templates from existing publications by using the Save As command from the File menu. The Save As dialog box contains the Template check box option which allows you to save the file as a template. All templates are stored in the TEMPLATE directory.
- ▶ To permanently change a template, you must use the Open Existing Publication File from the File menu. This opens the template file instead of a copy of it. Any changes you make to this file and save change the template itself.
- ▶ You can use the Windows File Manager to organize your publication files on disk. You can create directories and subdirectories and copy and move files from one directory to another.
- ▶ To run the File Manager, you click on the Directory icon in the Main program window.

Chapter 13

Professional Techniques: Newsletters, Brochures, and Business Forms

In This Chapter

▶ *Newsletters—how to make newsletters consistent and eye-catching*
▶ *Beautiful brochures—from inexpensive mailers that you can print yourself to glossy, high-quality brochures with four-color photographs*
▶ *Flyers—one of the least expensive ways to advertise but certainly not the least effective*
▶ *Saving money and helping your business by always having the proper business form*
▶ *Bids, quotes, and proposals—landing the contract that others miss*
▶ *Business cards—creating advertisements you can carry in your pocket or purse*

Making Publisher Pay for Itself

The previous twelve chapters of this book provided the basics of how to use Publisher to lay text, graphics, and other objects on pages. Although they include a number of imaginative FYIdeas and other tips, the text was more "how to." You needed that to garner the basics and bring you up to speed in Publisher, but you also need to know some techniques that deal with real-life publications. That's what you'll get in this chapter.

You bought Publisher and this book to save you money, and to learn how to create your own desktop publications either at home or in the workplace. So now it's time to shift your creativity into high gear. While this chapter continues to give step-by-step instructions on performing various tasks in Publisher, far more importantly it will give you ideas, *lots* of ideas. Sparks to ignite and then fan the fires of your own soaring Publisher-aided abilities.

Yes, it's time to get really excited about Publisher now, because what it lets you do *is* exciting! The examples in this chapter give only an overview of the many publications you can create with Publisher. You will find that Publisher is more than just a desktop publishing program—it's a *creativity enhancer!*

> **FYIdea:** *Paper!* Stock up on several colors of regular 8.5-by-11 inch paper at your office supply store. Having a selection of colors on-hand often spurs creativity. Pastels are best; they provide good contrast for the text, WordArt, pictures, and other objects you'll be printing out. If your local office supply store has a limited selection, call Paper Direct at 1-800-A-PAPERS. They have one of the largest and most unique selections of papers you'll find anywhere. Ask for their free catalog.

Tips on Newsletters

No matter what kind of business you're in (even if you're not in a business), you'll need to communicate with people—to pass along information. An excellent and inexpensive way to get your message out is to publish a *newsletter*—a very small newspaper, usually printed on 8.5-by-11 inch paper.

Publisher gives you all the tools you need to create your own newsletters. You can do everything from within Publisher, including writing the story. However, keep in mind that Publisher is a page layout program. It does not offer the advanced features of a word processing application or a paint or draw program. As you get more advanced, you'll want to add a word processing application, a more sophisticated drawing program such as CorelDraw!, and a scanner to your computer. Even without these advanced tools, however, you can use Publisher to create an attractive and effective newsletter.

So, let's do it.

A Newsletter Framework

The best way to start is to run Publisher's Newsletter PageWizard. It creates the framework for a three-page newsletter (although you can have the PageWizard create a newsletter of any number of pages). You can later refine that framework into the precise format that best serves your needs. The following steps tell you how to begin.

1. Start Publisher or pull down the File menu and select Create New Publication.
2. Press the PageWizards button, select the Newsletter Page-Wizard from the list box, and press the OK button. The initial screen of the Newsletter PageWizard appears—it has an old-fashioned typewriter on it.
3. Press the Next button. A graphic representation of the newsletter's front page appears, and you are prompted to specify an overall style for the newsletter.
4. Select Classic, Modern, or Jazzy. As you click on each option, the representation of the newsletter at the left changes to show how that style will look. Click on the Next button when you are satisfied with the style. The next screen asks you to specify the number of columns.
5. Choose One, Two, Three, or Four. Again, the screen changes to show the effects of your choice. Three columns is pretty much the standard for newsletters. Press the Next button when you are done. The next screen prompts you to type the name of the newsletter.

6. Type the name of your newsletter to replace The Gazette. You can always change this name later by editing it in Publisher's work area (the title created here is a WordArt object). Again, press the Next button to continue.

   The title of your newsletter should be something short and snappy that tells the reader what kind of business or organization the newsletter is about. For a plumbing company you might use *The Wrench Turner*, or *Shocking News* for an electrical supply house. The possibilities are endless.

7. The next screen asks if you plan on printing on both sides of a sheet. Answer Yes to add space on the right side of odd pages and on the left side of even pages. This extra space is called a *binding margin* and leaves you room to staple the pages of the newsletter together. If you don't want a binding margin, answer No. Press the Next button to continue.

8. The next screen asks how many pages you think you'll need for the newsletter. This question is not very critical. You can always add new pages by selecting Insert Pages from the Page menu. The page headings and other elements will be copied faithfully to the new pages. So just guess at what you need and click the Next button. The next screen lists special items commonly included in newsletters.

9. Choose one or more of the four options listed—Table of Contents, Fancy First Letters, Date, Volume and Issue—by clicking the appropriate check boxes to turn the option on or off. Then press the Next button.

10. In the following screen, select the language in which you want the month, table of contents title, and sample text to appear (*Ja, erlich ist Das Deutsch Magazin*), and press the Next button.

11. The appropriate headings will be in the language you chose and you are now asked if it's okay to create the newsletter. Press the Create It button to give PageWizards the okay.

Sit back and watch as Publisher puts together the basic framework of your newsletter.

Customizing the Newsletter

As you saw in earlier chapters, Publisher documents are made up of seven basic objects—text frames, picture frames, WordArt frames, rectangles, rounded rectangles, ovals, and lines. While the newsletter you just created may look complicated at first glance, it's not. There are just those seven basic objects, which you can now select and manipulate.

General Guidelines for Effective Design

As you are laying out your newsletter, be consistent. Use the same effects throughout; don't throw in a hodgepodge of confusing images. The following guidelines will help you lay out your newsletter consistently and effectively:

- ▶ Choose a standard font for the stories. For headlines, vary only the size of the font.
- ▶ Make sure all captions are handled consistently. Don't use varying fonts and type sizes.
- ▶ Carefully align the objects on the page. If you draw a line to enhance the publication, make sure it aligns with some other object, such as a headline or picture frame. This will help unify the page.
- ▶ If you are including ads, use the *inverted pyramid rule*— place larger ads at the bottom of the page against the outer margins (the left side of even pages and the right side of odd pages). When you look at facing pages, such as page four and five, the text will be in an inverted pyramid, as shown in Figure 13.1.
- ▶ Make effective use of white space. White space makes a publication seem less intimidating and helps the reader see where one element ends and another begins. Avoid overusing white space, as well. In general, newsletters should have more white space than you see in newspapers.

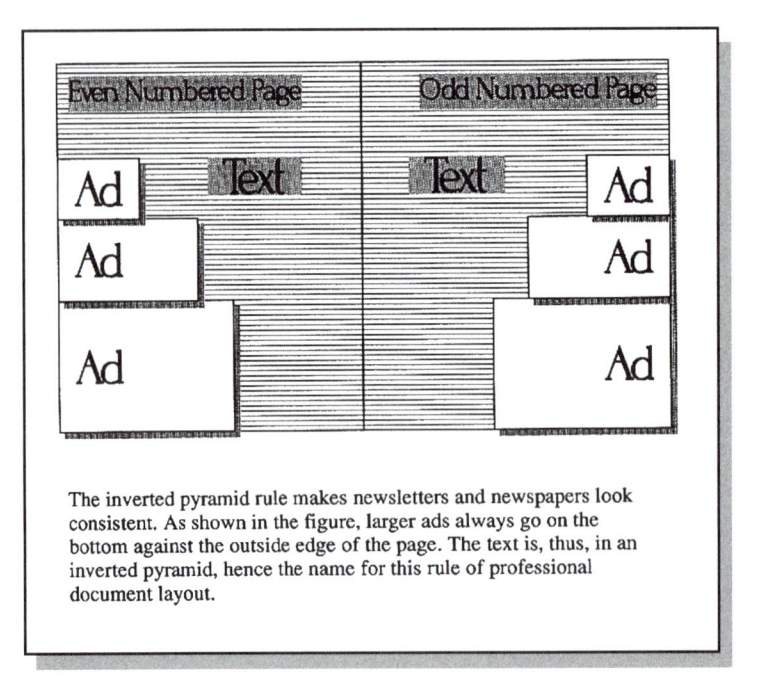

Figure 13.1 Use the inverted pyramid rule when including ads on facing pages.

It may sound picky, but things like this not only make you look professional, but more importantly help the reader comprehend your publication. As you become more familiar with layout, you'll start seeing the techniques and tricks used in other newsletters and newspapers. Such design tips will carry over to many of your publications.

Modifying the Banner

The *banner* at the top of the front page of the newsletter is a WordArt object. To change it, select it and then pull down the Edit menu and select EDIT WordArt Object. In the resulting Microsoft WordArt dialog box (as described at length in Chapter 9), you can edit the wording of the banner, change the font, stretch it vertically, add shadowing to the letters, arch the name, and perform several other tricks to create an eye-catching banner.

Now, save to disk what you have so far, and do so regularly from now on as you work. You don't want to lose your changes in the event that the power flickers.

If you want to start all over with the banner, select and delete the WordArt object. Next, select the PageWizard tool on the Toolbar (the one with the hand holding a wand). Move the mouse pointer (now a cross hair) into the work area, and draw a box where you want the new banner to be. Select the Newsletter Banner PageWizard. Respond to the PageWizard dialog boxes to create the new banner. When you are asked for the style of the banner, select Other Great Ones and press the Next button. Look at the four styles there—they have some real possibilities. Figures 13.2 and 13.3 show some possible designs for your newsletters.

Figure 13.2 A newsletter the author has published using Publisher for his own company.

Like all other objects except lines, WordArt objects have borders. Don't overlook the wonderful effects of BorderArt. For example, if you are creating a newsletter for a real estate company, an obvious border selection would be Cabins. To put a decorative border around an object, pull down the Layout menu and select BorderArt. For an interesting effect, add a gray shade as the background (for a WordArt object, put an X in the Color Background check box in the WordArt dialog box), then add the Crazy Maze BorderArt by using the BorderArt option on the Layout menu.

Figure 13.3 A newsletter banner using Crazy Maze BorderArt.

Depending on the style you picked when the Newsletter PageWizard asked you for Classic, Modern, or Jazzy, the objects containing the month and volume number of your newsletter will be text or WordArt. Either way, you can edit them easily enough to the current month and number of your newsletter.

Making Your Newsletter Graphic

On the front page of the newsletter is a picture frame with a placeholder picture. You can replace this with a photograph or artwork appropriate to the main theme of your newsletter (see Chapter 7 for information on how to insert and manipulate pictures).

If you do not want a picture or graphic on the front page, you can delete the picture frame. Select the frame and press the Del key. Also, delete the text box that was there for the caption. You can then select the text frame below (assuming you started with the three-column format as was suggested) and resize it by grabbing the middle handle on the top and pulling it up to fill the space that the picture frame occupied.

> **Tip:** Now would be a good time to save your newsletter again. It's *always* a good time to save!

Because readers like illustrations, consider adding more pictures to your newsletter. To add a picture frame, select the picture tool in the Toolbar and draw a picture frame where you want to add a picture (text will flow around the frame and make room for it). Insert a picture from Publisher's ClipArt library or insert some other graphic into the picture frame. You can even make the picture frame two columns wide, or wider if you like.

> **Tip:** If you see a stray line or other object in the newsletter that you can't seem to select, remember that you may have objects on top of each other. Select the top object and press Ctrl+Z or select Send to Back from the Layout menu. Then select the object you want to work with.

Adding Stories

Although the Newsletter PageWizard creates the overall layout and text frames you need for your newsletter, it does not write stories for you. You must import or type the text you want to use for your stories.

> **FYIdea:** When writing a story, don't be heavy-handed—don't preach. If you sell trucks, for example, and are publishing a newsletter to help you sell more trucks, you will find that subtle stories work far better than stories that take a hard-sell approach. You might include a story about a company that bought your trucks and is saving on maintenance costs, or a human interest story about a truck driver who drives one of your trucks. In other words, convey a subtle sales message by telling a story rather than by coming right out with a sales pitch. Reserve that for ads.

In a three-column newsletter, the Newsletter PageWizard sets up three separate text boxes, one for each column. The left and right text boxes have headline and *kicker* boxes above them. The headline is the title of your story. The kicker is the smaller headline about the larger one (also called a *tag line*). You can use kickers to categorize the story such as *Business* or *People in the News*. Kickers may also emphasize the main headline. For example, if your company just added a new service truck, your headline might be *Service Fleet Expanded* with a kicker of *No Expense Spared*. Headlines and kickers will be either text frames or WordArt. It depends on the style of newsletter you picked as it was being created.

Once your headline and kicker are in place for your lead story (which goes in the text box on the left), you are ready to place the text in the large text frame in the left column. Refer to Chapter 4 for information on importing text. While you can certainly type the stories directly into the text frame, you'll find that it is much easier to create the story in a full-fledged word processor and then import it. If the story does not fit in the text frame, link the frame to another frame, as explained in Chapter 4.

Now you can go back to the front page and start creating your second lead (beginning in the right column), the same way.

> **FYIdea:** People like to read about people. If you are putting together a company newsletter, include information about the people in the organization. You can get a fairly good black-and-white, hand-held scanner for around 150 dollars. You can use the scanner to scan in photographs of key employees or the employee of the month. You can then import the scanned image into a picture frame.

Helping the Reader Navigate

If you link a story in one frame to another frame, you need to tell the reader where to look to find where the story is continued. You do this by adding *continuation tags*. After linking the text frames, go to the last line in the first text frame. Draw a one-line-high text frame at the bottom of the linked frame, and (in a smaller type size) type a continuation tag—for example, `Continued on Page 3`. Right-justify the text to push it against the right margin. Consider bolding the text to make it really stand out.

Next, go to the top of the text frame on the page where the story is continued and create another continuation tag telling the reader where the story is continued from. It is often useful to include an abbreviated version of the headline above the text frame to help the reader find the text and remember what it was about.

> **FYIdea:** *News Releases!* A good way to get free advertising is to send out a news release to the media. If you have some newsworthy event, use Publisher to do a nice-looking news release and send it to the local papers and radio stations. The *Newsletter* PageWizard is a good starting point for a news release format. You can use the newsletter format to create a one-page news release. Also, be sure to send the release to a specific person on staff rather than to a generic person such as "the business editor"; you'll have better luck by working with real people.

If you need additional pages for your newsletter, go to the last page of the newsletter, pull down the Page menu and select Insert Pages, or press Ctrl+N. If you are using the Insert Pages dialog box to insert pages, don't change anything except the number of new pages you want; Publisher will create these pages for you with the newsletter heading, page number, and text frames in place (this information is all in the background if you want to modify it for the entire newsletter).

Adding Ads

Although the greater part of a newsletter will consist of stories and/or pictures, many newsletters also contain advertisements. The newsletter may contain a separate advertisement page or have ads dispersed throughout the publication. You may even be able to sell advertising space to local area merchants in order to help offset the cost of the publication, or to make a profit. Publisher includes an Ad PageWizard that makes it a snap to produce and place ads into your newsletter. A sample ad made with the Ad PageWizard is shown in Figure 13.4. The following Quick Steps lead you through the process.

Q Putting an Ad in a Newsletter

1. Turn to the page on which you want the ad to appear. — The correct page is now on your screen.

2. Click on the PageWizard tool in the Toolbar, and move the mouse pointer into the work area. — The mouse pointer changes to a cross hair.

3. Use the rulers and layout guides to draw a box of the desired size and dimensions where you want the ad to appear. — Text, if present, will move to accommodate the box. When you release the mouse button, the PageWizard dialog box appears.

4. Select the Ad PageWizard. — The Ad PageWizard takes over Publisher and guides you through creating an ad.

5. Respond to each dialog box in turn until the Ad PageWizard displays the Create It button. — Responding to each dialog box gives the PageWizard the specifications it needs to create the ad.

6. Press the Create It button. — The Ad PageWizard begins creating the ad. □

The Coupon and Calendar PageWizards also generate useful additions to newsletters, and the Table PageWizard gives you an easy way to enter any data that appear in columns.

Reproducing the Newsletter

Once you've finished creating your newsletter on-screen, spell-check it again, save it, and then print it out. Before you run off a hundred copies of your masterpiece, read through it once again. You'll often find that mistakes that you missed on-screen jump off the printed page. Once you have a clean printout, copy your newsletter. If you are going to reproduce the finished newsletter yourself, you can copy the pages to create your own 1- or 2-sided copies.

Figure 13.4   An ad made with the Ad PageWizard.

> **Caution:** If you are mailing the news letter without an envelope, be sure to leave room for a postage stamp, recipient address, and return address on the back. If you are folding it in thirds, this will be the lowest third of the back page (which must be an even numbered page).

Any quick copy shop can reproduce the newsletter for you. Keep in mind that even though you print the master copy on white paper (as you should), you can copy it on colored paper; you can even use different colors for different sections.

> **Caution:** Get a quote before having your publications printed professionally. The use of fancy paper and a lot of colors can increase the reproduction costs dramatically.

If you need a lot of copies and are going to have the newsletter reproduced on a printing press, you should also consider the number of pages you have. The most economical way to print a newsletter is on 11-by-17 inch paper, folded in half to make 8 1/2-by-11 inch pages. That way, the print shop can print two pages at a time, or even four at a time—two on the front and two on the back. For this to work, the total number of pages has to be divisible by four. So your newsletter can be four, eight, or twelve pages, etc., but nothing in between.

Tips on Brochures and Flyers

Brochures and *flyers* are commonly used in business to describe a company's goods and services or the goals of an organization. A brochure may consist of from one to several sheets of paper, printed on both sides. A flyer is usually only one sheet of paper, which performs the same function as a brochure.

Choosing the Right Brochure Type

There are two kinds of brochures. The simple kind, as generated by Publisher's Three-Fold Brochure PageWizard, is a single sheet of paper that can be folded in thirds and used as a mailer, or put in literature racks for interested people to pick up. In the latter case, you'll want to put something on the front of the brochure to *make* it interesting.

The second kind of brochure is the fancy several-page, 8.5-by-11-inch brochure printed on glossy paper with four-color photographs. You can produce the masters for these using Publisher, but obviously you'll need to go through a commercial printing company to have them printed. Still, you'll easily save hundreds of dollars for your company in setup costs, and you'll maintain greater control over the finished product.

> **Tip:** If you want to include color photographs, leave empty frames where they go. The print shop people will have to make color separations for the photographs and put them in place during the printing process.

Large brochures are expensive, so you'll need to call around and get quotes from printing companies before investing your time in creating one. You need to know how many color photographs are to be included (there is a separation charge for each), the total number of colors (four for color photographs plus however many other colors you are using), the number of pages, and the type of paper.

You will also be asked such questions as "Are there any bleeds in the brochure?" A *bleed* occurs when the printing goes all the way to the edge of the paper, as shown in Figure 13.5. This can be a pattern, an overprinted color, or whatever, but it does entail an extra charge because of the way the piece has to be handled on the press; it has to be printed on oversized paper and trimmed to the correct size. You can save money by not using bleeds.

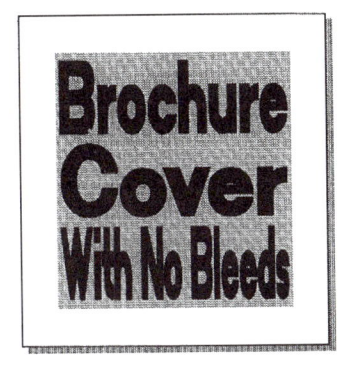

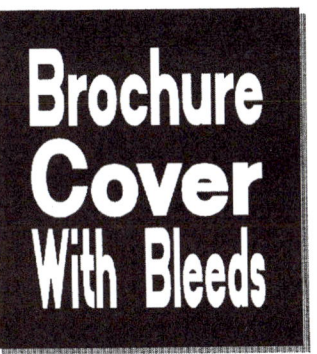

Figure 13.5   Printing a bleed consists of printing ink to the edge of an oversized sheet of paper and trimming the excess.

> **Tip:** To create a large brochure, try using the Newsletter PageWizard to create the pages you need. When asked to specify the number of columns, select One or Two. By using the Newsletter PageWizard rather than Three-Fold Brochure, you'll get the benefit of newsletter headings and page numbers. By using only one or two columns, you can use the newsletter format to create the more open design of a brochure. By *open*, I mean you can use more white space to set off pictures and frames of text.

Publisher, by the way, includes a catalog template, which you can use to create an oversized brochure. To access it, press the Templates button in the Start Up dialog box and select catalog from the template list box.

Using Flyers

A flyer is really just a big ad. You can use the Ad PageWizard or the Coupon PageWizard to make it; just draw a box as large as the margin guides on the page. You can also use Publisher's Flyer template to create a flyer like the one in Figure 13.6. Flyers work very well for seasonal events or sales—Memorial Day Blow Out, July 4th Clearance, Halloween Sale With Prices So Low It Scares Us, and so forth. You see stacks of flyers everywhere, and now that you have Publisher, some of these flyers can be yours.

Don't try to get too much information on a flyer; a flyer works best if uncluttered (brochures and newsletters are better for imparting a lot of information). The Ad PageWizard is a good choice because it lets you put a large, attention-getting slogan on the flyer, a striking but appropriate piece of ClipArt or other illustration, a minimum of explanatory text, and your company or organization's name, address, and phone number. Flyers get people in the store, or to the meeting, *then* you can give brochures, newsletters, and catalogs to those who are really interested.

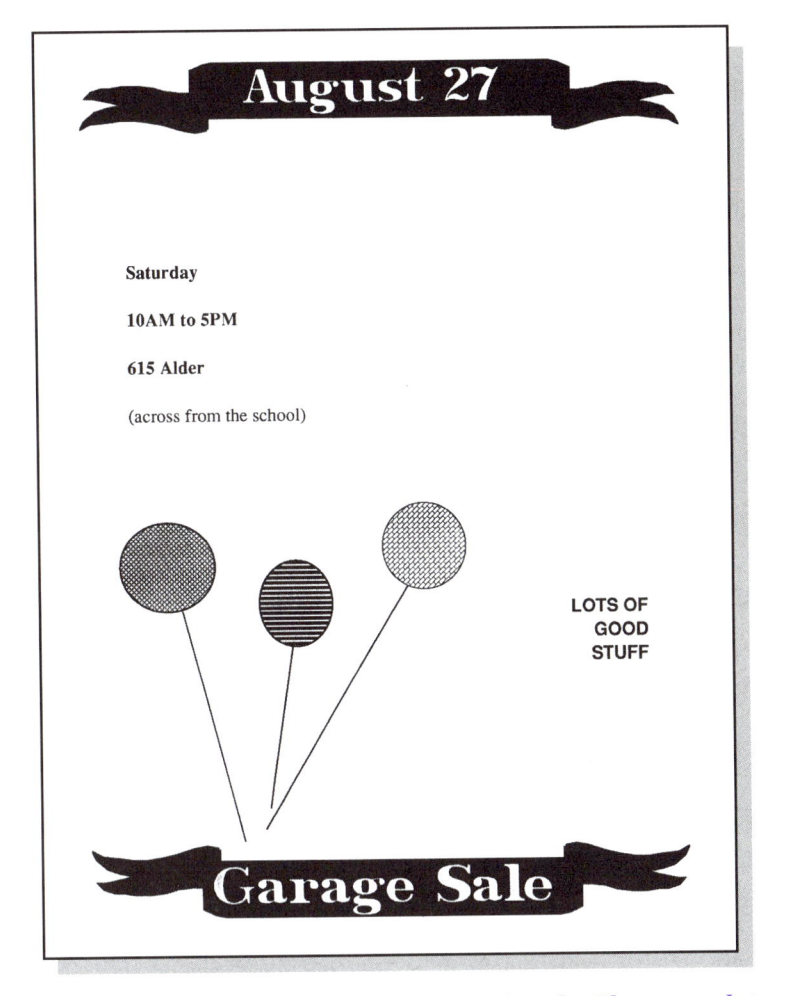

Figure 13.6 You can create a flyer using the Flyer template.

> **FYIdea:** *Paper Airplanes*! Yep, Publisher includes a Paper Aeroplane PageWizard, that will produce several styles of planes with a separate instruction sheet on how to fold them. (See Figure 13.7.) Make up some of these with your advertising messages on them and give the planes away. Even high-powered executives, in the sanctity of their offices, will fly paper airplanes!

Chapter 13

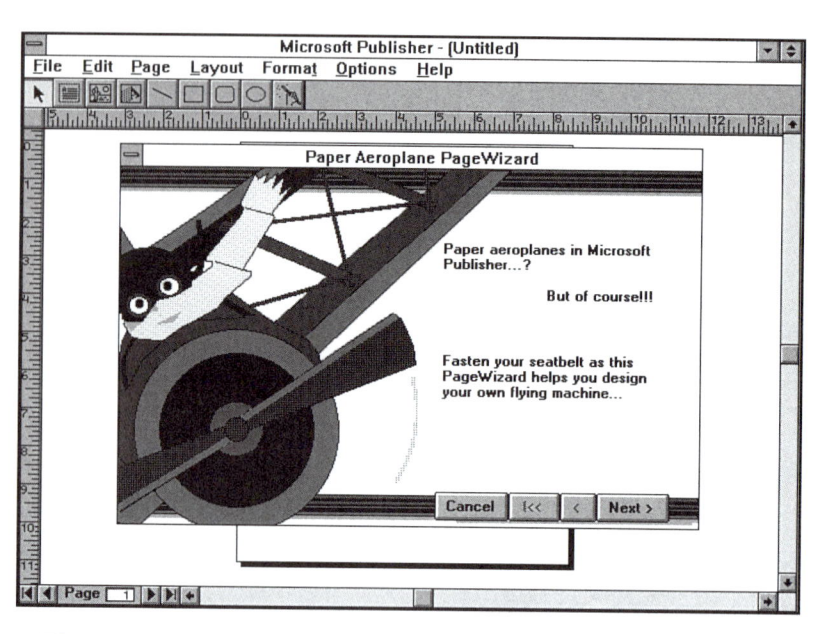

Figure 13.7 The Paper Aeroplane PageWizard is a fun, effective way to get your message off the ground.

Tips on Bids, Quotes, and Proposals

Bids, quotes, and proposals are three different categories of business communication that do the same thing—they help you sell your company and your products and services. Quotes and bids are very similar; they both tell a prospective client what you can do and how much it will cost. They differ in that a bid is submitted to respond to a request, whereas a quote is a generic statement of the kind of work you do for a given amount of money. A proposal differs from both bids and quotes in the amount of detail required. Proposals require you to supply a great many details usually laid out in a specific format. For government proposals, the organization will usually set the guidelines for the proposal.

Business Replies

Perhaps the most important thing any business can do is to answer a query with a professional, attention-getting reply. Although typing a response letter on company letterhead is better than nothing, you want your letter to stand out. Use Publisher to add ClipArt appropriate to your product or services, or import a scanned image of some of your products or of a project you completed.

> **FYIdea:** *Letterhead and Envelopes!* Publisher gives you two templates for designing letterhead—LTRHEAD1 and LTRHEAD2, and two matching envelope templates—ENVELOP1 and ENVELOP2. Start with these predesigned envelopes and letterhead and add your own touch, such as creating a logo or typing a slogan.

Submitting Bids and Quotes

Companies, schools, governments, and other institutions wanting to purchase goods or services often call for *bids* or ask for a *quote*. They want to know how much it's going to cost before they appropriate the required funds. The time to put together your bid is now. Assemble a bid template with all the artwork already in place. Leave spaces for all the information and prices that you want to include in the bid. That way, you can reply to every bid that comes along in a flash. Simply insert the prices, print out the customized bid, and send it off to your prospective client.

Instead of sending your bid to a prospective client, hand-deliver it. Offer to explain the prices and answer any questions up front. If a person gets to know you, he or she will be more likely to call you back and give you a second chance in case your competitor underbids you. Keep a copy of the bid handy for when the person calls.

> **FYIdea:** *Wrapping Paper!* You can't buy customized wrapping paper at the five and ten. Use Publisher to create a pattern on nicely colored paper consisting of appropriate ClipArt and a WordArt message such as "A Little Token for a Valued Customer." Duplicate the pattern many times using the Copy and Paste options on the Edit menu. Print the page on colored paper and wrap a small gift in it. Customers and clients will appreciate the thoughtfulness and you will stand out in their minds.

Writing Proposals

Proposals are similar to quotes and bids in that they tell a prospective client or customer what you can do at what price. They differ from quotes and bids, however, in that they must supply a great deal of information requested by the prospective client. The client usually provides specific instructions on what the proposal must include, often defining a page limit, an outline that must be followed, and other stringent guidelines. To write the proposal, you'll need to do some homework about the company or organization requesting the proposal.

Once you've gathered the necessary information, you can begin creating your proposal. A good way to start is to use the Report template to create the overall layout. The first page of the report might contain a statement of the customer's problem or the project involved and an overall statement that explains how you would approach the problem or complete the project. Subsequent pages could include details giving the customer a time table, a list of parts required, and a list of hours, including prices for parts and labor.

> **FYIdea:** Use the Calendar PageWizard to create a production schedule for your proposal. By letting your client know up front how long it will take to fill an order or complete a project, you may gain an edge over the competition. Be sure to set realistic dates, however. If you fail to meet your dates, you may do more damage to your company's reputation than if you had never set the dates in the first place. Create matching schedules and distribute them to your production team. Put inspirational slogans at the top, along with the company logo. By setting your goals in a concrete form, you can boost productivity.

Tips on Other Business Forms

Publisher's Seven Business Forms PageWizard—which creates Customer Refund, Expense Report, Fax Sheet, Invoice, Purchase Order, Statement, and Quote forms for you—is an excellent starting place for you to create a complete library of customized forms for your business or organization.

However, those seven forms are just a starting place. Keep in mind that Publisher also contains a library of templates. And several of these templates are business-oriented. To access a template, start Publisher or select Create New Publication from the File menu, and then press the Templates button and select a template from the list. When you press the OK button, Publisher loads a copy of the template and displays it in the work area. For more information on working with templates, refer to Chapter 12.

The templates that come with Publisher include templates for business cards, catalogs, envelopes, flyers, labels, letterhead, memos, price lists, product information sheets, reports, resumes, and membership rosters. To create customized templates for your company or business, load the template, modify it as needed, and then save it as a template under some other name. Do the same for the forms and other documents you create from scratch.

Tips on Business Cards

You should carry one of the most important keys to business success in your pocket or purse. No, not money but *business cards*. Business cards help you earn more money by helping you reach more customers. Although you can't gain any business without a first contact, you won't keep any business if you don't follow up on your calls. One of the best ways to follow up is to provide a business card during your initial meeting. A prospective customer is then more likely to call you back.

Business cards are an inexpensive way to help people remember your name, and to give them your company's address and phone number. Doing business cards in Publisher is also so fast and inexpensive that you can print special versions for various promotions or sales. Because many quick print shops will do 500 cards from camera-ready artwork for about 20 dollars, you can have cards for all sorts of occasions.

Here's an example. The author of this book has written many other books. As each new book comes out, he designs a business card promoting that book, as he has done for *The First Book of Microsoft*

Publisher (see Figure 13.8). Giving these cards to bookstore owners and other interested people sells a lot of books. You can do the same thing for your own products.

Figure 13.8   The author's business card for this book. The typewriter on the card was swiped from the opening screen of the Newsletter PageWizard with the Collage screen capture program, and then imported into Publisher as a picture.

To help you create your own business cards, Publisher includes three business card templates. Take a look at the template, `bizcard1.pub` to begin. The template document is a business card for the Rattlesnake Grocery in New Mexico. It consists of a picture frame (the desert scene), a text frame (the name and address of the business), and a thick line at the bottom for decoration. That's all, just those three objects (see how easy it is to design a business card!).

> **Tip:** If your printer can handle heavy card stock, you can print the business cards yourself. Select all the objects that make up the business card and use the Copy command to copy the objects to the Windows Clipboard. Then use the Paste Object(s) command to paste eight copies of the card onto a blank page. Use the rulers and guides to align the cards. You can then print eight business cards per page and cut them apart.

You can also use Publisher to make really fancy cards, having several colors, and even color photographs on them. These, like the four-color process brochures described earlier in this chapter, will require the assistance of a commercial print shop to do the four color separations and actual printing, but you can still do all the design, leaving a frame for the picture. Even for a multicolor card without a picture, however, expect to pay perhaps several hundred dollars per thousand depending on the design.

Regardless of how expensive the card is, Publisher will save you money in designing and setting it up, and let you have *your own* design instead of a stock one out of some printer's catalog that scores of other companies in your own city or town might have.

Putting the Promotions Together

Now that you know how to create the promotional materials your business needs, it's a good idea to put together a coordinated promotional plan for your company or organization. With Publisher, you can create everything you need from business cards to flyers, brochures, and a regular newsletter.

Remember, selling is a matter of percentages—the more people you tell, the more products you'll sell. Take junk mail, for example. Our mail boxes are full of it every day! Why do companies keep sending out mailing after mailing when a good percent of it gets thrown away? Because the small percentage that *does* get read not only pays for the mailing but also makes them a good profit. That's what you should and can do now, play the percentages.

No piece of correspondence should go out of your office, no bill should be paid, that does not include a flyer or business card. It costs you practically nothing, and that small percentage that does get you extra business is well worth the effort.

What You Have Learned

In this chapter, you learned how to put Publisher to work creating the publications you need to run your business or to publish from your home. Specifically, you learned about the following techniques:

- ▶ Publisher's Newsletter PageWizard sets up the basic framework for your newsletter. You can then import text into the text frames, import graphics into the picture frames, and modify the newsletter in other ways.
- ▶ Newsletter banners are WordArt objects. You can modify these by choosing Edit WordArt Object from the Edit menu. You can also use the Border, BorderArt, Shading, and Shadow options on the Layout menu to make banners stand out even more.
- ▶ If you import a story into a text frame and the story is longer than the frame, you can connect the frame to another frame to accommodate the overflow. You should then go back and insert a continuation tag at the bottom of the first frame and the top of the second frame.
- ▶ The Ad and Coupon PageWizards are very useful for adding advertisements to your newsletter. Sometimes selling a few ads can offset the cost of producing the newsletter and may even generate a profit. To add either of these items, click on the PageWizards tool, draw a box the size you want, and then select the Ad or Coupon PageWizard. The PageWizard will guide you through the rest of the process.
- ▶ Creating brochures and flyers is easy in Publisher. You can use the Three-Fold Brochure PageWizard to create a simple brochure, the Newsletter PageWizard for longer brochures, and the Ad PageWizard for flyers.
- ▶ Using the Seven Business Forms PageWizard, and all of the various templates provided with Publisher, you can develop an entire library of business forms for your company or organization.
- ▶ Business cards are a wonderful way to advertise your goods, services, or organization. Publisher comes with three templates and a PageWizard to help you make cards.

Appendix

Installing Microsoft Publisher

What You Need

- ▶ An IBM PC-compatible computer running Microsoft Windows 3.0 or higher
- ▶ At least one megabyte of RAM (random-access memory)
- ▶ A hard disk with at least four megabytes of free space
- ▶ A graphics display of at least EGA quality, preferably VGA
- ▶ A mouse or similar pointing device
- ▶ A printer with graphic capabilities installed in Windows

Running the Installation Program

Most of the installation process is animated, meaning that the SETUP.EXE program that comes on the first Microsoft Publisher distribution disk will make most of the decisions for you. To install Publisher, follow these Quick Steps:

Appendix

Installing Publisher

1. Load Windows and go to the Program Manager.
2. Insert the Microsoft Publisher Installation disk, disk 1, into drive A or B.
3. Pull down the File menu and select Run.

   The Run dialog box appears.

4. In the Command Line text box, type **a:setup** if you are using drive A or **b:setup** for drive B. Press the OK button.

   The Publisher setup program begins running and displays the Welcome screen, shown in Figure A.1.

5. Read the first screenful of information and then press the Continue button.

   The Setup Options screen appears, as in Figure A.2, asking if you want to perform a Complete installation or Custom installation.

6. Press the Complete Installation button to install all the Publisher files or Custom Installation to install selected files. While a custom installation may save space, you probably cannot predict what parts of the program you will need. It's better to install everything now.

   A progress dialog box appears, showing you that Publisher's program files are being copied from the floppy disks to your hard disk, as shown in Figure A.3.

7. Follow the on-screen dialog boxes and swap disks when prompted.

Depending on the speed of your computer, it may take some time for the installation program to copy the necessary files to disk. ☐

At the end of the installation process, the program displays a dialog box asking if you want to Run Publisher or Return to Windows. Select the desired option.

That's it for installation. A simple process of just a few minutes, and you are now ready to begin using Microsoft Publisher. Turn to Chapter 1, and start working...or playing. Enjoy! Publisher really is great!

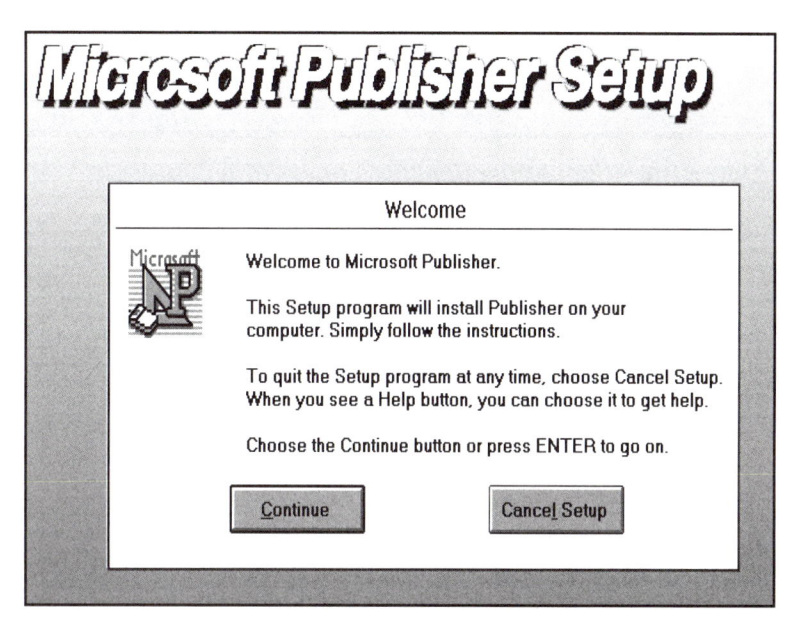

Figure A.1 The Microsoft Publisher Setup program's Welcome screen. Click on the Continue button or press the Enter key to start installation.

Appendix

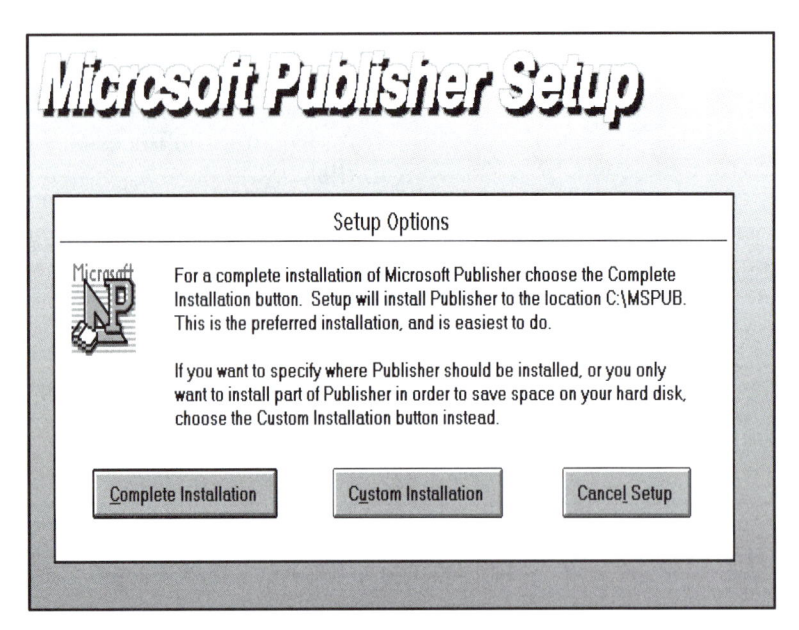

Figure A.2   Choose the Complete Installation option unless your hard disk is nearly full.

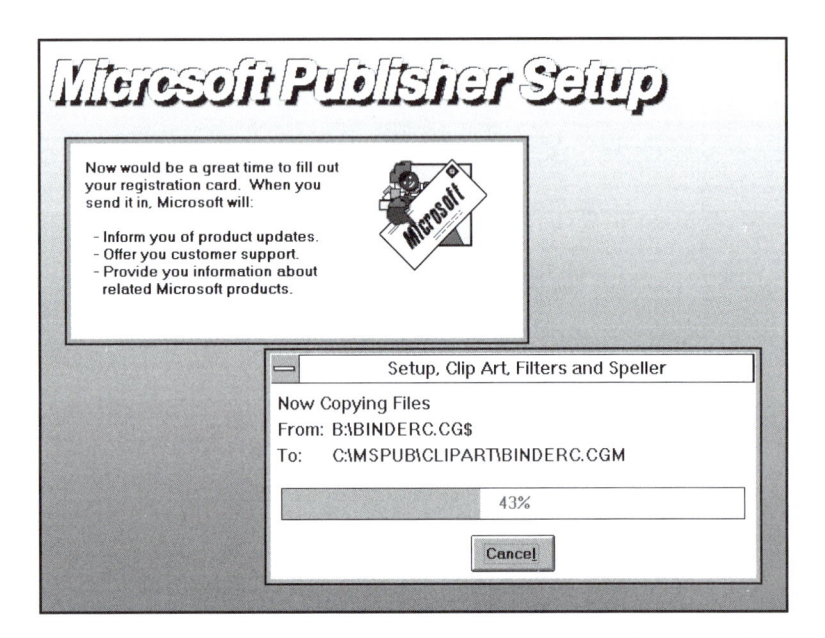

Figure A.3   Watch the installation progress and change disks as prompted.

Index

Symbols

(...) ellipsis, 23, 28
* (asterisk) wild card, 114
? (question mark) wild card, 114

A

About Microsoft Publisher, 37
active window, 8, 15
Actual Size, 26, 54
Ad PageWizard, 44
Add, 131
advertisements, 256-259,
   319-320
     camera-ready, 257
     guides, 320
     size, 257-258
aligning objects, WordArt, 248
anchor point, 175-177
anchoring
     cursor, 122
     highlight, 121-122
     text frames, 107
applications window, 11-13, 21

Apply, 240
arrow pointer, 7
arrows, 117
   lines, 183
   pointer
     mouse, 32
     two headed, 15
   scroll, 27
ASCII (American Standard
   Code for Information
   Interchange) files, 113
autoflowing text, 112
Automatically Create Text
   Frames, 263

B

Back, 35
background, 97-98, 264-265,
   271-272
   hiding, 266
   mirrored, 269-270
   objects, hiding, 266
   page numbers, 267-268
   rectangles, 265

backups, 59-60
banners, newsletters, 63, 314-316
base color, 285-289
Best Fit, 244
bids, 326-327
binding margin, 89, 312
bitmap files, 207
Blank Page, 18, 279
blank pages, 263
bleeds, 323
blocks
    commands, 120
    marking, 120
    text, 120-126
Book, 82
Border, 107, 182, 219-220
Border dialog box, 106, 182-183, 219-220
BorderArt, 107, 191-228, 315
BorderArt dialog box, 224
borders, 106
    color, 223
    dragging, 16
    frames, 218
    grabbing, 15
    line, 218-220
    lines, 218
    moving, 17
    thickness, 223
boxes
    drawing, 92
    shadows, 175
Bring to Front, 191
brochures
    template, 295
    three-fold, 44, 64-65, 322-324
Browse, 35
business
    cards, 294, 329-331
    forms, 43, 49, 64, 328-329
    replies, 326-327

buttons
    Blank Page, 77
    connect, 108, 116-117
    Create It, 52
    Find Next, 129
    minimize, 14
    Next, 55
    PageWizard, 41
    PageWizards, 55
    pins, 246
    Replace, 129

C

Calendar PageWizard, 44
Calendar tool, 44
calendars, 44, 66
calibrating printer, 278-280
call outs, 252-254
camera-ready pages, 257, 284
Cancel command button, 30-34
captions, newsletters, 313
cards
    business, 84-85, 294, 329-331
    free standing, 82
    side-fold, 83
    top-fold, 83
catalogs, 295
centimeters, 96
Change, 131
Change To, 130
Character dialog box, 30
Check All Stories, 130
check boxes, 31
Check Spelling, 130-132
Check Spelling dialog box, 130
circles, 178, 255-256
clicking, 8
ClipArt, 198-201
clipboard
    drawings, 203-205
    text, 110-112

Close, 131
Close Publication, 60
codes, formatting, 112
collating, 281
color
   base, 285, 289
   borders, 223
   four-color, 285
   lines, 182-183
   objects, 185
   paper, 310
   printing, 283-289
   process, 284-285
   separated, 284-289
   shades, 286
   spot, 284-285
   text, 247
Color Background, 242, 248-249
Color dialog box, 29
columns
   newsletters, 62, 311
   tables, 70
command buttons, 30
Complete Installation, 334
composite shapes, 189-190
connect buttons, 108, 116-117
continuation tags, 318
Control menu, 14-16
control-menu box, 12
COPY command, 283
Copy Picture Frame, 214
Copy Text, 123
copying
   picture frames, 210, 213
   text blocks, 123
Coupon PageWizard, 45, 69-70
Create Directory, 305
Create Directory dialog box, 305
Create It button, 52
Create New Publication, 45-48, 55, 77, 279
Create New Publication dialog box, 43-46
crop marks, 84, 282, 289
crop pointer, 33
cropping, 209-210
cross-hair pointer, 32
cursor
   anchoring, 122
   keypad, 10
   pointing, 10
   selection, 32
customer refunds, 49
Cut, 188
Cut Picture Frame, 214-215
Cut Text, 124-125
cutting
   picture frames, 213
   text, 110, 111

D

Danish, 52
Default Printer, 74, 77, 277
Delete Page, 264
Delete Picture Frame, 214
Delete Text Frame, 136
deleting
   objects, 188
   pages, 264
   picture frames, 214-215
   text blocks, 125-126
   text frames, 135
desktop, 11
desktop publishing (DTP) program, 1-3
dialog boxes, 23, 28-32
Directories, 58
directories
   changing, 304
   creating, 304-305
   files, 306-307
   icon, 303
   managing, 303-304
   opening, 304

paths, 58
subdirectories, 304
template, 300
tree, 114
window, activating, 304
disks, printing to, 282-283
distortion, 195
document icons, 10
documents, PageWizards, 55
DOS, 4-5
draft quality printing, 281
dragging
borders, 16
mouse, 8
objects, 181
drawings
importing, clipboard, 203-205
paint programs, 189
drives, changing, 304
drop shadows, 187-188, 234-235
drop-down list boxes, 30
Duplicate All Objects on Page, 263
Dutch, 52

E

Edit menu, 119
Edit Object, 206
Edit WordArt Object, 250
editing
objects, WordArt, 249-250
templates, 302
text frames, 119
ellipses connect button, 117
Ellipsis (...), 23, 28
end marks connect button, 117
envelopes, 295, 327
exiting Publisher, 37
expense reports, 49, 64
extensions
file name, 58
graphics, 202

F

F3 (Exit), 37
facing pages, 88
fan-fold paper, 278
Fancy First Letter tool, 44
faxes, 48-49, 64
styles, 50-51
File Manager, 303-307
File menu, 56, 113
files
backups, 59-60
bitmap, 207
folders, 59
formats, 113
graphics, extensions, 202
managing, 303-304
metafiles, 207
moving between directories, 306-307
names, 57-58
native, 207
opening, 292-294
printing to, 281
protecting, 59-60
saving, 56, 57
text, importing, 112-116
Fill, 247
Find, 127
Find dialog box, 127-128
Find Next button, 129
Find What, 127-129
Finnish, 52
flyers, 295, 322-325
folders, 59
Font, 241
fonts, scale, 276
WordArt, 242-243
footers, 264, 269
formats, 113
formatting codes, 112
forms, 51-55, 328-329
Forms PageWizard, 48-49
Forms PageWizards dialog box, 41

Frame Columns and Margins
  dialog box, 209
Frame Margins, 209, 225
frames, 102
  borders, 218
  deleting, 135
  designing, 217
  handles, 134
  linked, 118-119
  moving, 133
  overlapping, 229-230
  picture, 102, 194
    centering, 197
    copying, 210, 213
    creating, 195-197
    cutting, 213
    deleting, 214-215
    handles, 211
    importing, 194-195
    moving, 210
    objects, 205-206
    pasting, 213
    resizing, 210-213
    selecting, 198, 211
    square, 197
  reshaping, 133
  resizing, 133-134
  shading, 231-233
  shadows, 234-235
  text, 102-110
    anchoring, 107
    creating, 104-106, 263
    editing, 119-120
    handles, 105
    importing, 110
    linking, 118
    moving, 110
    multiple, 108-109
    selecting, 108-109
    shadowing, 107
    square, 106-107
    too much text, 116
    typing in, 116
    width, 117

  transparent, 134-135
  WordArt, 102
French, 52
Full Page, 26, 81

G

German, 52
Go To, 36
Go to Background, 98, 265
Go to Foreground, 99
graphical user interface (GUI), 4-5
graphics, 193-194
  icons, 6
  newsletters, 316-317
graphics-based text objects, 238
Greeking text, 296
Greeting Card & Invitation PageWizard, 65
greeting cards, 44
grids, 70
groups
  program, 6
  text frames, 109
guides
  ad, 320
  changing, 87
  hiding, 90
  magnetic, 89
  mirrored, 88
  moving, 87
  pages, 86
  revealing, 90
  snaping, 89

H

hairline, 182
handles, 179
  frames, picture, 211
  objects, 33
  side, 134
  text frames, 105, 108, 134
  top and bottom, 134

headers, 264, 268
headings, 70
Help, 34-36
    menu, 37, 103
    window, 35-36
Help command button, 30, 34
Hide Layout Guides, 90
Hide Object Boundaries, 229
Hide Rulers, 25, 93
Hide Status Line, 28
hiding
    background, 266
    guides, 90
    objects, 266
    rulers, 93
Highlight Story, 121
highlighting, 120-123
hollow letters, 247
How to Use Help, 37

I

I-beam pointer, 33
Ignore, 131
Import Picture dialog box, 199-201
Import Text, 113
Import Text dialog box, 113-115
importing
    ClipArt, 198-201
    drawings, 203-205
    files, 112-116
    pictures, 194-203
    text, 110-112
Index, 35-37
Index Card, 83
inkjet printers, 276
Insert Object, 205
Insert Object dialog box, 206
Insert Pages, 82, 262, 287
Insert Pages dialog box, 82, 263, 287
inserting pages, 262
installation, 333-336

Introduction to Publisher, 37
inverted pyramid rule, 313-314
invitations, 44, 65
invoices, 49, 64
Italian, 52

K

keyboard shortcuts, 23
    Alt+P (PageWizards), 46
    Alt+H (Help menu), 37
    Alt+T (Template), 300
    Alt+W (Windows menu), 5
    Ctrl+A (highlight story), 122
    Ctrl+C (Copy), 214
    Ctrl+Esc (Control menu), 15
    Ctrl+F (move to front), 191
    Ctrl+G (Hide Layout Guides), 90
    Ctrl+K (rulers off/on), 93
    Ctrl+M (Go to Background), 98-99, 265
    Ctrl+N (insert page), 82, 263, 319
    Ctrl+P (Print), 61, 279
    Ctrl+Shift+← (stretch highlight), 122
    Ctrl+Shift+↑ (stretch highlight), 122
    Ctrl+Shift+→ (stretch highlight), 122
    Ctrl+Shift+↓ (stretch highlight), 122
    Ctrl+Shift+End (stretch highlight), 122
    Ctrl+Shift+Home (stretch highlight), 122
    Ctrl+Shift+Tab (Move to Previous Frame), 118
    Ctrl+Tab (Move To Next Frame), 118
    Ctrl+V (paste), 188, 214

Ctrl+W (Snap to Guides), 89, 279
Ctrl+X (cut), 125, 188, 214
Ctrl+Y (Hide Object Boundaries), 229
Ctrl+Z (Send to Back), 191, 317
Shift + → (stretch highlight), 122
Shift + ↓ (stretch highlight), 122
Shift+← (stretch highlight), 122
Shift+↑ (stretch highlight), 122
Shift+End (stretch highlight), 122
Shift+Home (stretch highlight), 122
Keyboard Shortcuts option, 37
keyboards, 7, 10
keywords, 35
kicker boxes, 318

L

labels, 81, 295
Landscape, 77
landscape orientation, 49-50
Language? dialog box, 63
languages, 52, 63, 66, 312
layered objects, 190-191
layers, 229
layout, viewing, 26
layout board, 1-3, 87
Layout Guides, 87, 269
Layout Guides dialog box, 87-88, 269
letterhead, 295, 327
Line, 182
Line dialog box, 182-183
Line tool, 103
lines, 178
   arrowheads, 175, 183
   borders, 218-220

color, 182-183
hairline, 182
shaded, 187
straight, 174
thickness, 175, 182-184
tool, 91, 103, 174
WordArt, 255-256
linking
   frames, 118-119
   text frames, 118
list boxes, 30
logos, 271-272

M

magnetic guides, 89
mailing labels, 294
Main window, 5-6
margins
   binding, 89, 312
   picture frame, 208
marking blocks, 120
Match Case, 128-129
Match Whole Word Only, 128
Maximize, 16
maximize buttons, 12
measurement
   centimeters, 96
   points, 96
   rulers, 95-96
memo template, 295
menu bar, 13, 19-21
menus
   bar, 13
   closing, 21
   Control, 14
   control-menu box, 12
   conventions, 22
   Edit, 119, 188
   File, 28, 56, 84, 113
   Help, 37, 103
   Layout, 87
   Options, 119
   options, 22

    Page, 26, 54, 79, 98, 116
    pull-down, 20-24
    Windows, 17-18
message boxes, 68
metafiles, 207
Minimize, 16
minimize button, 12, 14
mirrored background, 269-270
mirrored guides, 88
mouse, 7-8
    moving windows, 15
    point and click, 3
    pointer, 32
        arrow, 32
        crop, 33
        cross hair, 32
        I-beam, 33
        moving van, 33, 181
        resize, 33
        selection cursor, 32
        windows, 13
    resizing windows, 15
Move, 16, 306
Move dialog box, 306
moving
    files between directories, 306-307
    frames, 110, 133
    guides, 87
    objects, 180
        selected, 211-212
    picture frames, 210
    text blocks, 124-125
    text frames, 133
    windows, mouse, 15
moving van pointer, 33
multitasking environment, 125

N

native files, 207
news releases, 319
Newsletter Banner tool, 44
Newsletter PageWizard, 62-63

newsletters, 43, 310
    ads, 319-320
    banner, 63, 314-316
    BorderArt, 315
    captions, 313
    classic, 311
    columns, 62, 311
    continuation tags, 318
    customizing, 313
    graphics, 316-317
    inverted pyramid rule, 313-314
    jazzy, 311
    kicker boxes, 318
    modern, 311
    PageWizards, 311-312
    stories, 317-318
    styles, 62
    table of contents, 312
    tag lines, 318
Next button, 55
Norwegian, 52
Note-It PageWizard, 68-69
Note-It tool, 44
Number of Pages? dialog box, 63
numeric keypad, 10

O

objects
    background, hiding, 266
    basic, 102
    color, 185
    combining, 189-190
    composite shapes, 189-190
    cropping, 33
    deleting, 188
    dragging, 181
    drawing, 91, 175-176
    duplicating, 263
    graphic, 174
    handles, 33, 179
    layered, 190-191

lines, 182-184
moving, 180, 211-212
picture frames, 205-206
resizing, 181-182
selecting, 8, 179
   as a group, 180
   individually, 180
   multiple, 180
shading, 184-187
shadows, 187-188
sizing, 92
stretching, 177
styling, 245-247
text, graphics-based, 238
WordArt
   aligning, 248
   creating, 241-242
   editing, 249-250
   sizing, 244
   text, 70
OK command button, 30, 34
on-screen rulers, 90
Open, 18, 45
Open Existing Publication, 292, 302
Open Existing Publication dialog box, 292-293
opening
   directories, 304
   files, existing, 292-293
   templates, 297-299
option buttons, 32
Options menu, 119
orientation, 78-79, 277
ovals tool, 103, 174
overlapping frames, 229-230

P

page control, 27
Page menu, 54, 116
Page Setup dialog box, 79
Page Wizards, 46
pages, 261

assembling, 101
background, 264
blank, 18, 77
books, 82
camera ready, 284
deleting, 264
duplicating objects, 263
facing, 88
full pages, 81
guides, 86
height, 80
inserting, 262-263
layout, 79-87
   viewing, 26
numbers, 267-268
orientation, 49-50, 78
paging control, 20
previewing, 80
setting up, 79-81
size, 79, 85-86
viewing, 93-94
width, 80
zooming, 94-95
PageWizards, 18, 39-42
button, 41
Calendar, 43-44, 66-68
Coupon, 42, 45, 69-70
documents, creating, 54-55
fax sheets, 48,-52
Forms, 48-55
Greeting Card & Invitation, 44, 65
maneuvering, 47
Newsletter, 43, 62-63, 311-312
Note-It, 68-69
Paper Aeroplane, 44-45
Seven Business Forms, 43, 49, 63-64
starting, 45-46
subprograms, 41
Table, 45, 70-71
Three-Fold Brochure, 44, 64-65

tools, 44
window, 53
PageWizards button, 55
paging, 27
paint programs, 189
paper
   colored, 310
   fan-fold, 278
   orientation, 79, 277
   positioning, 278
   size, 76
   tractor feed, 278
Paper Aeroplane PageWizard, 45
Paste, 188
Paste Object(s), 214
Paste Special, 206
Paste Text, 124
pasting
   picture frames, 213
   text, 110-111
   text blocks, 123
picas, 96
picture frames, 102, 194
   centering, 197
   copying, 210, 213
   creating, 195-197
   cutting, 213
   deleting, 214-215
   handles, 211
   margins, 208
   moving, 210
   objects, 205-206
   pasting, 213
   pictures, importing, 194-195
   resizing, 210-213
   selecting, 198, 211
   square, 197
pictures, 194
   cropping, 209-210
   distortion, 195
   importing, 198-203

text, wrapping around, 207-208
white space, 208-209
tool, 102
point and click, 3
pointers
   arrow, 7, 15
   changing, 33
   cross hair, 32
   I-beam, 33
   mouse, 8, 13, 32
      crop, 33
      moving van, 33, 181
      resize, 33
   Resize, 135, 182
   selection cursor, 32
pointing
   and selecting, 7
   cursor keys, 10
points, 96
Portrait, 77
Portrait Orientation, 277
portrait orientation, 49-50
ports, 75
Portugese, 52
PostScript printers, 276
preview area, 80
Print, 61
Print command, 84
Print Crop Marks, 84
Print dialog box, 84, 280
Print on both sides? dialog box, 63
Print Quality, 281
Print Setup, 74-76
Print Setup dialog box, 74-78, 278, 281
Print to File, 281
Print To File dialog box, 283
printers
   calibrating, 278-280
   dot-matrix, 276
   HP Deskjet, 276

inkjet, 276
laser, 276
paper, 277-278
ports, 75
selecting, 74-75, 276
setting up, 74-77, 277-278
printing, 275, 280
bleeds, 323
collating, 281
color, 283-289
crop marks, 84, 282, 289
double sided, 63
draft quality, 281
full page, 81
lines, length, 279
multiple copies, 281
pages, multiple, 63
quality, 281
quick, 61
ranges, 281
to disk, 282-283
to files, 281
process color, 284-285
program groups, 6
Program Manager window, 5, 6
programs, 6
proposals, 326-328
publication files, 293-294
Publisher, 17-19
Publisher Window, 19
pull-down menus, 24
purchase orders, 49, 64

Q-R

Quote business form, 49
Random Access Memory
  (RAM), 56
Rectangle tool, 92, 103, 174
rectangles, 255-256, 265
Replace, 129
Replace button, 129
Replace dialog box, 129
Replace With, 129

replacing, 125-129
reports, templates, 295
requirements, system, 4
reshaping frames, 133
Resize pointer, 33, 135
resizing
  frames, 133
  objects, 181-182
  picture frames, 210-213
  text frames, 134
  windows, 15-17
Restore, 16
resumé, 295
reversing text, 250-252
Rounded Rectangle tool,
  103, 174
rulers, 19, 25, 92
  hiding, 93
  objects, 91-92
  on-screen, 90
  snapping, 91-92
  units of measurement,
    95-96
  zero point, 91
Run, 334
Run dialog box, 334

S

Save, 28, 34, 56, 60
Save As, 34-56
Save As dialog box, 29, 34, 60
Save dialog box, 34
saving files, 56-59
scale fonts, 276
Scale Picture dialog box, 214
scanners, 318
scratch area, 20, 26
scrolling, 13, 20, 26-27
Search, 35
Search dialog box, 35
searching, 119, 127-129
selecting
  picture frames, 211
  printers, 276

Send to Back, 191
Settings, 96
Settings dialog box, 33-34, 96, 126
Seven Business Forms PageWizard, 63-64
Shading, 107, 186, 231
shading, 184
    foreground, 271-272
    frames, 231-233
    lines, 187
    objects, 185-187
    text, 247
Shading dialog box, 175, 186, 231
Shadow, 107, 187, 248-249
shadows, 175
    drop shadow, 187-188, 234-235
    objects, 187
    text frames, 107
Show Status Line, 28
Side-fold Greeting Card, 83
sidebars, 254-255
Size, 17, 242
sizing
    objects, 244
    windows, 13
sizing buttons, 12
Skip ALL-CAPITAL Words, 130
Snap To Guides, 89
Snap to Rulers, 91-92
Spanish, 52
Special elements dialog box, 63
Specific Printer, 75-77
spell checker, 119, 130-131
spot color, 284-285
squares, 178
Start Up dialog box, 20, 41-43, 46
starting programs, 17-18
status bar, 28

Stretch Vertical, 248-249
styles
    Arch down, 245
    Arch up, 245
    Bottom to Top, 245
    button, 246
    objects, 245-247
    Plain, 245
    Slant Down, 246
    Slant Up, 246
    Top to Bottom, 245
    Upside Down, 245
subdirectories, 304
Swedish, 52
Switch To, 15
system requirements, 4

T

table of contents, 63, 312
Table PageWizard, 45, 70-71
tables, 70
tag lines, 318
Task List dialog box, 15
techniques, 309
Templates, 18
templates, 18, 40, 291
    brochures, 295
    business cards, 294
    catalog, 295
    copies, 298
    creating, 300-301
    customizing, 301-302
    directory, 300
    editing, 302
    envelope, 295
    flyers, 295, 325
    labels, 295
    letterhead, 295
    mailing labels, 294
    memo, 295
    opening, 297-299
    reports, 295
    resume, 295

Tent Card, 82
text
   autoflowing, 112
   blocks, 120-126
   boxes, 31
   color, 247
   cutting, 110-111
   Greeking, 296
   importing
      clipboard, 110-112
      files, 112-116
   objects, editing, 70-71
   pasting, clipboard, 110, 111
   reversing, 250-252
   searching for, 127-128
   shading, 247
   special effects, 250
   spilling, 104
   stories, 109
   wrapping around pictures, 207-208
text frame tool, 102
text frames, 51-52
   anchoring, 107
   creating, 104-106, 263
   deleting, 135
   editing, 119-120
   handles, 105, 108, 134
   importing, 109-110
   linking, 118
   moving, 110, 133
   resizing, 134
   selecting, 108-109
   shadowing, 107
   square, 106-107
   too much text, 116
   transparent, 134-135
   typing in, 116
   width, 117
Three-Fold Brochure PageWizard, 64-65
three-fold brochures, 322-324
title bar, 12
toggling keys, 10

toolbar, 19, 24-25
tools
   drawing, 173, 176
   line, 91, 174
   ovals, 103, 174
   PageWizards, 43
      Ad, 44
      Calendar, 44
      Fancy First Letter, 44
      Newletter Banner, 44
      Note-It, 44
   picture frame, 102
   Rectangle, 92, 103, 174
   Rounded Rectangle, 103, 174
   text frame, 102
   WordArt Frame, 102
Top-fold Greeting Card, 83
tractor feed paper, 278
transparent frames, 134-135
Type Replaces Selection, 126

U

Undo Delete Objects, 136, 215
Undo Delete Page, 264
Undo Delete Text, 125

W-Z

white space, 208-209, 313
Whole Word Only, 129
wild cards
   * (asterisk), 114
   ? (question mark), 114
windows
   active, 8, 15
   application, 11-13, 21
   control-menu box, 12
   directories
      activating, 304
      creating, 304-305
   Help, 35-36
   Main, 5-6
   menu bar, 13, 19

mouse pointer, 13
moving
   Control menu, 16
   mouse, 15
PageWizard, 53
paging control, 20
Program Manager, 5-6
Publisher, 19
resizing, 15-16
rulers, 19
scroll bars, 13, 20
size box, 13
sizing, 12-14
title bar, 12
toolbar, 19
work area, 13, 20
Windows menu, 17-18
WordArt, 237-241
   advertisements, 256
   call outs, 252-254
   circles, 255-256
   fonts, 242-243
   lines, 255-256

objects
   aligning, 248
   creating, 241-242
   editing, 249-250
   sizing, 244
   styling, 245-247
   text, 70
options, 248-249
rectangles, 255-256
reversing text, 250-252
sidebars, 254-255
special effects, 250
text alignment, 248
WordArt dialog box, 240-242, 314
WordArt Frame tool, 102
work area, 26
WYSIWYG, 5
zero point, 91

Reader Feedback Card

Thank you for purchasing this book from SAMS FIRST BOOK series. Our intent with this series is to bring you timely, authoritative information that you can reference quickly and easily. You can help us by taking a minute to complete and return this card. We appreciate your comments and will use the information to better serve your needs.

1. Where did you purchase this book?

- ☐ Chain bookstore (Walden, B. Dalton)
- ☐ Independent bookstore
- ☐ Computer/Software store
- ☐ Other _____
- ☐ Direct mail
- ☐ Book club
- ☐ School bookstore

2. Why did you choose this book? (Check as many as apply.)

- ☐ Price
- ☐ Author's reputation
- ☐ Quick and easy treatment of subject
- ☐ Appearance of book
- ☐ SAMS' reputation
- ☐ Only book available on subject

3. How do you use this book? (Check as many as apply.)

- ☐ As a supplement to the product manual
- ☐ In place of the product manual
- ☐ For self-instruction
- ☐ As a reference
- ☐ At home
- ☐ At work

4. Please rate this book in the categories below. G = Good; N = Needs improvement; U = Category is unimportant.

- ☐ Price
- ☐ Amount of information
- ☐ Examples
- ☐ Inside cover reference
- ☐ Table of contents
- ☐ Tips and cautions
- ☐ Length of book
- ☐ Appearance
- ☐ Accuracy
- ☐ Quick Steps
- ☐ Second color
- ☐ Index
- ☐ Illustrations
- ☐ How can we improve this book? _____

5. How many computer books do you normally buy in a year?

- ☐ 1–5
- ☐ 5–10
- ☐ More than 10
- ☐ I rarely purchase more than one book on a subject.
- ☐ I may purchase a beginning and an advanced book on the same subject.
- ☐ I may purchase several books on particular subjects.
- ☐ (such as _____)

6. Have your purchased other SAMS or Hayden books in the past year? _____
If yes, how many _____

7. Would you purchase another book in the FIRST BOOK series? _____

8. What are your primary areas of interest in business software? _____
   ☐ Word processing (particularly _____)
   ☐ Spreadsheet (particularly _____)
   ☐ Database (particularly _____)
   ☐ Graphics (particularly _____)
   ☐ Personal finance/accounting (particularly _____)
   ☐ Other (please specify _____)

Other comments on this book or the SAMS' book line: _____
_____

Name _____
Company _____
Address _____
City _____ State _____ Zip _____
Daytime telephone number _____
Title of this book _____

Fold here

NO POSTAGE
NECESSARY
IF MAILED
IN THE
UNITED STATES

BUSINESS REPLY MAIL
FIRST CLASS   PERMIT NO. 336   CARMEL, IN

POSTAGE WILL BE PAID BY ADDRESSEE

SAMS

11711 N. College Ave.
Suite 141
Carmel, IN 46032–9839